THE PHILOSOPHY OF RIGHT

*****

Rights in Civil Society

ANTONIO ROSMINI

THE PHILOSOPHY OF RIGHT

Volume 6

Rights in Civil Society

Translated by
DENIS CLEARY
and
TERENCE WATSON

ROSMINI HOUSE
DURHAM

Translated from
Filosofia del Diritto
Vol. 2, Intra, 1865

Typeset by Rosmini House, Durham
Printed by Bell & Bain Limited, Glasgow

ISBN 1 899093 20 6

Note

Square brackets [ ] indicate notes or additions by the translators.

References to this and other works of Rosmini are given by paragraph number unless otherwise stated.

Abbreviations used for Rosmini's quoted works are:

AMS: *Anthropology as an Aid to Moral Science*
CE: *Certainty*
CS: *Conscience*
ER: *The Essence of Right*, vol. 1 of *The Philosophy of Right*
OT: *The Origin of Thought*
PE: *Principles of Ethics*
RF: *Rights in the Family*, vol. 5 of *The Philosophy of Right*
RGC: *Rights in God's Church*, vol. 4 of *The Philosophy of Right*
RI: *Rights of the Individual*, vol. 2 of *The Philosophy of Right*
SC: *The Summary Cause for the Stability or Downfall of Human Societies*, vol. 1 of *The Philosophy of Politics*
SP: *Society and its Purpose*, vol. 2 of *The Philosophy of Politics*
USR: *Universal Social Right*, vol. 3 of *The Philosophy of Right*

Foreword

The preceding five volumes of the English translation of Rosmini's *The Philosophy of Right* have dealt with the essence of right (vol. 1), individual rights (vol. 2), the principles underlying social right (vol. 3) and the application of these principles to theocratic society (the Church, vol. 4) and to domestic society (the family, vol. 5). In this sixth and final volume, Rosmini applies the same principles to civil society, the third and last of the great societies necessary for 'the perfect organisation of mankind', the kind of society which is the inevitable consequence of even minimal development as mankind increases in number and exercises its native talents.

Rosmini's aim is to show how civil society, in all its principal manifestations, is related to right, and dependent on the appropriate exercise of rights for its well-being and progress. To achieve his purpose, he deals first with the man-made nature of civil society. Of particular importance here is his insistence on the good which determines the essence of this society, the sole purpose of which is to regulate the exercise of family rights in such a way that no family is a nuisance or encumbrance to others.

'All this,' Rosmini claims, 'is achieved by disposing adequately the *modality* of the rights of all.' With this fundamental affirmation, he rejects in a single sentence every theory giving rise to a totalitarian State as the source and bestower of rights, and every assertion that rights can be exercised irrespective of the consequences to the well-being of others.

The 'modality of rights' refers, for Rosmini, to the exercise of rights, not to rights themselves. Rights, whether vested in an individual, in the true Church or in the family, are inviolable; the exercise of rights may be regulated, given certain conditions, by civil society which exists for that very purpose. But civil society must never damage the individual person, nor the collective persons formed by Church and family, which precede civil society. The form, laws and activity of civil society serve solely to ensure the good of these persons; the aim of civil society is achieved when all persons are enabled, through the activity proper to civil society, to exercise more perfectly the rights which are their due. While the good which is the object of right is unchangeable, the form which that good takes is, if separable from the good itself, subject to reasonable modification by civil society.

An essential element of the philosophy of right is to state the universal conditions according to which civil society should undertake this immense and daunting task of regulating the exercise of rights.

These conditions will inevitably be influenced by the origin of civil societies which, for Rosmini, goes hand in hand with the growth of government in the assembly of families that make up such a society. The origin of different forms of government — monarchic, aristocratic, democratic — explain the diversity of civil societies found in history. Each expression of government will have its value according to circumstances; each will be worthy of those circumstances only if it regulates all its activity with the highest regard for justice, both distributive and commutative. Civil society is not the fount of morality or right; it is subject to them in its activity, and clearly confined by the limits they impose.

Chief amongst the human needs giving rise to civil society is the interior perfection, satisfaction and peace of the human spirit. There will be no lasting cohesion within any civil society which ignores this need. On the other hand, gradual fulfilment of this need provides the necessary stimulus to the removal of family and national selfishness, which blocks the development of the brotherhood of mankind and its concomitant benefit of universal civil society. In Europe, we have already seen the fusion of family and social elements worked out through three thousand years of history. The vital role of the Christian Church in the past development of European nations will be re-enacted as it plays its non-political part in a new European union, and beyond that in the world union for which mankind is surely destined.

In the final sections of this work, the profundity of Rosmini's philosophical principles is equalled by the depth of his analysis of sources of injustice in the civil body, of the nature and activity of organisms in civil society, and of sanctions enforcing civil ordinances. In dealing with these issues, he offers acute reflections on subjects which extend from the need for a free press to the purpose of penal sanctions, material force and public opinion. Finally, he considers the better construction of civil society through the practice of justice, through the principle of balance, as he calls it, and through the social inequalities dependent on nature. From this point of view alone, without taking account of more general principles, this volume is, after a century and a half, of great relevance to modern theory and practice in the field of civic activity.

DENIS CLEARY
TERENCE WATSON

Durham,
July, 1996

Contents

PART TWO

THE SCIENCE OF RIGHT IN CIVIL SOCIETY DISTINGUISHED FROM POLITICAL SCIENCE

PART THREE

THE ORIGIN OF CIVIL SOCIETY

PART FOUR

OCCASIONAL AND EFFICIENT CAUSES OF CIVIL SOCIETY

SECTION TWO
RIGHT IN ALREADY CONSTITUTED CIVIL SOCIETY

PART ONE
POSSIBLE ELEMENTS OF INJUSTICE IN CIVIL SOCIETY CONSIDERED AS SUCH

PART TWO

THE ORGANS OF CIVIL SOCIETY AND THE SOCIAL FUNCTIONS DETERMINING THEM

PART THREE

APPENDIX TO THE PHILOSOPHY OF RIGHT — THE BETTER CONSTRUCTION OF CIVIL SOCIETY

CONCLUSION

SOCIAL RIGHT

SPECIAL-SOCIAL RIGHT

Part 3
RIGHT IN CIVIL SOCIETY

DOMINATING and GOVERNING civil
society are not the same thing.

Arist. *Polit.* 1: 4

[INTRODUCTION]

1560. I now have to take in hand the most complicated, thorny
and highly litigious part of social Right, split as it is by disparate
opinions and encumbered with fierce resentment, hatred and
love — stained even by blood. Sometimes these things spill over
from society itself to disturb the tranquil reign of philosophy;
sometimes they come to light as the illegitimate offspring of
philosophy and then return to disturb and upset the very foundations of society.

Nevertheless, provided the beneficent light of truth and the
authority of immortal justice is revealed to the eyes of human
intelligence in all its purity and light, we can rest assured of the
power of the progress of social Right in healing the atrocious
evils which afflict this contentious branch of knowledge and
suffering humanity. If only I could help in some small way to
bring this hope to fulfilment!

This fierce longing may provide the reader with the true
reason for the zeal which perhaps made us forget our weakness
when we undertook to write this volume and its predecessors,
which form a unity with it. Certainly, the sympathy of many
kind and noble spirits has been of great encouragement in
enabling us to persevere with such a difficult undertaking.

Having relied until now on the benevolence and wisdom of
good, learned people, we have to recommend an even more
difficult volume on social Right to those same gracious qualities.
In doing so, we promise to carry out straightforwardly our
investigation of what is true and what is just, without being
influenced by passion, as far as we are aware. This is precisely
what the learned require of us; this is the sole benevolent sup-

[1560]

port, the sole recognition (I dare not say assent) they will want to give to our impartiality and to the human purpose which presides over our efforts. This has such value and esteem in our eyes that, in comparison with the severity of the ignorant and the malice of pessimists which is so ready to oppose honest efforts and all good principles, it will have no power to disturb us.

1561. How do we begin the exposition of the philosophy of Right relative to civil society? Because it is impossible to know the Right of any society whose nature is unknown, we have to proceed according to the order found in the previous books and begin by placing the nature of civil society in the clearest possible light. After that, we shall indicate, by reference to this nature, the Right presiding over civil society. It is true that in dealing with theocratic and domestic society, we spoke only briefly of their nature, which we indicated hand in hand with our exposition of Right in these societies. Here however we have to deal at length with the nature of the City before discussing civil Right.

The difference in approach is explained by the simplicity of the two preceding societies which we find comparatively easy to understand. Civil society, on the other hand, is extremely vast and complex, and requires great mental abstraction to be conceived in all its purity. Too many people, having already shown themselves incapable of this, are unable to reach the pure nature of civil society. We can see this from the multitude of treatises which, instead of clarifying and determining this nature, have obscured its concept endlessly by making it discordant and inhuman. In fact, the connection between the *Theory of society* and *Right in society* is such that every error posited in the former germinates most harmful opinions in the latter, which in turn give rise to a succession of cruel misdeeds.

1562. Does the theory of civil society, which according to us has to be dealt with first, really belong to the branch of knowledge called 'Right'? It cannot be denied that the *constituents* of society, which form it into a jural entity, belong to the science of social Right. Nevertheless, the *first jural acts* which give rise to society are posited by individuals who, while still living in the *state of nature*, associate at some time prior to the presence of society. Strictly speaking, those jural acts pertain, as we have noted elsewhere (*Rights of the Individual*, 1059), to individual rather than social Right. We have, in fact, dealt with them under the heading of individual Right. However, we have to return to the argument here and treat it carefully. It is a precious thread leading us from individual to social Right and showing the connection between the two.

We shall explain, therefore, as clearly as possible, the Theory of civil society and the relationship of this theory with its corresponding Right before we move on to unfold the same Right in already constituted civil society.

SECTION ONE

THEORY OF CIVIL SOCIETY

1563. To reveal the nature of civil society in relationship to the Right presiding over it, we have to investigate four things:

First, the *concept of civil society*, which provides us with sufficient knowledge to speak about it.

Second, the *concept of its Right.*

Third, its *jural origin*, that is, those acts and jural constituents with which human beings lawfully institute it.

Finally, the *occasional causes of civil society*, that is, the stimuli that serve as starting points from which human beings set out to form civil society.

The present section will therefore have four parts:

PART 1. The essence of civil society

   „   2. The notion of Right in civil society

   „   3. The jural origin of civil society

   „   4. Occasional causes of civil society

PART ONE

THE ESSENCE OF CIVIL SOCIETY

CHAPTER 1

**The more general differences contradistinguishing
the three societies necessary for the perfect organisation of
the human race**

1564. In order to reveal the essence and character of *civil society*, and present it to the reader in its genuine forms distinct from all other societies, we begin by comparing it with *theocratic* and *domestic* society which are already known to us as a result of our previous books. The more universal differences between these societies and civil society must now be accurately noted.

Article 1.
Three principal constituents characterising societies

1565. To make this comparison, we have to pay attention principally to the following three elements constitutive of all societies:

1. The fellow-feeling of the person who unites with others in society. This fellow-feeling contains the acts we have called *factors of societies* (*Universal Social Right*, 38).

2. The concept of special society, that is, society intuited in its possibility.

3. The good desired by means of a given society.

These three elements are, as it were, the beginning, the core and the aim of society. Fellow-feeling as cause precedes the existence of society; and the good derived from society is its end and effect.

Article 2.
DE FACTO and *DE IURE* societies

1566. The *concept* of society, that is, society intuited as possible, preserves its condition as an ideal being even when the society known by means of that concept has already been realised. The ideal being remains unchanged in nature in the presence of the real being, although the human spirit unites the intuition of the idea and the perception of the reality in such a way that a single being is formed of both. Consequently, the complexity of the being is extremely difficult to recognise.

Fellow-feeling, on the other hand, and the *good* which a society is directed to produce, can be thought equally both in their concept, that is, as possible, and in their subsistence, that is, as real.

1567. A subsistent society, in so far as it subsists, is called a *de facto society*. This expression signifies both its subsistence and the state or mode of its subsistence, altogether independently of the questions: 'Has it the right to subsist or not?' and 'Does it subsist in a way that conforms to Right', or 'Are there things alien to the prescriptions of Right in the state in which it subsists?'

1568. Right can prescribe that a given society must be realised. This is the case for jurally obligatory societies (*USR*, 141). Moreover, Right determines many conditions about the state and mode in which a society must subsist when it actually does subsist.

1569. The concept of society considered only in so far as it contains these dictates of Right shows us society as it must be jurally. This ideal society, determined according to the norms of Right, is called *de iure society*.

1570. Do *de iure societies* subsist independently of human activity? This question leads us to discover the first difference between civil and domestic society on the one hand, and theocratic society on the other. It leads us to recognise that only theocratic society does not require human activity for its *de iure* existence. Let us see how this comes about.

Article 3.
All *de facto* societies can be called MAN-MADE

1571. All *de facto* societies need the *fellow-feeling* of the human beings who associate (*USR*, 38). Every *de facto* society, therefore, can be called the work of human beings in so far as they place it in being through acts of will. It follows that every *de facto* society is *man-made* and cannot be called *natural* in all the extension of the term.

Article 4.
Theocratic society alone exists *per se* as a *DE IURE* SOCIETY, independently of human activity

1572. But this is not the case with *de iure* societies. The definition we have just given of *de iure society* shows that a society can exist *de iure* without human activity when it possesses the following two characteristics:

1. Its concept is *full*, that is, the concept represents the society completely in such a way that human beings have nothing of their own to add to it. In other words, everything is already determined in the very concept in which the society is intuited and contemplated; nothing is lacking for its realisation except human consent.

2. Human beings are morally obliged to give such assent.

1573. This final characteristic can be verified in all three societies necessary for the perfect organisation of the human race. Human consent is always and absolutely obligatory in the case of *theocratic society*; there can also be a moral obligation to give consent, and so to associate, in many cases concerned with *domestic* (*conjugal*) and *civil society*.

1574. However, the first characteristic is not verified in all three societies: the concept of society which has to be actuated is not always presented to human beings furnished with all its determination; some determination may have to be added. This is not the case with *theocratic society*, which is entirely determined by the author and perfector of creation. Human beings simply have to receive it and give their consent, or rather act as though they were already members of it. Jurally, a human being is a member as soon as he wishes to be.

If we reflect more deeply and consider the natural and necessary act of the human will which tends to being and universal good, it seems that there is naturally in every human being a first fellow-feeling at least for the society of the human race, which we have acknowledged as a vestige and outline of theocratic society (*Rights in God's Church*, 635–636).

1575. The case is different with *domestic* (*conjugal*) *society*. This is not determined by its concept alone, which lacks the indispensable determination of the person of the spouse. When human beings come to actuate this society, they must not only add their consent to its concept but first choose of their own free will the person with whom they will associate. In other words, they have to complete the *concept of the society* they wish to make.[1] This *de iure conjugal society* does not exist, therefore, except as a result of the act of free will of those who unite.

1576. Still less is there any *de iure civil society* prior to *de facto civil society*. As human beings establish and realise *de facto* civil society, they come to form *de iure* civil society. The latter does not exist completely in its concept until people have determined with their own will a number of things in addition to those necessary for making domestic society fully possible. In other words, they must determine not only the persons of the members, but also the form and mode of civil association.

We conclude: only *theocratic society* exists as a *de iure society* prior to human activity.

1577. Nevertheless, *domestic* and *civil society* can, as we said,

---

[1] The concept of something is *full* when it has everything necessary to serve as an example for anyone who wishes to *realise* it (*The Origin of Thought*, 402–405; 657–659). — In the case of marriage, it may be objected that the determination of the person does not pertain to the concept of society because the concept contains nothing *real*. This is indeed true, but only because the *de iure society* of which we are speaking is not totally comprised in the concept; it is not purely *an ideal society*, but a *possible society*. Now the *possibility* is either logical, and to that extent has its foundation in the idea; or it is also *physical*, and to that extent requires *real conditions* which, in our case, is the determination of the person. The *concept* of domestic society does not contain everything that makes the society possible; in order to make it fully possible, we must add the real determination already mentioned.

be obligatory for human beings placed in certain special circumstances. This obligation also becomes jural relative to persons for whom neglect of this obligation is harmful.

1578. Once the obligation of association in these societies has been fulfilled by giving consent, consent itself becomes a new title of other obligations which have social responsibilities as their object.

1579. The objects of the *right* that correspond to such obligations are distinguished in the same way. First, there is the *right* to compel association upon the person who has the jural obligation to associate; next, there is the right to compel the person associated to fulfil consequent, social duties.

Article 5.
Considered in relationship to the good which they propose as their proximate end, the three societies can be distinguished by calling one divine, the other natural and the third man-made

1580. The difference we have noticed between the three societies is shown by consideration of their *concept*, and by the human fellow-feeling which fulfils the concept and actuates the difference. We must now compare the third of the three constitutive elements which we have already posited. By this, I mean the *good* to which the societies are proximately and immediately ordained.

1581. The good making up the aim and effect of theocratic society is the eudaimonologico-moral perfection which we acquire by uniting ourselves to divine things and to God himself. From this point of view, the first society deserves to be called *divine*.

1582. The good towards which domestic society tends is the satisfaction experienced by human nature 1. in the full union of the two forms in which human nature subsists, and 2. in the increase of human nature, the effect of full union, as a result of which the species is perpetuated and individuals are multiplied. Domestic society, which has the development of human nature as its proximate end, can rightly be called *natural*.

[1578–1582]

1583. What is the *proximate good* towards which civil society tends?

Civil society is a union of families, or fathers of families.[2] In the state of nature, one family, although independent of all others, can be in conflict with them because of uncertain rights, or be damaged by them, or even helped and advantaged. Civil society is then gradually formed in order to regulate these divergencies. It is an institution which tends to provide peaceful co-habitation amongst several families, without harm to any and to the advantage of all.[3]

1584. It is therefore clear that:

1. *human nature* exists prior to *civil society*;

2. it exists with all its natural development, that is, through the multiplication of individuals and the perpetuation of the species, by means of *domestic society*;

3. *civil society* (as separate from domestic society) begins to exist only when the human race, divided into several families, feels the need of some agreement between them;

4. the *proximate end* of civil society is to regulate the relationships between several co-existent families so that all may live in the way most secure and advantageous for each of them;

5. human understanding has to take many steps before it can think of constituting civil society by conceiving it as suitable for the aim we have described. It has to rise to the *order of reflection* by which human beings consider the disputes be-

---

[2] As I have already noted, the word *paterfamilias* has a more extensive meaning according to Roman laws; it is in this sense that I take it here. 'The *paterfamilias* is said to have dominion in a house, although he may not in fact have children. We indicate not only his person but his right. We also call a minor, *paterfamilias*; and when the *paterfamilias* dies, all those who were both heads and subjects now begin to have their own individual families. Each one takes on the name of *paterfamilias*. The same happens when someone is emancipated. This person, too, has his own family as the effect of his right (*Digest*, bk. 50, t. 16: l. 195).

[3] All the sages of old taught that civil society was simply 'the union of more than one family for the sake of regulating the modality of their rights to common advantage'. Aristotle (*Polit.* 1, n) will serve as an example for the Greeks, Cicero (*De Off.* 1: 17) for the Latins. According to them, there was no doubt that civil society originated from union amongst families. The writers of the Revolution sought to overthrow this natural, human principle. We shall come back to it.

[1583–1584]

tween various families, and understand that they must first be determined according to equity and prudence, without violence, and then carried out accordingly.

1585. Civil society does not begin, therefore, with natural and *spontaneous knowledge*, but as a result of *free reflection*. In this respect, it is not the work of nature, but of human activity. It can suitably be called *man-made* because its *good*, its proximate end, is not given by nature but found as a result of human genius and art.[4]

Article 6.
The end of civil society

1586. We now have to define more precisely the *good* which constitutes the proximate end of civil society. This good determines the essence of civil society by specifying it and gradually distinguishing it better from other societies.

1587. The object of rights is *that which is good*.[5] *Societies*, precisely because they all have some *good* as their proximate end (*USR*, 48), also have as their proximate end the complex of *rights*

---

[4] Although human beings who found a civil society must have arrived in their intellectual development at the level of *free reflection* of which we are speaking, it does not follow that persons without the use of free reflection, such as babies, the mentally handicapped, etc., cannot be members of civil society. Egger excludes them from civil society on the grounds that they cannot give their consent to this society. We must first consider, however, that these persons are true subjects of rights (*RI*, 26–43). Secondly, those who are subject to the power of their father are governed by the principle that the father's consent alone is sufficient for the whole family to belong to any association whatsoever. Thirdly, we need to bear in mind that entire groups of descendants can be considered associated, granted the consent of the first founders of civil society. In fact, all jural acts such as buying and selling, etc., endure after the death of those who carried them out. Civil society, because it is a decent, useful, perpetual contract, requires that no child can withdraw his consent from the association. Fourthly, the representative of an infant or a mentally-handicapped person, etc., does a truly beneficent work which is in no way absurd because civil society is a good for those who belong to it, and each subject of rights can be represented. When society itself treats these persons as its members, it does not harm but benefits them.

[5] Cf. *The Essence of Right*, 252–255.

to which those goods are referred. We have already distinguished between societies which have as their proximate end *rights* themselves and societies which have the *modality of right* as their proximate end (*USR*, 138). We said that civil society pertains to the second kind (*RGC*, 966).

In fact, civil society is the union of families brought about for the sole purpose of suitably regulating the relationship of their rights in such a way that no family is a nuisance and inconvenience for any other. The aim is to make their co-existence peaceful, secure and mutually helpful. All this is achieved by disposing adequately the *modality of the rights* of all. It is certain that fathers of families who freely unite in civil society do not intend to renounce any of their connatural rights or those acquired according to individual, theocratic or domestic Right.[6] They unite precisely because they intend to act for the better preservation of their own rights. They want to understand the matter together, in a friendly way; they want to attend to their rights reasonably and prudently (prudence is the offspring of reason) so that in exercising them no one may harm another, and each may help all. If the *modality* of rights were not wisely exercised to avoid collisions and protect this harmonious

[6] This principle, which is the basis of *political freedom*, is today held by all schools, and even by the better part of all parties. C. L. Haller himself writes: 'Sonnenfels held this. — And Sieges who, except for the false fundamental principle of the social contract, sees with total clarity and holds in the highest degree the spirit of true *private-freedom*, inveighs with his overpowering genius against those who are never content with tricking out and endowing their new sovereign, the people, with the private rights they concede. He wanted to leave everything possible to private persons, and thus distinguished himself from other revolutionaries. I myself, the defender of tyrants according to almost all the German critics, go even further and maintain that *nothing at all* was conceded to the rulers and that they can require nothing in return. This is the simple truth in theory and in practice' (T. 1, not. 65 in chap. 9). How extraordinary to see that the elements which truly make up freedom are least understood in France, where freedom is more talked of than anywhere else in the world! To be convinced of this, it is sufficient to note the sophism which serves as a foundation to the entire discourse made by Guizot in the House of Nobles on May 9th of this very year, 1844. He considers himself the upholder of all *individual liberties* without realising that freedom of association in decent and religious societies, which he greatly undermines in his speech, is precisely one of the most precious, individual liberties.

exercise which leaves each one with the greatest possible freedom to develop, the few, when multiplied throughout the earth, would have been unable to preserve intact the goods and rights of their families, or to increase and enjoy them peacefully.

The ordering of the modality of rights is, therefore, the aim of civil society.

Article 7.
Difference between the proximate end of civil society and the proximate end of theocratic and domestic society

1588. At this point we find a new, very notable difference distinguishing the three societies necessary for the perfect organisation of humankind. *Theocratic* and *domestic society* have as their proximate end certain *goods* or rights. Civil society has for its end solely 'to remove the obstacles, and to dispose with appropriate foresight the circumstances most favourable to preserving, increasing and enjoying the goods and rights proper to the first two societies'.

1589. If *theocratic* and *domestic society* have certain goods (objects of rights) as their proximate end, and civil society has as its end simply the *most useful, appropriate modality* of these goods, it follows that the first two societies are ends relative to the third, which is a means. In other words, civil society, according to the spirit of its institution and its very nature, must simply serve the other two.

1590. The comparison between the three societies can be completed by noting the distinction between the *rights* forming the proximate object of *theocratic* society and the proximate object of *domestic* society. Here it will be sufficient to recall our general division of human rights into two classes, the first of which has as its object what is good for the human person, the second what is good for human nature in so far as this is distinguished from person (*RI*, 56–67). On earth, theocratic society has as its immediate end the rights which refer to *what is good for the person*; domestic society, the rights which refer to *what is good for nature*.

1591. We may summarise as follows. *Theocratic society* tends to obtain for human beings the good proper to the human person; *domestic society*, what is good for human nature; *civil society* tends to regulate the modality of rights which refer to these goods so that the first two societies may prosper by attaining fully the end for which they were constituted by God and by nature, which is the minister of God's divine power and will.

Article 8.
Corollary: civil society must never harm theocratic or
domestic society; rather, it must minister to them

1592. It is clear, therefore, that civil society has been instituted to further the two preceding societies, theocratic and domestic, divine society and natural society. It is also clear that the essential, all-embracing duty of civil society is to organise itself and act in such a way 1. that it never damages either of the two primary societies which precede it, and 2. that its *form*, *laws* and *activity* serve solely to ensure the safety, peace and prosperity of theocratic and domestic society.

1593. As we know, ends are greater than means. It is therefore undeniable that theocratic and domestic society have a more noble and elevated character than that of civil society.

CHAPTER 2

Definition of civil society

1594. We need to consider here that *civil society* has perhaps never received, as far as I can see, a precise, adequate definition from publicists. I reach this conclusion because they do not seem to have known reflectively, nor meditated upon, the proper object of civil society, that is, 'the regulation of the modality of the rights of citizens'.

1595. The reason preventing them from such reflection is probably that *States* in their *de facto* existence are almost never *pure societies*; they also contain *seigniory*. As a result, the *social* and *seigniorial* elements, confused in civil societies, did not

[1592–1595]

receive the care and attention necessary for distinguishing and separating them. *Civil society* was assigned the mixed, uncertain object which is normally present *de facto* in *States*. Pure civil society was taken as the union of human beings which we normally call *State*, or even *Power* when it is considered in relationship with other, similar unions.

1596. Moreover, although the various *States* in which nations settle and organise themselves as a result of innumerable accidental factors contain a mixture of these two *social* and *seigniorial* elements, the proportions of the elements in the combinations vary; some are more characterised by seigniory, others by society. This would explain the various opinions of authors on the nature of civil society and its government, opinions which are then immediately re-presented in the field of reality by bitter, active groups. In fact, every author who has undertaken to define civil society has proposed, as the type of his definition, one or other of the *States* which actually exist. The author who composes his definition on the model of a State where the social element is greater than the seigniorial condemns as absolutist another author who has deduced his definition from a State in which the element of seigniory is more extensive than that of society. And in the same way, the second kind of author accuses the former of excessive liberalism. This painful contrast of feelings will never be resolved as long as the two jural elements, the seigniorial and the social, have not been well distinguished by separate definition and then by evaluation of the various admixtures made possible by Right.

Article 1.
Distinction between civil society, State, and Power

1597. Having noted this, we think it necessary, in order to avoid the same error, to distinguish very carefully the notions of 1. *civil Society*, 2. *State* and 3. *Power*. We shall call *State* civil societies as they actually exist with all the seigniorial elements which to a greater or lesser extent they retain in their constitution. When these *States* are considered in their relationship with others, we shall call them *Powers*.

[1596–1597]

1598. We shall restrict the name *civil Society* to the true, proper meaning of the words, that is, to *pure society*, abstracting from every *seigniorial* element. This element does not form part of the essence of societies, as we have seen; its nature is the opposite of that proper to the *social element* (*USR*, 28–31).

Article 2.
Erroneous definitions of civil society

1599. As confirmation of what has been said, I want to place before the reader the principal definitions which have so far been given of civil society. It will be easy to see that all of them lack the *proper object* which specifies such society and assigns it its end. It will also be clear that some authors, who err from excess, endow civil society with an end greater than it actually has; others, who err from defect, with a lesser end.

§1. *Definitions which err from excess*

1600. The following definitions attribute to civil society a more extensive aim that it actually possesses:
   1. Vattel's definition:

   Nations, or States, are political bodies, societies of human beings joined together for the purpose of obtaining their own welfare and advantage by means of united forces.[7]

   2. Bonald's definition:

   Society in a general or metaphysical sense is the union of similar beings for the purpose of reproducing and preserving themselves.
   In another sense, more restricted and appropriate to the particular argument with which we are dealing, society is the relationship between associated persons, that is, the relationship between power and the service of good, and the advantage of the subjects.[8]

---

[7] *Droit des Gens*, t. 1, §1.
[8] *Législation primitive*.

3. Maurus Schenkl, along with many other authors on *ecclesiastical Right*, first defines society in general as:

> A state in which human beings find themselves bound together under a perfect obligation to attain a certain end.[9]

He is then satisfied with assigning temporal good, or the temporal well-being of the subjects, as the proximate end of civil society, in contradistinction to the Church, to which he assigns spiritual well-being as end.[10]

4. Martignoni's definition:

> The City is a union of many human beings associated through mutual consent, having supreme power and directed to procuring civil bliss.[11]

5. Baroli's definition:

> The State or the City is the independent, perpetual union of a sufficient number of human beings and families under a legitimate power for the sake of obtaining mutual security of the rights of each (justice), as well as the universal and complete growth of human beings in humanity, that is, the resultant common well-being, which is to be promoted with means that cannot be posited without the union and efficacy of great forces.[12]

1601. At this point, it is sufficient to consider these definitions to realise that none of them accurately determines the proper, unique aim of civil society; none of them distinguishes the regulation of the modality of rights from rights themselves. In rights lies the *good* possessed by each human being; in their *modalities* no good or right exists properly speaking, although the purely equitable, prudent regulation and harmony of modalities is the most efficacious means of safeguarding rights and assisting their development and growth. In other words, these

---

[9] *Institutiones iuris ecclesiastici, etc.*, §1.

[10] 'The Church has the attainment of the spiritual well-being of its members as its proximate end; it achieves this with its own means. The City has temporal well-being as its proximate end (in so far as temporal well-being is subordinate to the final end and spiritual bliss of human beings),' §20*.

[11] *Principi del Diritto di natura e delle genti*, vol. 3, p. 3.

[12] *Diritto naturale publico interno*, §2.

definitions define arbitrary societies, mingled with a seigniorial element, which place in communion (*USR*, 108) *goods* and rights, or their *administration*.[13] But they never define civil society in its sole function of regulating the modality of this administration.

1602. Publicists who confuse the *remote* with the *proximate end* also belong to the class of those who assign an exaggerated end to civil society. There is no doubt that moral perfection and human bliss is the final and principal end of civil society, but this is also the common end of all societies, and indeed of all human activity. It is not, therefore, the proper, immediate end of civil society, which has to form part of the definition of civil society; it is not what we are seeking.

1603. Again, there were others who placed the end of civil society in goods of a general nature which can be obtained only through civil organisation. Of these

a) some were so enthralled with organisation itself, which they saw as something beautiful to behold, that they admired it as a copy of the organism of the universe.[14] It is certain, however, that people do not associate for the sake of offering their union as a beautiful, delightful spectacle to contemplating minds. They are doing something *helpful* to themselves, even if others see it as something *beautiful;*

b) others posited the end of civil society in the good of the State or in the good of the majority or in some external good, produced by the social organisation. But this is nothing if separated from internal, moral good. United with moral good, it is indeed a kind of completion and splendour of moral good, but only at a superficial level. It is not the whole, nor the better part;[15]

c) others, finally, posited the end of civil society in the

[13] The word *respublica* indicates a communion of goods. This was the practical concept that the ancients formed of their civil societies, to which consequently they accorded an absolute power to interfere with anyone's goods. Yet, how many today long for the *republic,* and claim to be liberal!

[14] Nibler.

[15] People holding this view wish to encompass all the moral sciences under the title *Civil Philosophy* by making them dependent on the teaching about external society in such a way that they have no existence of their own; they are simply servile parts of political science.

increasing progress of civilisation.[16] The progress of civilisation is not, however, an effect of civil society alone, but of many other causes conspiring with it, and even preceding it as its source.

§2. Definitions of civil society which err by defect

1604. The following, on the contrary, unduly restrict the proximate end of civil society:

1. All those who, with Samuel Coccejo, define the City as 'the assembly of many families brought together for the sake of safeguarding right'.[17] *Security* as an end was embraced in modern times by a great number of publicists.

> After a speech by Fichte to the rulers of Europe, in which this author, whom we have just quoted, spoke against the doctrine that a sovereign must watch over the happiness of his subjects (he maintained that this teaching was the poisoned source of all our miseries and a proposition that had its origin in hell), the system which established *security of right* as the sole end of the State became prevalent.[18]

1605. *Security of right* as the end of the State was presented under several aspects. Baroli, whom we have just quoted, expounds it as follows:

> According to Cicero, followed by Hobbes and Pufendorf, civil society springs from fear on the part of the weak who join together to resist tyranny and injustice on the part of the strong. The end of the City for these authors is, therefore, to ward off such fear. Lampredi's opinion is more or less the same. He accepts fear of force and violence from others as the proximate end of the City which he posits in

[16] Troxler expresses the same thought in different words. According to him, the end of civil society is 'the development of humanity both as archetype of the people and natural image of humanity itself.' Civil society is not sufficient for such development which requires many other conditions and factors.

[17] *Introductio ad Henr. L. B. De Coccei Grotium illustratum* (Diss. Proem. 12, bk. 3, §199).

[18] Baroli, *Diritto naturale pubblico interno* (§*1).

[1604–1605]

the removal of this fear, that is, in the happiness and security of the members. Genovesi also posits this as the end of civil society. Martini, Egger, Bauer and many others posit a contract as the foundation of civil society, and acknowledge security of right as the exclusive end of this society.[19]

1606. 2. Ortes, in a little known book,[20] posited *common reason* on one side and *force* on the other. For him, the Church was the depository of common reason, and the temporal Power the administration of force.[21] He maintained that government arose from both these elements.[22]

1607. We shall examine this concept later. For the moment it is sufficient to note that this system posits as the end of civil government: 1. the knowledge of common reason; and 2. the security of common reason obtained with the use of force. Of these two elements, the former is over-extended (Ortes takes common reason to include everything that pertains to morality and religion); the latter, security, is too restricted, as we said.

1608. 3. Others, such as Schmalz,[23] restrict the end of the State to the maintenance of *external freedom*.

1609. 4. Rotteck is much nearer the truth when he posits the proximate end of civil society in the full vigour of the law of right, that is, in the *security* of right itself, and in the *external freedom* of the citizens.

1610. The best regulation relative to the modality of rights and their administration has as a principal consequence these two effects of *security* and *jural freedom* in its widest possible use.

---

[19] *Ibid.*

[20] This admirable thinker published the work we refer to in 1780, without date and name, under the title *Della Religione e del governo dei popoli*, etc. etc., (bks. 1–3).

[21] 'By the *ministry of the temporal Power* I mean the force common to all, that is, the force in which each person posits his own particular force so that the former may defend the reason of all against the particular force of each' (bk. 2, c. 2).

[22] 'The Church represents reason; the temporal Power represents the common force directed to the effect under consideration. This is the result of the common consent. It must be said, therefore, that the government of peoples takes its origin from these two ministries of Church and temporal Power. The two together form the ministry of such a government' (bk. 3, c. 3).

[23] 'The State is instituted therefore solely for the maintenance of exterior freedom' (*Le Droit des gens européens*, bk. 1, c. 1).

But besides these, it also produces other advantages. It increases this freedom, that is, the members of civil society can, when united, do far more for the good of all than they could before their union took place.

1611. Moreover, *security* and *freedom* are effects of the *regulation of the modality of common rights*, which alone is the truly proximate object of government. It will be helpful to establish precisely the immediate object of governmental action because this is the sole way in which to determine the *sphere of means* of government and indicate how security itself, jural freedom itself, must not fall under government protection except by wise regulation of the modality of which we have spoken.[24]

Article 3.
True definition

1612. The definitions we have presented are therefore insufficient and erroneous, and have to be superseded by a new definition which assigns to civil association its proper object, the

[24] *The immediate object* of society is not the same thing as the *effects* it produces. The *effects* are innumerable; their series has no term because the causes and effects that bind them cannot be broken. Many of these effects, such as inevitable damage, can fall outside the *intention* of those who govern; they may even be extraneous to the *intention* of the art of government. Others are totally outside human foresight. Another cause of many divisions amongst the authors was precisely the way in which they defined the *object* of society from its *effects*. As a result, some restricted it unduly, others amplified it excessively; some erred simultaneously by defect and excess, as those did who assigned as the object the production of some particular, determined good. They erred through excess by making the object of civil society the *matter of a right*, instead of the sole *regulation of the modality of rights*; and they erred through defect by restricting their view of civil government to a single good, rather than to every good and to every right. Sonnenfels can be included amongst these authors; following in the footsteps of Rousseau, he posited increase in *population* as the end of the State, just as others had insisted on the development of *agriculture*, or the *production of material wealth*, or the *greater enjoyment of pleasure*, etc., according to the various philosophical systems from which they set out and to the extent that they fixed their attention on one rather than another of the innumerable effects produced by civil government.

modality of rights. This definition runs as follows: 'Civil society is the union of a certain number of fathers[25] who agree that the modality of the rights which are administered by them should be regulated perpetually by a single mind and a single (social) force in order to better safeguard these rights and ensure their most satisfactory use.'

1613. We say that civil society is a union of fathers not because wives and children cannot be considered as members of this society, but because they have to be represented by the fathers who sum up in themselves the rights of all their subjects (*RF*, 1528). All members of a family subject to the father are to be called *relative*, not *absolute citizens*, in accordance with the distinction we made between absolute and relative owners (*RI*, 1279–1293). In other words, they are citizens considered in relationship to other members of the society, but not in relationship to the father whose subjects they are. They become *absolute citizens* only by jurally leaving the paternal family. In this way they themselves acquire the state of fathers and represent themselves in the City.

1614. *Absolute citizens* constitute active, governing, civil society as long as no special form of government has been instituted; relative citizens pertain only to passive, governed society.

CHAPTER 3

The modality of rights, and the characteristics accruing to civil society from it

1615. We now have to examine with greater care this proximate end of civil society, the *regulation of the modality of rights*. The aim of the study is to determine more accurately the nature of civil association. We shall do this by describing those characteristics which accrue to civil society as a result of such modality.

[25] 'Fathers' includes women who possess their own right, as we have said (*Rights in the Family*, 1552).

It is these characteristics which separate civil society from other societies and enclose it within a precise sphere of action.

Article 1.
Various species of modality

1616. Right and the *mode* in which right exists, or in which it is used, are different and sometimes independent things. This independence is verified every time the *mode* of a right can be changed without the possessor of the right losing any of his goods, his pleasures, or his reasonable contentment. In such a case, this mode is not a right, but something distinct from and independent of the right. Indifferent actions also, which bring neither good nor bad to human beings, are modalities; they cannot be called rights.

Moreover, commutation in which a person's goods lose nothing of their value either *in se* or in relationship to the reasonable affection felt by the person who possesses them, does not prejudice rights; the change is only in their modality.

Again, if one person tries to save another from imminent harm by removing some good or right inferior to the damage to which he would otherwise be inevitably subject, we have a change in modality, not the subtraction of a right.

Modality of rights includes all these cases.

The distinction between modality and right originates therefore from the principle that the object of right can only be that which is actually good; whatever is indifferent cannot be the object of right.[26]

1617. But that which is indifferent for the person who possesses a right may not be indifferent for others. In this case, the former has the obligation to permit the variation of the modality of his right, and others to whom this is of assistance have the right to demand it.

1618. In the state of nature, therefore, before the existence of civil society, people were obliged to enter into conventions which determined the modalities held by their rights whenever

---

[26] *ER*, 252–255.

such modalities, which were indifferent to their possessors, brought good or harm to others. Such conventions were established until to some extent it was felt necessary to draw up general, permanent regulations. At this point, civil society was instituted.

1619. Here we have to consider those special characteristics that distinguish civil society from other societies which, like civil society, have the modality of rights as their proximate end. Note that in dealing with these *characteristics* we shall consider civil society in its general, abstract notion, not in any of its particular forms.

These necessary abstractions should not make the reader suspicious. Abstractions cause error when they take the place of subsistent things. When used as surveyors employ them (as principles applicable to subsistent things, but with due regard for all the irregularities present in actually existent matter), they lead to the perfection of knowledge and of society itself.

1620. In reasoning abstractly about civil society, we intend to explain that which results from the pure concept of civil society (without harm to particular, real rights) rather than that which civil society should be in reality. There is a considerable difference between our way of dealing with civil society in the abstract and that of 18th century philosophers. For them, civil society found through abstraction *was to be the norm*; for us, it is only a *possibility*. They describe a society which, according to them, is necessary, that is, a society which human beings have an inalienable right to form for themselves. We describe a hypothetical society, completely distinct from the real rights of human beings. Real rights can never be violated. The society of which we are speaking, which may or may not come into existence, can be and is modified in different ways by real, subsistent rights.

With this as our premise, we can now show the characteristics of civil society as we think they result from *its simple concept* without any adjunct of knowledge in the mind beyond that of civil society, and without any calculation about what pertains to the forms or real circumstances affecting subsistent civil society.

Article 2.
How civil society is distinguished by its characteristic of universality from other societies which have the modality of rights as their proximate end

1621. As we said, civil society is not the only society that has the *modality of rights* as its proximate end. We have pointed out several others (*USR*, 138, 141). How are they distinguished from civil society?

Societies which have the *modality of rights* as their proximate end are either *partial*, if they are concerned with some part of human rights, or *universal*, if they include all these rights. Examples of partial societies which have as their proximate end the modality of rights are companies which insure goods in transit, against fire, and so on; certain societies which deal with life assurance, and any private society set up to protect rights, or to further litigation, and so on.

Civil society alone is the only universal society of such a kind, and can indeed be defined as 'that society which has as its aim the modality of all the rights of the associates'.

1622. Civil society, which has as its aim the regulation of the modality of all rights, has the consequent faculty of regulating the modality of the rights of the family. It cannot, however, encroach on the value of such rights whenever its ordinance is such that it may prejudice domestic society. If there is some doubt about this, the judgment of the family, the competent judge about its own goods, must be consulted or heard.

1623. For the same reason, civil society can regulate the modality of the rights of theocratic society (*ius circa sacra*). However, only the rulers of the theocratic society are the competent judges who must decide if the regulation harms the rights and goods of the society itself.

1624. When misunderstood, the *universality* with which civil government is endowed has produced various systems of despotism. This comes about through failure to consider that such universality is restricted simply to the *modality* of rights in relationship to which alone there may be some part of truth in a principle which is so often abused to bring the Church to heel, that is, 'the Church is in the State, not the State in the Church.'

[1621–1624]

Article 3.
And by the characteristic of supremacy from other modal societies

1625. Because of its *universality*, civil society is also characterised by *supremacy*. In other words, 'civil society is supreme amongst all societies which have the modality of rights as their proximate end.' Consequently, civil society has to regulate all similar societies.

Article 4.
Errors resulting from mistaken concepts of these two characteristics

1626. Misunderstanding of *universality* and *supremacy*, the two sublime characteristics of civil society, has occasioned many errors, as we shall see immediately. Errors arise through insufficient attention to the fact that these characteristics are relative only to societies which have the *modality of rights* as their proximate end; they are not relative to societies which have rights themselves as their proximate end.

1627. The origin of many absurd, tyrannical systems of public right is found here: the *universality* and *supremacy* of civil society have not been restricted within the *order of the modality of rights*, but absolutised.

Hobbes' system arose from badly conceived *supremacy*. This sophist saw that it was necessary to recur to some absolute in the series of human societies. He saw that it was imperative finally to reach some supreme society, force, judgment. This ultimate society, according to him, was called 'civil society'. Thus, by means of a simple entitlement arbitrarily and falsely attached to a concept, civil society was rendered infallible, the sole norm of every action. Hobbes made the society he had conceived the monstrous body which he then called indifferently 'civil society' and even 'ecclesiastical society', according to the objects with which it dealt.[27]

---

[27] *Quam nos civitatem, populus et clericus appellat Ecclesiam (De homine,*

His error did not consist in having formed such a bizarre ideal of society; to conceive any society whatsoever in the abstract is not an error. He erred in wanting to posit his totally imaginary society in the place of true, subsistent civil society. Hobbes' society is not civil society, just as it is not ecclesiastical society; it is an abstraction, as we have said, drawn out mentally from all societies.

What path did Hobbes follow in reaching such an error? — He drew an analogy between the supremacy of civil society and the supremacy of the society that he had conceived. — How do these supremacies differ? — The supremacy of civil society refers only to societies concerned with the modality of rights; the supremacy of Hobbes' society is absolute over all societies and all individuals. In fact, the supremacy of civil society does not imply any seigniorial power over other societies or over individuals; it implies no power whatsoever as long as we are dealing with rights, rather than the modality of rights. Relative to rights, there is perfect equality, between individual and civil society (*RI*, 1649–1688), just as there is between independent persons. Hobbes omitted to posit this limitation because he had not grasped the extremely important difference between *right* and *modality*. He did not see how greatly the nature of civil society differed from that of his imaginary society. Hobbes' poor understanding of the *supremacy* of civil society was the fount of his mistakes.

1628. The *universality* of civil society was equally badly understood. Its false concept generated many illiberal, tyrannical systems, among them that of certain Protestants who against all reason posited this gratuitous affirmation: 'The Church is in the State, not the State in the Church.'

1629. They were ignorant of the different character of the two societies; they did not see that civil society is *universal* only relative to the *modality* of rights. As far as rights themselves are concerned, civil society does not even exist. Rights are not its

---

c. 14 and c. 15: *Cum enim voluntas Dei nisi per civitatem non cognoscatur, etc.*). Thus he reduces religion to horrible pharisaism, to mere legality. The definition of his City, whether true or not, impious or not, has to be believed by faith.

[1628–1629]

object, but the object of other societies, and in general of domestic and theocratic society.

Article 5.
Third characteristic: perpetuity

1630. Another characteristic of perfectly constituted civil society is *perpetuity*.

1631. This does not mean that civil society can never be dissolved. It does in fact dissolve itself effectively through disastrous wars and other causes which shatter its bonds (*RI*, 1660, 1875). It is characterised by perpetuity in the sense that it is perpetual in the intention of the members who compose it, in its laws and in its provisions.

1632. This requires some explanation. When we say that civil society is perpetual in the intention of its members, we do not mean that they intend to oblige themselves never to leave it. This would be absurd and against the principles of universal social Right (*USR*, 454, 470, 472–475). Rather, because civil society is of its nature perpetual, the members intend to join it forever, without however renouncing their right to change their allegiance.

1633. At this point, many things have to be taken into consideration relative to the way in which the bond of any special civil society is dissolved. First, we have to see if the society is truly civil, or mingled with seigniory. It is clear that the bond-servant cannot leave his master at will.

1634. The question takes on another aspect, however, if we consider a pure civil society whose governors, outside the ambit of civil authority, have no other right of seigniory.

1635. I think that this distinction allows us to reconcile the two differing opinions of authors about 'the right to emigrate'. Those who consider civil society as seigniory deny citizens free emigration because they consider them as bound to service [*App.*, no. 1]. And these authors are correct when this seigniory or seigniorial element is verified. The bond-servant must remain with the master until redeemed from servitude (*USR*, 181).

1636. Authors who consider purely civil society agree that citizens have this right on certain conditions; they also are

[1630–1636]

correct. These conditions are that civil society has no account to settle with the person who leaves it. For example, the emigrant must not be employed by or bound to the civil society through some special convention, or in debt for any loan, or be the cause of positive prejudice or harm through his departure.[28] I say 'positive prejudice or harm' because a simple lack of greater usefulness does not authorise a society to keep its members (*RI*, 702–704).

1637. Stable goods which the emigrant does not wish to sell but retains in the territory of the civil society are to be considered on a par with the other stable goods of foreigners.

1638. If he wishes to sell them, he must be the master; there is no reason for imposing a *departure tax* on him.[29]

1639. However, it does not seem unjust to impose a *departure tax* on an absent citizen if through his absence he devotes less to the society, proportionately speaking, than others who remain in the State, ever ready to serve it even with their own personal work. This does not apply if the absentee, through his absence, shares to a lesser extent in the benefits of his homeland.

Article 6.
Fourth characteristic: the prevalence of force

1640. Civil society, therefore, must regulate the modality of rights of its members *universally, supremely and in perpetuity*. It cannot do this, however, without possessing *a prevalent force* with which to overcome any obstacle opposed to the regulation of the modality it has decreed.

[28] Lampredi's condition to the right of emigration is too vague: 'We say that it is lawful on the basis of the same principles which we have established when dealing with this subject, provided the society has no interest in the matter.' A society always has an interest in retaining a citizen who possesses some ability or faculty. If Lampredi were correct, the only persons with a right to emigration would be the helpless poor.

[29] Rotteck's authorisation of the imposition of such a tax seems to be contradictory in the light of what he has said about the right to emigrate. By selling his goods, the emigrant does no *positive* harm to the society, does not injure social rights; he merely makes use of his right of ownership.

1641. *Prevalence of force* is, therefore, a characteristic of civil society.

1642. It is of course sufficient for this force to be effective however this may be achieved. It is certainly not necessary for the *civil government* to have at its disposition a *material force* greater than all the material forces present in the society — this is sometimes impossible. But it is at least necessary that its *regulation of modality* be effectively respected and practised by all. This normally results from a fusion of partly moral, partly intellectual and partly material forces, whose proportion can depend upon purely accidental circumstances. This fusion of forces constitutes the *prevalent power* of government. If the force of moral opinion is lacking, or errors and prejudices against the government have to be overcome, the government needs to increase its material forces in order to exist and be able to govern usefully. It thus fulfils its condition of existence, that is, the prevalence of its power over all opposition.

Article 7.
Fifth characteristic: the end of civil society is the common good together with the tendency to equalise the share of utility

1643. Civil society leaves intact the *rights* of all individuals, and of the two societies which precede it in logical and chronological order. It is instituted to regulate the *modality* of these rights in such a way that all rights may be preserved, and those who possess them may use and enjoy them in peace, and increase them. Because civil society (granted its universality) extends such protection to *all* rights, its aim is the *common good*.

1644. The *common good* must be distinguished from the *public good*. These two matters are confused with consequent serious harm to the science of public Right and to humanity which, because of this confusion of concepts, searches in vain for a suitable social constitution. The *common good is the good of all the individuals* who make up the social body and are subjects of rights; the *public good is the good of the social body* taken as a whole or, according to some opinions, taken in its organisation.

[1641–1644]

1645. The *principle of public good*, substituted for the *principle of common good*, prevailed in pagan societies.

1646. Christianity fought this unceasingly, but was able only little by little to eradicate such a harmful error from people's minds and to wipe out in civil governments such an unjust principle of activity. Even now, civilised Christian societies are still not free of it, although they are working to free themselves.

1647. When the *principle of public good* is substituted for that of the *common good*, *utility* is substituted for *justice*. Politics, having taken Right into its bullying hands, now governs it as it pleases.

1648. The following false principles, which tore humanity apart in every age while pretending to help and save it, result from this profoundly unjust principle:

1. Right is nothing more than utility.[30]

2. *Salus Reipublicae summa lex* [the preservation of the State is the supreme law]. — The absolute right of preservation.[31]

3. *Expedit... ut unus moriatur homo pro populo, et non tota gens pereat* [It is expedient... that one man should die for the people, and that the whole nation should not perish].[32] Assassination of the individual carried out legally by the society (*RI*, 1647–1703, 1747–1757).

4. Reasons of State justify any violation.[33]

5. Everything must be decided by majority vote (*USR*, 243–310). Tyranny of the majority over the minority.[34]

1649. The civil State is instituted to protect and improve *all the rights* of its members. It acts against its natural function, the function for which it exists, if it harms rather than helps a single one of its members for the sake even of benefiting all the others, or proposes to attain the good of *some of them*, even the elders or the majority, and not that of *all*. In other words, if it is

---

[30] The reader can see a confutation of utilitarian authors in [Rosmini's] *Breve esposizione della Filosofia di M. Gioia, Parte Pratica*; and the *Storia de' Sistemi intorno al principio della morale*, cc. 4 and 5.

[31] *ER*, 329–331.

[32] Jn 11: 50.

[33] This system has been applied to a great extent in modern times. See vol. 27 of the *Collezione*, pp. 462 *ss.*

[34] Cf. *Society and its Purpose*, 476–486.

satisfied with acting for the so-called *public good* rather than the *common good*.

1650. The obvious question at this point is: 'If civil society must have as its object the common good of all its individual members, how is this good to be distributed amongst them?' To reply simply that 'utility must be spread out equally', as several publicists have done, is obviously mistaken.[35]

1651. If utility has to be made equal for all, two citizens, one of whom has contributed the equivalent of one hundred units to a society, and the other a single unit, would have to receive equal earnings. Everyone feels the injustice of such a system (*USR*, 341). *Parity of utility, understood in this sense*, presupposes or leads to *absolute democracy*. In such a system, this kind of democracy would be the only jural form of civil association. The law which allows every member to enjoy the same portion of social advantage cannot be reasonable except on the supposition that every individual has posited the same capital in the society — which is against nature. The *right of ownership* does not have equality of possessions as a condition; inequality therefore is present within the sphere of Right. Wanting to make possessions equal by force is the same as starting to institute civil society with the disavowal of right; it means building society on injustice and arbitrary will.

1652. What has to be understood, on the contrary, is that civil society comes together not to disestablish rights, but to protect and favour them by acknowledging them as they exist prior to civil society. Moreover, because no right is excluded from its protection, the utility that members must draw from the ordinances and operations of civil society must be equitably divided in proportion to the quantity of rights they possess. The social contribution depends for its existence on this proportion. Those with more rights have assigned more to the protection of society, and must contribute more to the burdens of society. Consequently they must obtain greater advantage from the protection it provides. Those with fewer rights have put less

[35] Some authors did intend to speak of the *relevant share-quota* of utility when they gave this reply. Understood in this way, the answer is correct, but its expression is still defective.

under the protection of society, contribute less to it and must draw less advantage from it.

1653. The object of civil society, therefore, in regulating the *modality* of the rights of the members, must be to equalise the SHARE-QUOTA OF UTILITY which members can derive from the institution and management of society; it does not consist in equalising utility itself among the members. This is the *equable distribution of common good* to which legislative thought and the government of civil society should constantly tend if it wishes to walk in the way of Right.

1654. It must be noted finally that it is extremely difficult to attain in full the balance indicated by the *share-quota of utility*. Proximity to this end will be proportioned to the wisdom of the government and of the people themselves.

1655. There are, therefore, two duties of social government: 1. to increase in itself, and in the people, the enlightenment with which civil society can always come nearer the attainment of the balance we have described; 2. to tend to the equalisation of the share-quota utility with all the enlightenment and means it possesses[36] while disregarding every private or party interest.

1656. We shall conclude by perfecting the formula that expresses the proximate end of civil society: 'The end of civil society is the regulation of the modality of the rights of all for the common good by means of A CONTINUOUS TENDENCY to equalise the share-quota of utility.'

Article 8.
Sixth characteristic: the end of civil society is also the public good if this is directed to the common good

1657. As we said, the phrase 'public good' means the good of the social body, not of its single parts. For example, at Sparta, where everything tended, as in all pagan societies, to the public good, defective babies were thrown into the Eurotas to ensure

---

[36] No more can be required of any government; no one is held to the impossible, as we have said (*RI*, 735–771).

[1653–1657]

a society of healthy and robust citizens. The life of these innocent children was sacrificed to the *public good* which thus became a tyrant ruling *common good.*

1658. But in what part of the social body does the good of that
body lie? — Of necessity in the principal part of the body, which
is always formed by those citizens who control social authority.
Consequently, the good of the social body, which is called *public
good* under different forms of government, changes place. In the
democratic form of government, public good is normally made
to consist in the good of the *majority.* Under an aristocracy,
public good is understood as the good of the *noble families* who
govern the State. Under a monarchic form of government, the
good of the family which governs the State becomes the principal portion of public good; the good of the families and bodies
bound to the monarchy by service and alliances form a considerable part of the public good.

This is natural. The good of that part of the social body on
which the constitution, life and movement of the body depend
is undoubtedly more important for the general good of the
social body; and it is this part which possesses social authority.

1659. What we have said here about the principal seat of *public
good* under different forms of government has to be distinguished from the artifice used by *political parties*, each of which
endeavours to make the masses believe that the public good is
served by its triumph.[37] The parties appear to be right when
society is disturbed and stands in need of harmony and recom-
position, but for the moment we can ignore this special, exceptional case.

1660. We ask, therefore, if civil society can in some way have
public good as its end? It can indeed, but on condition that *public
good* is subordinated as a means to *common good*, which is its
sole proximate end.

1661. The following principles flow from this reply:

1. Not a single right of individual citizens (the complex of
these rights is the common good) can be sacrificed for the sake
of the public good. — *Sacrificed* means being destroyed or

---

[37] Cf. *SP*, 277–282 for a distinction between *political parties* and *legitimate
forms of government.*

damaged without recompense, when the right or its worth[38] could otherwise be saved.

2. *Public good* must be preferred to *private good* once the rights of individuals have been safeguarded. In this case, public good will undoubtedly further common good.

Article 9.
Seventh characteristic: the end of society is also private good, provided concurrence or opportunity for this good is open to all

1662. In addition, when first the common good and then the public good have been safeguarded, the private good of individuals and families can and must be pursued, provided one condition is observed: the opportunity for obtaining private good through the action of society must be open equally to all families and all individuals. It must not be restricted to particular individuals or families or bodies.

1663. When this condition has been verified, all citizens have equality of opportunity, and private good itself becomes part of the common good. The good that one family or individual gains today from civil society is gained tomorrow by another individual or family when they are placed in the same circumstances with the same opportunities. Private good, alternating between families and distributing itself evenly over a certain period of time, is absorbed and changed into true common good.

Article 10.
Corollaries from the two preceding articles

1664. There are three areas to which civil society can extend its ordinances for the sake of obtaining *public good*:

---

[38] We add 'or its worth', because it is possible to imagine a case in which society, by preserving for John Smith a right which is worth one unit, may then leave him exposed to the loss of other rights worth nine. In such a case, society could certainly dispose of John Smith's one-unit right. Its loss would be more than compensated by the preservation and defence of his nine-unit rights. As we have said many times (*ER*, 252–255), right is constituted by *worth*, not by a simple *faculty* without worth.

[1662–1664]

1. It can make all the ordinances helpful to public good but without causing damage to any of its citizens. These ordinances must not in any way affect those who gain no advantage.

2. It can impose natural, slight actions, not burdensome or damaging, on its citizens for the sake of public good. These actions are not to be harmful to the person who does them; they can be considered as modalities of rights.

3. Civil society can also limit the inoffensive freedom of citizens, that is, their rights to actions and things (*RI*, 79–84), provided this causes the citizens no trouble nor arouses any jural resentment in them.

1665. In the second place, what can civil society do for the private good of determined persons or families?

First, it cannot harm some persons or families, nor exclude them from concurrence, or opportunity, in order to favour certain others.

Second, for the sake of private advantage, civil society can regulate the modality of the first two areas, mentioned above relative to public good. It cannot do this, however, relative to the third area, which touches the limitation placed on others' freedom, unless it has a firm intention of never preferring private to public good. Indeed, it can favour private good only for the sake of public good, just as public good must be favoured in subordination to the common good. This is the case when dealing with the acquisition of some good. The opposite is true when dealing with the avoidance of evil. Society must prefer not to do harm to a private individual even for the sake of obtaining the safety of all the others. Conversely, it cannot do some good to the individual unless this good comes about without any damage or diminution of public good.

1666. Besides this, civil society can make ordinances about the ownership held by particular persons when such an ordinance is to their indubitable advantage. In this way, civil society simply regulates the modality of their rights without touching the rights themselves. What is taken away on the one hand is amply compensated for on the other. Activity of this kind is the exercise of the right to benefit others, which is proper not only to civil society but to each person. Indeed, civil society has a special office in this regard relative to the end for which it was instituted because 1. the common good results from the good of the individuals and 2. the good of the individuals has a useful influence on the common good.

1667. In the third place, civil society has the right to do the following for the common good: restrict inoffensive freedom of private individuals in the three areas indicated; restrict the freedom of the public at large and of the commonalty; use the ownership held by particular persons provided they are compensated as individuals or sufficiently compensated by the share they have in the common good. Civil society can also reach out to the ownership held by the commonalty or a body or a determinate number of persons provided full recompense is made in both cases. Finally, it can lay hands on the ownership of the commonalty (the right to tax) if the commonalty, that is, *all* the individuals forming it, are recompensed proportionately through the good which will be obtained.

We sum up: the powers of civil society and the limits beyond which it cannot go without fault relative to its members are:

1. It can make ordinances about *inoffensive freedom* as follows: for the good of individuals who belong to it; for the public good provided individuals experience no jural resentment; for the common good. It offends against individuals if it disposes of their freedom irrespective of any of these three aims and without the conditions we have indicated.

2. It can make ordinances about the *ownership* belonging to individuals when the aim is their own greater good; when the aim is the common or public good; and when the individual shares in what is being done through adequate compensation for the harm suffered. Civil society offends particular persons when making ordinances about their ownership if the ordinance does not aim at the good of the individual himself or the public or common good, or without advantage or full recompense to the damaged owner.

3. Civil society can make ordinances about public freedom when the aim is the public good or the common good. It offends the public in making ordinances about its freedom if such aims are not effectively verified.

4. It can make ordinances about public ownership, or the ownership held by a body or an indeterminate number of individuals when this is done for the common good, and for a common good sufficient to compensate all the citizens who

have been harmed. It offends the public if it makes ordinances about its ownership without aiming effectively at the common good, and at a common good sufficient to compensate all the citizens who have been harmed.

5. It can make ordinances about common, inoffensive freedom for the common good. It offends all the citizens if it makes ordinances about their freedom without this aim.

6. It can make ordinances about common ownership when the aim is a common good sufficient to compensate all the citizens for their loss. It offends the rights of all the citizens if it makes ordinances about their ownership without aiming at the common good, and at a good sufficient to recompense all their losses.

The social power to alter the modality of rights extends to these six branches of ordinances.

Article 11.
Eighth characteristic: civil society needs external means to fulfil its end; it is an EXTERNAL society

1668. All the regulations which civil society can impose relative to the *modality* of the rights of the members cannot be put into effect without the use of external means, persons and things. Every social activity requires the use of functionaries, and the consumption of things of worth which economists call 'riches'. Civil society can therefore be called *external society* with respect to the means necessary for its *action* (*USR*, 105–107, 125–127).

1669. Like all human societies, however, its constitution has an *internal* or spiritual *part* as well as an *external part*.[39]

---

[39] Cf. *SP*, 149–168.

Article 12.
Corollaries of the eighth characteristic

§1. Corollary 1: *civil society does not necessarily include all human beings*

1670. Simple consideration of the general concept of civil society — an association of several families or heads of families for the sake of regulating for common advantage the modality of the rights they possess — shows that its essence does not extend either to all human beings or to all those who are found in a given territory, but only to those who do in fact associate.

1671. Nevertheless, although civil society does not need to include all heads of families in order to be what it is, we still have to see if it can, according to Right, aggregate them all to itself. The answer to this question follows from its eighth characteristic.

1672. Civil society has as its end the protection of *rights*. All human beings have rights for which they want more or less general protection. From this point of view there is nothing to impede anyone from belonging to civil society.

1673. Civil society cannot exist, however, without the use of external means. These have to be provided for it by the members who seek safeguards and protection for their rights. It is clear that not all human beings can provide the means, at least with the regularity and surety that society requires. It follows therefore that in a civil society regulated with perfect equity there is no place amongst the citizens for those unable to contribute anything of substance to the society and incapable of providing the necessary taxes by regular work.

1674. No one may conclude from this that the concept of civil society demands the possession of land. There are other riches which can be used for the purpose.

1675. Nor does this concept require territory of one's own in which the associates dwell continually. Nomad families or even adventurers can join together in some civil association,[40]

---

[40] Schmalz is wrong in denying this on the basis that a society of human beings without fixed, proper territory cannot protect all the rights of which man is susceptible. The premise is true, but this does not prevent the existence of a true civil society between people. Not all civil societies are perfectly equal

although this may not be suitable for providing them with all the goods possessed by peoples permanently attached to a territory.

1676. Finally, we must note that, according to this concept of society, the sole condition upon which someone can be admitted as a citizen is that he has sufficient means to live and to pay his contribution.[41]

§2. Those excluded from citizenship retain their extra-social rights

1677. This does not mean that those who cannot attain citizenship are therefore lacking in rights, nor that citizens and the City itself have no obligation towards them. Civil society and its members are in the *state of nature* relative to those outside the society. Both society and its individual members, as well all human beings present in civil society without belonging to it, are jural persons and as such equal (*RI*, 1647–1688). Natural, rational right must be maintained amongst such jural persons with equal respect on both sides.

1678. Again, members of civil society and those not belonging to it are nevertheless associated in *theocratic society*. They are equally obliged to respect mutual rights and to fulfil the mutual obligations which they have as equal members of this divine society.

1679. We have noted that *civil society* amongst the pagans had absorbed all things. It recognised no society superior to itself and no right other than that established by itself. This horrendous tyranny of *civil society* was abrogated by God through the fact of Christianity. Civil associations now have to acknowledge

in their organisation and effective in obtaining their end, but this does mean that they lack the essence of civil societies. If the word 'State' is reserved for civil societies established in their own territory, I would willingly admit that ambulant civil societies should be called something other than 'States'. Cf. *Le Droit des gens*, bk. 1, c. 1.

[41] Those altogether lacking in goods must not be excluded from *civil society* because they have no independence, as Kant requires, but simply because they cannot pay their contribution, a necessary condition for the existence of civil government.

that they cannot dispose in any way of human rights, all of which they have to respect whether the subjects of these rights exist within or without civil society. The only authority possessed by civil societies is that of regulating the *modality* of the rights of their members — nothing more.

This truth has been accepted in various degrees in all Christian legislations, although not all have followed it in practice. The Austrian Code is explicit and clear: 'Every human being has innate rights which are known through reason alone; each human being, therefore, is to be considered as a person.'[42]

§3. Corollary 2: *it is not absurd for an individual to belong to several civil societies contemporaneously*

1680. Just as it is not absurd for a man to be in the state of nature without belonging to any civil society, so it is not absurd for him to belong to several civil societies contemporaneously.

1681. The reason for this lies in the distinction between *jural person* and *individual person*. The jural person, although formed from more than one real individual (*RI*, 1649–1650), can be unique; similarly, a single real individual can contemporaneously be more than one jural person. The latter is simply a complex of rights administered with unity of will.

1682. It is not repugnant, therefore, when considered in itself, for one complex of rights in an individual to be placed under the protection of one civil society, and for another complex of rights belonging to the same individual to be placed under the protection of another civil society. In this case, the individual takes a

---

[42] §16. — Although this paragraph speaks only of *innate rights*, it must be extended to all rights, even *rights acquired* under a just title when human beings are found in the extra-social state. Affirming that such rights are known by reason alone is in opposition to their being known through the positive ordinance of the civil legislator, although it does not exclude the rights and duties known through divine revelation. The word *person*, as we have said on other occasions, is a noun indicating dignity and power. Right is in fact a *power*; it indicates a jural state formed by a complex of rights adherent to a human being. Each human, therefore, even outside the civil body, has a jural state; he is a jural person whom society must respect for the same reason that it wishes to be respected itself.

[1680–1682]

suitable procurator[43] as his representative in his absence, and pays the *contribution* necessary to provide the two social bodies with means of action.

1683. It is not necessary to the essence of civil society that it should include all human beings. As a result, mankind is divided into different civil associations. The proximity of related families, or even simple proximity of place, does indeed unite them, but as relationship becomes more distant and communication more difficult, they find themselves divided and distributed in several commonalties. Geographical, linguistic, intellectual, moral, spiritual and religious differences all contribute to the growing isolation. In this case, there is nothing to prevent an individual's acceptance as member in two or more of these commonalties provided he contributes his quota of expenses and activity in person or through others, according to varying social constitutions and conventions.

1684. A difficulty would arise if an individual belonged to two societies at war with another. This however would not be a case of mere Right. It is impossible for both societies to be acting justly, and the individual would simply have the obligation to act in favour of the just side. If the justice of the case were doubtful, an obligation to decide the matter peacefully would exist, but no *casus belli* (*RI*, 462, 501, 505, 1026). Our citizen would then either have to abstain from taking part or do what he could to pacify the two societies. If one side refused, and thus committed an evident injustice, he would have to abandon it. The difficulty about belonging to two civil societies would be reduced to the disturbance and harm arising for citizens with dual nationality and possessions in both territories.[44] If negotiations did not succeed and right on both sides were still doubtful, the citizen belonging to both societies could refer judgment to the societies themselves as competent judges, while he himself

---

[43] Society guards every good and right posited in it, but nothing more. Individual activity is not an *essential* element of civil society; the activity of a jural person is sufficient. We did indeed say that civil society regulates the modality of all the rights of the members, but 'members' must be understood here as a jural person.

[44] The principle that the same person could belong to two or more cities was in fact acknowledged by governments. Often, several cities admitted the same family to citizenship.

remained as passive as possible except for the contribution prescribed by both societies.

1685. The question of *citizenship*, which belongs to *social right*, must not be confused with that of *servile subjection*, which belongs to *seigniorial right*. A person cannot properly speaking be a bond-servant of more than one master; but he can be a citizen of more than one City.

§4. Corollary 3: *external means must be provided for civil society by the members in proportion to the quantity of rights which they place under the protection of the society*

1686. Civil society regulates the modality of all the rights of its members, that is, of all rights to whose modality its power extends.[45]

Every member therefore of civil society receives an advantage proportioned to the quantity of the rights he places under the protection of the society. It follows that he must contribute to the society a share-quota of the external means necessary for its existence and administration. This quota will be in proportion to the quantity of rights whose modality is regulated. Such is the only principle suitable for directing the equable distribution of taxes (*USR*, 338–341).

[45] A citizen possessing some good or right outside the power of the civil society to which he belongs receives no protection or advantage in respect of them. Hence, they do not belong either to the civil society or to the jural person that is a member of it. The goods may be in the territory of another civil society, located amidst families who belong to another society. In this case, it is the second society which protects them and regulates their modality in relationship with the rights of the other families who belong to it. The owner of the goods will therefore have to contribute to the second society the quota necessary for the protection of the goods. We could ask here if the citizen of one society, when harmed by another society in whose territory his possessions lie, could be protected forcefully by the first society against the injustice. He *could* be protected just as persons in the state of nature can provide mutual assistance to repel unjust aggression or defend themselves against unjust harm. But the society is not *obliged* to do this under any title of society. The relationships between two independent societies belong to *individual Right* (which is called *Right of the nations*), not to *social Right*.

[1685–1686]

§5. Corollary 4: *in civil society members must enjoy a degree of social power equal to the share-quota they contribute, except for the judicial part*

1687. It follows that the persons contributing are those who posit civil society in being and provide its action. Hence, rigorous justice requires that radical[46] and autocratic social power, if not alienated, should be distributed amongst the contributors in proportion to the size of their contribution. This, as we said, is proportioned to the quantity of their rights, whose modality is regulated by the society; it is also in proportion to the advantages they receive from the association (*USR*, 214–310).

1688. I said 'except for the judicial part'. In fact, two parts in civil society have to be distinguished with the utmost care:

1. The part relative to justice — this is not arbitrary, but fixed by jural, rational law.

2. The administrative, prudential part — the political part in the strict sense — which consists in determining and choosing from amongst the *just activities* of the society those which are most beneficial to the *common good*, that is, to the end of the society itself.

If there is a question of justice, neither majority voting nor a greater quantity of rights (a majority of jural persons) should prevail. Each person is obliged to submit to the law of justice, even if this is suggested by a single individual or by a person foreign to the society (*USR*, 305–310).

1689. *Judicial power*, understood in its greatest extension, must be placed in the hands of the wisest and holiest people who can be found; administrative or strictly political power must lie either with the majority vote or with unanimity, and is of its nature distributed amongst the members according to the quota

---

[46] If radical power is still in the hands of fathers, they can at will choose officials, to whom they entrust *executive power*. The suitability of these officials, and the distribution of offices according to merit, will depend upon the enlightenment of will found in the fathers. Mistaken choices would not necessarily be unjust, therefore, although they would lead to damage. Any law, however, which antecedently excludes someone from simple *passive concurrence* for such posts, without factual proof of unsuitability, is always unjust because it violates relative jural freedom (*RI*, 83, 273).

of their contribution to the external means with which the
society endures and carries out its activity.[47]

§6. Corollary 5: *is an electoral patrimony to be set in the case of representative governments? If so, what kind of patrimony should it be according to rational Right?*

1690. At this point, we can also consider the jural solution to
the very important question of electoral patrimony which is
subject to so many controversies in representative governments.

It is clear in the first place that establishing a *fixed patrimony*
is not absolutely necessary. The amount of contribution needed
for a right to a say in the choice of deputies must, of course, be
established, but this personal contribution, which we can call
capitation, can vary from year to year, according to the amount
spent on the administration.

1691. Again, if deputies are nominated for a certain number of
years, citizens must be able to have their say in the choice,
provided they can assure the State of their ability to pay the
capitation for that number of years. If, later, the capitation is not
paid, the right to vote is lost.

1692. I said that setting such a patrimony is not *absolutely*
necessary. Circumstances and experience can well render it
necessary if it becomes clear that without it social administration would be rendered uncertain, hesitant or too complicated.
In this case, the patrimony would have to be *income* which
stably assured for the civil administration the contribution of a
fixed capitation calculated according to an abundant median.

1693. Electors with a greater number of votes must assure for
the State an *income* corresponding to that number.

[47] Here, we can only mention this important question in passing. It is
developed in Part 3 of Section 2.

[1690–1693]

Article 13.
Ninth characteristic: civil society has neither seigniorial nor profit-making power; its power is purely beneficial

1694. In the state of nature, the modality of rights was and is regulated by each individual, by each partial society. Was this need to regulate the modality of one's own rights in relationship with that of others good for the owners of rights? In the first place, it was a burden because, as we said, modality is what can be done about a right, prescinding from the good the person draws from it. In addition, modality also brought responsibility from the point of view of conscience, and often became a burden superior to the forces of the person who bore it.

1695. On the other hand, it was good for individuals to have this freedom to regulate the modality of their own rights. With it they possessed the means of governing or harming, of diminishing or increasing the good coming from their right. Entrusting others with such regulation is a delicate and dangerous matter. Every owner wants either to have it in his own hands or be able to put it in safe hands. With the introduction of civil society, all owners, depriving themselves of this modality, placed in common the right to regulate the modality of their own rights. This, accompanied by the contribution of external means, is the common *fund* of civil society.

This explains why individuals or families did not deprive themselves of their own goods when they entered civil society, but only of the trouble of regulating the modality of their rights. This is not a advantage unless considered in relationship to the danger of abuse that might be feared if modality fell into other hands. Moreover, families, in ceding such a burden to civil society, have not in any way ceded the right to abuse modality, but only the faculty of regulating it advantageously, or at least with more advantage than they could have achieved by themselves.

Of its nature, therefore, civil society has no seigniorial or profit-making power. It is simply a *beneficial power*. Its function is to remove a burden from all families and establish for them peaceful cohabitation, with constant progress and development in every kind of good.

[1694–1695]

Article 14.
Tenth characteristic: civil society is a multi-quota society

1696. A society composed of members who put in common a greater or lesser fund, and receive different degrees of advantage from it, is a *multi-quota society* (*USR*, 131). It is clear from what has been said that this is the case with civil society.

1697. This quality does not harm anyone, but is of assistance to all. Nor does it render society *unequal* (*USR*, 141); all citizens have the same law before which they are equal.

1698. If *jural persons*, taken as an equal complex of rights, are distinguished from *real persons*, civil society is uni-quota relative to jural persons. The *complex itself of rights* with which a subject is vested gives a title to the same degree of power and to the same degree of benefits arising from it.

Article 15.
Civil society can accidentally seem unequal

1699. Civil society acquires the characteristic of *unequal society* if some bond of *seigniory* intervenes in it. Because the *law determining seigniorial rights* is different from the *law determining civil rights*, the members of such a society are not subject to the same law. This inequality does not arise from the nature of society, however, but from the heterogeneous element accidentally inserted in it.

CHAPTER 4

Government in so far as it flows from the essence of civil society

1700. We continue to describe civil society as it is shown in its *abstract concept*. We ignore its accidental modifications and *de facto* titles, which we shall deal with later. We now need to

[1696–1700]

demonstrate how the constitution of a government grows from this *concept*. Government is so essential to society that without it society cannot be fully conceived. The principles already posited contain the germ of government suggested to the mind by the essence of society. We must develop it.

Article 1.
The sense in which fathers of families, by associating in civil society, cede the regulation of the modality of their rights

1701. We said that fathers, by uniting in civil commonalty, cede to it the regulation of the modality of their own rights. This needs explanation. In doing so, they do not deprive themselves of the faculty of regulating this modality, but oblige themselves to regulate it *in common*, rather than *in private*, each one by himself.

1702. Before civil society, each father regulated only the modality of his own rights. After association with others, he regulates not only the modality of his own rights, but the rights of all the other fathers. If he loses anything, he regains it to his great advantage.

Article 2.
Radical governmental authority resides in the associated fathers

1703. Every governmental power, therefore, resides as in its seat and root in the collectivity of associated fathers,[48] although the power is present in unequal, not equal quantities, as we said. The vote of the fathers carries weight proportionately to the accumulation of their rights, to their contribution, or to the

[48] Samuel Coccejo, after deducing civil authority from the authority placed in common by fathers, adds: 'It is easy to see from this why only heads of families, not individual members of families, are called to meetings. Only heads had the right to command. Coming together in the City, they subjected themselves and what they had to the common will of the other heads' (*Dissert*. Proem 12, bk. 6, c. 1, §612, 9.

consequent advantage which they obtain from society — three things which must remain in constant, proportional equality.

Article 3.
The authority of the representatives

1704. The associated fathers, who possess governmental authority in proportion to the quantity of their contribution, can exercise this authority for themselves, or by means of their representatives or procurators (*USR*, 255–258).

1705. The fathers' *governmental authority* is divided into two branches: *legislative authority*, which makes laws, enactments and ordinances, and *executive authority* which puts legislative matters into execution.

1706. The fathers may exercise authority either on their own account, or by means of others, although even here they are bound by a moral, jural obligation to proceed with order, harmoniously and peacefully.

1707. In modern societies, they usually exercise legislative authority by means of 'representatives' or political 'deputies'.

1708. The limits to the authority of these representatives are:

1. All the limits of the civil authority of the fathers represented. This civil authority does not extend to the *rights* of the associates; it is limited to the *regulation of their modality*. — The *rights* of the associates are the object of *political obligations*; *modality* constitutes the object of *political rights*.

1709. 2. In addition, all the limits pertaining to their mandate. — The representatives must remain within the sphere of the modality of rights, regulation of which is the aim of civil association, without attempting to dispose of the rights themselves of the associates. They must also remain faithful to the express or presumed will of the fathers whom they represent as simple mandataries.

1710. Nothing more needs to be added here, except that fathers cannot limit in their political representatives the necessary faculty of regulating equably the modality of rights. They have to concede this faculty whole and entire (if they themselves do not wish to intervene in the deliberations). Doing otherwise would be equivalent to impeding the aim of civil association. This should be noted carefully. The associates have a duty to attend personally or through their procurators to the regulation of modality, the proximate end of civil society.

Article 4.
Executive authority in officials, or government in the strict sense

1711. Legislative authority can be exercised by many individuals united in an assembly where people deliberate and establish necessary ordinances by vote. This is not the case with executive authority which is divided into more or less general, special and particular functions that require the presence of individuals to whom the execution of deliberations is entrusted.

1712. The fathers can either choose these officials for themselves or through their deputies. The persons deputed to choose the officials can constitute a ministry or even a different assembly from the legislature, or even carry out the choice themselves.

1713. Choosing one rather than another way of electing officials pertains originally to the radical authority of the fathers. They can and must agree to establish their way of acting through a majority of *political votes*[49] which they give by means of the legislative assembly they themselves constitute or through others acting as their procurators.

Article 5.
Moral duties governing the choice of political deputies and officials

1714. The fathers must choose as legislative deputies those persons who are 1. most prudent; 2. most trustworthy (persons whom they trust most to act for the greatest interest of their families, with proper regard for justice); 3. most conciliatory

[49] By *political vote*, I mean that which corresponds to capitation.

[1711–1714]

(persons who will come more easily to agreement with other deputies without harm to the partial interest they represent). — This last quality is the object of moral-civil duty, that is, duty arising from the good that all the members of a civil association have to seek.

1715. Relative to the choice of officials constituting government in the strict sense, the fathers must choose in general the persons most suitable for the office. Thus, they should choose

1. for the *administrative* and *political* branch, persons in whom greater prudence and ability is united with uprightness and justice;

2. for the *judicial* branch, persons *a*) well-known for their integrity; *b*) endowed with greater knowledge of Right; *c*) less subject to temptation — for general, special or accidental reasons — to depart in their judgment from the direct line of the most perfect justice (*RF*, 1411).

Article 6.
The independence and dependence of political deputies and officials on the fathers

1716. *Political deputies* and *officials* enjoy the independence which gives social offices a very different nature from that of mere *services* (*USR*, 404–414).

1717. Consequently political deputies are independent of the fathers in their obligation to respect the rights of all; they depend on the fathers in the way they regulate the modality of these rights.

1718. *Officials* are independent of the fathers:

a) In their obligation not to exceed the sphere of the *modality* of rights in executing laws. — Laws themselves which exceed these limits, obviously cease to be laws. They cannot be put into execution without breaking the moral-social law.

b) In their obligation to carry out laws that are not excessive, or which can and must be presumed not excessive. — Having established the laws, the fathers must leave them to be executed unless they legitimately derogate or abrogate them.

1719. Officials, in cases where they operate illegally, are

dependent on the fathers but have the right to be judged by arbitrators, tribunals (if they have been set up) and especially by the social tribunal (if this exists) (*USR*, 310).

CHAPTER 5
Alienation of social authority

Article 1.
The civil authority of the fathers can be alienated in whole or in part

1720. Choice of *deputies* and of *officials* does not contain any *alienation* of civil authority; it is simply an *exercise* of civil authority. Nor is it limited by the degree of independence connected with the office of deputy and all other social offices; this independence arises from the law of justice which can never be violated by social authority. Authority is said to be limited only when it exists with an extension whose sphere is restricted. Authority cannot be limited where it does not exist.

1721. Nevertheless, limitation of authority can come about through an act of the fathers when they alienate a part of it. We have seen that all rights, except some congenital and inalienable rights, can be ceded by those possessing them, can be sold to others; in a word, alienated. Hence, *social authority* can be alienated by the fathers in whole or in part (*USR*, 313–314, 386–403). In fact, there is nothing to prevent the fathers from choosing, for example, a family in whom they place in perpetuity their own executive or even legislative authority.

1722. This is perfectly possible to conceive. In this case, they would have constituted a more or less absolute hereditary monarchy.

Article 2.
Alienation of the social authority of the fathers introduces a slight seigniorial element into social society

1723. With the constitution of this monarchic power, a very limited *seigniorial element* has entered civil association.

1724. In fact, ceding civil authority in perpetuity to such a family does not spring from the essence of society. It is a contract pertaining to *individual Right*, and to this extent resembles dominion which springs from willed subjection (*RI*, 531–532).

1725. In fact, we have seen that every social office is a power (*USR*, 404–414), and that having in one's own hands the faculty of regulating the modality of one's own and others' rights is a good, on account of the danger which could occur when such regulation is handed over to the judgment of another.

1726. Nevertheless, it is true that the family vested with social authority has no power beyond *social* power. In other words, it does not go beyond the regulation of the *modality* of the rights of the citizens. This is why we insisted that the *seigniorial element* is extremely limited in this case.

1727. This element is reduced, therefore, to the following headings:

1. To the *title* through which the vested family possesses such authority. This is held not through *social title* but *cession*, which resembles ownership and dominion acquired indirectly.

2. In the *irrevocability* of this cession which is presumed to be made in perpetuity.

3. In the annexed *right* of *competence*. The person who possesses such authority is also the *competent judge* of its exercise. The fathers cannot judge that a monarch errs, except in almost self-evident cases (*RI*, 610–612, 631, 713). In every other case, they hold the condition of *dependents*. The monarch, however, retains the total moral-jural obligation of regulating modality to the best of his knowledge according to the principles of justice and prudence.

[1723–1727]

Article 3.
How the social contract was conceived in the last century

1728. What we have said enables us to evaluate the social contract as it was conceived in the last century. This system was invented to explain the way in which people, in positing jointly the modality of their own rights, formed civil society. However, because the modality of particular rights cannot be conceived as posited in common without its being entrusted to particular persons administrating it, that is, to government, two very distinct questions were confused; the question of *society* was muddled with that of *government*.

In fact, granted the presence of a government which administers the modality of rights, civil society certainly exists. It remains true, however, that government is one thing, and society another. Government is the power that administers the modality of rights; society posits jointly the modality of particular rights and makes it a single administration. Confusing these questions opened the way to two different paths, which led to two opposite systems. One group focused on *government*, and claimed to reduce and, as it were, sacrifice society to government; the other focused on *society*, and claimed to sacrifice government to it.

Those focusing on government started from the fact that humanity is furnished with governments; those focusing on society started with an abstraction because there are no societies without government. One side claimed to defend governments, the other, society; one side reasoned according to the data of experience, the other on theoretical principles; one side sustained absolute authority, the other made authority dependent on the social contract. Where does the truth lie?

1729. If we have to make a judgment about a formed government, we already have persons in whose hands lies the regulation of modality. Here, justice requires simply that we search for the *title* by which authority of this kind is placed in the hands of those who govern, or by which this authority is possessed. In such a case we have to form a judgment about the title, just as we judge about the title to any other right whatsoever. This title is a fact; if we find it valid, the government is legitimate, if invalid, illegitimate. The titles by which rights are acquired can be various and all equally valid; the right to govern is subject to the same rules of justice as other rights. It is an error, therefore, to maintain that this right can be attained solely through a single title, or a single means (we shall deal with the various means of acquiring a title later). Those claiming that the social contract is the only means for obtaining this right err because they gratuitously restrict the various means and title to one alone. They confuse the question of the *essence of civil society* with the question of the *origin of civil society* and governments. The *essence of civil society* remains the same, but the origin of governments can vary. Government is a right and, as we have said, a right is acquired in various ways amongst which immemorial possession is sufficient, even without information about the primitive title (*RI*, 1047).

Elsewhere, we have confuted the opinion of those unable to understand the origin of the right of ownership without presupposing some convention amongst the first humans [*App.*, no. 2], that is, without an express or at least tacit contract in the division of land (*RI*, 334–343). We agreed that such a convention between individuals is indeed a way (when it actually takes place) of acquiring the right of ownership, but we added that this way does not exclude other equally legitimate ways such as occupation of what is unoccupied. Granted the principles which determine various ways of acquiring rights, all that remains is to examine the title with which an individual or collective person holds the power of government, and see if it is just.

The error of the supporters of the social system is very obvious, and necessarily overthrows civil societies and their already constituted governments, the greater part of whom are not founded on the title of contract, but upon other titles which can thus easily be declared illegitimate. But how can such a systematic theory arise?

1730. As we said, the theory arises from considering civil society in the abstract. If civil society is considered as it really is, that is, as subsistent, rather than abstract, very different results are seen. In the first case, the titles upon which the legitimacy of governments is judged exist in fact; in the second, positive titles are lacking, history no longer gives us any light on the matter, and we ourselves set aside the facts of its origin with such a method. Only the essence of civil society stands before us, and this certainly consists in the union of the modality of particular rights, that is, modality administered with unity of mind. But this concept lacks any real person who may have acquired for himself the exclusive right to such administration. As a result, administration of the modality of particular rights belongs, in this hypothetical case, only to the whole body, and is shared by its members according to their contribution. The only way of conceiving how this modality can be brought together is mutual consent and pact on the part of those who make up the association. It is under this aspect that we disapprove of the social contract because it is used erroneously to explain the origin of governments rather than the origin of society. It claims to be the sole origin of governments rather than one amongst many; it becomes a necessary rather than a merely possible title.

1731. We conclude by distinguishing the four questions which have been confused and treated as one by publicists:

1. What is civil society? — The commonalty of fathers who want the modality of their rights to be regulated by a single social mind for the shared, better good of all.

2. What is government in civil society? — The collective person or the individual who regulates the modality of the rights of the commonalty.

3. What is the jural origin of society? — The common consent of the members.

4. What is the origin of governments, that is, what are the ways according to which a collective or individual person holds the administration of the modality of the rights of the commonalty? — There are different ways, which we shall enumerate shortly. Only by prescinding from all positive and factual ways are we left with the social contract itself, the origin in this case both of society and of government.

PART TWO

THE SCIENCE OF RIGHT IN CIVIL SOCIETY DISTINGUISHED FROM POLITICAL SCIENCE

> No one is to harm another unjustly for the sake of promoting the common good.
>
> St. Thomas, *ST*, II–II, q. 63, art. 3

1732. What has been said will receive greater light from consideration of the various possible origins of civil governments. Later we shall examine these origins at greater length. But first we need to clarify any mental confusion about the science of Right in civil society and the science of Politics. These two branches of knowledge have been confused and muddled by sensist philosophers and utilitarians. We begin, therefore, by carefully tracing the distinction between these two disciplines, both of which are needed for the art of government.

CHAPTER 1
The proximate and remote ends of societies

1733. We have discussed elsewhere the proximate and remote end of civil society,[50] and shown that the *proximate end* must be regulated by the *remote*. Related to the latter, the former stands as means to end. The office of wholesome, complete *political science* is to lead civil society to attain its *proximate end* without prejudice to the *remote end*, which the proximate must help and serve.

We also said that the art of leading civil society to its proximate

[50] *SP*, bk. 2.

[1732–1733]

end is *politics in the strict sense*; the art of subordinating the proximate to the remote end pertains to *political philosophy*. This is the moral and more excellent part of politics.

CHAPTER 2

The difference between politics and social right

1734. Political science should be carefully distinguished from *social Right*. *Politics* shows how society is led to the attainment of its proximate end; *political philosophy* shows how the proximate end of civil society is ordered to the remote, final end.

What remains for the science of *Right*? Let us begin by comparing *Right* with *political philosophy*.

1. First, Right is a much more restricted branch of knowledge than political philosophy which aims at leading civil societies to that final perfection wherein these societies become suitable means for obtaining *virtue and happiness*, the supreme good of associated human individuals. That which is *just* is only one particular element of this supreme good. Virtue extends much further than simply 'giving to each member what is his own', which is the object of civil-social justice.

2. Secondly, political philosophy, although it intends to bring society to the perfect state most favourable to the supreme good of individuals, does not determine this good. This is done by the *moral law*, of which *jural law* is a part. [51]

Political philosophy does not expound what pertains to the philosophy of right, which however it needs to hold present as a prior datum if it is to regulate its own progress and carry out the work assigned and committed to it, that is, to harmonise successfully the perfect state of society with right. Social Right, therefore, is a branch of knowledge anterior to political philosophy before which it places what is *just*, precisely as ethics precedes social Right in an even more general way by placing before it what is *upright*, in other words, moral good in all its

[51] *ER*, 293–317.

extension. Political philosophy, enlightened by these two branches of knowledge, can see and find with certainty, by using its own proper means, the perfect state of society most favourable to moral perfection, a state which it must actuate in the associated individuals.

1735. *Politics* itself differs from the science of social Right in the way that what is *useful* differs from what is *just*. Politics seeks what is useful for societies; social Right shows what is just, irrespective of other considerations.

1736. *Political philosophy* provides the middle ground needed to avoid collisions between these two sciences and arts, one devoted to what is useful, the other to what is just. Political philosophy aims, we said, at tempering and dispensing *political utility* in such a way that it never prejudices or violates *what is just*; having preserved in all things what is conformed to justice, political philosophy directs and orders the utility sought by social government in such a way that all associates may become as fully and completely virtuous as possible.

CHAPTER 3

The utilitarians' false definition of right confuses the two sciences of politics and Right

1737. The two sciences of politics and Right, which we have just distinguished, were confused during the last century. This was the sad effect of the dominion gained over minds in that unbalanced time by the sensist school which did all it could to obscure and distract people's attention from the objectivity of the moral law. Consequently it destroyed the concept of right, which it replaced with the study of utility.

1738. The darkness veiling the eyes of the mind to moral light has not yet passed completely; thought is still imprisoned in the narrow confines of subjective feelings. It must be helpful therefore to return briefly to what I have said more at length elsewhere. Let us see how *right* was conceived in this Italy of ours. Beccaria wrote:

> Notice that the word 'right' does not contradict the word 'force'; the former is rather a modification of the latter, that is, THE MODIFICATION MOST USEFUL FOR THE MA-JORITY.[52]

It is true that the word *right* does not contradict the word *force*; we have shown this. [53] It is also true that right is a kind of modification of force to the extent that force protected and directed by jural law becomes right. But it is totally false, impossible, unjust and immoral in the extreme that this modification should be conceived as what is useful for the *majority*. On the contrary, *right* exists without any relationship whatsoever to the majority; it exists between two persons alone where there is neither majority nor plurality. Moreover, *right*, whether it belongs to the majority or minority, or even to a single individual, can never be sacrificed for the good of the majority, whatever the size of the majority. Otherwise, the majority would be jurally the worst possible tyrant over the minority; it would be the sole depository of right; the minority would be deprived of all its rights and excluded from society and law (*USR*, 216–286). Present-day philosophers have in their books justified and reproposed a more wicked *servitude* than that abolished by Christianity.

1739. Romagnosi is more cautious, but no less unwholesome. He dresses up similar teaching in his normally attractive, decent way of writing. He says, for example:

> What is *useful* and what is *just* are not contraries, just as *force* and *right* are not contraries. Right, substantially speaking, is not and cannot be anything more than *regulated force*; in the same way, what is just is not, and cannot be, substantially speaking, anything more than a regulated activity, some utility which of its nature conforms to the rational, moral order. [54]

[52] *Dei delitti e delle pene*, §2.
[53] *ER*, 246–251.
[54] *Assunto primo*, §17.

[1739]

This could not be better said. He speaks of
1. a *rule* given to force, and
2. expressly posits this rule in the rational, *moral order*.

If we stopped here, there would be nothing to contradict in Romagnosi's theory. But we have to penetrate his mind more deeply. We have to see what he means by the *moral order* which must regulate force. At this point precisely, we can see the fallacy underlying the high-sounding words. According to him

> Morality in its philosophical sense consists in the faculty of acting freely according to a previously known norm. [55]

Leaving aside the many other observations which could be made about this definition, we note that 'acting according to a previously known norm' is not what the whole world understands as morality. Artists and cobblers act according to previously known norms; every craftsman acts according to previously known norms. But we do not say that the faculty possessed by the artist, the cobbler or any other craftsman is morality. If we keep to Romagnosi's expression, we have to say that the meaning he gives to morality is different, very different indeed, from that found in the same word used by everyone else. The definition is, however, much more defective than that. As well as norms pertaining to the sphere of morality it includes immoral laws, such as those used by highly sophisticated villains. Thus villainy itself can be and has been reduced to an art with its own *previously known norms*.

Let us see if Romagnosi explains himself better elsewhere, perhaps by determining the specific difference between the norms of which he speaks.

1740. He declares his true intention in places where he denies that individuals can act according to any previously known norm except that of their own advantage. He asks, as though it were outside controversy: [56]

> Isn't it true that no one can act according to any previously known norm other than that of his own advantage? Can individuals go outside themselves and act for motives other

[55] *Assunto primo*, §4.
[56] *Assunto primo*, §8.

than those which determine their own will? In a word, is it possible for anyone to act except for self-love? Self-love is taken here as the general will to remain in as satisfactory a state as possible. — The law of self-interest is as absorbing and imperative for human beings as the law of gravity is absorbing and imperative for bodies.'[57]

Romagnosi's rational, moral order is clarified here; he leaves no room for doubt. It is that order which reason suggests to individuals as best for themselves, the order for attaining the greatest possible advantage to self, for satisfying self-love as much as possible, for obtaining one's own interest — the only motivating power for man, and a power as absorbing and imperious for him as the law of gravity for bodies. The word *morality*, used so often by this publicist, along with the expression *rational, moral order, natural law, just* and *upright*, and so on, can no longer deceive anyone. They mean something altogether different from their common sense significance; individual utility[58] as suggested by self-love has been substituted for

---

[57] The great objection made by all *idealists*, whether sensists or transcendentalists, is: 'How can a man go outside himself?' — Their difficulty in answering this kind of question arises from their inappropriate use of the words GO OUT, LEAVE, WITHIN, OUTSIDE which are proper to bodies alone, but do not apply to the spirit. Not realising that such words, when applied to the spirit, can have only a metaphorical sense, they ask themselves in all seriousness: 'How can the spirit go outside itself?' In fact, the spirit has neither inside nor outside; it neither goes out nor returns. It would have been very easy for them to escape from the maze (in which they had lost themselves because of their use of *a priori reason guided by imagination*) if they had made *psychological observation* their guide rather than argue about the spirit with a badly applied analogy taken from what occurs in bodies. We have already shown: 1. that the idea and concepts present to the intelligent spirit are not the spirit itself (relationship of diversity); 2. that the idea and concepts have no relationship of *place* with the spirit, nor can it be said that they are inside or outside it; their sole relationship is that of being *intuitable* and *intuited*; 3. that in human *feeling* there is *activity* and *passivity*, and that the second indicates one force acting in another, an *anotherness*; 4. finally, that by means of *ideas* applied to *feelings*, the human being knows *subjective* good (his own), and *objective good* (not his own) — the former *acts* upon him, the latter has a moral *authority* very different from the action of the former.

[58] I say 'individual utility' because self-love knows no other, and because we are dealing with *final utility* which holds the place of end for human activity. Romagnosi explains: 'Granted this, we do indeed find isolated forces

morality. The honourable word 'morality' has been pinned on
'self-interest'. The whole system is nothing more than a barely
conceived cover-up. It is clear that in this sensistic, utilitarian
system, teaching about what is just is reduced to teaching about
utility; the only possible rational order is that which leads every
man to act according to his own greatest utility. This is the sole
order of justice, uprightness and morality; what is just has been
absorbed by what is useful.

1741. As a result of applying this system to teaching about
society, the *science of Right in civil society* is confused with, or
rather swallowed up by that of *Politics* which has for its object
the direction of civil society to the greatest total advantage of the
citizens. It is clear that equating justice and morality with such
advantage is equivalent to claiming that Politics and Right are
one; Right is abolished and Politics reigns alone, or rather
tyrannises over mankind. We reject these inhuman principles.
We grant Politics the faculty of governing for the sake of the
greater public good, but in subordination to *Right*, from which
it must humbly receive the law which conditions and limits its
activity. *The greater public good* is conditioned by the *inviolate,
particular right of each individual, whether citizen or alien.*

We continue now with our exposition of the *philosophy of
civil right*, and will return when we can to the exposition of the
philosophy of politics.

and tendencies, but not common tendencies unless each one finds in the
common tendency satisfaction for his own self-love. In order to effectuate the
essential, rational constitution of society it is indispensable that *personal
interest* be identified with *social interest*; each individual, acting for others,
would see that he is acting for h imself' (*Assunto primo*, §8).

[1741]

PART THREE

THE ORIGIN OF CIVIL SOCIETY

1742. From what has been said we see that the essence of civil society consists in its constitution as a power to administer the modality of the rights of a certain mass of human beings. Because this power is unique and supreme, it is called 'sovereignty'.

1743. The origin of civil society is multiple. But careful consideration shows that investigating its origin means investigating the origin of the institution of the power which administers the modality of the rights of a certain mass of human beings; in other words, investigating the origin of governments.[59]

1744. The reason for this is that civil society presents two parts:

1. A mass of human beings with individual rights.

2. A power called *government* that administers the modality of these rights.

Consideration of only one of these parts must result in false conclusions about the origin of civil society.

If civil society is considered simply as a mass of human beings, all its origins are necessarily reduced to a social contract, as we have seen.

If on the other hand only its government is considered, everything is reduced to an absolute power, or to a particular origin of absolute power, such as fatherhood, prevalent force, etc.

But when our thought includes both these extremes, so that we compare them and note their mutual relationship, we find an easy way to reach the real and complete origins of civil society.

The primary relationship between society and government is normally such that society is created only when government is created. To find the legitimate ways by which society is normally formed, we need therefore to find and list the legitimate

[59] Aristotle defines a republic by assigning it a government (*Pol.*, 3, 4). Thus, according to him, the origin of civil society is to be found in the origin of governments.

ways by which governments are formed. This is the task we must now undertake.

CHAPTER 1

Principles pertaining to individual Right, which are necessary for explaining the origins of governments

1745. We first recall some principles of individual Right which must be kept clearly in mind in meditating on the origins of governments and, through them, on the origins of civil society.

1746. These principles are:

1. 'Myself' must be distinguished from 'mine'. 'Myself' indicates personship, that is, subsistent, inalienable right; 'mine' indicates all other rights, alienable and transferable from one person to another.

2. The quality of rights transferable from one subject to another must be seen as something entirely independent of the titles by which rights were acquired. Rights are transferable, even if the titles are not. When the transference of rights is legitimate, new ways of acquisition, called *indirect* or *derived*, result (*RI*, 1072), that is, new *titles*, which differ from the original and posit right in being. For example, although the title to possession of an estate may be occupancy, the estate can be sold to another person who then possesses it by title of sale, because the title of first occupancy is not transferable. Similarly, a father can in certain cases leave civil government to one of his sons, although he cannot leave fatherhood because this title is not transferable. In a word, we can say that the transferability of rights comes directly from their nature and is independent of the nature of their first, original titles.

3. Relative to others, we have the right to do that which does no harm to them and helps us, that is, to occupy anything not occupied by others. 'Anything' means not only material things but actions and responsibilities; in other words, everything that can be considered as good and thus form an object of right.

[1745–1746]

CHAPTER 2

Titles of right to govern; those of first acquisition and those of second acquisition

1747. It follows that the title by which a person (individual or collective) may acquire the power to regulate the modality of all the rights of a certain mass of human beings is first of all divisible into two classes, called *first acquisition* and *second acquisition*. By 'titles of second acquisition' I mean those which transfer such power from one person to another.

1748. The origins of civil governments are as numerous as the titles of first acquisition.

The titles of second acquisition should also be indicated because civil power, when modified by its transference from one person to another, gives rise to at least a new form of government, if not a new society.

CHAPTER 3

Titles of first acquisition

1749. These divide into two classes. One class gives a person, whether individual or collective, the right to administer civil government. It also gives *a greater right*, with which the right to govern is necessarily connected. Fatherhood is an example. Properly speaking, fatherhood is a title of dominion over children, and necessarily includes the right to regulate the modality of the children's rights, that is, to govern them. The other class gives a collective or individual person the simple right to govern, *separate from any other right whatsoever*. I shall deal with both kinds.

Article 1.
Right to govern, arising from a preceding right of ownership and of dominion

§1. *The title of absolute Being*

A.
God considered as civil ruler over human beings

1750. The first, absolute and essential title arising either from a preceding right or from ownership is the title of creation, God's title. It bestows ownership over the being of things (*RGC*, 536–631).

If such a master did all he had a right to do, he would do it alone. Human beings would do nothing; second causes would be destroyed.

To explain the existence of second causes, we need to distinguish right from its use. A person who possesses some land can allow others to work it and profit from it. This is God's state: although he possesses every good and all rights, he allows human beings to make use of many things to their advantage. This explains human powers and rights, and the truth of the adage, *omnis potestas a Deo* [all power is from God].

1751. Consequently, all human powers and rights, relative to God, are precarious. We use what belongs to the supreme Being, not to ourselves. We call this use 'right' because we cannot despoil another of it. The word *right* expresses a relationship, not something absolute.[60]

1752. It is clear however that the adage, *omnis potestas a Deo,* is abused by those who wish to remove the second causes brought into being by human power; the adage in fact authenticates and confirms second causes. It is also abused by those who apply it solely to civil powers. It does in fact apply to all powers equally. Again, it is abused by those who claim to deduce from it the civil power of any particular person, as if the power were poured down directly from heaven. The sacred phrase explains only the origin of civil power in general, not the special titles with which a particular person is invested. Finally, the adage is

[60] *ER*, 322–328.

[1750–1752]

abused by those who use it to extend civil power unrestrictedly: for them, it indicates the respect due to authority without in any way determining the limits of authority

B.
Continuation — Theocracy among the Hebrews

1753. In the case of the people of Israel, God was not content to let human beings administer and use civil things over which he retained dominion; he wished to administer them himself. This was the case when he removed some of the second causes, and seemed to leave no royal power to any human being. He himself acted as king, and expressly told them so; otherwise, the Hebrews would not have known that he wished to administer directly what he usually left to human beings to administer.

The first title of this civil administration was his positive will. But he did not want this to be the only title; he wanted a human title, of total seigniory. It was not a title of *conquest* but, in contrast with the title invented by the first sovereign human beings, of merciful *liberation* from the slavery of Egypt.[61] The resulting form of government was both the most *absolute* and the *least despotic* because he used his absolute power for the greatest good of those he governed. It was absolute, because he joined *State ownership* and *seigniory* to civil power whose object is the *modality of rights*.

God, therefore, as a powerful person, made himself known to the enslaved Israelite people whom their master wished to oppress and destroy. His covenants were these: 'He would redeem them from such great slavery, and the people on their part would serve him alone' (title of seigniory), and: 'He would let them conquer the fertile land of Canaan on condition that he, as their valiant and invincible captain, maintained direct dominion over them, and they were his settlers' (title of State ownership). In this way, God, having acquired all rights over persons and lands (even apart from his essential seigniory as God), could dispose of their modality. He was thus invested with the authority of civil head.

The absoluteness of this power rendered his liberal, equable

[61] Ex 20: 2.

government most gentle. There was no extreme inequality of fortune. Any inequality in any need could be levelled out directly by the master. And in order not to provoke comment among the rich by doing this at irregular intervals, he maintained equality of patrimonies (a supreme law of ancient republics). For this he established institutions, like the institution of the sabbatical year, when debtors were absolved, lands that had been sold were restored, and bond-servants freed; everything was returned to its first state. Leviticus says: 'The land shall not be sold in perpetuity, for the land is mine; for you are strangers and sojourners with me. And in all the country you possess, you shall grant a redemption of the land'.[62] And relative to persons, it says: 'If your brother becomes poor beside you, and sells himself to you, you shall not make him serve as a slave: he shall be with you as a hired servant and as a sojourner. He shall serve with you until the year of the jubilee; then he shall go out from you, he and his children with him, and go back to his own family, and return to the possession of his fathers. For they are my servants, whom I brought forth out of the land of Egypt.'[63] The reason for such gentle government, unique among the ancients and unbelievable in modern times, is its absoluteness: all the earth and every person belongs to the monarch. Clearly, *absolute government* is vastly different from *despotic* government.[64]

C.
Possible errors caused by applying the principles of Hebrew theocracy to other civil societies

1754. Over-exclusive attention to this extraordinary mode of government among the Hebrews, and failure to distinguish sufficiently between natural and supernatural positive relationship, seems to have led Bossuet into many errors about civil

[62] Lev 25: 23–24.

[63] Lev 25: 39–42.

[64] Montesquieu distinguishes three governments: *republican, monarchic* and *despotic* (bk. 2, c. 1). Despotic government, however is not government, but the corruption of all government. This explains why the author of *De l'esprit des Lois* was reproached for sometimes putting fact in place of right.

[1754]

power, laws and even natural right.[65] The authority of such a great man requires that I indicate his errors, but I do so with apprehension born of reverence. Because the errors are systematically connected and result as it were in a single error, I note the principal places where in my opinion the great prelate departs from the truth.

1. Sometimes he seems not to acknowledge that the supreme principle of morality is the light of our reason. According to him, there can be no real obligation without *positive* knowledge of God. Thus, the people cannot form an inviolable covenant except in the presence of God known in this way.[66]

---

[65] This school is wrongly called *Catholic*. Catholicism is not restricted in this way in its doctrines; it is as extensive as truth. When the first Presbyterians sailed to North America to escape persecution, and founded the first colonies of the United States, they took the mosaic laws as their model because they considered these laws divinely inspired and therefore the best. The consequence was legislation steeped in blood: things which, in the present state of humanity, are considered politically as minor failings, were subject to the death penalty. Such legislation, taken from the Bible, and essentially Hebraic and Protestant-like, soon had to be changed. Catholicism does not lead to such errors because a divine, living magisterium resides within it, a magisterium that is necessary precisely because it protects human beings against political errors of this kind which are natural to people who listen solely to the voice of God communicated long ago to human beings and recorded in the Bible.

[66] 'The people could not unite by themselves in an inviolable association, if the agreement were not founded on a higher power, such as the power of God who is the natural protector of human society and unfailing vindicator of every contravention of law' (*Politique etc.*, bk. 1, art. 4, prop. 7). Soon afterwards he says: 'Plato, in his *Republic* and his other book on laws, proposed only those laws which he wanted confirmed by the oracle prior to their acceptance; it is in this way that laws would become sacred and inviolable.' It is true that a little earlier Bossuet had taught that all laws are based on the first law of all, the natural law, that is, on right reason and *natural uprightness* (art. 2) which undoubtedly come from God. When he says therefore that an agreement is valid only when positively concluded, we are not clear whether he means according to natural uprightness, or in the presence of the supreme Being revealed by some external sign. I think that an agreement is undoubtedly valid even if it lacks God's supernatural, positive confirmation, provided it is made according to the laws of natural uprightness which certainly contain a divine element. Arguing from Bossuet's example from Plato, whose laws are sacred and inviolable only when confirmed by the oracle, it seems that the bishop of Meaux requires a direct revelation of the

2. Hence, where he discusses the nature and properties of royal authority, he does not say what it actually is, that is, the administration of the modality of the people's rights; he simply says it is sacred. But this tells us nothing about the nature and limits of the authority. Furthermore, the secondary cause is absent from his discussion, because he says nothing about the title through which sovereignty takes form and comes into the hands of a collective or individual person, or of one family rather than another.[67]

3. Because no importance is given to the principle of morality originating in reason, the explanation of the existence of human rights is sought in the institution of society. Consequently Bossuet makes the right of ownership come from society itself. This destroys natural Right. Generally speaking, he says: 'Every right must come from public authority.'[68]

4. He extends the limits of this public authority too far. For

divine will for laws to be inviolable. We must not, in my opinion, confuse God's will manifested naturally through reason and natural uprightness with his will manifested supernaturally through revelation. In both ways, God's will is *inviolable*; only when manifested through revelation is it properly called *sacred*.

[67] Bk. 3, a. 2 — Both *royal* and *paternal* authority are inviolable, but properly speaking they are called *sacred* only in the case of Christian rulers whom the Church has consecrated. The dignity which the ruler has in himself must not be confused with the august characteristic he receives from the church ceremony. The Hebrew kings had this characteristic of being *Anointed of the Lord*. Precisely because Bossuet always sees the Hebraic regime as the type of every government, he easily applies it to all other sovereigns. The quotation from Sirach which he uses to prove this contradicts him: God 'appointed a ruler for every nation (this is what he does with all peoples because all authority comes from God), but Israel is the Lord's own portion' (this is what he did in particular with the people of Israel) (Sir 17: [17]).

[68] 'If government is removed, the earth and all its goods become common to all human beings, like air and light. — According to this primitive, natural Right, no one has a right to anything whatsoever; everything is open to all.' What kind of right is this where no one has a *right* to anything whatsoever? Can it ever be lawful, even where no government has been instituted, to take over what another has occupied? A little later he concludes: 'From this arises the right of ownership (that is, from Joshua's distribution of land). In general, every right must come from public authority; no one is allowed to invade anything, to take something for himself by force.' I have already shown that if ownership could not exist before the institution of civil government, it could not exist after (*RI*, 330–359).

[1754]

example, he says that under a regulated government no individual has the right to occupy anything.[69] On the contrary, civil society cannot and must not entirely remove the state of (extra-social) nature among human beings. The right to occupy unoccupied land must remain theirs, even after the institution of civil government.

5. He deduces individuals' rights from public authority (as was the case among the Hebrews where the head of the society, in addition to government, also held ownership of land and seigniory of persons). Consequently, he attributes to law, that is, to the will of public authority, full power not only over the modality of rights but over the rights themselves; indeed, it is the law that distributes and grants them to human beings, in the same way that a master who possesses some good allows another to enjoy the use of it, as we have seen. He thus considers it reasonable that law should enact, as it did amongst the Hebrews, ordinances of pure beneficence for the poor, not of pure justice or protection.

§2. The title of fatherhood

A.
Fatherhood is a greater power than civil power and, in the state of nature, contains the latter

1755. Generally speaking, anyone who possesses a right over something has the right to determine the modality of its use.

1756. A father naturally possesses every right over his children (*RF*, 1455–1513). He can therefore regulate the modality of any rights that might belong to them.

The power to regulate the modality of rights, separated from every other power, is called 'civil power'. It is therefore included in the *patria potestas*. Let us look at this concept in greater detail.

1757. In parental society, the father aggregates, the child is aggregated. Moreover, the one who aggregates also gives existence to the person aggregated who thus depends on the aggregator through a necessity of nature, not through submission of

---

[69] *Politique etc.*, bk. 1, a. 3, prop. 4.

will, just as effect depends on cause. Although the child when born and grown subsists without the father, his intelligence reminds him that his life comes from his father who produced it and took possession of it from the beginning.

To know how *civil authority* is included in but distinguished from *paternal authority*, let us recall what we have said about paternal authority. Three things are distinguished in the grown-up child and member of parental society:[70]

1. A passive substance, which constitutes human nature and has been received from the father:

2. A personal energy by which he can obey the law of uprightness without concern for pleasure or pain, or obey the law of pleasure without concern for uprightness:

3. A light of reason which continually shows him the universal law of what is upright and what is just.

The *light of reason*, together with the *free energy* by which he can follow that light, is the exclusive property of the human being. Even slaves have it and cannot be deprived of it. But the first thing, that is, the *passive substance* of the child, pertains to the father, who has the duty to use it in accord with morality.

1758. As we have seen, usurping another's right is not the same as making immoral use of one's own right (*RF*, 1481–1482).

The moral rule, which directs the way we must *use* our right is: 'Use what is yours according to its natural end.' Hence the father, who has power over all the rights of his child (except the inalienability of person), is equally obliged to use those rights morally, that is, according to their natural ends.

1759. This explains the two limits of the power of fatherhood: 1. the moral precept governing the right use of what is one's own; 2. respect for the personship of the child.

[70] The relationship between father and child is *beneficent* and *seigniorial* but not *social* as long as the child has not acquired sufficient use of reason to realise that he has goods in common with his father, with whom he lives. Prior to this, relationships between parents and children pertain to *individual Right*. We have discussed them under this heading (*RI*, 772–894). Father and child are in a *state of nature* until the child becomes a *social being*; at birth, he is this only potentially. Assigning the period of *puberty* as the moment when parental society begins, as Zeiller does (§166), indicates to some extent the arbitrary nature of the discretion found in the souls of writers who have applied themselves at length to the study of positive laws.

[1758-1759]

1760. Despite these limits, *patria potestas* is far greater than civil power. Its object are *rights* themselves, whereas the object of civil power is simply the regulation of the *modality* of rights. Obviously, in the state of nature, civil power is included and absorbed in that of the father.

B.
Continuation — Possible errors resulting from the application of the principles of *paternal authority* to *civil authority*

> If the theory I am defending implies the nega-
> tion of paternal regime, at least in an absolute,
> rigorist sense, I would not think of forbidding
> paternal feelings and virtues to governments.
>
> Vinet, *Essai sur la manifestation des
> convictions etc.* Foreword.

1761. As we have seen, the system of those who confuse *civil* with *theocratic power* is excessive and erroneous. The same must be said of the system of those who confuse *civil* with *paternal power*, and maintain that the former has the same nature and extension as the latter.

This is the conclusion of authors who derive civil government from paternal power, as the sole source. An example, in England, is Sir Robert Filmer.

It was easy to foresee that this would give rise to another arbitrary system of the greatest absolutism. The father has all authority over the children and possesses absolutely the rights which they possess relatively to other human beings. Civil authority which becomes the same as paternal authority, and no longer needs to be restricted to the regulation of the modality of rights, is invested with the most absolute *seigniory*.

1762. In my opinion, the principal mistake of authors of a system so contrary to historical witness depends upon a single omission. They rightly saw paternal regime as the gentlest of all and the most suitable for doing the greatest good, but failed to see that paternal government within the four walls of a home is gentle and powerful in effecting the good of the children because of the love placed in the hearts of the parents by nature.

[1760–1762]

This love is not transferable to other human beings. If indeed a father were able to hand over to another all his authority, he still could not give up a single particle of the natural affection he has for those he has generated. Moreover, despite such great affection, which *in reality* tempers the absolutism of *paternal right*, we so often see within the domestic circle tyranny on the part of inhuman parents. Today, civil society feels obliged to remedy this situation by laws and penalties destined to help tormented children.

C.

Continuation — *Patria potestas* is a particular, not a universal source of civil governments

1763. There is however an element of truth in Filmer's thought. Sidney, his famous opponent, simply fell into the opposite error when refuting him.

Sidney denied the possibility that civil power was derived from paternal power and thus arose from paternal power. He should have been satisfied with establishing that while this paternal origin of civil governments can sometimes be verified and has in fact been verified, it is not the sole origin of civil government. A civil association or government could be established by other jural ways.

If we suppose that human beings are immortal and their numbers grow, the first father would indeed by his nature be the monarch of the human race. Government would be his, nor could any greater human power rise on earth. The organisation of this great body would naturally be committed to the will of the first genitor. The primitive, natural form of civil government would have to be a universal monarchy, a consequence of paternal power (*RF*, 995).

1764. But the first head dies. It is clear that paternal power belongs to him alone, as Sidney observes, and cannot be passed on. But can civil authority be passed on by inheritance? Sidney's arguments[71] demonstrate that although this is not necessary, it is not absurd. Nevertheless, according to him, this kind of government is not passed on by natural succession.

But could it not be passed on by the father's command and

---

[71] *Discours sur le Gouvernement*, A. Sidney, tom. 1, sects. 12 and 14.

express declaration? If the father dies without leaving to one of his children the civil government he exercised over them, the siblings remain independent of each other. But could not the father constitute one of them head and governor, and oblige the others to obey him in matters concerning the *modality* of their rights, for the good of the family or relatives? Can it be proved that paternal authority does not extend so far, when it is naturally unlimited and absolute? If the father can pass on other rights, why not this right? It is true that the father possesses the civil government of his children by the title of fatherhood, a non-transferable title, but we have already said that a right's transferability or alienability depends by nature not on its title but on the right itself. Hence a right possessed through a non-transferable title (the title of the first occupier, for example) can afterwards be possessed by others through a new title substituted for and arising from the first, as in the case of all derived titles, or titles of second acquisition. Can the title of the genitor's authoritative will never be substituted for the non-transferable title of fatherhood? Cannot the firstborn, or someone else preferred by the father, take on the government of his siblings by means of this title? I see no absurdity here, and nothing contrary to the analogy of right. The right of government is by nature transferable, even though the title of generation, which imposes this government first of all on the father, is not transferable.

1765. It is said that antiquity offers no example of a moribund father leaving to one of his children the right to govern his siblings, who are obliged to obey him. I think this is incorrect. Noah certainly subjected the descendants of Canaan to the servants of his brethren, as well as to Shem and Japheth.[72] Isaac constituted Jacob master of his brethren who, in the words of Isaac, would have to bow before Jacob.[73] Jacob set the sceptre of Israel on the house of Judah until the coming of the Messiah.[74] The kings of the Hebrews chose as their successor the child whom they preferred.[75] Mattathias divided the power of gov-

---

[72] Gen 9: [24–27].
[73] Gen 27: [29].
[74] Gen 49: [10].
[75] 1 Kings 1: [33–35].

ernment between his sons Judas and Simeon.[76] In the East, where civil society developed with the natural increase of the family, in which all the relatives remain united,[77] the head of the tribe and city was frequently constituted by the will of the dying genitor.

1766. The following facts will convince us that, according to Right, civil power can pass from the father to one or more children:

1. Paternal authority is a *complex right*,[78] that is, a union of several rights, each of which can be distinguished from the others.

2. The right to govern the modality of the members' rights does not detract from anyone else's rights; on the contrary it helps them. The power, relative to its object, is beneficent not seigniorial. The father's ordinance therefore does not prejudice but helps the children, provided he acts suitably and wisely.

1767. A father uses his authority wrongly if his ordinance lacks the two characteristics of *suitability* and *usefulness*, that is, if his choice of head is not required by circumstances or did not fall on a child suitable for governing. The children could agree to correct the part of paternal ordinance which contains an abuse; if they could not emend it, they could abandon it. This would not offend the dead father's right in any way; on the contrary it would conform to the intentions that he must have had, and did in fact have, or must be presumed to have had.

If the paternal ordinance is truly *suitable* and *useful*, the children must accept it, and, in my opinion, are jurally obliged to do so. This obligation can be enforced by anyone who suffers harm from its violation.

1768. 3. Finally, the most convincing proof of the father's faculty to divide civil, governmental right from the fullness of his power is this: in the system of social contract it is the fathers who divide and separate this right, by alienating it and transferring it partly or totally to other hands, that is, to civil government, which they institute. Consequently, to maintain that the right of governing civilly cannot be separated from the power of

[76] 1 Macc 2: [65–66].
[77] Cf. *SP*, 371–391.
[78] *ER*, 322–333.

[1766–1768]

fatherhood is to leave the existence of civil governments without any jural explanation.[79]

§3. *The third title: seigniory*

1769. Anyone who has bond-servants, that is, persons obliged stably to his service, is clearly also the person who regulates the *modality* of their rights by general ordinances. In this way he is their *civil ruler*.[80]

1770. Let us imagine that servitude is total, and that the master does not grant his bond-servants freedom to regulate the modality of their communal rights. He may do this either to prevent their withdrawing from a task to which he has obliged them, or because he has a reasonable fear that they will abuse the faculty of regulating the modality of their rights, to his or their own harm, or finally because this faculty is a power that has come into his ownership through some legitimate title. In this case, the master may not only regulate the *modality of their rights* but is obliged to do so by the moral law in such a way that they live peacefully together and that the rights of all are maintained and can be used to their greatest advantage (*USR*, 170–190). If this were not the case, his seigniory would degenerate into wicked dominion, harmful to human nature, like the dominion of slavery.

1771. We must note that, in the case of *civil rule* joined to *absolute seigniory*, the master who possesses and administers *beneficent rule* is not himself a member of the society; he is outside it. It is not contradictory for the person who governs,

---

[79] Laws acknowledge a father's faculty to confer on another person a part of his power over his children, for example, the right to feed, educate and govern them. This was practised even more extensively among the Romans in *adoption*.

[80] Here the master is considered in the state of nature, not in constituted, civil societies where he is a member, not a monarch. However, wherever slavery is practised, we find civil governments leaving the civil regulation of the slaves almost entirely to the master. As we said, this renders civil governments weak and imperfect (*RGC*, 869–871).

[1769–1771]

even with his own power, to remain outside the society he governs.[81]

1772. This would make the ruler a *benefactor*, not a *member;*[82] as such he would have a more noble moral state than that of a member.[83]

§4. *The fourth title: ownership*

1773. *Civil rule* has its origin in another title, ownership of land.

1774. Let us imagine a human being in the state of nature who occupies a certain area of land and has it worked by relatives or settlers. Other families come and establish themselves on his land with his free consent or pay him rent. Because he can make laws for all those whom he allows to live on his property and who need him in order to subsist, he can naturally make himself their *civil ruler.*

1775. However, the families and individuals who are not his bond-servants remain at liberty to leave the territory (right to emigrate) and thus withdraw from his civil government.

1776. Furthermore, the circumstances do not require the owner, as civil governor, to become a member of the civil community; relative to it he can simply be the *civil ruler.* On the other hand, he can associate himself with all the families who, although lacking stable goods in the land where they live, could have wealth of some kind, or productive abilities, and could share with him the expenses of civil administration.

1777. We saw that God wished to found the external sovereignty he administered among the Hebrews upon these two titles of *seigniory* and *ownership.*

In Egypt, the landowner and the civil ruler are often combined almost entirely in one person; this is more or less the case with

---

[81] Cf. *SP*, 111–131.

[82] *Ibid.*, 91–101.

[83] The Gospel itself speaks about this union of *seigniory* and *government*: 'Those IN AUTHORITY over them are called BENEFACTORS' (Lk 22: 25). But the spirit of the liberator of bond-servants is much more social and beneficent: 'But not so with you...'

[1772–1777]

Mehemet Ali. The practice is very ancient in Egypt. Towards the end of the 18th century BC, when starvation threatened the Egyptians, they sold their lands and themselves to the king who fed them. Certainly, Pharoah already possessed sovereignty, but let us suppose that civil society did not yet exist. Joseph, foreseeing the famine, would have been able to make himself owner of the lands and lord of the people, and consequently, their civil ruler.

Hence, a great benefit such as liberation of a people from cruel slavery, or salvation from extermination by fierce enemies, starvation or drought, etc., can certainly bring the liberator legitimate ownership of the land and of the persons liberated. Here again we have sovereignty.

1778. Someone may say that this is a case of contract. Undoubtedly contract is present, but its objects are land and services rendered by people, not sovereignty. In fact many contracts concern land and service rendered by persons because a contract is made with each of the possessors. But once dominion over land and persons has been acquired, a contract for civil sovereignty is no longer needed: it is a necessary consequence, an element indivisible from ownership and dominion.

1779. We must note however that this title of *ownership* of land is not as absolute as the previous titles.

Let us suppose that some wealthy families have received permission from a landowner to live in his vast territory, and that they do more good than harm. If we consider *crude* right alone, the owner can certainly offer an alternative to the families: either to vacate the land or submit to his civil rule. In addition, he is the only *judge competent* to decide the fittingness and equity of such action. But because it is possible to appeal from even a competent judge to *evident reason*, the families have no obligation to obey if their residence is obviously not only harmless but helpful. This would reduce their resistance to the use of 'the right of everyone to use another's things in a truly harmless way' (*RI*, 1622). It is true that the implementation of such extremes is difficult, but not impossible.

1780. Hence, based on the hypothesis, we see:

1. that free families ought to work for a stable, common regulation of the modality of all those rights which might collide with the landowner's rights;

[1778–1780]

2. but they could have an active vote in the formation of the regulation, and retain part of the civil government.

§5. *Comment on the* titles *already discussed*

1781. Whenever dominion over *being, life, service* rendered by persons, *land* and generally over the *means of subsistence* embraces a number of persons, it can be legitimately extended to *civil rule.*

The titles are theoretical and often practical *ways* of setting up unique regulation of the modality of the rights of many individuals, that is, government, civil association.

1782. Because the four ways of dominion mentioned above basically include *civil rule*, they give their possessor the *right of coercion*, by which dependent persons can be subjected to civil regulation.

Article 2.
The right to govern, independent of the right of dominion and of ownership — Two classes of titles to this right

1783. So far we have considered the titles to civil rule of *first acquisition which are contained in rights of dominion and ownership.* We must now discuss the other titles of first acquisition which give a person (collective or individual) civil rule *separate from and independent of seigniory and ownership.*

1784. They are primarily divided into two classes:

1. Those arising from a *unilateral* action, that is, from an act of the person assuming rule.

2. Those arising from many acts of fathers, who come together to establish civil rule as the supreme moderator of the modality of rights.

1785. The first are the means by which civil society is formed from top to bottom, so to speak. The second are those by which civil society is formed from bottom to top. Haller wanted to exclude the second way of forming civil society, but in my opinion its rational legitimacy cannot be doubted, nor are historical examples lacking, as the present fashion of studies tells us.

I will indicate the ways of formation and the title to civil rule of both classes. But first I must present two theses which derive from what we have already said and throw greater light on the way by which civil society is constituted by unilateral or joint action.

Article 3.
Titles of civil rule which consist in an act of the person assuming it

§1. *Preliminary teachings — Civil rule is a good for its possessor and its subjects*

A.
Civil dominion is a good for its possessor

1786. Civil sovereignty is a responsibility, a service, but also an undeniable good for the person possessing and exercising it (*USR*, 311, 404–410).

I do not appeal for proof to experience, which shows that all human beings greatly desire sovereignty as the greatest good on earth and shed blood over it. Such madness could come from human depravity and the abuse people intend to make of sovereignty by sometimes directing it to their own good rather than the good of those governed. I want to speak about sovereignty free from the benefits expected from these abuses. Indeed, sovereignty loses most of its attraction when these advantages are removed and remains a purely laborious administration of the modality of one's own and others' rights. The person invested with sovereignty cannot profit from the smallest good pertaining to others. Upright, civil government needs to be able to proclaim continuously to the people the words of Samuel: 'Here I am; testify against me before the Lord... Whose ox have I taken? Or whose ass have I taken? Or whom have I defrauded?

[1786]

Whom have I oppressed? Or from whose hand have I taken a bribe…? The Lord is witness against you… that you have not found anything in my hand.'[84]

The union between pure, honest sovereignty and magnanimous poverty is not contradictory. Sovereignty offers no right to self-enrichment and holds no seigniory over the rights of others; its only power is to regulate the modality of those rights. No external, real good is necessarily joined *per se* to civil sovereignty.

1787. Nevertheless this office is highly desired. What does its good consist in? Three things:

1. The esteem and gratitude of those governed. — The head of civil society is necessarily legislator, leader and judge; this presupposes wisdom, strength and justice. A sovereign endowed with these sublime qualities, whether he possesses them all personally or in his ministers, is the defender and pacifier of his people; in short, he is their continual benefactor. Hence, reverence, affection and national gratitude belong to him. The esteem, gratitude and love of our fellows draws in its wake great social happiness for the upright spirit of the person able to enjoy them; indirectly, they bring a great quantity of goods and legitimate affluence of all kinds.

Sovereignty is a sublime office from which gifts of spirit and soul can shine before all, and great benefits flow ceaselessly over humanity; it can conquer the hearts of an immense number of our fellows. It must therefore be considered a most precious good in this life.

2. The protection of the sovereign against dangers from the abuse of government to which the subject is exposed. — The sovereign, considered as an individual, need not fear that another will harm the subject's rights under the pretext of governing their modality. This advantage becomes more notable in proportion to the wealth of the sovereign considered as a private person, so that the person most interested in the regulation of the modality of rights among a people in the state of nature is the one who owns the most. This individual is most interested

---

[84] 1 Sam 12: [3–4].

in the constitution of good civil society and good government, and must naturally desire to keep it within his grasp.

3. Sovereignty is a school of wisdom and virtue. — Heroism, magnanimity, and a serene, all-embracing, wise mode of thought are engendered in the person exercising sovereignty. Ruling families preserve traditional practices and examples, while experience gradually perfects them in the art of educating their children to great office. Everything contributes to the formation of character and royal blood, a character eminently distinguished by a certain mysterious splendour of nobility, generosity of enterprise, independence, exercise of mercy and constant practice of benefits (*USR*, 159).

B.
Civil rule is beneficial for the governed

1788. The word *subject* does seem to express the concept of some kind of servitude; some degree of servitude is certainly present when *civil society* is not pure but mixed with *seigniory*. But if *subject* means simply 'citizen', a person civilly subject to a governor, it expresses only the lightest servitude resulting from the alienation of civil power. We have already seen that all servitude consists in the right one has over the actions of another for one's own advantage. Civil sovereignty has no right over actions and things; its task is to regulate socially the modality of the members' rights.

It is very necessary and helpful for those possessing rights to have the modality regulated by a single mind and power; civil society and its government are a benefit for citizens. Any burden imposed comes from abuse, not from the institution of a single mind to regulate the modality of rights. If indeed regulation requires some sacrifice of rights, the sacrifice, as we saw, has to be compensated in such a way that the person making it loses nothing of the good he could otherwise have kept.

1789. To say that modality could be regulated in a far more helpful way than by this kind of institution is not a valid objection. All we can justly claim is that the institution should act in such a way that

1. no individual good is harmed, and no rights are affected (commutative justice);

2. the good it does is equably distributed (strict distributive justice); and

3. this good is the greatest obtainable by the wisdom of the ruling mind, granted that the ruler has taken every care to be enlightened. Because no one can determine the limit of this wisdom, it is reasonable for everyone to be content with what the government can and does achieve.

1790. Government which fails to adhere to these conditions abuses its power. The evil, however, comes not from the nature of government but from its poor administration, from human wickedness.

Clearly, civil sovereignty does not involve any loss of rights; it is not even a limitation of good, but a benefit to those governed.

§2. *Corollary to the first thesis: civil rule is a suitable object for a right of ownership*

1791. The first of our two theses gives rise to the following. Civil rule, although only an office for regulating modality, is a suitable object for a right of ownership, provided it contains the goods listed above, because good is a necessary condition for constituting right.[85]

The argument can be further developed by the application of jural reason from which we can derive the titles giving rise to the acquisition of such a right.

§3. *Corollary to the second thesis: peaceful occupancy is a valid title to civil rule*

A.
Peaceful occupancy

1792. Moreover, we can show by legitimate deduction that

---

[85] *ER*, 252–255.

occupancy peacefully consented to is a just way to acquire sovereignty or civil rule.

1793. In fact, according to individual Right, everyone can take possession of an unoccupied good, provided the occupancy harms no one.

In the state of nature, where the administration of the modality of rights does not generally exist, such an office, although unoccupied, is a good for the person who comes to occupy it without harming but rather helping others. Anyone therefore can legally occupy it. Occupancy is a just way of acquiring both the right of civil rule and every other right.

1794. If family heads did not in fact associate peacefully in the way discussed earlier, some individual, or special society, might reasonably undertake to administer the modality of everyone's rights to the advantage of all, provided they had the force necessary to assert their rule. No one would have the right to obstruct this person or persons although everyone would have the right to take action against abuse of administration, and to request sufficient guarantees in accord with the norms governing rights of defence and guarantee. The good sense of mankind acts in this way and always has done. The voice of upright nature ceaselessly suggested it to those who formed the first civil societies without unjust violence. Often they recognised wisdom in someone or imagined a person inspired by heaven, and either asked that person to be their legislator and civil ruler or, if the person took the lead, submitted spontaneously and accepted his laws and decrees as a great benefit. They felt an infinite gratitude towards him, acclaimed him, deified him. Some individuals were considered on a par with Hercules or Theseus because of the strength and bravery with which they defended their peoples; others, like Orpheus or Amphion, took control of the multitudes by their wisdom and eloquence; others, like Numa, ruled by their piety. In short, numerous individuals gained civil rule through occupancy, persuading whole nations of their capacity to guide them, defend their rights and hold the reins of civil government. To condemn as unjust everything that happened in this way when the first societies were instituted would be mistaken and temerarious. The voice of nature always suggested the dictates of justice to

[1793–1794]

the people. What they accept and what is done in the matter is not unjust unless the people manifest jural resentment.[86]

1795. It may still be objected that although eminent individuals, using their talents, could place themselves at the head of nascent civil societies, the people legitimised the move by open or tacit fellow-feeling. Consequently, the acquired right of these individuals to govern must be sought in the will of the people, in a social contract.

On the contrary:

1. The people's judgment and consent does not in this case concern the right of civil rule but the exclusion of someone from the right. The people, being in the state of nature, can and usually do exclude those who want to govern them without sufficient sagacity or strength. They exercise a just right of defence, a right whose strength corresponds to the danger and extent of the offence threatened under the pretext of taking possession of sovereignty.

The right to occupy sovereignty is therefore subject to the same exceptions as the right to occupy anything whatsoever. If my neighbour or someone else wishes to occupy some unoccupied thing, he has the right. But if I have a well founded reason to fear that his occupancy will invade my rights, I also have the right to prevent his occupancy if he will not give me sufficient guarantee to dispel my fear. This is the right of a people, or rather of each person in the state of nature, against anyone wishing to occupy sovereignty.

1796. 2. If my neighbour's occupancy causes me no fear or he gives me sufficient guarantee to dispel all reasonable fear, and I do not wish to occupy the thing myself, it is indeed true that he occupies some good with my tacit or expressed consent. It is not true however that my consent gives him the right of occupancy or that I put him in possession of the occupied thing. It is also true that the person who occupies sovereignty in the state of

[86] Aristotle says: 'All those raised to the level of king were benefactors of the cities and provinces over which they presided either through preserving the fatherland from forced servitude, like Codrus, or through freeing it from servitude, like Cyrus, or through conquering provinces and establishing cities, like the kings of the Lacedaemonians, Macedonians and Molossi' (*Pol.*, 4, 10).

[1795–1796]

nature does so with the people's tacit or expressed consent, but it is by no means true that the people's consent is that which grants sovereignty or the right to occupy it. This is the inoffens-ive freedom which no one receives from another, although each individual can limit its exercise when they have good reason to fear its abuse.

1797. We conclude:

1. Occupancy is a legitimate way of taking possession of unoccupied sovereignty to which no one has an acquired right.

2. A people cannot give or remove this title, but they can prevent its exercise when, in accord with jural reason, they fear injury to their right.

B.
Continuation — Lack of resentment against attempted occupancy is the sign of its legitimacy

1798. Jural resentment is symptomatic of injured right (*RI*, 638). History frequently witnesses to individuals who have quietly become heads of nations without any resentment on the part of the people; indeed some nations have joyfully welcomed them. There can be no doubt that such leaders occupied govern-ment legitimately.

This tacit, peaceful and spontaneous consent is the clearest *sign* that the person assuming civil rule neither usurped it nor invaded others' jural freedom. This kind of freedom had not yet developed; there was no capacity for governing at the time when those outstanding individuals used their own more developed freedom to undertake it, as they were fully entitled to do by *jural law*.

1799. Resentment, we should note, is a symptom of injured right when human beings are guided by nature. But they also become irritable and show resentment when they are debased by passion or deceived by rebellious persons, even though right is not injured. Modern error, which gives right a material, mech-anical stamp, supposes that evil itself can become a right. Today, people think that when they have a right, they can use it capri-ciously, free from any obligation to conform to reason and fittingness. Rousseau said that people have a right even to harm themselves. What could be more foolish or inhuman! On the contrary, a people is jurally obliged to allow unoccupied sovereignty to be occupied, and cannot capriciously expel the person who has taken the sovereignty; indeed, he can force them to reasonable, civil submission both in a case of right of jural claim and in that of jural freedom, that is, in a case of legitimate occupancy. But I will speak about this forced, civil submission later. For the moment, let us continue our examination of peaceful, spontaneous occupancy.

C.
Continuation — Peaceful occupancy is the cause of three forms of government: monarchic, aristocratic and democratic

1800. *Occupancy* of civil dominion is not complete until the fellow-feeling of all has been given to it either in fact or verbally. It does not yet exist as a title giving a right to civil rule.

1801. Consequently, two cases can be verified wherever someone proposes verbally and attempts in fact to establish a civil society where it does not exist:

First Case. The other family heads (in the state of nature, as we have supposed) refuse the proposal of the individual who aspires to form a civil government, and will not unite with him for the good regulation of the *modality of rights*. If this refusal is prejudicial to the individual, he can force them to agree to the foundation of a civil commonalty. Later we will consider the jural laws which bind and limit this kind of forced foundation.

1802. *Second Case.* The others consent to the institution of civil societies in one of three ways:

1. They can consent unanimously, handing over to the person who aspires to government the *regulation of the modality of their rights*. This consent, whether expressed or tacit, completes the occupancy. — The resulting form of government is *monarchic*.

2. In consenting to the proposal to found a civil society, some of the fathers may wish to take part in the government; others may not wish to have this responsibility and expressly or tacitly renounce it. Granted the declaration of those who wish

to take part, the individual who wants to occupy the government can no longer do so alone because the others' consent is lacking. Consequently he has no right to use force. Those who say they want to occupy the sovereignty together with him have the same right to do so as he. The civil rule must be regulated by all those who desire it; it rests with those who have claimed it through the tacit or expressed consent of others who either do not wish to share it, or do not think or know about it, or cannot share it. Each of the claimants must partake in proportion to the mass of their rights. — Here the government is *aristocratic*.

3. Finally, all the fathers may both consent to the institution and wish to take part in the civil rule. With this act of their jural freedom they become co-occupiers, none of whom can be excluded provided they pay their contribution. — The form of government that results from this kind of *occupancy* is *democratic*.[87]

1803. The last form clearly supposes a greater development and activity of *reason* and *jural freedom* in human beings. Allowing another *to occupy civil power* indicates that human reason still does not see the consequences of the power to govern and that human freedom does not have the means to profit from it. Hence, because jural freedom remains almost dormant, the people appreciate that in their present state it is more useful to be governed than to govern.

1804. Furthermore, because civil rule cannot exist unless someone occupies it, we see the great error of the theory that places it in the hands of the people, as if it exists there naturally

---

[87] Signor Baroli's affirmation does not seem true to me: 'Wherever civil society had to be instituted for the first time, provident nature always determined that the person required as sovereign possessed exclusively the qualities necessary for his vocation. The fear that many claimants to the crown would arise in nascent States is totally vain and imaginary. The person truly called presents himself automatically in a most natural, human way, so that he cannot but be recognised, much less his vocation opposed' (*Il diritto naturale pubblico interno*, §22). On the contrary, history is full of violence and struggle. Those who obtained supreme civil power peacefully and legally were mostly brave men chosen by the people to defend them against ferocious enemies. But whatever the merits of this historical information, an author of Right must discuss all jural cases whose concept contains nothing absurd. We have made it our duty to do so.

before its institution. Neither the people nor the fathers have civil rule by nature; its institution requires some element of action. If the people desire it, they must occupy it and, by doing so, they (or a number of individuals who wish to possess it) become subject to the same jural law affecting individuals. When fathers unite, come to a mutual understanding and determine a way of reliably regulating in common the modality of their rights, sovereignty is instituted and occupied by the people. Only now is it a democracy, not before: *Tolle unum turba est, adde unum populus est.*

Article 4.
Fragment of a philosophical history of civil society

§1. *Mixed titles to civil rule consisting* of seigniory and ownership preceded *pure titles*

1805. Before presenting further titles to *pure civil rule*, that is, titles divided from every other right of ownership and seigniory, it will be helpful to look at the historical order, and properly speaking, the humanitarian order, in which these titles arose in the world. We must do this to understand the kind of progress revealed by the institutions and foundations of civil societies among mankind. It will serve as a fragment of a *Philosophical History of Civil Society*, a work yet to be undertaken.

1806. I have said that it was and still is difficult for human beings to divide the modality of rights from rights themselves, and govern the former without invading the latter. Only time can perfect and refine civil power by separating it from every other power. We certainly cannot claim that human beings of the remotest antiquity were able to make a perfect distinction, even mentally, between *rights* as such and their *modality*. Great development of the *faculty of abstraction* is needed to achieve this, and we have seen how slow this development is in the masses. Whatever strength we attribute to the ancients' *faculty of thought*, we cannot grant them much *abstraction*, which comes only after a long time and varied experience. It is time

[1805–1806]

which presents us with the series of successive events. It composes and dismantles things and occurrences, varies their forms and their countless accidents, which then become abstract. Time alone leads the mind to divide and subdivide things, to distinguish and subdistinguish, to separate out individual relationships, circumstances, ownerships. In this way the human mind is educated to abstract.

1807. To distinguish the modality of rights from rights themselves is a profound and difficult abstraction, but nevertheless necessary for separating *civil power* from all other power. Because the ancients lacked the force of abstraction, they did not and could not have the pure, clear idea of civil government — they were able to conceive this power only as united and incorporated in other powers, not totally separate from them.

1808. This important observation explains very many facts in ancient societies. Civil government is a benefit for the governed on one condition: it must be limited to the regulation of the modality of their rights. If civil government, by that title alone, directs the rights themselves of those governed, it is no longer a benefit but a continual violation of particular rights, a pure despotism. The governments of all the ancient nations were of this kind. Civil government in antiquity was as extensive as its force: if the force was supreme, the government was a supreme, seigniorial power in the full meaning of the term; the emperor's house was truly *divina domus* [a divine house].

1809. The first government to exist among human beings was paternal. The danger was not, generally speaking, that such government might exceed its power because the power was supreme and universal; all that was required was its reasonable exercise. Nature generally taught fathers to use this reasonableness within their homes, and taught the children the fullest subjection. Consequently, the children hardly ever felt the resentment caused by violation of rights. During the lifetime of the fathers, the children lived together under a single head; later, they separated.

The father could indeed have divided civil power from his paternal authority and passed it on to one of the children, but that would have caused many difficulties.

In the first place, there was no evident need; children did not need common government in the first ages of the human race.

The reason is obvious but worth noting. Our mind and faculties cannot attend simultaneously to many things. We cannot think of the advantages to be obtained from the common administration of the modality of our rights before we have thought about the rights themselves. The first human beings were concerned with their rights, not with the modality of these rights. Their needs and desires were few, the terrain to be cultivated extensive, the flocks abundant — everyone was intent on enjoying domestic happiness. The first, spontaneous movement of families must have been to separate rather than unite.[88] Thus each family lived a long time by itself in complete independence, totally occupied with its own internal sphere. This explains the division of languages and cults: these arose from the almost solitary life which the families must have led for a long time, concentrating on themselves and fleeing relationships with others.

Secondly, relationships with others easily caused dissensions through wickedness and through the selfishness that increased in each family because of their solitary living, and through that lack of abstraction, of which we have spoken, which made it impossible to distinguish one's own right from another's in the same matter. If one family had to govern others, it would have so easily become tyrannical, believing it could dispose of things as it liked and totally unable to conceive how its government must be limited to regulating only the modality of others' rights without in any way disposing of the rights themselves.

Civil government, therefore, divided from *patria potestas*, served no purpose in the earliest times. Because people were sufficiently occupied in forming their rights, they had neither time nor desire to busy themselves with the modality of rights. Regulation of the modality would have been harmful and insufferable, because there was no one who could exercise it without disposing under such a pretext of every good and every right of others.

[88] We have the history in Genesis.

[1809]

§2. *A republic is more suited to civilised pagan nations; a monarchy, to Christian nations*

1810. We have noted that in its infancy humanity had so little ability in using the faculty of abstraction that it was unable to separate modality from rights; it could not administer modality alone without believing it could invade rights. We have therefore the following important corollary: 'Monarchy was less suitable for ancient nations; whatever their civilisation and culture, they had to favour a republic.'[89]

1811. If a single person governs only the modality of others' rights, he does them no harm; his action is beneficial. But the opposite is true if he thinks he has the right to do anything whatever that helps him govern, even to regulate particular rights. This is the principal error of ancient governments: civil governments of antiquity thought they had an unlimited power, at least relative to everything concerning the general good, which they understood as the good of the majority, the good of those influential in government. According to this principle, the *veteres migrate coloni*, the division of land among soldiers, the prohibition of cultivating the land in certain provinces, the mass punishment of entire cities and provinces, and many other political ordinances which directly removed the goods and life of individuals, were universally justified. The system was expressed in the maxim: 'The well-being of the republic is the supreme law,' which later became 'reasons of State'. All this took on an aspect of justice in the eyes of the people for the reason already given: human beings had not separated the modality of rights from rights themselves. Aware of the need for a power over modality, they included in it a power over rights; civil power was necessary and seen to be just and respectable.

[89] Lycurgus, who tried to inculcate the following maxim, which is a general expression of all that the ancients claimed to achieve, states grandly: 'Each citizen is a property of the fatherland and, relative to the fatherland, has no right whatsoever over him- or herself.' According to this principle, citizenship entails the most absolute slavery. Rousseau had the same ideas and granted civil society ownership of its citizens: 'When the ruler has told a citizen that it is necessary for the State that he die, he must die.' Understood in a strict sense (as we have a right to do, according to the whole spirit of the author), these words suppose that society is owner of all particular rights, and that the minority is swallowed up by the majority.

[1810–1811]

Because power over particular rights seemed inseparably connected with the modality of rights, it followed, as I said, that power over the latter implied power over the former, and because power over the latter could not be denied, power over the former, no matter how burdensome, could also not be denied. To lighten the burden, another method was used: to make civil power as tolerable as possible, all individuals, or at least many of them, were made part of civil power. In this way republics were born. In republics, individuals themselves carry out civil administration. Those who get into government, that is, the most powerful, do not find it intolerable if civil administration extends to regulating rights as well because, after all, it is they themselves who regulate their own rights.

1812. It will be objected that this seems contrary to many historical documents: Justinian states that 'when peoples and nations began, government was in the hands of kings;'[90] in a word, republics succeeded monarchies.[91]

I certainly said that a *republic* must have been a more suitable form of government for ancient peoples. Their faculty of abstraction had developed so little that they could not conceive *civil government* in its purity. But this does not mean that this form was chronologically the first. Ancient peoples did not immediately know which form of government was most suitable and fitting to their circumstances. They attained this knowledge only after long and painful experiences, in the way that the greatest discoveries are made gradually, after long and hesitant research. We should not be surprised therefore that kings replaced family heads, whom they resembled, and that republics followed kings.

1813. Many reasons for appointing a single head influenced the first fathers to unite in civil associations:

1. The thought of a single head is certainly the simplest for the human mind.

2. The task of government was far beyond the intellectual power of many. Because jural freedom was so little developed, most preferred to be governed rather than govern.

3. Government as the source of common good was

[90] *Epit.*
[91] Haller has maintained this for a long time.

perceived as an idea, not a fact; no one suspected the abuses which experience would later reveal.

4. Probably the sole purpose for uniting at the beginning was *defence*, which requires unity of strength. Hence, the fathers chose commanders-in-chief rather than kings, uniting under the strongest and most valiant personage.

5. Finally, *patria potestas* was so obvious that they could not avoid using it as a natural model for civil power.

1814. These observations remain valid even if we suppose that ambitious people exerted no violence on the institution of civil society and that everything was done according to *jural law*.

However, although history may indeed witness to a tendency in human beings to make the idea of justice a reality, it also reveals the various ways this task was thwarted by the uncontrolled force of passions. Passions are often more active, more vehement than the rational feeling of justice; they prevent its action and bring forth a deformed, lifeless child, a repulsive monster instead of beautiful offspring. This is what we find at the historical foundation of civil societies.

1815. The first cities mentioned in history were built by violent men, like Cain and Nimrod.[92] Consequently, Bodin, Böhmer and others ascribed the origin of States to force and to the desire to dominate. Certainly, some kingdoms arose from these passions and their accompanying violence.

1816. However, when tyrants of this kind wished to found kingdoms for themselves, they did not always have to deal with the ignorant, the weak and the deprived, people with whom they could do as they liked. Sometimes those they wished to subject rose in their own defence. Thus united, they appointed a head, the strongest and bravest among them, through whom they hoped to escape the threatened slavery or feared tyranny. This explains why Hobbes and many others ascribed the origin of civil society to the fear of tyrants and the need for defence.

1817. We should not be surprised therefore that in the beginning some monarchies appeared as a result of tyranny or the need for defence.

1818. But after these monarchical forms had been founded and

[92] Gen 4.

wars ended, they must have become unbelievably burdensome. As we said, the ancients were unable to separate *civil rule* from *full dominion*. Nor could they conceive how the modality of rights could be regulated without control over rights themselves. This explains the change of monarchies into republics, which occurred, however, only where a people had attained sufficient intellective development to be able to rule themselves. They activated that quantity of jural freedom which made them feel the need to govern themselves. This is what happened among the Greeks, Romans and generally among all ancient settlers. In other peoples, laziness and restricted development rendered the evils of tyranny more tolerable than the irksome effort and thought needed to avoid them.

1819. This explains the rapid change to republics among all pagan, civilised peoples. It explains why all Greek and Roman authors extol this form and vaunt it above all others, and why the greatest, most generous and just characteristics of such times emerged in all their splendour wherever this form of government was established.

1820. But the move to escape the oppression of a single human being ran into other obstacles. Accidental disorders arose in republics where the multitude governed, particularly through the manipulations of the ambitious and party struggles. When these evils, accompanied by corruption of morals, reached a certain level, the people were forced back to government by one human being. Any nation that has made some progress can tolerate only a certain level of evil. This explains why neither government by a single person nor by all endures for long among the most alert peoples of the pagan world; the forms of civil rule have nearly always oscillated between the two extremes.

1821. The faculty of abstraction in the human race was developed by Christianity.[93] Christianity led people gradually, although unconsciously, to the very important separation we are discussing, that is, the separation of the modality of rights from rights themselves. This alone leads to the perfect idea of

[93] *SP*, 839–843.

civil government, and would itself be enough to declare the Christian religion a sublime benefactor of humanity.

Civil government, reduced to all the purity of which it is susceptible, is government proper to Christian nations. Monarchy is therefore more suitable to these nations than a republic.

1822. When a monarch limits himself to regulating the modality of rights, preserving intact the rights of all, he is the great benefactor of the nation. In this case the monarchic form loses all its dangerous and burdensome content, which it never did in antiquity. On the other hand, a republic preserves its defects, and is therefore greatly inferior to Christian monarchy.

1823. Moreover, in Christian peoples every seed is developed. Hence, as good and evil grow,[94] a republic necessarily becomes much more difficult, while the dangers it presents increase. Furthermore, it lacks the guarantees that moderate monarchies can give peoples: the gentleness of reigning families, traditional affections and virtues, hierarchical order, ancient inviolable customs, fundamental constitutional laws.

1824. A rigorous democracy has probably never existed, and could not exist, at least not for any length of time. Civil power needs a prevalent force, not found in democracy without perfect agreement, which is rarely achieved and even more rarely endures steadily for any length of time.

If however civil power is placed into the hands of a small number, the rest, whether few or many, are easily sacrificed to them. Moreover, the many, the majority, are always excluded if the republic is huge and possesses provinces. On the other hand, if a body of citizens governs, it is almost impossible for the civil administration to be purified, that is, limited to the modality of rights, although government by one person can very easily accomplish this. A body of citizens, especially those whose authority is prevalent in a group where members are both owners and civil governors, attaches no importance to the limits of civil authority. No one commands in their house; they command themselves, or at least they think they do. Hence their inclination to despotism and their low esteem of those who do

[94] *Ibid.*, 715–722.

not share in government, especially of those whose fortunes are usually much less than theirs.

I said they at least *think* so, but often they are deluded. In fact, in a republican government equity is considered satisfied if all ordinances are based on a majority vote. In this case, the minority is sacrificed to the majority. If we prescind from inflamed passions, we see that all the difficulties of a republican government stem directly from its form. History confirms this theory: it reveals the extent to which many republican governments openly regulated individual rights. If we compare the laws of different forms of government, we will see that republican laws have always entered more boldly where they do not belong, and more resolutely controlled every kind of ownership among the citizens. Sumptuary laws, which limit the exercise of particular rights, are proper to republics; goods, life, morality and the very religion of the citizens are seen as things belonging to the republic. Whenever a republic is born, even today, it manifests its despotic character and regards the citizens as servants or things of the State. Its symbol is Ruault's motto: 'Everything, both body and goods, belongs to the State.'

Article 5.
The title of occupancy (continued) — Forced occupancy of civil rule

1825. Let us now return to the discussion of *occupancy* of civil rule, a title of first, direct acquisition.

We have already asked whether a person who wishes to occupy civil rule can, according to rational Right, force others to submit to him as regulator of their modality of rights. Generally speaking, the answer is 'No', but there are special cases where even *forced occupancy* can be an upright, jural title to civil rule.

1826. The answer must be 'No', generally speaking, because there is certainly no place for forced occupancy when peaceful, harmless families willingly agree to the stable regulation of the modality of their mutual rights. In this case, no single father or family can exclusively occupy civil rule (the supreme right to regulate the modality); all the families are disposed to occupy it. A policratic government therefore is the only form possible.

1827. *Forced occupancy* of non-existent civil rule can be effected in only two cases:
1. when just self-defence requires it;
2. in the just defence of others.

§1. *Forced occupancy of civil rule as the sole means of self-defence*

1828. We have seen that rational Right obliges human beings to agree in certain cases, and that they must exercise their rights in a way helpful to others without reducing their own good. We have also seen that as a result of this rational law one human being can require others to exercise their rights in one way rather than another, when this brings equal good to the possessor of the right and reduces obstruction to others' freedom (*USR*, 161–167). Civil society is simply an extensive agreement by many, or rather, an extensive, enduring determination agreed upon for the regulation of the modality of rights to mutual advantage. A person therefore could require from others (still in the state of domestic society) the establishment of a civil society, that is, that their modality of rights be regulated in common in a determined way, because helpful to himself and without harm to them. Moreover, if they refuse with total unreasonableness, he could force them to this, because their refusal would offend his right.

1829. Let us imagine that a person with great possessions lives among barbarian people who have not yet associated in civil society. Although he has occupancy of vast lands worked by his bond-servants, his property is never safe from the rapacity of his neighbours, who lack both laws and customs. Furthermore, this ferocious, strong and wild people refuse to submit to any social order, rejecting all guidance and despising the threats and cajolements of the landowner. Surely he is allowed to put pressure on them and force them to a regular, civil life? It is true that the yoke, being contrary to their practices, would be burdensome. But because these practices are depraved and lead to vices, the barbarians have no right to maintain them with harm to others; no one, as I must go on repeating, has a right to vice. Here we have an obvious case of the legitimacy of forced occupancy of civil government.

The ancient inhabitants of Sicily, described by Homer, are one of the many historical examples of people in this condition. He describes the Cyclops as

> huge barbarians, who live alone and neither sow nor cultivate fields. They do not meet for common counsel, and have no idea of rights. They live in caves in the mountains, each laying down the law for his children and wives. None cares for anyone else.

In short, they are a people in a state of domestic society, entirely lacking civil society. Moreover, they are inhospitable, cruel, wicked, proudly despising divinity itself.[95] Surely, no one lacked the right to compel these monsters to duty and make them return to the fold of humanity?

§2. *Forced occupancy as a means of defending others*

1830. That which can be done in defence of self can be done with laudable generosity if defence of others.

The *defence of others* can have as its object not only some particular, unjustly oppressed individual, but violated, tortured humanity itself.

1831. Certain vices against nature are reasonably considered by publicists as just titles of war, for example, cannibalism. It follows that whenever savage, immoral hordes and large gangs of robbers cannot otherwise be brought to a human state, every ruler has the right to go to war, and to govern them under just civil rule. In this way he brings them the greatest benefits; his conquest gives him the most human, beneficial title to govern them civilly. And there are still many peoples in this state today.

1832. A *right of conquest* must therefore be acknowledged.

The abuses of this right have been immense; its use is, and

[95] *Odyssey*, bk. 9.

[1830–1832]

always has been, exceedingly dangerous. But God forbid that we should exclude it for this reason from a treatise on Right. We do not dictate arbitrary laws. As faithfully as possible we copy the laws written in the eternal mind and write them down. We are not legislators, but simply recorders for the divine legislator. In any case, the right of conquest under discussion has no place among civil and Christian nations: a family may be conquered, but not a nation, at least not a civil, Christian nation.

Article 6.
Titles of civil rule arising from a common, combined act of many fathers

1833. I have said that *many* or *all the fathers* can agree to occupy civil sovereignty, that is, constitute themselves as a government. This form, which requires a contract between them, is a title resulting from a combined act.

§1. *Occupancy by a body of people — As a result of choice*

1834. Moreover they can all choose one or more persons on whom they confer government. There is nothing contradictory in this origin of civil society.

Let us suppose that the fathers come together after living independently and governing their families. After some increase in numbers, they experience the advantage to be had from agreement and the establishment of a common administration regulating the modality of their rights. Finally, they decide to come together and, in assembly, unanimously constitute a government. In this case the government is certainly legitimate, and civil society has begun to exist with full right.

1835. We need to distinguish here between different actions and successive states:

1. The state of separate families without any relationship between them, or without any stable, universal relationship.

2. The idea and proposal to unite, and the effective union or

mutual understanding of the family heads, which we call 'people'.

3. The result of this agreement and mutual understanding, that is, the establishment of a government.

1836. Civil society, and consequently civil power, exists only when the third action is verified.[96] Previously only families co-existed, but without the civil bond which formed them into a body, a society.

1837. This highlights the absurdity of the statement that civil power resides always and inalienably in the people. In fact, while the human race is in the state of family society, civil power does exist, but only in individual families. In this case, because it is absorbed by paternal authority, it is not yet called civil power or government which, as we have seen, applies solely to the jural relationship of many families.

1838. Hence, prior to the existence of civil society, a people as such has no political rights; they do not form a body, exist as a collective person, have unity. The word 'people' is misused when applied to family heads, or whenever a merely mental, potential union, non-existent in reality, is attributed to them. The ancients were correct to refuse the name 'people' to the co-existence of many human beings who were not all dependent on a government.[97]

1839. In the state of nature, therefore, no political right pertains to the *body* of family heads; such a body does not exist. But what of the right of individuals? They have no right *in*, but only *to*, civil power; their right is simply that of the *jural freedom* pertaining to every human being, as we have seen. Through this

---

[96] Baroli says: 'Some authors maintain that a mere *contract of union* suffices for the jural origin of a State, except for aristocratic and monarchic States. Others, like Pufendorf and Egger, accept the necessity of three known levels of contract: *union*, *constitution* and *subjection*. The last level does not take place in a democratic State' (*Il Diritto naturale pubblico interno*, §28). We must note however that *civil subjection* is found in every government, but not *servile subjection*, which does not exist even in purely *civil monarchies* and *aristocracies*.

[97] 'According to Africanus, the republic is what belongs to the people. But a people is not every association of human beings, irrespective of the way they associate. The people is that association formed by *de iure* consent, and brought together to be of mutual assistance' (Cicero, *De Republica*, bk. 1).

right of freedom, which allows everyone to occupy all the unoccupied goods he finds, human beings can also occupy government provided it is unoccupied, and provided they have the aptitude and others do not object. This right therefore pertains equally to everyone. Hence, many, and even all together, can attempt occupancy. In this last case, which produces the democratic form of government, the people obtain the *right in civil power* which, as I said, they did not previously have.[98]

1840. If this is true, how are the titles of *occupancy* and *popular choice* distinguished? In the same way that occupancy of land through spontaneous will is distinguished from occupancy through invitations, requests and the help of friends.

Family heads, gathered together to establish a government, can choose a king or some outstanding individuals to govern them. The choice simply means they are inviting these worthy people to assume the burden of governing them and, because the family heads consider government better occupied by others, are renouncing their own freedom to occupy government. If the occupancy takes place *without this explicit choice*, the fathers' consent is spontaneous, tacit and as it were unconscious. In the case of an *explicit choice*, the consent is explicit, reflective, formulated, fully conscious and vested in contractual form (*USR*, 313).

1841. But the decision of the family heads can take another direction, if they wish. They can keep the government for themselves while choosing magistrates or ministers to act on their behalf to represent the government. Thus, although they would bring into existence a *representative government*, they themselves would occupy *civil rule*, absolute government.

Representative government can be 1. by one person or 2. by many. In the first case, the fathers choose a ministerial head of the nation, who has executive power, while the legislative power is retained by the national body. In the second case, they choose two or more consuls or a body of magistrates, as they wish.

[98] Horn fittingly wrote: 'Because neither individuals nor the multitude as a loose association possess majesty, they cannot bestow it on a king' (*De Civit.*, bk. 2, c. 1). If we substitute 'civil rule' for that mysterious, obscure word 'majesty', the truth is clear.

It is imperative however that the fathers, before having the right to constitute a representative government, occupy absolute government — there is no representative without some absolute to be represented (*USR*, 313–314).

1842. Hence, the people's right to be represented is not to be considered an exclusive, inalienable right, but a right common to all those who have some absolute power. In absolute monarchy, magistrates effectively represent the ruler; in every government they represent the person (individual or collective) who possesses absolute power, autocracy.

1843. We must note here that the people, even when they retain civil authority, can never exercise it fully on their own behalf. Although absolute power is present equally in republics and monarchies, it is not present in the administrative branch. In monarchies the absolute power, present in the king, can for the most part be exercised by him. For this reason alone, popular government, rather than monarchic, is normally called representative.

§2. Interpretation of choice

1844. We must now ask various jural questions.

If the united family heads choose a leader to govern them, does this person have absolute power, or simply representative power? The question must be answered according to circumstances and the precise formula of choice. In the absence of these, the choice must be interpreted according to the rules of contracts (*RI*, 1166–1176).

1845. Chief among these rules is that of noting carefully the nature of a contract. The nature of the contract by which someone is given direction over a people assigns to him either complete civil power or only some share of the attributions and duties of civil power. Power is complete when the person is given total direction of the modality of rights; partial when he is chosen to regulate only a part of the modality of the people's rights, in some particular circumstance, in case of some urgent, transitory need. The choice of a commander-in-chief in time of

[1842–1845]

war would be a case in point. The ancient Germans did this when choosing their rulers.[99] Thus recourse was sometimes had to a wise man to obtain wise laws. Such choices are for particular purposes; when these are fulfilled, the authority conferred ceases. Those chosen can be viewed as having responsibility, that is, as ministers, representatives, councillors, masters, directors, etc., but not as absolute, permanent monarchs.

1846. The case is different when someone is chosen as head of civil society in general, without limit of duties or time. Such a choice should be interpreted as an invitation to occupancy of absolute authority or, if the people have already been constituted, as a transmission and alienation of popular authority.

1847. It can happen however, and history offers frequent examples, that a person who has been called to occupy, or has himself occupied, a part of civil authority, gradually occupies it all. Thus, many absolute monarchs began by being simply commanders-in-chief or legislators or priests. The errors of publicists arise precisely from their relying on one or other of these origins to deduce all political regimes. Other origins are excluded.[100] The vast nature of human systems, however, admits them all, and history offers us examples of them all.

[99] P. Cluver shows in his *Germania* that 1. government among the ancient Germans was military; 2. the king was chosen by the people; 3. the people obeyed the king as long as it pleased them. The Lombards placed a staff in the hand of their king as a sign of their choice. The Visigoths lifted the chosen king on a shield.

[100] Haller is too restrictive in determining the origins of civil society, even though he ranged more widely than his predecessors. For him, Filmer and Adam, who derived all government from *patria potestas*, Gatterer, who derived it from leaders of armies, and other authors, who derived it from priestly power, were far too exclusive and systematic. Haller accepted these three origins, but history offers others, which we have indicated.

[1846–1847]

CHAPTER 4
The origins of civil governments in history

1848. Publicists like Pufendorf, Montesquieu, Sonnenfels and others, who make States pass successively from anarchy to democracy, aristocracy and monarchy, err only in the desire to apply to history what is perfectly acceptable in theory. Euclid first presupposed the point from which he posited the line, from which he posited the surface, from which he posited the solid — an excellent order for science, but contrary to the order of nature. The order of ideas is always opposite to the order of facts; confusion in their relationship causes error.

Even if we identify all the theoretical elements and arrange them according to the order of concepts, we see that in history these different elements are modified and altered without any apparent regularity according to circumstances.

1849. So far we have dealt with the titles which could have initiated civil government among human beings in the state of nature. It is untrue that no trace of any of these titles is visible in history. On the contrary, history reveals traces of them all, but not in the order which we have given them according to the law of concepts. They are historically mixed with every expression of human passion and vice: justice is found next to violence, beneficence in the midst of the horrors of cruelty. Before I discuss the titles of second acquisition, I shall make some observations on the historical order of the titles already dealt with.

1850. The first historical question is: 'Of what kind was the first civil government to exist on earth?'

We have already answered: it was civil government joined with ownership; it was divine, paternal, seigniorial, proprietary government.

1851. The second question is: 'Was the first civil government pure, that is, separate from dominion and ownership?' The answer seems of little importance because it depends on the circumstances and the opportunities which made families associate.

[1848–1851]

1852. Two things must be distinguished in the progress of the human race:
1. The ordinary, continuous course of growth in perfection.
2. The extraordinary accidents which affect this course by accelerating or delaying it.

These two forces, one ordinary, the other extraordinary, are also evident in the establishment of civil societies, which are formed through either regular, almost natural progress, or precipitous, irregular movement.[101]

1853. Although the ordinary course of things is continuous, we cannot infer that it is always more powerful than the extraordinary accidents, or that it obtains its end more quickly. Sometimes extraordinary accidents find things so disposed that extraordinary interventiion accomplishes in a short time what the ordinary process would accomplish only imperfectly and after a long time. Sometimes they delay interminably what the ordinary process would have obtained without them.

1854. The ordinary, developing course of humanity results from the active qualities common to all human beings; this is the course of the *masses*. The extraordinary course is due to the extraordinary abilities and activities of certain *individuals*, and to their vices and virtues.

1855. Civil society, formed by consent and by contract amongst family heads, must be seen as the effect of the ordinary course of things; civil society subjugated by a conqueror, whether just or unjust, can only be considered as the effect of an extraordinary accident. Because extraordinary accidents cannot be foreknown, it is possible for civil societies to be produced by some extraordinary event which precedes the slow course of nature. We find undoubtable traces of this in the giants mentioned in Scripture, who were violent men, conquerors and founders of governments, or more exactly, of seigniories. After the Flood, the race of Ham evidently spread wide and for a short

---

[101] Authors divided these two ways in which civil associations, considered in themselves, arose. Some declared the origin of civil society to be *natural*. Horn writes: 'The City is the work of nature, produced in a natural order and sequence, that is, out of the family and the abundance of offspring' (*De Civit.*, bk. 1, 4, 6). Others declared the origin to be the work of violence and tyranny, etc.

[1852–1855]

time ruled on the earth. Later they were conquered and dispersed in every direction, particularly by the Japhites.

1856. Nevertheless, the slow course of natural development continued amidst this violence. The number of families had to increase before they could unite in civil society. Although they all originated from one father, their characteristics were different; they had something proper to themselves and something common to the paternal family. These two elements mingled in varying measure; sometimes the common element dominated, sometimes the proper element.

With the passage of time, one of two things had to happen: either a violent man would appear who would subject his brethren — the extraordinary case — or families would continue to multiply, and events follow their ordinary course.

1857. The ordinary course of the multiplication of families could be conceived as follows. First, families needed to feel the discomfort of living together in the same area. Then, because of the shortage of food and material comforts, disputes and quarrels arose. It was then natural for them to discuss means of remedying this unsatisfactory state, as Scripture says: 'They said to one another.'[102] But these discussions did not produce a civil society, nor did time render such society indispensable; the people were able to provide for their needs in other ways. Hence, we must believe that civil society, in common with all other spontaneous humans operations, was formed only when need forced it on the people.

Certainly, the first remedy for excessive multiplication must have been separation, which was suggested by the people a hundred years after the Flood. Before separating, however, they united to build the tower of Babel.

The mutual withdrawal of families kept them in a state of domestic society for a further period. The fathers themselves preferred to emancipate their children rather than exercise civil rule over them; the strong will of the offspring for development and extension aroused their need for independence. Sometimes their insubordination, their ferocity, forced their fathers to exercise a very gentle government even in the home, and to bear and

102 Gen 11: [3].

deplore their mistakes silently rather than correct them severely. Sometimes they had to be dying before they could punish or reward their children by calling down curses and blessings, as Jacob did with Ruben, Simeon and Levi. If the children grew more insubordinate or upset the domestic peace for any reason whatsoever, the fathers preferred to expel them outright from the home, giving them full independence. Abraham acted in this way with Ishmael, whose character was similar to that of Esau, Isaac's son. Noah evidently did the same thing earlier, like his three sons, who lived a long time after the Babel dispersion. The father possibly went west, the children spread to the east. The fathers therefore, instead of maintaining civil government over all their children, took the way of general peace offered by vast, unoccupied territory. They let them separate to found new families independent of each other.

The first dispersion, and the most impressive, was that of Babel, but it was not the only one; similar separations had probably occurred many times. We see that Abraham and Lot separated: 'The land could not support both of them dwelling together,' Scripture tells us, 'for their possessions were so great that they could not dwell together, and there was strife between the herdsmen of Abram's cattle and the herdsmen of Lot's cattle... Then Abram said to Lot, "Let there be no strife between you and me, and between your herdsmen and my herdsmen; for we are kinsmen. Is not the whole land before you? Separate yourself from me. If you take the left hand, then I will go to the right; or if you take the right hand, then I will go to the left".'[103] Lot chose the well-watered lands of Sodom and Gomorrah, and separated from Abraham.

As long as lands were extensive and spacious, and people were few, there was naturally no place for civil society. This was the time for acquiring *rights*, not for *regulating their modality*. Arguments and disputes were avoided by families moving away from each other. Luxury was not known, and every family lived in peace and abundance.

Not long after the dispersion of Babel, the Hamite, Nimrod, established a kingdom. A violent man, he upset the natural

[103] Gen 13: [6–9].

[1857]

course of events. Assur, who gave his name to the Assyrian monarchy, is possibly the son of Sem, conqueror of the tyrannical descendants of Ham.

1858. New irritations must have been experienced, as human beings continued to multiply. Emigration became more difficult and troublesome, especially for those who had turned to agriculture and had already formed the first concept of a fatherland. Unoccupied land became ever further away, and mountains, rivers, deserts and sea obstructed progressive dispersion. The effort of transporting oneself with all one's possessions and leaving one's native land made a fixed habitation pleasant, while the discovery of various skills rendered such movement intolerable and impossible. The necessity now arose of discovering how best to stay together and regulate the modality of everybody's rights, so that the land could hold a greater number of peaceful persons supplied with what was necessary.

Two means of solving the difficulties were now tried: *weapons* and *law*, that is, tyranny and the establishment of equable civil societies.

The first wars aimed at establishing settlements; swarms left the hive to search for somewhere to settle and feed themselves. The Israelites, for example, drove the Canaanites out of Palestine: of these some were destroyed, others took flight, and some, Newton suggests, went either into Egypt where they found other Hamites, descendants of Mesraim, already settled, or made their home on the African coast.

Many civil societies must have had a peaceful foundation. In Abraham's time we see communities subject to kings, and to priests, whatever the means the latter had used to occupy the royal dignity. However, the smallness of these kingdoms, the names of cities taken from the family heads and the peaceful, domestic disposition of the priestly dignity indicate the separation of families from each other.

1859. During this time, when people tended to disperse rather than establish a fixed dwelling, progress in founding civil societies must have been slow and haphazard. The period can be considered as extending as far as the death of Jacob, five and a half centuries after the dispersion of Babel. It is an age of uncertainty, not reported in profane history precisely because civil societies do not exist; for the whole of its duration, human life was long.

1860. In the following period, when the fathers lived much shorter lives, civil government became more necessary to preserve general peace and happiness; dispersion was too difficult. The profane history that has come down to us with dates is almost entirely Greek and begins nine or more centuries after the death of Jacob — centuries of legend, full of unreliable traditions. The search for profane records of the historical origins of civil society at most produces origins of societies that appeared late in a corner of the world. Greece itself is very small compared with so many nations of the earliest times whose reliable history is almost entirely lacking. The error of authors who over-generalise Greek history, substituting it and Roman history for humanity, has often been pointed out. A great number of publicists who considered the golden age of the Greek poets as the state of nature based many of their useless theories on it.

1861. Whenever one or more families settled in new territory, they started a new world. Their transformation into nations involved experiences similar to those of the first family of Noah. I say 'similar' and not 'equal' because, as we have noted, every family possesses a proper element in addition to the common element. Furthermore, each is subject to the action of a different climate and has to procure its means of sustenance in different ways. The children who come afterwards also bring to the world their own element which, although accidental relative to us who cannot foresee it, is predisposed by Providence with infinite wisdom. In this way new challenges arise, and all the possible origins of civil society become a reality one after the other.

1862. We can note generally that the origins of civil society among the nations springing from the families of Noah's three sons exhibit in some way the character inherent in lineages.

The Hamites, more wicked and sensual than the others, widespread in Africa, were destined to be *bond-servants*. The Semites, a very intuitive race who spread through Asia, aspired to *absolute domination*. The Japhites, among whom reasoning prevailed over intuition, settled in Europe and showed themselves

most apt for civil society. All this accorded with the will of their
father.[104]

Among the Hamites, civil societies must have been almost
non-existent due to dissipated living and brutality. They could
be violent, were always superstitious and, after material prosperity of short duration, were destroyed and subjected to base
servitude.

The Semites must have been conquerors; the seigniory they
practised was the origin of civil societies.

Only the Japhites were able to separate civil society from
ownership and dominion, and conceive the idea of pure, abstract, civil government. The Hamites, having a debased intelligence and enslaved by the tyranny of material imagination,
could not rise to abstraction; their debased intelligence
prevented their having a calm, just spirit. The Semites, a people
of sublime, contemplative intellect, which they devoted to the
faculty of thought, made very slow progress with the faculty of
abstraction. Only the descendants of Japhet were characterised
by their skill and ease in using their intelligence to separate one
thing from another, to distinguish and to abstract.

The ability to conceive divine things without being able to
abstract and divide them certainly elevates and perfects concepts. It disposes human beings to become enthusiastic, to open
themselves to great and sublime designs, and to be capable of
executing them. The simplicity of their ideas is matched by the
absoluteness of their wishes; the means used for their enterprises are now complete and full. But the same manner of mental
conception, when applied to limited, human things, is very
defective, with the consequent loss of many a good, which
abstraction could have saved. Using our intelligence to divide
one thing from another does reduce our energy for thinking,
and slows our activity, but it compensates by goading us on to
find remedies and solve difficulties. This may indeed make us
fussy, dull and content with indifferent solutions, but it also
renders us patient, persevering in our tasks and happy in the
most complex undertakings. Neither virtue in all its simplicity
nor pure vice is normally found in people endowed with prompt

---

[104] For the story of Noah's three sons, cf. Mons. Marchetti's *La felicità in
problema* etc., Imola, 1823.

[1862]

abstraction. Our action varies according to the partiality of our vision; we are not controlled by enthusiasm, but guided by cold reason. This is the character of the Japhite; it is more mobile, more developed than that of the Semite; it is able to rise from decline and, to some degree, from corruption itself. This explains why among Europeans the origins of civil governments were laid down and perfected in the ordinary course of events, whereas among Asiatics they arose almost solely in the extraordinary case of conquest, and never became perfect.

The Semite conquests were directed against the violent Hamites whom Josuah drove into western Asia where they still remain. The Semite, Mohammed, attacked them in Africa. The Japhites, despite their humanity, searched them out and exterminated them in America, where Japhet spread widely, three thousand years after Noah's prophecy. The Asiastics themselves became subject to the Europeans, but were not destroyed — the descendants of Japhet did not destroy those they conquered but associated with them in a single civil commonalty. The political mission of Japhet therefore is to found PURE civil societies. Who knows how much harm the refugees from Canaan did to Carthage, or what harm Egyptian and Phoenician blood may have brought to Greece?

1863. We must also note, when discussing the origin of civil societies, how historians record one form of government more easily than another. When a monarchy is established, civil society undoubtedly exists. This is not the case with popular government that exercises only little action. Thus nearly all historians say that the first form of government was monarchic,[105] without considering what form preceded it. Homer's description of the isolated Sicilian families, who had neither common laws nor assemblies, presupposes that the custom, practised by family heads, of uniting and deliberating matters of mutual utility was found among other peoples. We have here a trace of very ancient popular government preceding the age of the Cyclops. Homer does not say they had no king but that they did not meet together, that is, they had no civil society.

1864. In the ordinary course of events a head is usually con-

---

[105] Aristotle, *Polit.*, 1: 1; Cicero, *De Legibus*, 3; Sallust, *Jugurtha*; Pausanias, bk. 9; Justin, bk. 1; Tacitus, *Ann.*, bk. 1.

[1863–1864]

stituted for a military need only. Aristotle, who sees the origin of the king in paternal rule, clearly states that in the absence of a father the *eldest* of the family took command. He also says that the growth of the family gave rise to the town, and that four towns united to make the city.[106] This can only be a special case. Granted the very tenacity of paternal traditions,[107] this case cannot explain the origin of all civil societies; it is a case proper to peaceful families, all of whose children follow a regular course. A more frequent origin of the monarchic form seems to be that of the choice of a commander-in-chief when a multitude needs to defend itself or wishes to conquer. If that commander-in-chief makes himself the stable governor of the people whom he leads, it is natural to say that civil society began with him; under him the society begins to have strong, visible influence, and takes on regular, solemn forms — prior to him, there was little organisation and few formalities.

1865. Among the Hebrews, we cannot really say that an external, executive government existed for the four hundred years from the time of Moses to the first king, Saul. A commander-in-chief was chosen according to need. Because Hebrew

[106] Aristotle's observation that the city was originally composed of four towns seems a very ancient tradition. In the formation of the first historically known civil societies the number four is constantly before us. Scripture states that four places formed the kingdom of Nimrod (Gen 10: [10 Douai]). The rabbis claim that every leader of the peoples had four places to govern. The royal palace at Nineveh is thought to have been divided into four towns, minor cities, just as Jerusalem was divided into four small cities. Cicero says that the metropolis of Sicily was composed of four great cities (bk. 6, *in Verr.*). According to the artist, Fabius, Romulus divided Rome into four cities (Varrone, bk. 4, *De ling. lat.*); the same is claimed for the Etruscans. An author has observed that the Trojans were divided into four parts, and that the Indian castes were four. The use of the word 'tetrapolis' also seems to prove the fact. A fragment of Xenophon says that in ancient times a country city was called a monopolis, a rich city a dipolis, the principal city of a province a tripolis, and the royal palace that presided over the others a tetrapolis. Julius Caesar also says: 'Every Helvetic city has four towns (bk. 1, *De Bel. Gal.*).

[107] Among the Tartars, family government was constant (the same can be said about other Asian peoples). Consequently they guarded their genealogies like treasure, and used them to see who was head or *mursa* of the lineage. This head represented their first father and exercised the authority of judge in time of peace, and champion in time of war. Eventually the family of Genghis ruled the others.

theocracy had a popular form prior to a royal form, popular governments existed before the kings. These governments however are nascent rather than perfect civil societies; they supply contingent needs and restrain the few disorders which arise when life is simple.

1866. Civil society grows and becomes perfect in proportion to needs. This is precisely why popular governments naturally become ever more restricted and eventually monarchic. On the other hand, internal vice increases, and, even without the need of defence against external enemies, necessitates a stronger, more organised government. This probably explains why God complained about the Hebrews who requested a king. In Deuteronomy,[108] foreseeing the time when they would need a king, he had already decreed what this king would have to observe. Evidently, the complaint did not so much concern the request for a king, but the need motivating the request, that is, the increase of vice. Hence God's words to Samuel: 'They have not rejected you, but they have rejected me from being king over them.'[109]

CHAPTER 5

Titles of second acquisition

Article 1.
The two parts of right concern: 1. the FORMATION OF RIGHTS, and 2. their TRANSMISSION — The modes of second acquisition pertain to the latter

1867. We have said that titles of second acquisition are those by which constituted civil government passes from one person (collective or individual) to another. Can a treatise on the origins of civil society deal with titles of second acquisition, if they presuppose the prior existence of civil society? Strictly speaking, such a discussion pertains to the part of Right dealing with

108 Deut 17.
109 1 Sam 8: 7.

the *formation of rights*, not their *transmission* (*RI*, 1031–1043); it concerns not the *forms of rights* but their *titles*, the ways of acquisition by which a particular person becomes the subject of rights.

Article 2.
Discussion of titles of second acquisition completes discussion about the formation of civil society

1868. Nevertheless, a right, when transmitted from one subject to another, can sometimes change form, as happens in the transmission of the right of civil rule. I must therefore add something about the transmission of civil rule to what I said about the formation and origins of civil society.

1869. We must distinguish three easily confused things: 1. civil society; 2. government of civil society; 3. the form of this government.

Civil society cannot exist without government, and government cannot exist without a determined form. Furthermore, civil society does not exist except by means of government, and government does not exist except by means of a determined form. Hence, the origin of civil society must be sought in the origin of governments (where, in fact, I have sought it), and the origin of governments must be sought in the origin of the forms of governments. I have already shown this in part, and will complete the demonstration by discussing the ways of second acquisition.

Note that I do not intend to provide here a complete treatise on the *transmission of civil rule* from one person to another. The matter has been amply dealt with by publicists. Moreover, in *Rights of the Individual* I posited the principles of reason which must regulate the *transmission* of rights in general. These principles can be applied, with a few comments, to the transmission of the right to civil rule. My intention therefore is to discuss only the modifications of form which civil rule can undergo when transmitted from one subject to another.

[1868–1869]

Article 3.
Three ways of transmitting civil rule

1870. Any power whatsoever can be communicated from one person (collective or individual) to another in three ways. The person communicating the power

1. does not despoil himself of it but both retains and communicates it;

2. despoils himself of it, making it pass to the ownership of the person to whom he wishes to communicate it;

3. retains total ownership of it; the person to whom he communicates it simply becomes an instrument for exercising his power, a representative or minister to whom he entrusts the executive part of the power whose ownership he does not cede.

In all three ways, the person who possesses naturally transmissible power can ordinarily communicate it as he wishes. Relative to civil rule, history provides examples of all three, in each of which power can be communicated with or without limit.

1871. Examples of communication of civil power, in which the communicator is not deprived of the power, are those cases where a ruler associates another person with himself in exercising civil rule. Communication is full when rulers hold civil rule in perfect communion, as the Roman emperors did equally among themselves; or partial, when, for example, Emperors communicated it to Caesars.

1872. In the second way, the person despoiling himself of power and consigning its ownership to another can do this wholly or partially. If he despoils himself entirely, he can will

1. everything to pass into the ownership of the person to whom he consigns it;

2. to transmit only a part, or more exactly, to transmit the right of regulating the modality of rights not arbitrarily but according to certain laws which aid the ruler to regulate the modality better and more easily.

In the case of feudal rights, particularly hereditary rights, a portion of civil power together with a portion of seigniory was communicated to the invested family.

An example of total consignment of authority is royal, unconditional abdication in favour of children or others. The third case however obtains when political conditions (fundamental laws, civil constitutions) are imposed on those to whom the royal authority passes: the person who communicates disposes of his entire authority, without this passing in its material integrity to the person to whom it is transmitted. I say 'material' because directive laws, if involved, are not properly speaking a limit to civil authority, but rather a help to better government, as I said.

1873. Finally, in the third mode the person to whom the authority is communicated is only a delegate, representative, minister of the person communicating the authority. The communicator has the faculty to limit the power by means of the *mandate* constituting his vicar; the formulas of this mandate are the law to be followed by the mandatary.

I will make a few observations on each of these three forms of civil power communicated through transmission.

Article 4.
Civil power communicated to another's ownership without loss of power in the communicator

1874. Power can generally be communicated either fully or partially, without loss to the communicator, in two ways:

1. by natural jural connection between the person to whom authority is communicated and the communicator;

2. by act of will.

1875. If power passes by means of a natural bond or connection, the quantity of power that passes is determined by the nature of the bond.

If power passes through a purely willed act, the quantity is determined solely by the will of the person transmitting it.

1876. In both cases, the *form of power* undergoes modification because it no longer exists solely in the person who originally possessed it but also in the person who participates in it.

1877. However, the difference in the two cases means that the modifications undergone by the *form* of the power, when this is communicated without its being lost to the communicator, are of two kinds:

[1873–1877]

1. If power is communicated entirely to the second person so that the two persons possess it *in solido* and equally, its form is changed in one way.

2. If the second person to whom power passes, either through a natural bond or the will of the communicator, receives only a part of it, its form is changed in another way.

1878. A ruler who chooses a colleague and makes him equal with himself in sharing government has changed the form of the power. If he chooses many colleagues instead of one, he changes the monarchy into a kind of aristocracy by an act of will.

The ruler however may communicate only a part of civil power to many of his favourites or fellow officers, making them dukes, princes, counts of cities and particular provinces. In this case he retains the general direction of all these dignitaries, but changes the form of full monarchy into a form mixed with feudal government. Once again he does this by an act of his will.

1879. The natural bonds through which power is communicated to a second person, without its being lost to the communicator, arise from the relationship between creature and creator, son and father, wife and husband. On the other hand, the willed communication of power comes about solely through an act of the communicator's will and acceptance on the part of the receiver.

1880. The first of the three natural bonds mentioned above has its own characteristic. God possesses all power in an inalienable, invisible way so that, when he communicates some of it to human beings, he does not produce a *modification of the form* of pre-existent authority but creates human authority.

When a father communicates his power to his child, the form of the power is modified. On the other hand, when God communicates power, its form is not modified but produced simultaneously with the power. Before the child is born, a visible form of power exists in the father, but before humanity receives power from God, no particular form of power exists; God is invisible and infinite. In human beings the *form of power* is proper; in God, *power* itself is proper. Thus, because there is no government without form and no society without government, society and government are communicated to human beings when the corresponding form of power begins to exist in them. Although this explains the saying that all authority comes from

[1878–1880]

God, we cannot say that human beings possess their authority in communion with God, still less that God remains without authority.

1881. In human generation the father communicates with the child in respect of power and its external expression. The same must be said of husband and wife; they are different members of one body, each of whom acts for the whole, and harms or helps the whole.

1882. Furthermore, a supernatural generation is made known to us by faith. Christ receives power from the Father analogously to the way the human child receives power from his genitor and is made heir of all paternal riches. Christ calls human beings to be his companions as hereditary, adoptive sons. Hence, the origin of visible and invisible ecclesial society. Divine power was communicated to Christ in a natural way that is, relative to the two natures through the generation of the Word and the Word's union with Christ's humanity. The communication of Christ's authority to other human beings is not made by a bond of nature but an act of his will called forth by the likeness of nature.

The great difference between ecclesial and civil society is seen especially in the unique, totally special mode by which ecclesial society receives its form, namely, 1. in generation of the child by the father, and 2. in adoption; in other words, in the union of the two modes *natural* and *willed* through which one person's power is communicated to another.

Article 5.
Power transferred to another's ownership and lost by the person communicating it

1883. Every change in forms of government peacefully carried out through transference comes about in one of two ways:

1. The person who comes to government either occupies a larger part of the power that was previously unoccupied, or leaves vacant a part that was previously occupied.

2. Power in the hands of a person (collective or individual)

[1881–1883]

passes wholly or in part into the hands of another person whose members differ in number from the first.

1884. The form of government does not change when it passes by hereditary means or in some other way from one person to another if the quantity of power or the number of people receiving the power remains unaltered.

1885. The form of government can be changed by a person who holds absolute, autocratic, civil power either by altering the number of persons possessing the power or by changing the quantity of power itself, provided however that those governed consent either expressly or spontaneously and tacitly, or at least that no jural resentment is aroused in them.

1886. Civil power held by a moral or individual person is rarely limited; indeed, the quantity of its exercise generally increases. The principal reason is that the existence of pure civil power helps civil society. Consequently, when civil power is constituted, it is very difficult to let power decrease: it is either kept wholly as it is or increased by an injection of energy or by extension to new regulations of modality. Changes in the form of governments normally come about therefore either through increase in the quantity of power together with more extensive administration of the modality of rights, or through change in the number of members composing the moral person who possesses the power.

If Alfred's will were to have been understood in the way David Hume and Edward Burke thought,[110] it would have allowed the English, after his death, to choose the form of government they preferred most. This disposition could have caused a change in the form of government relative to both the number of governing persons and the quantity of reducible power. The change would depend on the energy and degree of activity of the new government.

1887. The fundamental laws added to certain monarchic governments do not always change the form of power because they do not reduce or increase authority. They simply direct and clarify it, by ascertaining that the monarch does not exceed the

---

[110] The interpretation given to Alfred's will by these authors was refuted by Count von Stolberg in his life of Alfred.

[1884–1887]

limits of civil power, and by helping him to use it to the greatest possible advantage.

1888. Governmental form changes when the three powers are divided and parliaments are instituted. In this way the different branches of civil authority are really divided.

The form of government is also changed by the addition of conditions which are not simple rules of conduct but agreements whose execution imposes and regulates the people's duty to submit.

1889. Examples of changes in the form of government through every manner of increase or reduction of the number of persons are found in history. Either many persons restrict the power to a smaller number, or one or several persons extend it to many.

In Sparta, the popular magistrate of the Ephori received an increase of authority from the king, Theopompus, who told his wife he had reduced his royal authority to secure it better for his children.[111]

Through the famous royal law the Roman people, by transferring their supreme authority to emperors, deprived themselves of it.[112]

I cannot agree that history offers no example of authority passing from a whole people to their ruler. Whatever our view, the institution of the Roman empire is itself an enlightening, irrefutable example, even if we consider the royal law to be invented by those sycophants of rulers whom we call lawyers. Something similar is also to be seen among the Hebrews. The transference of civil authority from the hands of a people to those of an individual is not at the origin of civil society but of a particular form of government. At the time of the Hebraic and Romans republics, society and government already existed, and did not cease to exist when those republics changed to monarchies; the popular form ceased and the monarchic form began.

---

[111] Arist. *Polit.*, bk. 5, c. 11.

[112] Some modern authors maintain that the constitution of the Roman empire was made more despotic through legal formulas. This was attributed to the baseness of a few jurisconsults who lived under the emperors and had been slaves and children of slaves. Be that as it may, it is certain that despotism really existed. Legal formulas, which never cease to be added, are easily accepted, and contribute considerably to the increase and strengthening of despotism.

[1888–1889]

1890. Let us sum up the ways in which a people can co-operate in bestowing civil power on a collective or individual person:

1. In the state of nature or domestic society they can co-operate with tacit or expressed fellow-feeling. They permit or help a person (collective or individual) to occupy unoccupied civil power, but do not confer the power. They place no obstacle to power, but do nothing that could make another individual powerful; they simply help the person who wishes to occupy civil government — they are a friend helping another friend to occupy what is unoccupied.[113]

2. When civil society is already established and the people possess the supreme power *in solido* (as in a democracy), they can transfer the power, despoiling themselves of it totally, either to one person, in which case their action establishes a monarchy, or to many persons, in which case their action establishes a more or less aristocratic form. In each case they are simply disposing of some ownership. They are doing what any absolute ruler can do who, without any conditions, cedes his crown to one of his sons or to a brother or to a body of powerful persons or anyone at all. He is merely doing what every human being can do: donating and disposing of what is his, as he likes.

Article 6.
Delegated civil power

1891. The transmission of ownership of civil power must not, as we have said, be confused with delegating representatives who exercise power in the name of the owner and in accord with his instructions.

If we confuse the *transmission of the ownership of power* with

[113] We see here the weak side of Grotius, which allowed Rousseau to make the following reasonable objection: 'Grotius says that a people can give itself to a king. He therefore agrees that a people is a people before giving itself to a king.' Rousseau bases his system on this objection. But I deny that a multitude is a *people* before the institution of civil society, and can perform acts such as giving itself to a king. A multitude can only *consent* to whoever wishes to govern it, or concur in the occupancy of the civil power. If however a multitude has already become a people, formed as a democracy, it can give itself to a king, consigning to him the civil power it had occupied.

[1890–1891]

delegation to exercise power we fuse two totally different systems into one, that is, the system of social contract.

1892. The most contradictory consequences were drawn from the social contract. From it, Hobbes derived the most horrible despotism exercised by a single person. A century later, the French revolution, and later still the German illuminati, used the social contract to reduce all principalities to the most democratic republics. All this is explained by the fact that the system, although one in name, is really two in substance. I will first speak about what they have in common, which produces the confusion, and secondly about what is proper to each, which allows us to understand their difference.

We begin from the principle that the people are the source of civil authority, and that no collective or individual person can possess this authority legitimately, if it is not conferred by the people. This is the common element of both systems. Their difference is as follows.

In Hobbes' social contract, the people *transfer* the ownership of civil power to the governing person (autocracy). In Rousseau's, the people do not transfer the ownership, which he declares inalienable, but simply choose persons as their *representatives* who exercise the authority which they cannot exercise through themselves.

In Hobbes' system the people are deprived of all civil authority, and the sovereign has absolute power. In Rousseau's, the people always remain the sovereign, and sovereigns are their ministers. Hence they can change their ministers, limit their authority as they please, punish them, etc.

1893. Both systems are certainly false, and err from the start by maintaining that the people are the source and natural owner of civil authority. On the contrary, in the state of nature the people have no civil power and do not constitute a social body. In this state, neither civil power nor the common administration of the modality of rights exists. Civil power, which is only possible, is not and cannot be held by anyone. If we consider the people as having taken unanimous occupancy of this power, we have indeed a special, very rare case on which however no general theory can be founded. Occupancy of civil power by the people could never explain the origin of civil society in general, but only the origin of a particular form of government, that is, popular government. This very serious error, common to both systems, arose from a limited view which elevated a particular fact to the level of general theory.

1894. In addition to this common error, each system sins by its own defect. In Hobbes' social contract, the only possible form of government is monarchic. Rousseau's social contract pronounces as unjust all non-popular or representative forms of government.

1895. But if we take from Hobbes the declaration that civil power is an alienable right transferable to another's ownership, and from Rousseau the possibility of representation, civil power can be conceived as having the same quality and character as all other human rights, that is, the person to whom civil power is proper can transfer it or entrust its administration to another. We therefore finish with two forms of government, *absolute* and *representative*, which the nations of the world acknowledge today in their treaties.

We should also note that Hobbes' political system springs from a more remote principle: his denial of the existence of justice prior to the social pact. This is a fundamental, disastrous error [*App.*, no. 3].

[1894–1895]

PART FOUR

OCCASIONAL AND EFFICIENT CAUSES OF CIVIL SOCIETY

1896. So far we have examined the nature of civil society and its Right (Parts 1 and 2), and the *manner* in which it is formed, that is, the jural acts from which it originates (Part 3). But knowledge of the *essence* of civil society and of the jural manner in which it is composed is not sufficient. Our theory has to take more account of real societies and investigate 'the stimuli that impel people to set up actual, civil society.'

1897. Note that this is different from the investigation already undertaken. The *jural manner* in which a society is formed is one thing; the *stimulus* that moves people to effectively form civil society is another. Society does not receive *real existence* from the *jural manner* of its formation; it receives only its *jural essence*, the form of justice, its legitimacy. The *stimulus* which moves people, and their real actions, is the source of society's actual realisation.

1898. However, it is not the case that teaching about these stimuli, which move people to come together in civil commonalties, pertains to *real Right*.[114] It, too, belongs to *pure Right*, to the theory of Right, because the stimuli of which we are speaking are *possible* stimuli (although, if we consider our mental progress, we see that the mind came to them from experience and history). We are dealing also with *specific* stimuli (types of stimuli), not with *individual* stimuli (realities corresponding to types). We must now examine the stimuli which move people to set up civil society.

---

114 Cf. *USR*, 142–145.

[1896–1898]

CHAPTER 1
Need is the general stimulus moving people to establish civil society

1899. Human activity does not become operative without some stimulus;[115] the stimuli which draw it from inaction to action are certain needs felt by human beings in certain dispositions.

1900. I say 'certain needs' because human inertia is not activated by every need; some excessive, wayward needs have the opposite effect. I say 'certain dispositions' because the various dispositions in which a person finds himself greatly change the effect of the pressing needs.

I cannot examine here the degree and quality of the needs or the kind of human dispositions suitable for usefully awakening latent activity. I have to refer the reader to what I said elsewhere.[116] Needs capable of arousing human activity, I shall call *instigating needs* to distinguish them from others which disturb human beings without moving them to action.

1901. Everything done by man depends upon his need for things. The same is true about the establishment of human society; people feel the need for it. This stimulus must also be present when fathers come together and unite in civil communion, and when they submit to some powerful figure who either requires their union or from whom they seek union. In the second case, they at least feel the need not to resist a person who has sufficient power to make them regret their resistance.

1902. The word *need* is very general. Its meaning extends to the disquiet posited in human beings by every kind of longing that desires satisfaction, even if the desire originates from speculative reflection on hoped-for advantages. However, the instigating need which must have influenced fathers to move towards civil association was that of avoiding evil rather than satisfying the desire for some good.

---

115 *OT*, 514–527.
116 *SP*, 670–707. — *Saggio sulla Moda*, obs. 3.

1903. It follows from this principle (human activity is unmoved unless stimulated by some need) that 'the quantity of effective action produced is in exact proportion to the quantity of the instigating need itself' and that 'the effect is proportioned to the quantity of action and the quantity of need.'

CHAPTER 2

Necessity of civil society for the progressive development of mankind

1904. Several authors, having abandoned fact and historical circumstances, set out to argue abstractly whether *civil society* was necessary or not. Naturally, they held two extreme opinions.

Some said that it was not necessary for the requirements and exigencies of human nature. They concluded that civil society is an entirely arbitrary union of human beings. This decision gave rise to the system of the *arbitrary social contract* which at present seems to have almost no supporters.

1905. Others exaggerated the unconditioned need for civil society and invented an abstract moral-jural obligation pertaining to all human beings without distinction of time and place.

For the most part they started from an equivocation by substituting *society* for *civil society*. Having demonstrated the necessity for the former, they concluded that the latter also was necessary. They did not notice that society had been instituted before civil society; domestic and theocratic society already existed.

1906. Romagnosi belongs to the second group of authors, and writes:

> Only in society, and by means of society, does the child, emerging from infancy, acquire the use of reason;[117] only in society or by means of society can the human being receive adequate experience of good and evil, resist damage from

---

[117] Cf. *OT*, 514–527, for the possible development of the use of reason without language communicated by *society* (or even by gregariousness).

[1903–1906]

material objects and wicked people, and turn nature to his own utility by dominating it.[118]

That is well said, but it proves only that man has a need for society in general; it does not prove the absolute necessity of the special society we call *civil*.

Romagnosi is conscious of the weakness of his argument and later confines his affirmation of the jural necessity of civil society to: 'at least after a determined period'. He posits the question, which he answers affirmatively, in the following way:

> Are the conditions in which we live — the agricultural and commercial, educated and enlightened, political and regulated conditions — such that *at least after a determined period* they have to be adopted under pain of violating the inflexible duties established by the rational order? If we do not investigate this, we shall find ourselves bereft of the first, true foundation of right that authorises all the codes, so-called, of civilised peoples.[119]

1907. I do not dispute that there are times and circumstances when civil society becomes a matter of jural duty. This is indeed what I wish to say. But my reasons are not those of Romagnosi, who is too contemptuous of the time prior to civil association. His claim depends upon substituting for *history* the *romance* believed only by philosophers who use it as a foundation for their nebulous theories. Romagnosi's phrase, 'Just as man, therefore...', indicates his assurance that the 'facts' he is dealing with lie outside every possible discussion. He says:

> Just as man, therefore, is born in perfect ignorance, naked and helpless in the midst of the world's great forest, so the economic, moral and political state of human societies had to begin, progress, develop and perfect itself gradually through the sole work of societies themselves, and simply as the result of internal impulses and the force of natural, external circumstances. A long, preceding period was necessary in which, after lengthy experience, many mistakes and happy and sad events, the passage was finally made by rough, ignorant humans to the use of reason and

[118] *Assunto primo*, §7.
[119] *Ibid.*

of enlightenment. Naked, weak man, lacking useful tools, moved on to a state of laboriousness, comfort and enjoyment; isolated or confined to families, he moved on to the state of tribe, people and nation.[120]

In a word, Romagnosi, in order to describe social progress, starts from the *beast-man*, as he calls him: 'the beast-man, weaker, less safeguarded morally and physically than any other.'[121] Certainly, these expressions are not to be taken literally, but they do give us a good idea of the false, exaggerated style of the sophists of the last century.

1908. As far as I know, no sensible person now accepts the foolish notion of a beast-man suddenly arriving at the state of human life. However, the thread of our argument calls for a few brief observations on the quotation from Romagnosi.

1. Romagnosi describes the origin of man as follows: 'Man, therefore, is born in perfect ignorance, naked and helpless in the midst of the world's great forest.' We could ask if man appeared in this forest like a mushroom, or born from other humans. The first hypothesis we can leave entirely to sophists, whose inclination to leave the truth suspended has always rendered them the most credulous people on earth. Those who hold the second hypothesis will say that humans were born from other humans, and that the story of the natural development of mankind can only be discovered by going further back and investigating the intellectual and moral state of the first humans from whom all others arose.

2. But Romagnosi, writing in the 19th century as though he were an eye-witness, declares that man *was born* in the world's great forest as the archetype of ignorance and savagery. In this state 'in which he was weaker than the great beasts and less secure against the buffeting of seasons and events than any other animal, he cannot normally make provision even for his own conservation.'[122]

Nevertheless, he not only preserved himself: 'After lengthy experience, the passage was finally made to the use of reason.' These are spineless fables which cannot furnish a solid founda-

[120] *Ibid.*, §9.
[121] *Ibid.*, §7.
[122] *Ibid.*, §7.

tion for any philosophy, above all for what is called *civil philosophy*. This cannot be the true method, the experimental method, with which to philosophise.

3. A teaching which relies simply on the imagination does not need to be refuted. Nevertheless, we shall call in evidence an up-to-date, undeniable fact. Even now, at this late date in history, savage populations exist whose lengthy experience over the course of millenia has done nothing to raise them a single stage nearer a moral, civil state. This is sufficient to show that the progress made in other nations is indeed a fact, but a *particular*, not a *universal, necessary* fact. It shows that 'the different states of infancy, childhood, youth and civilisation of peoples are not at all a necessary law of nature'[123] or, if it is necessary, that it is so only on the basis of certain conditions extraneous to humanity. In other words, mankind must receive help from outside, help which, sustaining and comforting it, moves it to take those steps forward. This help comes from on high, from the Creator who has never abandoned mankind.

1909. We have to reject such vain suppositions as Romagnosi's if we want to avoid deceiving ourselves and others; we must turn to history and psychological facts which are the fruit of observation, not the outcome of fantasy. The facts intrinsic to human nature, together with others present in the annals of the human race, bring us to conceive the different jural states of humanity in the following manner.

Comfort, material laboriousness, and physical enjoyment are not the only objects occupying human intelligence and feeling. Mind and sense are raised up to God; they conceive and honour the supreme Being, they long for the supreme Good and thus bring forth religion; they reach out from individual to individual and thus give rise to love, beneficence, society. Cultivated fields, house-building, suitable arms and adequate clothing are means of protection and enjoyment, but they do not constitute *moral perfection*, nor *human happiness*, although they indirectly assist its attainment.

The true worth of the human state cannot therefore be gauged solely from its exterior, but principally from its interior condi-

---

[123] *Ibid.*, §9.

tion. Nor does it depend principally on the development of the *analytic activity* through which more attention is paid to aspects of things, to specialised reflections and to minute details. This certainly helps economic, material development, but it does not raise directly by a single degree the comprehensive understanding, virtue or merit of mankind. Only spiritual and moral *synthetic activity* does this. These are undeniable data proper to human nature. But let us now look at what history tells us.

1910. It describes the first humans created by God in a state of domestic society. These were not savages, not *beasts*, nor lower than beasts. They were endowed with powerful, perfect faculties, and moreover immediately enriched with every kind of natural and supernatural knowledge enabling them to lead a moral, religious, happy life, and to teach the children they would generate. They were works of the hand of the supreme Being, and worthy of such a maker.

Nevertheless, their *intellective and moral* state, although without defect and furnished with all the abilities required for progress, can be conceived as a *very lowly state* relative to states to which they were to raise themselves successively according to the divine design, that is, the progress in merit and advanced spiritual life to which they tended. Their initial perfection was a seminal perfection; they were perfect as seeds are perfect relative to the great, fruitful plant they produce.

Their *eudaimonological state* was also perfect. They were untroubled and fully content. But even this state, compared with those to which they were gradually to climb, was *lowly in the extreme* — it was only a fertile seed promising increasingly full happiness.

The same can be said about their *economic state*. They had what was necessary and desirable in abundance, but their wealth would have increased together with their laboriousness. They would have discovered ever new, unsullied pleasures.[124]

The same is true of their social state, that is, perfect conjugal society. Their communal life, their harmony of spirit, was perfect; they were affectionate in daily life, open and frank, their

---

[124] Pleasures are different from contentment. They can be opposed to it, or lead to it. Cf. *SP*, bk. 4.

[1910]

wills fully united. Everything was held in common. And all this was simply the seed of another, greater society.

Mankind fell from this happy state. Along with their innocence, human beings lost the supernatural gifts. The essential elements of humanity remained the same, but a principle of corruption had entered the human heart whose poisonous action gave rise to our passions. The will, pliant under the passions, seduced the intellect, causing error and its concomitant ignorance (every error is ignorance, and the generator of further ignorance).

But the Creator did not abandon his creature. From that moment, the development of mankind was twofold: the development of natural goodness sustained by assistance from the Creator, and the development of the principle of corruption which had entered mankind. An implacable struggle began between the two principles; its outcome varied.

If we follow the course of the principle of corruption, we see that it leads certain groups to savagery. There is not a single example in history of one of these groups rescuing itself or being rescued by others from its abasement.

Other groups fell into barbarism, a very different state from that of savagery. Sometimes they were raised again, not it would seem by themselves, but by the help of civilised settlers and landowners, who brought them their own civilisation.

This was the case with the aboriginal Greeks at the root of Greek history. They were brought in a flash from the depths of barbarism to the highest stage of civilisation. The fables about the rocks of Deucalion and Pyrrha that were changed into men, and other fables refer to this. The history of this single, very modern period, the history of tiny Greece, was embellished by the imagination of poets and by the equally fertile imagination of philosophers; it was then converted into theory and taken as history typical of human civilisation (*RGC*, 639).

In fact, the *first philosophers* were the *second poets*, no longer popular, no longer disciples of the people as the first poets were, but teachers of the people, heralds of a new age, singers of nascent civilisation, who taught the peoples to scorn barbarism, the oldest part of their chronology. Hence the boast, sung so often:

> Orpheus, sacred interpreter of the gods,

[1910]

overran the forest-men by slaughter and conquest-
based treaties.
Hence, HE WAS SAID to tame tigers and rabid lions.
Amphion, who fortified Thebes,
WAS SAID to move rocks with the sound of his lyre
and to lead them where he would with gentle words.
Long ago this public wisdom discerned private matters,
this sacred wisdom profane matters.
It forbade promiscuity; gave rights to spouses;
Built cities; inscribed laws on wood.
Thus honour and a glorious name came to divine
prophecies and songs.[125]

The repetition, 'was said', makes it clear that already in Augustus' time[126] it was impossible even for poets to take seriously
the exaggerated fables of the first state in which men were called
tigers, lions, hard-heads. Our publicists, however, have recently
gone back to exaggerations of a similar kind and modelled a new
history of civilised human progress on pitiful Greek annals and
fables, echoed by the Latins. This is the foundation presupposed
by Romagnosi as the basis of his social Right.

1911. But we have to remember that the good, natural principle, strengthened and guided by supernatural aid, developed
and gradually showed itself contemporaneously with the principle of corruption which had entered mankind. This fact also
must not be neglected. It is true that the facts dependent on the
two principles are mixed in the history of nations, but the first
duty of historico-jural philosophy is to distinguish them according to their natural character. It must do this by drawing
from our observation of what occurs in human nature (and
history especially provides the information) all *natural and
specific facts*, which it must simplify, classify and consider in

---

[125] Horace, *Art. poet.*

[126] The esteem in which the learned held popular idolatry at this time is
clear from Horace's satire which begins with the words put in the mouth of
Priapus:
Once when I was a truncated fig, a useless tree,
An unknown carpenter refused to make a footstool.
He wanted me to be the god, Priapus. I am a god, therefore,
the terror of thieves and birds.
(Bk. 1, Sat. 8).

[1911]

their essence, in their mere possibility, as *possible titles* for equally possible rights that it has undertaken to establish.[127]

The most *natural* of all *specific facts* is the development of the goodness and uprightness of human nature irrespective of unsettling causes pertaining to another fact, the development of human corruption *opposed to nature*.

1912. If we begin, therefore, from consideration of the prior fact, that is, the natural development of mankind conceived as good, savagery and degradation will certainly not be our starting point. Prior to civil society, human beings will not be the beasts, inferior to all others, imagined by Romagnosi. We shall indeed have males still unassociated in civil commonalty, but not isolated. They will be united to women as intelligent and good as themselves. — We should also separate mentally from human beings, but neither forget nor destroy, the supernatural help that forms part of their history. It will be considered later on its own, as a fact of a different nature. As we said, we have to consider from the beginning each specific part separately to discover the rights to which each fact gives rise.

If we consider incorrupt human beings without reference to supernatural assistance, but furnished with everything pertaining to their nature (we ignore the source of what they possess), we find intelligence, morality, marriage and natural contentment. In this primitive state, human beings have no need, desire or thought of civil society. Their crafts and industries are few; there is no man-made wealth, no trade and politics. Nevertheless, these beings cannot be called savage or barbarous. Their few needs are accompanied by extremely simple, lively, but undiversified pleasures. Starting with the first man, that is with the first couple (*RF*, 1062), we can follow the course of their development and see parental society united immediately to conjugal society. In their turn, the children brought up by these parents increase in number. We see them as hunters, fishermen, shepherds, cultivators. As we follow them philosophically by observing the discovery of crafts and progressive human perfection, we note an endless development of their laboriousness. Domestic society grows into patriarchal society; the bonds of

---

[127] Cf. *ER*, 54–89.

tribal, civil and national societies follow in succession. All these are moral, jural, happy states, perfect in their being. We have no need to import into them corruption, barbarism and savagery.

It cannot be denied that each of these states has its own proper justice, its own proper virtue and moral perfection, its own ease, peace and happiness. And as long as the *period natural* to each of these states has not terminated, there is no moral duty to accelerate it, no moral duty to leave it for the sake of a more advanced state. In other words, there is no need for human beings to enter the state of civil society before such a state shows itself necessary, that is, before it becomes necessary (it is not necessary of its nature) for the maintenance of right. According to Romagnosi:

> It is a fact that the state of society of the nations, especially *European nations*, is agricultural and commercial from an economic point of view; a state enlightened by teaching, laws and religion from a moral point of view; and finally a state directed by laws, rulers and judges from a political point of view. — My question is: do at least these three states, generally speaking, truly pertain to necessary right?[128]

This is indeed the question. To decide it, we first have to define *necessary right*. This is Romagnosi's definition:

> For something to be qualified as necessary right, it has to be disposed in such a way that without it there would be no possibility of respecting the moral, rational order established as the norm of human actions.[129]

My only comment on this conclusion refers to that impersonal 'there would be no possibility'. For it to have a meaning, it must be translated as a personal phrase. Otherwise we would not know 'for whom there would be no possibility of respecting the rational, moral order.' In fact, there is no absolute impossibility for anyone about respecting the rational, moral order. Doing this depends upon free choice. If the obligation of forming a part of society were imposed only on the person for whom

---

128 *Assunto primo*, §9.
129 *Ibid.*

it would otherwise be impossible to observe the rational, moral order, everyone could withdraw by retorting: 'It is not at all impossible for me to respect the rational, moral order. That depends upon my free choice. Civil society therefore is not a matter of *necessary right* for me.' Romagnosi's impersonal phrase 'there would be no possibility of respecting the rational, moral order' has no sense unless it is understood personally; on the other hand, it cannot be rendered personal.

The phrase cannot be understood, as far as I can see, unless changed into: 'Without civil society, it would be impossible for one or more persons to act in such a way that the rational, moral order could be respected to their advantage by others.' Totally changed in this way, the phrase receives a correct, determinate meaning, and is equivalent to what we have said so often, that is, that 'each person has the right to constrain others, with whom he is in contact, to unite with him in *civil society* when this has become a means necessary for the conservation and defence of his own rights.' We say that the right of *jural claim*, proper to each individual and collective person, can in certain circumstances be activated by this sanction: constrain others to enter civil association. (*USR*, 160–167). In *these circumstances*, civil society has become *de iure* for the constraining person, and a *necessary obligation* for those who are constrained.[130]

1913. It is also possible to demonstrate that civil association can in certain circumstances become an *ethical obligation*. Romagnosi confuses *right* with *obligation*, and *jural obligation* with *ethical obligation*. When he wants to prove 'the necessity of agricultural and commercial life as a matter of rigorous natural right',[131] he presupposes the growth of a group of hunters for whom hunting is no longer a sufficient means for obtaining food. These people have no choice but to make war on adjacent territories or cultivate their own land, an aim which will be greatly helped by civil association. There is no doubt that people in this state have an *ethical obligation* to cultivate the land and to live on the basis of all the good work of which they are capable. This, however, is merely an *ethical obligation*. If such a

---

[130] Romagnosi's phrase 'necessary right' is also inexact in the sense that *obligation* is necessary, right is only *facultative*.

[131] *Assunto primo*, §10.

people wished to die of hunger, their madness would offend morality, but not right. No one has jural rights in his own regard; only moral rights.[132]

The same must be said about the way in which Romagnosi undertakes to prove the necessity of education, and of a political state.[133] If these institutions are necessary to live, and to live well, they immediately become an *ethical duty*. They become an object of *right* only in relationship to the person who needs them for just defence or as a guarantee of his own *rights*. When this person (individual or collective) begins to exercise the right that he has to demand from others their agreement in setting up these institutions, the others encounter a corresponding *jural obligation* to yield to his just requirements and reasonable claims.

1914. *Civil society*, therefore, is not a right *per se*, but becomes the object of *right* when certain given conditions actually come about, as they do at a certain age, at a certain stage of development of mankind. This age is often anticipated through the work of human waywardness which gives rise to an early need to recur to the formation of civil association as a secure or even unique means of guaranteeing defence of one's rights against villainous attacks.

1915. Equally, *civil society* is not essentially an *ethical duty*. It becomes such as soon as it takes its place as a necessary means of fulfilling one's duties. This also occurs at a certain epoch of humanity.

1916. It is harmful and historically inaccurate to paint in the blackest hues the period during which people lived in a state of domestic or patriarchal society without arriving at civil association. Although the moment for civil association had not arrived, morality flourished; human life was simple, content and joyous, characterised by magnanimity, generous affection and freedom of heart and life. The spirit was not oppressed; it had not been wearied under pungent, sordid longings for possessions, nor riddled by strife caused by ambition and envy, nor ground down by unending social trivialities, nor entangled in innumerable social protocols. It would have appeared, if seen

---

[132] *ER*, 278–280, 299.
[133] *Assunto primo*, §11, 12.

[1914–1916]

with bodily eyes, like a babe in swaddling clothes. As it savoured the captivating spectacle of immense nature, and understood its sublime language, the spirit raised itself joyously to contemplation of the Creator, and felt itself made for him. It is impossible to relegate life at that time to a lower level than present-day life, and equally impossible to deny it morality and right. But just as that former life of freedom cannot be applied to our own, later age, so the right proper to that time cannot be applied to us now. Nevertheless, we must not infer from this that the right suitable for us is the only right, nor that there is no good other than the good we enjoy, no other moral obligations than those found appropriate to our own circumstances and conditions.

CHAPTER 3

The steps by which civil society comes into being

Article 1.
Summary

1917. We must sum up and then go on to show how civil society continuously progresses by extending the sphere of its objects.

First, we defined civil society as 'society which aims at regulating the *modality* of all the rights of its members in the best possible way.' This abstract, general definition is sufficient to determine the duty of civil society in all its extension, and contains the principle which establishes the limits of its government.

We then asked: 'Do civil societies always in fact include a sphere as extensive as their aim? Do they always regulate to the fullest extent the modality of all the rights of its citizens?' The answer was 'No'. Nascent civil societies are ignorant of the immense frontiers of their own territory; they push forward almost accidentally and constantly discover new regions. Their advance is proportioned to the needs of new insights which arise

[1917]

as social ages evolve and higher reflections are formed by those who govern and those governed. People never form civil society nor multiply the objects of their government without being moved by determinate stimuli.

Next, we began to speak about these stimuli which, we said, were in general the needs that instigate human activity. We concluded that 'civil society could neither commence prior to the operation of needs instigating human activity, nor reach its most perfect organisation and fullest exercise except in proportion to the greatest impulse given to families by the action of increasing needs.'

At this point, we wanted to expound the way in which the activity of civil societies was stimulated and extended by needs. First, however, it seemed necessary to remove an obstacle from our path.

Some authors, by exaggerating the jural necessity of the City, seemed to claim that right, divided from the City, was impossible. According to them, civil society would have to exist *de iure* from the origin of humanity; the slowness of its progress would have to be considered as barbarous and alien to right. At this point, we showed that as *nature* gradually provides efficacious stimuli moving people to constitute and perfect civil society, so *the law of Right* imposes the obligation of civil society suitably and gradually at the appropriate time. Thus, the *progressive de facto order* relative to civil societies harmonises with the *progressive de iure order*. There are as many *jural states* as there are stages in human development. Some of these *states* are anterior to the institution of the City; some pertain to *the incipient City*; some to the *City as it progresses* towards greater unity and constantly expanding activity in the exercise of its power.

We can now take up the thread of our argument and explain the needs which successively require the work of civil commonalty and bring it by stages to ever greater perfection.

[1917]

Article 2.
Gradual formation and growth of civil society

§1. *The right of war and peace is anterior to civil societies.*

1918. Domestic society, in its restricted form with a single father, or in a more ample form with several fathers under the command of a supremo (patriarchal society), waged war prior to the formation of civil society. It also cultivated alliances with other domestic or even civil societies with which it found itself in contact. Thus Abram fought against the four kings[134] (an example of domestic society at war with civil society), and made a peace treaty with Abimalech, king of Gerar and with Phicol, head of his army.[135] Later, Isaac did the same.[136] Similarly, Jacob made an alliance with Laban.[137] In those early days, domestic society was sometimes more powerful and flourishing than *civil society*, and more to be feared. 'Go away from us because you are much mightier than we are,'[138] said the king of Gerar to Isaac, a simple father of a family.

§2. *The need of external defence for families is the only efficacious stimulus for the formation of civil societies*

1919. An extraordinary cause was needed before a *domestic society*, which could *per se* flourish and prosper, would decide to associate with others in civil commonalty. There were two possible causes: 1. the desire to offend other societies by subjecting and conquering them; 2. the need of defence against the assaults of other societies.

1920. The first cause, if it cannot be reduced to the second, is

---

[134] Gen 14.
[135] *Ibid.*, 21.
[136] *Ibid.*, 26.
[137] *Ibid.*, 31.
[138] *Ibid.*, 36: 16. — We have described the steps by which peoples pass from the state of nature to that of civil society in *Rights of the Individual*, 1052–1057.

normally unjust (*RI*, 680). It does not therefore furnish a jural occasion for the formation of the City. This, however, is the history of heroic undertakings in antiquity, and of bands who went sword in hand to places most suitable for them in the midst of peoples whom they subjugated and in great part destroyed.

1921. The second reason, that is, the need for *legitimate defence*, is therefore a good jural occasion furnished by events for the formation of primitive civil societies.

1922. But the need of *defence* is of two kinds: 1. the need of *internal defence*, within society itself, on the part of one member against another, and 2. of *external defence* on the part of one society against another.

1923. The need for defence within *domestic society* is seen very rarely. Nature gives sufficient guarantee to all members in their mutual natural affections. Moreover, such a need cannot be an occasion for establishing civil association.

A need for defence on the part of one member against another is certainly seen in the interior of civil society. However, because civil society has already been formed, this need draws citizens to make society perfect, not to constitute it. The same is true about the need for external defence of one civil society against another.

We conclude that the efficacious, jural stimulus, which moved fathers of families to come together in civil commonalty is the need for external defence of the family, that is, the need to defend one's own family against other powerful families, or against an already established civil society.

1924. In fact, the establishment of one civil society must have called others into being. Otherwise, the disassociated families would have been subject to the danger of harsh treatment, and brought under the yoke of families already civilly associated and thus more powerful.

1925. It follows that fathers were forced to bind themselves together more strongly and stably as they felt greater, more serious and more constant *danger* of harm which threatened their goods or freedom.

[1921–1925]

§3. *The circumstances which manifest a permanent need for external defence of families*

1926. I say 'more constant' because the *need for external defence*, if transitory, is not sufficient stimulus to fully constitute civil society, that is, a lasting aggregation of families (cf. 1630–1639). Associations of families do indeed exist for the sake of eliminating *momentary danger*, but they are destined to cease activity as soon as the danger has passed. In fact, they are not so much civil societies as *attempts* at civil society, unformed sketches, trials, rudiments of civil society, or mere alliances. History shows that associations of this kind normally precede the formation of lasting society.

1927. We need to ask, therefore, what are the *de facto* circumstances in which danger and the consequent need of defence is truly constant and consequently capable of impelling people to establish some means of constant defence. We also need to know what kind of circumstances present only momentary dangers, and lead to temporary proximity and groupings without any stable, lasting union of families.

Two circumstances need consideration: 1. violence which conquers or dominates; 2. the ordinary life of co-existing families. We shall examine both these accidental features to see when they produce continual or momentary dangerous circumstances.

A.
Conquests

1928. As soon as some violent person takes steps to subject others to his power, a *stimulus* to union is felt both by the person attempting violence, who cannot take on the masses single-handed, and by those attacked as they prepare to defend themselves.

I. Let us suppose that the violent party triumphs.

In this event, *seigniory*, not *civil society* is constituted. Nevertheless, *seigniory* in this case is necessarily followed by some form of *civil society*.

1929. The degree of imperfection in this kind of civil society goes hand in hand with the degree of domination found in the *seigniorial element*.

1930. Civil society arising from conquest is formed either by the conquerors alone, or by the conquered alone, or by both.

1931. Only in the final case is civil society well formed; only in this case does the *seigniorial element* have less effect and absorb less of the social element.

1932. Civil society is constituted by the conquerors alone when the conquered people are considered slaves, or divided and dispersed, bereft of civil rights. If servitude breaks even domestic bonds, the jural state of the people relapses to the *state of nature*. This does happen unfortunately, and has occurred several times in history.

1933. If the seigniory of the conquerors is less burdensome to the conquered, it becomes necessary to consider the state of the people at the moment of conquest. Either the people were still in a state of domestic society, or existed as a tribe, or were already in the state of civil society.

1934. In the first case, the people remain in the same jural state of family or tribe as that in which they were found. The family itself, however, and the tribe are the slave of the conquerors. This was the state of the Hebrew people in Egypt under the oppressive Pharaoh Amenophis when the heads of tribes and kin governed with the fathers of families.

1935. If the conquered people is already ordered towards *civil society* at the time of conquest, the seigniory of the conquerors is found at two levels: it either totally destroys every *civil bond* between the families of the new people, or it leaves the people in the state of *domestic society*. If the seigniory is milder, the conquered people retains some civil unity, and indeed draws closer together; it conserves either wholly or in part its laws, customs and religion, and simply lacks supreme civil power. Some rudiment of *civil society* remains, therefore, amongst this subjugated people, but in servile, not free *civil society* (*USR*, 112–122). It is very different from the civil society formed by the conquerors amongst themselves.

The conquests of the ancient Eastern peoples offer examples of all these different degrees of seigniory and corresponding servitude. Sometimes the conquered people are totally dissolved and only *individuals* remain (enslaved); sometimes the people

[1930–1935]

remain, but divided into *domestic societies* (enslaved); sometimes they remain in imperfect *civil societies* (enslaved). The Hebrews in Babylon are an example of the last case.

1936. The varying degrees of servitude found in conquered peoples is explained by the status of the conquerors. These did not form *civil societies*, but dominant *families*. Consequently, they tended to establish *seigniories*, not *societies*. The family[139] draws seigniory in its wake; civil society draws society. Whenever a *family* conquers, the conquered people remain as bondservants.

1937. If we consider *civil society* formed by the conquerors amongst themselves, we find that it also exhibits less perfection when dominated by the *seigniorial* and domestic *element*, and more when it absorbs and swallows the *social element*.

1938. This explains the distinction between *conquering families*, and conquering *individuals*.

The family was fully constituted in the East, and conquered without itself breaking up. It produced empires in which practically everything was *seigniory;* there was very little *society*. The opposite occurred in colonies. Unions of young bachelors, associated in order to found a city wherever it suited them best, did not draw any family element in their wake. They began with the foundation of *civil society* itself. They always established *republics*, that is, true societies, and only societies. This happened even if the marauding groups were under the control of a single person.[140]

Later these adventurers, who needed to find wives amongst the conquered people, had to associate with the people, not destroy or enslave them. At the same time, they could not trust the people who, given the chance, would certainly have ejected the violent, unjust foreigners. Fear of the conquered people must have endured for a long period in a newly-established colony. This was a permanent cause of unease and a constant danger which only lessened and ceased as races inter-married and attacks arose from common enemies. Conquerors and con-

---

[139] The family is of course a mixture of *society* and *seigniory*. As society, it is limited and cannot extend except through generation; *seigniory* can extend without limit.

[140] Cf. *SP*, 371–391.

quered soon fought together in the same war, defended the same cause of common defence, sought and received repeated pledges of brotherhood. In these circumstances, the *stimulus of lasting need* occurred which, as we saw, is necessary to induce human beings to form true *civil societies* characterised by stability and perpetuity. This stimulus is not necessary to the same extent for the conservation of civil societies after their formation.

1939. II. Our supposition is that the assailants conquered. This was almost always the case in antiquity. The reason for their success is obvious. The attacking side was prepared; the defenders unprepared. The latter, trusting in their long period of tranquillity, had been lulled into inactivity by natural, habitual inertia accustomed to peace. Nevertheless, we could imagine the contrary, and allow for a vigorous, triumphant defence. Here we already have a first stimulus to the union of families. The constancy of this union depends, however, on the length and obstinacy of the war, or the arrival of continual new dangers. It could happen, if the union necessary for maintaining one's own freedom and safety lasted a long time, that a people might be glad to preserve the union after the conflict had ceased. Or, during the conflict (and this is more likely), the ambition of some fortunate, talented commander-in-chief might lead to his becoming lord or civil head. Finally, the gratitude itself of the people could make head and ruler someone who had saved them on several occasions from extermination in battle. One example of this is the Hasmodean family who remained at the head of the Hebrew people after the long and glorious wars they sustained in defence of religion and fatherland.

B.
Accidental hostilities between families

1940. Setting aside the case of conquest as the result of passion for dominion or need to subsist, we normally find families living together in *peace*. *Hostilities* are rare *exceptions*, motivated for the most part amongst younger people by accidents such as insults, rivalry and love. Motives of this kind usually produce wars of only brief duration. They are not sufficient to stimulate the formation of civil constitutions which require perpetuity.

1941. Nevertheless, they often produce temporary alliances and associations which are rudiments and, as it were, attempts made by nature to produce civil society.

1942. Civil society begins from a bare outline and gradually arrives at full maturity unless some extraordinary accident impels it more quickly to maturity.

1943. *Civil society* can be imperfect either

1. because it is not yet fully constituted — essential imperfection; or

2. because the exercise of its powers is not fully activated — accidental imperfection. We shall show in the following chapter how this exercise is gradually activated. Here, our intention is to explain how civil society is gradually constituted.

1944. We note immediately that the *constitution* of civil society remains imperfect for three reasons: either

I. it lacks *perpetuity*, that is, it is not instituted in a perpetual manner; or

II. it lacks *unity*; or

III. it lacks *total power*. Let us consider all three imperfections.

I.
The period in which civil societies are still unformed, but temporary civil establishments are founded

1945. Some nations began to arise without any permanent need for the defence of which we have spoken. In these nations, the union of families in positive associations under a governmental power took considerable time to achieve a stable, perpetual character. Families remain at a kind of half-way stage between the family state and that of civil society, and vacillate between these states. Outlines or sketches of civil society appear, disappear, and reappear according to accidental needs.

1946. In the history of the Hebrew people the period of which we are speaking is that of the judges who were chosen for a time according to the people's needs. As long as the families and tribes descending from Jacob had no external enemies to fear, they lived together without a common government.

1947. A similar state of imperfect civil society, marked by lack of continuity and permanence, was found amongst the Germanic nations before they settled in Roman territory. They chose a chief to lead them in their wars. When these came to an end, all common government ceased. The families, or groups of families, returned to life in domestic or tribal society. The tribe is simply associated agnation, a kind of man-made domestic society.[141]

II.

The period in which civil societies tend to establish themselves but have still not reached unity of governmental power

1948. In this period, when families or tribes co-exist (granted the circumstances we have described) and bring civil association to birth gradually and painfully, some attempts at imperfect association appear. The reason for this imperfection is lack of unity in the government that is being constituted.

1949. In the period of Hebrew history prior to the institution of the monarchy (the period we have mentioned), civil power appears divided. In his will Jacob had divided the power, conferring primogeniture on the sons of Joseph, priesthood on Levi and rule on Juda.[142]

1950. It seems that the *primogeniture* conferred on Joseph and the *rule conferred* on Juda were the seeds or principles of unity that the dying patriarch intended to sow amongst his sons. *Primogeniture* was to be the principle of unity as long as they and their descendants remained in the tribal state. This was in fact their condition during the one hundred and ninety-nine

[141] The *tribal state* differs from that of *civil society* because the power recognised in the tribe is not limited to the regulation of the modality of rights as governmental power is in civil society. The chief holds the place of common father and exercises a dominion similar to paternal dominion. The bonds are those of *agnation*, another distinction between tribe and civil society. The respect and obedience given to the chief of the tribe is referred to the dead father whom he represents.

[142] 1 Chron 5: 1.

[1947–1950]

years they spent in Egypt after the death of Jacob; Joseph and his tribe probably prevailed during this time. *Rule* was to be another principle of unity. It was to be developed later when the people were formed into a perfect civil society through the choice of the kings. Jacob had clearly foreseen this, as Moses had after him when he wrote the law of the future kingdom one hundred and fifty years beforehand.[143] The priesthood was the principle of permanent unity which was to unite all the descendants of Israel whatever their social state.[144]

1951. The organisation of powers was still deficient during the time of the Judges, except for the stable priesthood of the tribe of Levi. Levi's priesthood supplied what was lacking to the other powers on the occasions when they organised themselves for a time on the basis of temporary need.

1952. It does not seem necessary to note here that the *unity* of the social mind and the governmental power of which we are speaking is not a material, but a formal unity. Powers, even when divided amongst many individuals, possess unity when they are ordered in fixed relationships and dependency that allows them to produce one single complex action.

---

[143] Deut 17. — Jacob's division of *primogeniture*, *rule* and *priesthood* amongst his son is already a great step towards the state of civil society. According to domestic traditions, these powers are normally included in *primogeniture*. The first-born, besides taking all or the greatest part of the inheritance, also exercised household priesthood, and received some part in paternal rule. Jacob, however, took from primogeniture (the basis of the tribe) its principal attributes, that is, rule and priesthood, and thus, by enlarging the bonds of domestic and tribal society, laid the foundations or seeds of civil society. All that remained for primogeniture was the right of inheritance to a double portion. Five centuries later, Moses restricted paternal authority still further with the law forbidding fathers to pass primogeniture to sons who were not in fact first-born. (Deut 21: 16–17). Again, the first-born exercised the priesthood before the Levites did (Ex 13: 2; 34: 19; Num 8: 16), although Moses soon introduced the levitic priesthood according to the ordinances laid down in Israel's will. Domestic and tribal society were modified in this way, and lost force and compactness to the benefit of emerging *civil society*. — Moses also considerably decreased paternal authority, even relative to the right to punish sons (Ex. 21; Lev 20: [2–3]; Deut 21: 18–21).

[144] The majority of the teachers came from the tribe of Simeon.

[1951–1952]

III.
*The period in which civil societies are still only partly formed
because they lack the institution of some essential power*

1953. Finally, in the period of time that humanity uses to pass
from the state of domestic society to that of fully formed civil
society, history presents us with attempts at society amongst
families. The efforts do not result in a full form of civil society
because part of the power essential to that society has not been
actuated.

1954. When Moses and Aaron received the responsibility of
leading the people out of Egypt, they had not yet occupied the
fullness of civil power, but only military command and political
representation before the Egyptians. Soon Moses became the
judge in the people's litigation. He then took possession of
another branch of civil authority. The people's need was the
stimulus leading to acknowledgement of his judicial authority,
which was simply the exercise of public beneficence. Later he
became *legislator*. When he chose rulers, tribunes and other
chiefs over the people, he made use of his authority to *constitute
lower magistrates.*[145]

1955. Moses' power ceased with his death; Josuah was only a
commander-in-chief. The judges who succeeded him exercised
various offices according to need.

> These judges declared war, commanded the army and con-
> cluded peace, although such tasks were not their only or
> principal duties. Some, such as Jair, Ibzan, Elon, Abdon,
> Eli and Samuel, did nothing in this respect. They were
> administrators of the supreme power, exercising the rights
> of majesty. They commanded, but had no power to make
> laws or to raise taxes; they were honoured, but without any
> external distinction or privileges. Moreover, they did not
> transmit their dignity to their descendants, but provided
> for the public good without any reward. Their aim was to
> save what was common to all, to conserve true religion and
> to see that God was the sole king in Israel.[146] Not all of

145 Ex 18: 25; Deut 1: 15.
146 Judg 8: 22–23.

[1953–1955]

them were even rulers over the entire commonalty; several presided only over certain tribes.[147]

Article 3.
Considerations on the transition periods between domestic and civil society

§1. *Importance of historical facts in this period*

1956. The period in which humanity struggled to escape from the straits of domestic society and expand to civil commonalty has attracted very little attention from philosophers. They seem not to have noticed the supreme importance of meditation on this moment when humanity passed imperceptibly from one state to another. Instead, they have been content to consider the state of domestic and civil society as if they appeared suddenly, fully complete and formed. They have limited their considerations to the fact of civil society as it exists in this Europe of ours, hoping to find its causes and origins in some hypothesis springing from philosophical imagination.

1957. The opposite is true. This extremely complicated fact that makes up our societies cannot be understood, explained or judged unless we consider intensely and profoundly the slow, varied work of human nature which produced it over many centuries. In a word, the theory of society must not be drawn from the unfertilised egg of a mere idea standing before the mind. History, with its extremely varied accidents, administers the conditions and positive data which, changed by the mind into possible conditions and data, can become suitable materials for constructing the theory.

1958. For the moment, we can draw some consequences from

[147] Jahn, *Archaeologia biblica*, §216.

what has been said. They will show both the possibility and the immense importance of this kind of historical study.

§2. Civil society passes to complete formation through a series of formless states

1959. The first consequence: it is a mistake to believe that nothing lies between *civil* and *domestic society*. Over and above *patriarchal society*, which is an *expanded domestic society* containing several fathers and families who obey their *living progenitor*, we have the *tribe*. This we have defined as 'a man-made patriarchal society, formed within the same agnation', that is, a feigned, patriarchal society between cognates and agnates.[148]

1960. Moreover, it is possible to conceive a long series of *formless civil societies* which are such because they lack the essential factors we have mentioned: 1. perpetuity; 2. unity; 3. totality of powers.[149] In the same way, a *civil-servile society* is also without form because it lacks *supremacy*, an essential characteristic of perfect civil society (1625–1629).

1961. Finally, a civil society reaches its full constitution, at least relative to its *essence* and *integrity*,[150] if, besides tending *de facto* and instinctively to regulate ONLY the modality of all rights to the common advantage, it has formed for itself 'a clear consciousness of its office and, after that, has acknowledged it as a fundamental written law.' This is what we await from future ages.

1962. Meanwhile, we remind our readers that if this is true, it must also be true that civil society cannot attain its full, perfect

---

148 I have shown elsewhere (*RF*, 1134–1139 and *RI*, 1340–1348) that *jural cognation* exists in nature as long as 'cognates remember and feel their cognation nourished by their mutual treatment as cognates'. We need to indicate this here to explain how the totality of mankind does not see itself as a single tribe, although they have all come from a single first father.

149 The lack of *stable organisation* injures simultaneously all three of these conditions, that is, perpetuity, unity and totality of powers.

150 It would be possible to distinguish the *essential* from the *integral parts* of civil society. I would prefer not to deal with this subtle distinction here, however. It will not help to clarify our concepts.

[1959-1962]

constitution unless *political Philosophy* has first presented the theory to the mind. Political philosophy must first separate the various elements mingled together in human societies and attribute to each its own jural law. Above all, it must with most scrupulous care separate from the seigniorial element what belongs to the social element. Then it must separate what pertains to the socio-civil element from everything belonging to other social elements. Finally, it must establish with unshakeable evidence that 'the supreme necessity of regulating the modality of all the rights of the members is the sole function of civil society.' This is the clear principle we inscribe in books; from books it must pass into peoples' heads and from there into their constitutions. All this, however, can only be the work of time, which passes quickly, and of the uprightness and civil wisdom of legislators as well as of those whose love is the boast of their fatherland and of humanity.

§3. *The chief obstacle to the full formation of civil society is family* selfishness

1963. Another consequence of supreme importance is this: the major obstacle preventing humanity from associating perfectly and peacefully in civil commonalties is *family selfishness*.

1964. This selfishness is the great evil proper to domestic society. Every society, every human institution has its own characteristic evil. Domestic society, founded on the father's *seigniory*, impresses the minds of the children profoundly and naturally with the concept of paternal *seigniory*. The concept of a man-made *society* such as civil society is not present to children from the beginning. When it does appear, its presence in their minds is weak; it may endure, but it is not the object of reflection and consciousness for some considerable time. All members of domestic society naturally operate according to the more lively model present to their minds, in this case, *seigniory*. The development of this principle is then confined to an endeavour to increase seigniory of the house. Thus, as we saw, empires and despotic governments spring from families.

1965. *Love of family* is *sui generis*, and immensely different

[1963–1965]

from *friendship*. Through friendship, the friend forgets himself in his sole care for the other; through love of family, human beings do not forget themselves, but confuse themselves with others.

Love of family is also different from *social benevolence*, through which individuals love the collective body to which they belong for the sake of their own advantage; they are looking to their own interests. Love of family is not a calculation, but a simple instinct of nature.

1966. Through *love of family*, all blood-relatives belonging to a family form a *single feeling-person*. This single feeling is followed by an intellective calculation that in turn flatters and ministers to the feeling. In a word, love of family is an extension and reinforcement of individual *self-love*. It is love of self which results from the fusion, in each person's feeling, of many self-loves. As such, it is rendered proud and bold through each member's consciousness that their common force is directed by a single idea, in this case, seigniory.[151] Hence, *slaves* were always considered by the ancients as part of the family, and very few authors before ourselves were coherent in teaching that so-called *patronal* society is not society at all (*RF*, 969–981). In fact, it was normally discussed under the heading 'socio-domestic Right'.

Universal affections (humanity) are extinguished in the family in proportion to the intensity in which blood-affection increases. The human heart is restricted and restrained; the smaller the number of members composing domestic society, the larger the number of strangers towards whom it tends to act unjustly.[152] The injustice is slight because the family possesses only a small quantity of force with which to exercise injustice.

1967. This narrowness of domestic society was felt so deeply by Cicero that the great man could uncover the origin of *justice* only by further extending the society of which the family is such a restricted form. He expresses his thought best of all perhaps in

---

[151] We describe the family as it is *per se* in mankind. It would be wrong to object on the basis of the family as it is formed and educated in our own civil societies. In these families, a great number of feelings are present foreign to those of the family itself.

[152] *SP*, bk. 1, 179–189.

[1966–1967]

the noteworthy passage where he speaks of the universal love of human beings. He describes it as

> born from that very first sowing through which children are loved by their procreators. Afterwards a whole house is united by marriage and race, and universal love suddenly springs forth, first through blood-relationships, then step-by-step through affinity, friendship, neighbourliness, fellow-citizens and closeness with companions and friends in public affairs. Finally, it embraces the whole of mankind. This spiritual affection, which *gives to each his own*, is munificent and equable, and protects what I call the 'society of human togetherness'; it is named JUSTICE.[153]

Cicero acknowledged justice on earth only when the love born within the heart of the family was propagated to all mankind. On the one hand, the *pagan* cannot rise above himself to conceive how the dignity of the individual, the foundation of justice, must be recognised even in the state of nature; on the other, the *Roman*, released from the straits of family, is capable of understanding the beauty and holiness of universal society.

1968. The enclosed nature of the family, the close union of a few separated from the many, the succession through generation of those bound together, is most suitable for preserving true and erroneous *religious traditions*, as well as useful and damaging, or good and bad *customs*. In turn, traditions and customs are new bonds drawing the family together and continually dividing it from other families. Families with different errors and vices easily hate one another, but they also develop unbelievable animosity, jealousy and emulation simply as a result of diversity of *indifferent customs*, and through the *different forms* with which they cloth the same feeling, the same thought. Families separated for a long time also develop their own dialects and languages which then become a new wall of division cutting them off from strangers, and a new bond uniting their own members.

1969. All these causes coalesce and render difficult the formation of lasting, perfect union between several families or tribes, that is, an entire civil society. Consequently, this kind of associ-

---

153 *De Finibus*, 5: 23.

ation is never wont to occur fully in a *peaceful way*. It needs some extremely violent accident either to move and pressurise families in acting against their own will to overcome many powerful obstacles, or to destroy and disperse families themselves for the sake of associating individuals.

1970. Nevertheless, humanity could not accomplish its destiny unless it succeeded in associating in civil groups. Providence, which leads mankind, undertakes to fight invincible selfishness, the obstinate spirit of independence, tenacious customs, inveterate prejudice, superstition, ignorance and the absolutism of families. It opposes these obstacles with tremendous force that often shakes the foundations of the family; it humiliates the family, breaks it up, tears it to pieces. These fragments then become suitable, purified material for the construction of a new, majestic, harmonious edifice of civil association in which mankind moves on, more united and free, towards its great end.

Providence, you see, is fully justified; it has a reason for arousing every now and again those warrior-geniuses who as conquerors devastate the earth before them. They are necessary for clearing the land on which will rise the edifice of civil society, a wider, more instructed, more liberal, more progressive society than domestic society, which is no longer sufficient.

1971. Careful examination of these ways of Providence will show the results of conquests from Sesostris to Napoleon, from Ghengis Khan and Tamberlane to the French revolution, from the Crusades to the European colonies in the New World. Without any exception, all the upheavals, sufferings and strife that humanity has had to suffer from the immense destruction and violence of wars and revolutions were directed by Providence to this tremendous end: to severing narrow, family restrictions and conquering the immense opposition which families maintain against the perfect formation of civil society, through the strong, excessively selfish constitution that unceasingly encloses and fortifies them. If humanity is to progress towards all good, civil society must be bound into mankind.

One does not have to assume the role of prophet to predict with certainty that these furies, who lead the hurricanes passing through nations like whirlwinds through fields white with the harvest, will reappear whenever certain families, developing according to their internal instinct, reach the stage of self-

[1970–1971]

isolation, independence and separation from other families that blocks the unbroken journey of mankind, led by God. The opposition caused by the family must be conquered, and will always be conquered. At least the most recent event, the French revolution, should be considered attentively under this aspect by the reader.

§4. *A reflection on the way France should act to lead the Arabs of Algeria to civilisation*

1972. Allow me to add a few lines to the preceding digression. They will serve as a corollary, and answer the following question: 'How can stationary peoples in a family or tribal state be led to civilisation if their civil society is still imperfect in some parts?'

1973. The knot of the difficulty has been clarified, I think, by what has been said. It is the old, hardened family which is opposed to progress. Like the snail, it uses its own secretions to build up for itself an ever harder, more impenetrable shell. The shell has to be broken, but not by ferocious conquests whose inhumanity can only be praiseworthy in the light of Providence. I have no desire to diminish the abhorrence and infamy called down on monsters who delight in shedding infant blood, reducing widows to tears, and bringing despair to the eyes of little children, old beyond their years. The problem is simply this: how must a Christian government act when it has the noble mission of bringing to civil life those generations of families who have surrounded themselves with the hardened shell of opinions, customs and man-made but extremely tenacious affections which form family morality or feeling? How can all this be accomplished, for example in the case of Arabs or Bedouins, through just, human means?

1974. The Romans, faced with this consideration, would have divided the men, women and children by transporting the men to settlements, providing the women with husbands from some other group, and giving the children a Roman education. Such violence might have served its purpose, but it would not cease to be unjust and cruel.

[1972–1974]

1975. This treatment could be partly justified only if it were considered a punishment for repeated rebellions, which could not otherwise be prevented. There is no doubt that Arab betrayal would be repressed efficaciously if the French decreed by law that

'Any tribe which broke faith and rebelled, after submission to France or bound to her by just agreements, would be punished as follows:

1. Unmarried men would be separated and put at the disposition of the French.

2. Polygamy is abolished. One wife, the first he had married, would be left to each married man. The other wives would be considered as unmarried.

3. The French arrangements for unmarried men would be these: *a*) young children of both sexes would be given a Christian education; *b*) young men would be transported to the colonies; *c*) young women would also be transported to other colonies.

4. Succession would be determined by law.

5. Rewards would be given to those who make progress in civilisation.'

1976. Penal laws similar to this, which represses rebellion in entire tribes, could be drawn up to punish faults on the part of families, as follows:

'1. A family convicted of unlawful communication with the enemies of France would be broken up as indicated.

2. Any married man gravely wounding a Frenchman would be deprived of all his wives except the first. If he had only one wife, he would be deprived of his children, who would be educated by France. If he were unmarried, he would be deported.'

France could make other peaceful ordinances in addition to these civilising but criminal laws. These ordinances would have the same aim of weakening the concentrated force of the Arab family. Nevertheless, the surest and most powerful means is always the preaching of the Gospel, followed, and not preceded, by instruction in the sciences and arts.

[1975–1976]

§5. A reflection on the ways used by Providence to form modern civil societies in Europe

A.
Theory

1977. The family, isolated over a long period and concentrated on self, acquires blind, selfish and internal affections which produce indefinable abhorrence and aversion towards other families, as well as envy, permanent hostility and obstacles to civil association. These things cannot be overcome except through the destruction of the family itself. Nevertheless, as we said, the family is the essential element of civil society. It must exist, but with expanded boundaries; *blind*, family *instinct* must be tempered by the *intelligence* presiding over civil society.

1978. We see this in European civilisation. It would not be far from the truth to say that the cause of civilisation in Europe is the mixture, in the right proportions, of family and civil elements.

1979. These two elements first had to be formed and instructed separately from one another; then they had to be suitably mixed. This was the design and work of Providence.

1980. After many partial, accidental vicissitudes, mankind came to be divided into two great parts called the *Roman* and *barbarian worlds*. Providence destined the barbarian world to educate and strengthen the *family element*; the Roman world to form and educate the *civil element*.

1981. The *family element* could certainly not grow and reach perfection in total separation from all civil society. Hence the presence in the midst of the barbarian world, charged with perfecting the family element, of imperfect, civil societies which, without impeding the strong development of the family element, contemporaneously protected and seconded it.

1982. Even less could the *civil element* exist without the domestic societies which it brought together. Hence the Roman world had families, but regulated on the model of the republic and in total agreement with the republic, whose growth they served; they were devoted to it and often sacrificed to it.

1983. The time came in which the two worlds had completed

the work assigned to each by Providence; one had brought the family to full strength, the other had drawn civil commonalty to full development. All that remained was to mix the two elements so that the fusion resulted in mutual moderation, not destruction. The outcome was a twofold, harmonious bonding of the human race which had not previously been seen on earth.

1984. This was a divine work. Some superior force was necessary for such an important fusion; some wise, beneficent mediation was necessary if the battle between the two elements was not to destroy either one, but bring about mutual acceptance, as brothers finally recognised one another after long separation and infinite, blind discord. That mediation was carried out by Christianity; the work was done through the fusion of the Germanic and Roman races.

1985. The time was ripe; change was necessary for the salvation of the world. Corruption amongst the Romans had almost dissolved marriage. Augustus tried in vain with laws and penalties to force citizens to marry. The Germans, still showing signs of Eastern tendencies, were constituted in families and tribes.[154] They were aware of *seigniorial right* [*App.*, no. 4], but had no permanent city. Their unity was weak and imperfectly governed.

1986. Christianity, the great mediator, took under its protection the two elements represented by the two races. By strengthening and sanctifying marriage through the sacrament and the Church, it prevented the loss of family society in Roman civil society. It conquered the powerful chiefs of the northern families who invaded Roman territory at the head of their barbarian neighbours. When these chiefs became sons of the Roman Church, they learned from their mother to prefer civil, peaceful government to military, family government. Through this sublime, powerful mediation the two races, successfully grafted together, were able to form a single race which inherited the good elements proper to each. These elements were now immensely increased, and assured in perpetuity.

1987. Without the work of Christianity, the struggle between

---

[154] 'In times of peace there is no common magistrate; the rulers of regions and country districts formulate right for their own subjects' (Caesar, *De Bello Germ.*, 1: 12).

family and civil elements would have been fatal for both races; the isolated elements, battling to the death, would have mutually destroyed one another. Christianity, however, restored marriage to the Romans and persuaded the Germans to accept civil living. The discord between the two races diminished, to be replaced by harmony in which each saw in the other the good things it required. Each was sufficiently instructed to know what it needed, and what it was avidly searching for. Otherwise, the barbarians would have taken only dissoluteness from the Romans; the Romans would have received from the barbarians only military anarchy in which civilisation perishes.

1988. This fusion between the races could not take place immediately. Religious influence needs time to make itself felt in the masses and produce its marvellous effects. At first, it seemed that the inrush of one race upon the other would disrupt all social bonds by simultaneously destroying the barbarian family and plunging the Roman City into anarchy. The effect, however, was wonderful beyond all hope. The barbarian family suffered a severe blow, but Christianity used this to render civil association easier; Roman government fell, but Christianity used its fall to render domestic association easier.

B.
History

I. *The first clash between the family element, which was the attacker during the barbarian invasions, and the civil element, which was attacked*

1989. The Latin *pagus* was ordered towards civil society; the Germanic *gau* was a seigniorial administration. When Roman territories were invaded by Germans, it was natural that the Roman regions should be ruled as German *gau*. Government was in fact in the hands of counts. The outcome was incipient fusion between the *seigniorial* and *social* elements.

The Roman inhabitants of the *pagus* were highly imbued with the preceding *concept of social order* which dictated their reasoning. This concept, firmly fixed in their minds, was a model in strong contrast with the German *gau* and government by counts. A people *en masse* cannot change the concepts it normally uses as standards of judgment with the same readiness and ease that it applies to words and social conditions. The opposite was true in the minds of the German counts who, dominated by the concept of the *gau*, had to apply it to the Roman *pagus* according to the same psychological law. They had to regard the *pagus* as a *seigniorial matter* because that was the concept directing their *gau*, which they wanted to introduce into the newly acquired regions.

The same can be said on a larger scale about kings and their subjects, and about all conquerors and conquered peoples. A common political language sprang into being because the conquerors imposed their own language as far as they could, while necessarily absorbing, albeit unwillingly, a part of the language of those they had conquered. But the shared language, which was gradually formed, concealed to a great degree the diversity of concepts as well as preventing or reducing the open struggle between them. The two sides, although appearing to agree in the use of language, held very different ideas.

Meanwhile, their common belief gave each side the time to modify its own ideas by associating them with those of the other side. It is altogether impossible for masters to govern without assimilating some part of the ideas of their subjects. They cannot rule alone if subjects do not co-operate in making government effective, or at least if subjects do not obey. Masters and subjects have to understand one another if they wish to live in peace. Inevitably, therefore, they must form for themselves not only a common language, but a common thought.

1990. The *castellans*, that is, officials who administered the territories indicated by divisions into kingdoms and duchies, were equal in authority to counts. The offices of *count* and *castellan*

> were in the beginning rewards distributed by barbarian kings to their *gasindi* or table companions (*anstrutiones*). Later these offices were given to *vassi* or vassals, and to other meritorious personal retainers who formed a kind of sacred legion around the king in time of war.[155]

[155] L. Cibrario, *op. cit*, bk. 1, c. 1.

[1990]

Similar *benefits* were given to other meritorious members of the royal family who were first called *beneficiaries* and later, about 1000 AD, *feudatories*.

1991. Kings and feudatories were heads of seigniorial families. They governed to the extent needed for the preservation and growth of the greatness of their own families. But because the element of Roman civil society had remained in people's minds, the multitude had other truly social requirements to which it was even more sensitive. Roman social hierarchy had been destroyed at the top, but it could not be entirely destroyed at the base. The stones forming the base had shifted, but not perished. These foundation stones were the *communes*.

II. *Causes that revived and re-ordered the* civil element *after its first defeat following the assault by the* family element

1992. *a*) First cause: the *Catholic Church.*

The Church took the *communes* under its protection because it always favours the *social element* as supremely human, moral and Christian.

> This patriciate (Cibrario is speaking of the *decurioni* after the barbarian conquests) no longer existed legally, and had lost all its worst features. Nevertheless, it preserved the prestige due to noble birth as well as some of that due to its wealth and, although it could no longer do harm, was capable of helping. The Arian Longobards — I am speaking of northern Italy — left the Romans free exercise of their religion, and allowed the people to choose the bishop. They allowed the bishop to remain as the spontaneous rather than legal JUDGE[156] of many disputes at law between Catholics, and permitted his favourable conclusions to be executed to the letter according to Roman law. The faithful had a kind of priestly government under the government of the Longobard heretics. The BISHOP was the natural head of the MUNICIPALITY, the ancient curial families the council.
> In this way the Catholic element helped to maintain a

---

[156] An essentially social authority.

form of municipality in the cities. Some larger cities, such as Milan, offer examples in the 11th century of assemblies between neighbours in every parish for the sake of common interests. In the countryside, parishes multiplied after the Councils of Orleans and Toledo in the 6th century. The parish formed a religious community which must have become accustomed to meeting and deliberating on temporal business relative to the upkeep of the parish itself.[157]

1993. The Church also contributed indirectly to re-ordering civil society after its overthrow by the families who invaded the empire:

1. By supporting morality, instruction and all peaceful practices amongst conquerors and conquered. This was a necessary prelude to the quality and dignity of citizens, for which these people were destined.

2. By defending the weak *communes* against the injustices and arbitrary cruelties of the feudatories.

3. By freeing slaves, who were declared before God equal to other humans and led, little by little, to external freedom. In addition the way was left open for them to attain the highest social offices as a result of their being admitted without distinction amongst the clergy.[158]

[157] *Ibid.*, c. 3.

[158] 'The priesthood and the liberal arts were precisely the two gateways through which it was possible to abandon the servile condition and rise in dignity. A bond-servant who appeared suitable to receive the subdiaconate was bought by the bishop and made a freedman. A tax-collector wealthy enough to pay for his child's education could hope to see him a teacher of grammar, a notary, or a judge of the sacred palace, that is, an approved jurisconsult. At this stage, it was easy for him to be freed from every trace of servitude, provided there had been no deceit' (Cibrario, *ibid.*, c. 2). — Christianity, after proclaiming the *equality* and *essential freedom* of all human beings, also influenced their external liberation in many different ways. Such methods of liberation, carefully mustered, would provide fine material for a book. For example, in some places all a bishop's slaves had to be freed on his death. This was the ruling of the Council of Chelsea, 806 AD, in England. The Council was composed of twelve bishops from various provinces, and presided over by Wulfred, archbishop of Canterbury. In the Council or Parliament of Attigny on the Aisne, called by Louis the Good in 822, it was ordered that slaves worthy of the clerical state should be publicly declared free before ordination. In certain monasteries, slavery was regarded as contrary to the Gospel. St. Theodore, the celebrated abbot of the Studium

4. By the crusades, which weakened family power and extended trade.

5. By the struggles generously sustained against the vice and overbearing force of certain German emperors whose tyranny and lust were refrained to the advantage of the Church, of freedom and of public prosperity.

1994. *b*) Second cause: the *insufficiency of seigniorial government.*

As I said, masters 'governed to the extent necessary for the preservation and growth of the greatness of their own families'.[159] This government, which did not extend to everything and did not satisfy all needs, made it necessary for people to help themselves. Thus a social element, separate from the seigniorial element, was preserved and tolerated first as a kind of abuse but later as a necessity. As we saw, 'need is always the stimulus which makes families resolve to contract bonds of a civil character amongst themselves.'

1995. The principal office of civil-social government exercised by counts, marquises, viscounts and in general the heads of the dominant families was that of *judge*.[160] However, they were unable of themselves to exercise judgment in everything and in all places because:

1. often they were too ignorant;[161]

monastery on the outskirts of Constantinople, offered the following counsel to his monks before his death (826 AD): 'You will not have any slaves as your personal or community servants. They are human beings just as you are, made in the image of God.'

[159] 'The rulers governed only their own affairs. They dealt with their subjects' affairs merely to the extent that such matters impinged upon their own' (C. L. Haller, *Ristaurazione della scienza politica*, Introd., c. 5, note. 2). These words of the celebrated publicist characterise exactly *seigniorial government*, but are never applicable to *civil government*, which can be exercised very well even by a single person (monarch). The capital error of Haller's unduly restricted theory is his failure to recognise the difference between *seigniorial right* and *social right*, and his application to civil society of ideas that pertain solely to seigniories.

[160] 'They were also called "judges" from their principal office, and are consistently indicated in this way in the laws of the Lombards. *Judiciary* was another name for a count's feud' (Cibrario, *ibid.*, bk. 1: 2).

[161] 'The counts should have been familiar with the law, but as soldiers were only too often illiterate. A legal decision of 874 AD was signed by Heribald,

2. their real interest was in retaining the executive power (*imperium, districtionem*). They were indifferent to the result of judgments in private controversies, provided the people were satisfied.[162]

Consequently, they were often glad to leave the *skapins*[163] and other jurisconsults, or even all the freemen, to take part in these judgments.[164] This meant leaving part of this branch of social government to members of the people.

1996. Moreover 'the barbarians generally left to the conquered peoples the faculty of living according to their native

count of the sacred palace, *qui ibi fui et propter ignorantiam litterarum signum sancte crucis feci* [I was present and made the sign of the holy cross because I was unable to write] (Chron. monast. Cassaur. *Script. Rer. ital.*, t. 2, part 2)' (Cibrario, *ibid.*).

[162] Hence the opinion of some historians who maintained that only the *skapins* were judges, not the count. 'This view is given great weight by a legal decision of Hunfred, count of Rietz, in 807 AD. In question was a *manso*, or plot of land, which had been taken from a certain Hrotelm, according to Hrotelm himself. After the witnesses had been examined, the count asked the skapins for their decision in the matter. But they said: "We judge according to the witness of these men and according to your enquiry, and so on" (Goldast, *Rer. Alamann.*, t. 2, p. 62)' (Cibrario, *ibid.*) 'This single example,' says Cibrario, 'seems to be contradicted by the tone of many other decisions.' On the other hand, he at least confirms something that is highly likely: that is, the lord often acceded to the feeling of the *skapins* and other men of law in private affairs of this kind where he had no other interest than seeing that the litigation was generally accepted as equitable.'

[163] The sworn skapins 'represented the commonalty of freemen from every city or land. Their other common name was 'judges' because their chief office was to assist the count in his legal decisions' (Cibrario, *ibid.*, c. 2). 'The skapinate also contained a municipal element in so far as it represented the people in their relationship with the judges. The skapin was an official of the people who helped and invigilated at the royal palace. It was to the skapinate that the descendants of the ancient decurion families were often elevated after the difficulties of the first occupation. In fact, after the new organisation of the communes, 'skapin' was the name given in France and elsewhere to those who in Italy were called experts or counsellors or savants. It is true that the same name does not identify an office, but there does seem to be some analogy here' (Cibrario, *ibid.*, c. 3).

[164] 'The count, the judges, the vassals, the skapins and franklins all had the right to ask questions during cases. However, there does not seem to have been any regular form of voting; everything was decided through acclamation' (Cibrario, *ibid.*, c. 2).

[1996]

law. Consequently, some of the *skapins*, natural judges in every legal decision, had their roots in Roman law, and could be called as expert judges on law and on litigants in legal cases or, as we now say, in litigation."[165]

1997. We should note here that almost all the regular clergy were governed by Roman law, and had considerable influence in such judgments. The clergy, natural protectors of the civil-social element, thus acquired new influence from the need to assign it a considerable part in judicial power, which is a branch of civil power.

We should also note, however, that for the same reason many judgments of this kind were left to the people, even amongst the barbarians. The master, provided he preserved his *imperium*, was not enthusiastic about taking upon himself the task of attending to litigation amongst his subject families, and was quite happy to leave any such decision to them. Cibrario says very aptly:

> There was some municipal element even amongst the barbarians. A decree of Clotaire II, appositely quoted by Beugot, requires that a person who has suffered harm in a territory should ask for compensation from the head and inhabitants of that territory: *centenium cum centena requirat.* The *centena*, therefore, as a body had some dominion over the territory where it dwelt if it was under an obligation to repair the damage others had suffered on that territory.'[166]

1998. For these reasons, the seigniorial government of the barbarian families was insufficient for the needs of the conquered people, and even for the conquering, governing families themselves. There was no way in which a certain *civil element* could be totally driven out and eliminated from the seigniorial element. Indeed, it was soon necessary to call it in aid for common needs. In addition, the insufficiency of the barbarian-seigniorial-family government, which was obvious in the ordinary state of things, was also felt ever more noticeably in the case of war.

[165] Cibrario, *ibid.* [*App.*, no. 5].
[166] Cibrario, *ibid.*, c. 3.

1999. Now

> in the case of war and sedition when the royal official, count or marquis, was absent, the government passed into the hands of the people — a people governs itself when governors are lacking. And in this case, government in the name of the people fell to the bishop, the religious head, together with the leaders of the people. These, as far as I can see, were indeed the minor vassals and skapins.[167]

2000. Moreover, Genoa, Pisa and other cities, especially those in Provence and Italy,

> found themselves at war on their own account from the 10th century, when the sovereign left them undefended, or when they had sought distant shores, or had protected trade and the honour of the home country in every way possible.[168]

To these circumstances, altogether favourable to the preservation and restoration of the *civil element* which at first had been oppressed by the *family element*, we have to add the need felt for Roman law by the conquering families for the formation of their own greatness. Their own laws, sufficient for their prosperity as *nomad* families on their native soil, were insufficient from the moment that the barbarians, enriched by cultivated lands, understood the right and advantage of *Roman territorial ownership*. Hence, 'the barbarians preserved Roman ordinances relative to agriculture'[169] and found themselves having to forge their own laws in other matters according to the example of Roman law.

2001. *c*) Third cause: *trade which enriches many plebeians.*

We ought not to believe that all the better families of the conquered people were eliminated. Some[170] remained as foundation stones suitable for the later construction of communes.

---

167 Cibrario, *ibid.*

168 Cibrario, *ibid.*

169 Cibrario, *ibid.*

170 'There is no doubt that many of the greater Roman families were exterminated or sent into exile at the first barbarian onslaught, especially under the Lombards. But many remained. I think it a serious mistake to believe that an entire rank of citizens was destroyed. The patriciate certainly

2002. Soon trade arose, which enriched many plebeians. New fortunes were so many that they necessarily attracted a part of government to themselves according to the law, which I indicated elsewhere, 'of the equilibrium between ownership and political power.'

> Trade, the enemy of servitude, could be exercised and was exercised, I believe, only by freemen. The prejudices of Germanic peoples did not apparently include the notion that attending to trade, understood in its broadest sense, would contaminate nobility of birth. This certainly was never the opinion of the Italians, who owe their resurgence to trade.[171]

2003. Man-made wealth, as we said, is the indispensable means for the formation of civil society. Trade, as the means of enriching families amongst the people, brought in its wake the *bond* necessary for their union. Anonymous communes took on a name, became powerful and later dominated.

> At the beginning of the 11th century, powerful cities, especially along the coast, were already enriched by trade and accustomed to uniting forces when threatened by war. Frequently abandoned by the weak successors of Charlemagne, they took heart and, under the quiet presidency rather than seigniory of the bishops, carried out acts of absolute independence. In 1006, Genoa and Pisa captured Sardinia.[172]

2004. *d*) Fourth cause: *the oppression suffered by the civil element from the seigniorial element of families.*
Seigniorial government, progressing in accordance with its nature, weighed ever more heavily,[173] and at first experienced no

had no further legal existence, but in losing everything that had made it hateful, it retained the prestige that arises partly from birth and partly from wealth. Unable to do harm, it was certainly able to help' (Cibrario, *ibid.*, c. 3). — Vesme and Fossati, *Vicende della proprietà in Italia, etc.*, Turin, 1836.

[171] Cibrario, *ibid.*, c. 2. — Eichorn, *Origine della Costituzione delle città tedesche*, in *Giornale di Giurisprudenza storica*, t. 1, p. 241.

[172] Cibrario, *ibid.*, c. 4.

[173] According to Cibrario, 'the lands and persons of tax-payers were burdened by innumerable calls upon them. The condition of franklins and servants of the glebe was deplorable. As we have seen, they were like mere

resistance to its desires. The conquered were oppressed, down-trodden and grateful to be alive. But they revived, as it were, from their moribund condition, and for reasons we have already explained gained a good part of the government which lordship found impossible to manage. In addition, they were enriched by trade, and united more closely in community. At this point, they began to oppose injustice with force which itself became offensive and unjust as it increased.

2005. The consequence was a renewed struggle, more bitter than before, between *civil* and *family elements*.

    1. *Cities arose against the dominant families.*

> Minor cities, still subject to the counts, grew impatient at their lot and easily fell into rioting. The arrest of Odilo, abbot of Breme, at the hands of Olderico Manfredi II, marquis and count of Turin, set off a revolt. 'All the citizens came together in their desire to free the abbot', says the chronicler. But the soldiers of the marquis prevailed.[174]
>
> At Asti, where the bishop was perhaps too devoted to the countess Adelaide, daughter of Manfredi, the citizens threw him out. Adelaide restored him to his see with force, and set fire to the city.[175]
>
> Everywhere the municipal element tended to take on a stable form, while already good, ancient customs were given the broader form of constitutions.[176]

2006. But we should follow this struggle in another description given by the same author. The length of the following quotation need not deter us. The particular facts of history are, we believe, necessary as additional proofs of our theories which are themselves founded on historical events.

    2. *The peasants rise against the dominating families.*

> Country people, forever straightened and oppressed by their immediate masters, and by the masters of the masters, sometimes abandoned the peace of their agricultural work

machines used for the cultivation of one plot of land or another' (*ibid.*).

[174] Chron. Novalicens. *Rer. Ital*, t. 2, p. 2, 760.

[175] In 1070 AD, according to the chronicle of Fruttuaria; in March 1091, according to the chroniclers of Asti.

[176] Cibrario, *ibid*.

to take up arms. We need not speak of guilds, which seem to have been groups of artisans prohibited by a capitular law of 779 AD. We mention, however, the revolt of the Stellinga, or Saxon restorers, who in 841 attempted to bring back paganism, the revolt of the peasants of Thurgau against the nobility and clergy in 992, and of the peasants of Normandy against Richard II about the year 1000. This century was particularly noted for revolutions, especially in Italy; rural people struck out not only for freedom, but for some kind of independence. Epidamnus the Coenobite has a memorable passage in which he describes the league of minor vassals against higher vassals in 1104, and adds: 'Some of those even in a servile condition conspired together against their lords and went so far as to establish judges, rights and laws (*iudices, iura ac leges*). The bishop of Milan and other elders (*seniores*) of Italy rose to dissuade them, if possible, from such insolence, but were unable to satisfy their demands until a written promise had been obtained from the king that the right of their fathers (*ius patrum suorum*) would not be violated.'[177]

In Germany also the more important rural people seem to have shown unrest at their servile condition. Ekhart the Younger complains about the situation in the houses of the monastery of San Gallo, and says that the senior cultivators (*villici majores locorum*), who are said 'to be puffed up because bond-servants are without fear', began to carry shields and shining arms. This was forbidden to bond-servants.'[178]

Other peasant-wars worthy of mention are those in Jutland and Scania against St. Canute and Absalon of Roskilde, archbishop of Lund (1180–1186); these were caused by higher tithes. Others again were: the war of the Stedingers of Frisia against the counts of Oldenburg, who attempted to subject the peasants in 1187, and then against the archbishop of Bremen about tithes and taxes in 1207; the rebellion of the shepherds of Flanders and Picardy led by the fanatical 'Great Master of Hungary' against the clergy in 1251; the horrible excesses of the hundred thousand peasants of Beauvais, Laon, Soissons and other parts against the nobles in 1338. We mention also the army of

---

[177] Cf. Goldstat., *Rer. Alamann.*, t. 1, p. 1.
[178] Cf. Goldstat., *ibid.*, p. 30.

rebels called *La Jacquerie* after *Jacques Bonhomme*, the scornful name given by the nobles to the English peasants led by Wat Tyler, Ball, Straw and Littester who rose against the pole tax imposed by John of Gaunt, counsellor of Richard II, in 1380.[179] Towards the end of 1387 the people holding small lands and fields in the Canavese, Vercellese, Vallese and Tarantaise regions rose against the nobles and tax-collectors, several of whom they tortured and killed. One of the rebels was John of Montelenghe, lord of the Val di Brozzo, who burned and overthrew the castles of Brozzo, Cly, Lessolo, Strambinello, Castellamonte, Astrutto, Arundello and Lorenzè. These rebels were called 'Tuchini', that is, according to some authors, 'All-for-one' (*Tuttiuno*).[180] None of these revolts, generally stained with atrocious cruelty, achieved their purpose.[181]

3. *The popes, to defend the mutual relationship between civil society and the Christian religion, favoured freedom for the communes.*

Cities and their surrounding lands were assisted in giving stable order to communes by disharmony between minor and major vassals and, more importantly, by the long, deplorable struggle between Gregory VII and Henry IV. The greatest assistance was, however, furnished by the special favour of the popes. This revolution, so long prepared, was finally completed in the last twenty years of the 11th century; not all the cities were able to share in the movement from the beginning. Counts were replaced by municipal magistrates; from the start judges and administrators, together with war-leaders, were at peace. Raimbaud of Oranges, consul of Nice, went with the leaders of his people on crusade to the Holy Land.[182] Later, offices were divided, with judicial authority going to the consuls of justice or legal decisions. The consuls of the commune attended to government by voting in secret council, that is,

---

[179] Wachsmuth, *Révoltes et guerres des paysans du moyen âge*.

[180] 'From Peter Pilori, found guilty of conspiracy, in Tarantasia from the rock above, against the nobles and Lombards, a fine of sixteen small gold florins'. The account is rendered by Hamlardo Gerbais, general treasurer of Savoy, 1386–1387 and by Peter Ducis, treasurer of the count of Savoy, 1390.

[181] Cibrario, *ibid.*, c. 4.

[182] Geoffrey, *Storia dell'alpi marittime*, bk. 7.

privately in minor business, and in general council, that is in the presence of all the people, in major matters. For a long time, the bishops in some places continued as head of the municipality. At Milan, they were for two centuries the heads of the order of the captains of minor vassals while the people and the generality lived under the government of the consuls and the *podestà*.[183] In other cities, their political influence ceased almost entirely.[184]

2007. *e)* Fifth cause: *weakness of the dominating families as a result of divisions and other accidents.*
    1. The *struggle between minor and major feudatories.*

Another great cause of disorder was the beneficiary system. The higher captains or vassals bore down through intolerable taxes and burdens upon their own lesser vassals who held land in feud from them.

The first to rise were the minor feudatories who rebelled against the great barons at the beginning of the 11th century. Conrad the Salic tried to settle this strife by reducing feudal customs to a body of laws which defined the rights and reciprocal duties of feudatories and vassals. As a result, the causes of disharmony diminished. The rules were called 'customs' to denote that they were not new laws but a choice made of the best, most just and most universal laws already introduced in the matter either solely according to the light of natural reason, or by argument from analogy with similar laws preserved through tradition in the memories of the old and the wise. These laws, which had served the people's needs for a long time, had also multiplied with consequent doubts about their original observance. At times, there were two contrary laws about the same point. For common peace, therefore, they had to be revised, ordered, chosen and approved. The remedy, however, was not sufficient, and Milan was the scene of fierce, bloody strife for more than a century.[185]

2008. 2. *The struggle between sovereigns and feudatories.*

Charlemagne wished to introduce unity of administration

---

[183] Cf. Corio.
[184] Cibrario, *ibid.*
[185] Cibrario, *ibid.*, c. 4.

into his vast empire, and weaken the power of the counts in order to remove their threat to the throne. He ordered new partitions and circumscriptions of areas in France, Germany, Italy and in Spain north of the Ebro. These divisions were geographic, and followed the course of mountains and rivers. At the same time, he had the foresight to increase their number so that they were not excessively large like the Lombardy duchies.[186]

In their turn, the nobles fought with the rulers:

The counts, who were delegated to guard the borders, soon obtained command of other areas. 'Count of the borders' is the same in German as 'marquis'. The marquises rose to great power from the 9th century onwards, as a result especially of relatives or in-laws of the king being given command of these border areas. These marquises, who were sometimes called dukes because their authority was effectively the same as that of dukes, constantly rebelled against royal authority. Boso, a duke or marquis, and Rudolf, a marquis, founded the two kingdoms of Burgundy at the end of the 9th century. Others occupied the throne of Italy until Henry II, called the Saint, defeated Arduin, marquis of Ivrea and king of Italy, and succeeded in reuniting the crown of Lombardy and the imperial diadem for many centuries.[187]

2009. Many lordly families were weakened or extinguished during the Crusades. It is true that a few of the very rich were strengthened but these, by becoming quasi-centres of society for lesser nobles, reduced the isolation of families and inserted a broader principle of society into less narrow-minded, savage families.[188]

---

[186] Cibrario, *ibid.*, c. 4

[187] *Ibid.*

[188] 'Even where lesser landowners had preserved their fiefs, they were less isolated than had previously been the case. The possessors of great fiefs became centres around which the smaller owners grouped themselves after coming to live there. During the Crusade, an effort had been made to follow the richest, the most powerful, and to receive help from that source. The lesser nobility had lived with their chief, had shared his fortune and with him had run the same risks. When the crusaders returned home, they lost neither this sociableness nor this habit of living with their superior. Just as the great

f) Sixth cause: *the weaker members' need of the already strong civil element as a defence against the strong and violent.*
2010. The civil element was preserved by the causes we have described. It grew in the municipalities and became a power alongside family power. At this point, the weak found it more advantageous to appeal for help to the civil power, and gather under its standard. This in turn rendered the civil element stronger and freer.
2011. 1. *Population in the communes was increased by people fleeing from feudatories.*

> One of the great means used by the free cities to increase their population and their power was to bestow citizenship upon people fleeing from barons and rulers, provided the fugitives had lived quietly in the city for a determined time. They (the sovereigns) gave the same faculty over fugitives to the local burghers, provided their master had not demanded their return, normally within a year and a day. The free communes were accustomed to digging ditches and erecting precincts on nearby hills for the twofold purpose of acquiring new subjects and providing new fortresses against external enemies. They enfranchised every person who built a house and lived within the precinct; they furnished the new population with the privileges of the motherland. Rulers followed their example. The result was a great rise in the number of new cities and towns founded by rulers or republics.[189]

2012. 2. *Lesser lords fled to the communes for protection against the oppression of the greater families, and thus reinforced the communes.*

> At the end of the 11th century, the lesser nobility, lords over one or two castles, were considerably oppressed by the great vassals, and fled to the communes which them-

fiefs increased after the Crusades, so the owners of these fiefs held greater courts in their own castles and had around them greater numbers of nobles who kept their own domains, but did not reside in them. The extension of the great fiefs and the creation of a certain number of centres of society in place of the dispersion which had prevailed until then are the two great effects of the Crusades in the heart of feudalism' (Guizot, *Histoire de la civilisation en Europe, etc.*, lecture 9).

[189] Cibrario, *ibid.* c. 5.

selves were seeking independence. Once there, and admitted to the top levels of the republic, they turned on their old tyrants and even allied themselves to kings for this purpose. For their part, the barons found themselves in difficulties on all sides. They had been ruined by the Crusades, which had given the communes the opportunity or satisfaction of enlarging their own trade. Little by little, the barons had been forced to sell or at least to pawn, without much hope of redemption, their ancient heritage; they had been compelled to sell certificates of enfranchisement to their subjects, and abandon part of their jurisdiction; they had fallen from their ancient power and were often obliged as time went by to have themselves received as citizens and to buy houses in the very cities where their ancestors had once ruled the roost.[190]

2013. 3. *Sovereign families favoured the communes for their own defence against the power of the greater feudatories.*

Civil society was in a state of disorder. The power of the great vassals, whom from now on we shall call 'barons', prevailed over royal authority in the monarchy. The barons were the hardest of tyrants over the soldiers who held their land in fief, and over peasants who groaned under the yoke of servitude. But above all, the power of these great men was dangerous and envied by sovereigns who founded new monarchies. The barons, turbulent and threatening, were unable to forget that they had seen one of their own rise by stages to the throne; new sovereigns soon saw in the abasement of the barons a hope of remaining on their own thrones. The ladder of promotion had to be overthrown if the barons were to be prevented from taking the first opportunity of reaching the height of power. For centuries, therefore, sovereigns put all their effort into weakening the power and pruning the prerogatives of the barons. Sometime this was done openly, sometimes with cunning. The communes were favoured; the claims, even the unjust claims, of the barons' subjects were favoured. Every complaint obtained a paternal hearing, while the royal judges and commissaries endeavoured to reform the decisions of the baronial judge and castellans.[191]

[190] Cibrario, *ibid.*
[191] Cibrario, *ibid.*

2014.

Long before, the kings had called another force into action against the excessive power of the marquises and counts. This was the Roman element which had, to a certain extent, been lessened or circumscribed under the first barbarian rulers. Charlemagne, by renewing in his own person the ancient empire and receiving its investiture, as it were, from the Pope, had recognised in it a supreme degree even of temporal power. He had moreover subtly eased the way to honour and responsibilities for Romans, descendants of the defeated power, who practised Roman law. Vast possessions had been ceded to bishops and abbots by barbarian kings converted to the Christian faith. Gifts of this kind became ever more frequent and abundant under the Carolingian kings. Later, to increase the authority of the bishops and lessen the dangerous authority of the counts, ecclesiastical immunity began to be extended, perhaps under the last Carolingian kings, but certainly in the 10th century. Some of the cities in which the bishops resided, and a part of their territory, then obtained immunity from the ordinary power of the counts as the bishops were granted the authority that counts had over these cities. At the same time here in Italy, the element of Roman municipality, which had been preserved *de facto* if not *de iure* even under the barbarian domination, was recognised and confirmed under the title of 'good custom'.[192]

2015.

On various occasions rulers, when they had to form a confederation with some free commune, accepted its citizenship.[193] We have already seen that in 1228, the Dauphin of Austria had become a burgher of Turin. In February, 1324, Odoard, count of Savoy, was enrolled for twenty years as a citizen of Fribourg which promised to defend him, within eight days of a request for help, on both sides of the lake as far as Saint Maurice and the river Emme. The city also promised not to grant citizenship to any of his subjects without his consent, or to hold them as guarantees except for confessed, recognised debts.[194] Confed-

---

[192] Cibrario, *ibid.*, c. 1.

[193] 'In the royal archives of the Court.'

[194] *Contrats entre la maison de Savoie et les princes étrangers*, fol. 662, *Arch. Camerale.*

erations were often confirmed by oath on the holy Gospels. On other occasions, the promise was made 'on one's own body'. This was a less solemn oath, made by holding up a finger,[195] *per fidem corporis, digito elevato.*[196]

III. *The struggle between* family and civil elements *was carried into the heart of renewed, mature civil societies and caused the rise of sovereign houses and modern nations*

2016. *a) Civil societies pass from defence to attack and thus, not content with the social element, absorb the seigniorial element.*
2017. The Roman element, that is, the social element, escaped the observation of the conquering families, who despised it. It was thus preserved in the communes where it flourished and grew powerful. The natural result was a desire of independence in the communes themselves and in the cities. This was soon followed by willingness to dominate over the weak. *Civil societies* thus passed from just defence to attack, and themselves became lords over the peoples subject to them, creating one cause of their own decadence.
2018.

> The communes, protected and supported by the arm of the Pope, and favoured by the kings of Sicily, had finally overcome Barbarossa after many difficulties. Barbarossa, although bearing the title of emperor of the Romans happily conferred on him by the jurisconsults, and believed by all to be the true successor of the ancient Caesars, was obliged to content himself with empty superiority. This indignity was inflicted on one who from the height of his throne had looked down on other kings as his vassals, had held the power of creating new monarchs, and granted through imperial investiture lawful possession over vast monarchies, 'feuds of the crown', as they were called in the appropriate language of the imperial jurists. Already, but

[195] *Ibid.*, fol. 477.
[196] Cibrario, *ibid.*, c. 8.

[2016–2018]

to a greater extent when they had conquered the lord of the world, the communes had enlarged their command over nearby lands and castles. Villages of little importance were happy to have a sound defence as a result of aggregation to the nascent commune. Later, greater cities and lands had to cede to pressure from ambitious, triumphant communes. We have already indicated the power of Pisa and Genoa even before 1000 AD. In 1140, Ventimiglia was forced to swear fidelity to San Siro and the people of Genoa. Milan subjected Lodi, Como and Cremona at the time of Barbarossa. In 1170, the men of Casal Sant' Evasio were subjects of Vercelli.[197] In 1199, the Cenedesi became citizens of Trevigi. The marquises of Monferrato, Savona and Ceva were sworn in as citizens of Asti in the 13th century, the counts of Biandrate as citizens of Vercelli[198] and Novara. As we know, they resembled rulers rather than barons. Bertold, patriarch of Aquileia, one of the most powerful sovereigns of Italy, became a citizen of Padua in 1221, and paid ransom to the city. Shortly after, the Dauphin of Vienna became a burgher of Turin to strengthen the alliance he had made with the city. Other examples of the height of prosperity enjoyed by the communes at the end of 12th and beginning of the 13th centuries need not be mentioned here.[199]

2019. *b) By admitting to their ranks the heads of powerful families, civil societies took on the discord between the family and civil elements. Their newly acquired power prepared the way for the decadence of the communes, that is, the decadence of the municipalities.*

The feudatories who became burghers and citizens of those small *civil societies*, whose power they feared and whose protection they invoked against the oppression of more powerful feudatories, were unable to change their old way of thinking simply by ascription to such communities. The concept of seigniory impressed in their minds necessarily followed them; they brought it into the heart of the civil societies of which they

[197] *Monumenta hist. patriae*, chartar. t. 1, col. 861.

[198] In 1170. — *Monumenta hist. patriae*, chartar. t. 1, col. 864.

[199] 'Sometimes lands of little repute and lesser lords paid notable sums to obtain citizenship from a powerful commune. See the chronicles of Sienna for examples of this' (*Rer. Ital.*, t. 15).

[2019]

had become members. They did indeed declare unambiguously at their enrolment that they were equal to all their fellow-members; this equality was the required *legal condition*. But their spirit was quite different; it retained its dominant instinct. At the same time, the communes thought themselves honoured and strengthened by accepting as equals in name and word feudatories whom they really considered as lords, as in fact they were. These men were rich and powerful, and more enlightened and alert in politics and government than the other citizens. As soon as the lords became members of civil societies, they found themselves in command, and were of great assistance from the beginning in providing a form and regular organisation for the communes. This provoked an appearance of extraordinary prosperity and fortune. Valiant lords who had fled to communes and cities to escape the oppression of other lords were accustomed to war; they were soon at the head of the armies of their scorned peoples, whom they freed or whose freedom they vindicated against those who held power or tyrannised and oppressed them. The lords acquired glory as popular leaders, as fathers of their country, or founders or saviours of the republic. But when the republics were assured of safety from external dangers, the greatest danger of all arose in their midst. The seigniorial, prevalent families, having increased their authority through the services rendered to the communes, and no longer distracted by anything else, aspired to civil command, or rather, ignorant of the nature of civil command, aspired to seigniory.

2020. There followed: 1. bitter strife between such families; 2. bitter strife between such families and the people. Again, *family* and *civil elements* were at odds in a conflict dependent for its severity on the proximity, cohesiveness and admixture of the elements.

2021. The outcome of these murderous discords varied:

1. Sometimes one citizen family overcame the others to become the more or less absolute lord of the commune — a *monarchy* was founded.

2. Sometimes several powerful families together dominated the people — an *aristocratic* government resulted.

3. Sometimes, the people won — a *democratic* form of organisation was founded.

[2020–2021]

4. Sometimes the government was separated in two, one aristocratic, one democratic — independent societies arose.

5. Sometimes finally, a foreign ruler, or an already sovereign family, favoured by such discords, was able to subject to itself the power of both nobles and communes.

2022. According to Cibrario, whom we are following here,

> Men of noble blood, whose ancestors had helped to attain independence, acquired a natural preponderance in the counsels of the republic through their wise conduct of public affairs and the blood they had shed in combat. No one envied that power as long as the fatherland was insecure or the exercise of authority was accompanied by troubles and dangers of all kinds. When things had settled, every spirit was aflame with the desire to command. Under the pretext that all private greatness entailed a diminution of public freedom, persecution broke out first against those who governed the republic with pride and violence, and then against the best and greatest citizens, who suffered a kind of ostracism. As far back as 1185, two years after the peace of Constance, Modena has records of rulers, *chiefs and vassals of the Mutiny*, whose ambition centred on a separate government. They were in fact forced to swear to support *the rulers of the city*, and to keep the peace among themselves.[200]
>
> In the same and following centuries, we find in many other cities and lands records of companies of patricians, under the names of families of hospices or inns, of baronies and of military societies. But they were unable to hold out for long against the pressure and impetus of the people as a whole.
>
> Where civil discord did not give rise to tyranny by a single person, it produced that of the people, which was perhaps worse, granted the changes, mobility and imprudence of its ferocity, often directed against itself. At Florence, the title 'Grandee' was given in mockery, or even as a punishment, because it was accompanied by the loss of every political right. The statutes of that republic tell us that one became a grandee 'for murder, theft and incest'.[201]

---

[200] *Antiq. ital.*, dissert. bk. 1.

[201] *Statuta Florentiae*, t. 1, p. 429.

In no other city was democracy so violent. At Milan, although it prevailed under Martin della Torre, it soon gave way to the rise of the Visconti, heads of the nobles.

At Florence, on the other hand, the ancient guilds of artisans became omnipotent to such an extent that the most noble citizens, in order to retain any civil right, were forced to beg for admittance to the guild of wool-workers or weavers. Once the order of moral ideas had been overthrown, it was common to see knighthoods granted as a reward for arson and theft perpetrated against the grandees by the lower classes. Weavers and potters who excelled in arson and robbery were made knights of the people. Others, tribunes in poor opinion with the people, were made grandees to exclude them from office; some grandees were made tribunes and, as often happens, denied their blood and the works of their ancestors for the sake of drawing near those who held power.[202]

If the people did not succeed in taking over the government, it tried to withdraw itself from its influence. It formed another government, called the society of St. George,[203] or St. Stephen,[204] or the society of the people.[205] There was also a Guelf section, headed by a foreign commander, such as the republic of a foreign power. If there was no commander-in-chief, there were four or more rectors, as in the republic itself, divided into a small and a great council. Everything was intended to paralyse the action of laws and lawful magistrates.

In some cities, the guilds of artisans formed part of the government. These craft unions were called *Paratici* in Lombardy, and ruled by priors and consuls,[206] or sometimes by one or more standard-bearers. The end of these societies was: 1. to get the greatest number possible of their members chosen for office; 2. to make the opinion of the society prevail in the councils; 3. to revenge every offence, even the smallest, against a member of the society by

[202] Cf. Capponi, the riot of the Ciompi, *Chronichette antiche*, p. 219.

[203] At Chieri.

[204] 'At Vercelli. There is some record of this from 1183, when the society of St. Stephen already shared in the government.' Cf. *Monumenta hist. patriae*, chart., t. 1, col. 921.

[205] At Cuneo, and in many other cities.

[206] 'At Novara, the consuls of the *Paratici* took part in government in 1194.' *Monum. hist. patriae*, chartar., t. 1, col. 1021.

punishing offenders in limb, life and possessions; 4. to prevent merited punishment for these vendettas falling on their perpetrators. It was these societies which preferred to call a foreign dominator to rule the country when they saw the nobles attaining the upper hand. They preferred this to serving their fellow-citizens. The final, perpetual victory would be gained, they thought, when they forced the nobles to serve at the very moment in which they were preparing to take up command again.

IV. *Summary of the stages through which civil society took the more perfect form it shows in our present European nations*

2023. Modern nations emerged from the struggle we have described between the family and civil elements. In fact, Providence brought that struggle to produce the most perfect civil state ever seen on earth, in the form of stable, unceasingly progressive civilisation. Antagonism is always the means used by the wisdom of the Creator to place and fix finite beings at the centre of good, despite their constant readiness to move blindly towards the outer limits.

2024. If the *stability* of modern nations dates from the 16th century, their *progress* dates from the 18th. Indeed this characteristic word 'progress' was not mentioned until people saw new nations, already sufficiently constituted, rise and move towards something better with peaceful, regulated, sure and inexorable tread. Historically, this epoch is assigned to the 18th brumaire in the 8th year of the French republic (9th November 1799).

2025. At this point we have to retrace carefully the stages by which modern societies were formed. These stages, securely indicated in history, are of great assistance in removing a world of prejudices and mistaken theories from the minds of those who imagine that civil society fell from heaven already formed, and cannot now be moulded or even touched by human hands without sacrilege. These stages, through which modern nations passed according to providential laws, were the following:

2026. 1st stage. *The Roman element remained nameless and bereft of legality, but a germ of new civil societies.*

[2023–2026]

Religion and Roman law, having survived the empire, were the bond amongst the conquered. But while the law no longer had an interpreter, this was not the case with religion. The bishops who governed the continuation of society amongst the conquered, were also the pastors of the conquerors. In the public acts of the time, great numbers of people appear not as a named body, but as individuals living near one another, that is, as co-existing.[207]

2027. 2nd stage. *Civil societies without legal existence, organisation or name begin to acquire an organisation and name as soon as seigniorial families enter them.*

As long as *civil society* was composed solely of the people, without recognition on the part of the ruling lords and without any corporate name, it was ignorant and incapable of any suitable organisation. When certain families of lords entered society, for the reasons we have given, they brought organisation to these civil multitudes who soon acquired the name of 'communes' or 'municipalities'.[208]

---

[207] 'In 1090, a certain Otto, called *Rifus*, and his wife Benedicta, sold a house and a stable "to all the neighbours of Biella". This shows that the commune of Biella still had no common legal organisation. However, the simple capacity that enables people to acquire, which the act reveals, has very important consequences for the history of the Italian municipality. Two years later, the inhabitants of Saorgio, listed individually as men and women, made a donation to the monastery of St. Honoratus of Lenno' (Cibrario, *ibid.*, c. 4). — It is noteworthy that women begin to be named here. — In a diploma published by Muratori, *children* are named together with the Prior of the city of Ragusa, Peter the Slav. This man 'with ALL alike, my nobles and non-nobles, old, young, adolescents, and CHILDREN also' restores certain goods to the abbot of St. Mary of Lacuna in the presence of the bishop, Vitale. This document dates to 1044, and leads one to believe that Ragusa was the first city organised under a municipal government. In stipulations of this kind, the introduction of *women* and *children* shows 1. a certain relaxation in the bond of domestic society; 2. the tendency men have by nature to accredit their own intelligence and feeling to others who do not share it.

[208] 'The counts of Biandrate condescended to make just treaties with the soldiers of Biandrate, that is, with the lesser vassals and feudatories who, with free and good men, were everywhere the principle and foundation of the communes which they had the good sense to strengthen by aggregating the people. In 1098, Asti was free and made an alliance with Humbert II, count of Savoy, the heir of its ancient lords. Novara, Vercelli, Nice on the sea, Turin, and shortly afterwards Chieri and Testona, and other smaller lands were free'

[2027]

2028. 3rd stage. *The organisation of civil societies consisted first in an explicit, free law to which were bound only those who wished to enter the society, not all the inhabitants of a given territory.*

We have seen that civil society does not of its own nature necessarily include all those who dwell in an area (cf. 1670–1676). In addition, the poor who are unable to pay the indispensable contribution to the social administration cannot be called citizens, according to natural right. Others may refuse to join, although later, under circumstances which become clear through the contrast and complication of interests, a jural obligation may arise for them to do so (cf. 1904–1916).

In the centuries when modern civil societies began once more to knit together, they appeared as leagues in which many, but not all individuals, bound themselves to protect their own interests. The number of these individuals varied, and came partly from the families of the people, especially those enriched through trade, and partly from seigniorial families.

2029. In medieval times at the beginning of our civil societies, good sense, the natural light of reason, had shown that the two principles we have indicated were principles of justice.

1. Association in civil commonalty is of its nature a free act. Civil society is not necessarily composed of all the people dwelling in a territory, but of those alone who willingly join it.

2. Only the person who accepts the obligation of paying the necessary contribution to the administration of this civil union is necessarily a member.[209] From then on,

(Cibrario, *ibid.*, c. 4). — 'I do not think that the word "soldier" can be understood in any other way at the time. Epidamnus the Coenobite, when speaking of the movement of lesser vassals against greater, says: "The pact based on lawful oath-taking arose in Italy. The lesser SOLDIERS, more oppressed than usual by the evil domination of their superiors, joined together to resist" (Goldast, *Rer. Alemann.*, t. 1, part 1). This is even more obvious from the preface to the law of Corrado on feuds (1037) which says that it came about "to reconcile the spirits of the seniors and the SOLDIERS." Shortly after, the document calls these "seniors" "greater vassals", that is, commanders-in-chief who are always placed in opposition to "soldiers" (Murat., *Antiq. Ital.*, t. 1, col. 609)'.

[209] Modern publicists distinguish between *passive* and *active* citizenship. I think that this is one of those false distinctions which in a remarkable way serve to confuse rather than explain the rights of individuals. To my mind,

the individual who could not or did not want to become a citizen put himself under the wardship of the ruler or the commune. For this protection, he paid an annual levy of a florin, or a gold coin, or a few pounds of wax, pepper, cane or some other product. Clerics, who did not pay tax with the people nor satisfy the other obligations of citizens, were not considered citizens, but foreigners under the special protection of the commune,[210] although more often than not they made no attempt to refuse requests for financial or military help, or assistance with transport, on extraordinary occasions.[211]

2030. *Foreigners* and *citizens* inhabited the same territory, therefore. Even now, the same distinction is partly preserved, except that a person who is a foreigner in one place is normally a citizen in another. Practically everyone is a citizen or at least a subject. At the beginning of civil association, however, many people existed in a totally extra-social condition.

2031. However, once communes were established, these nascent civil societies, which were not yet completely organised, felt even more than at present the need not to tolerate foreigners. Hence the choice with which these people were presented: either leave the territory or become members, that is, citizens.[212]

2032. Civil commonalty, having increased through continual aggregation, broadened to admit entire classes and conditions of

citizenship is an altogether simple, single concept: 'It is the state of the individual who as a member of civil society is obliged to pay his tax contribution to civil society, from which he receives his share of utilities.' There cannot be any middle state; either these conditions are verified, and citizenship is present, or they are not, and no citizenship is present. Only the state of extra-social, jural relationships remains (cf. 1677–1679).

[210] This unhappy exemption from the social contribution greatly damaged the clergy because it excluded them *de facto* from enrolment amongst the citizens. Being considered as *foreigners* also harmed the exercise of their holy ministry, which is supremely social. This false idea of the priest as excluded from civil society is still fixed in the minds of the people, although the very few ecclesiastics who have anything left after the despoliation of the clergy carried out in the name of civil society pay taxes like other citizens.

[211] Cibrario, *ibid.*, c. 7.

[212] 'Foreigners who wanted to live perpetually or temporarily in some territory had to become citizens, buy a house of a certain value and fulfil the other obligations of citizenship, which was granted by the communal council either in perpetuity or temporarily' (Cibrario, *ibid.*).

persons. Thus, practically all the inhabitants of the same territory were drawn into a single civil society.[213]

2033. 4th stage. *Civil societies were first temporary, then perpetual.*

Civil society conceived in its integrity and perfection is perpetual (cf. 1630–1639). But it does not become perpetual immediately. Just as it is not universal in the beginning — it does not extend to all families — so it does not begin its existence as an never-ending aggregation. Only the utility experienced through its existence makes it continue after its commencement without further thought of its suppression. This passage from temporary to perpetual society is also part of history.

2034. According to Cibrario,

> These groupings were first established temporarily on oath, as for example at Genoa, and then in perpetuity. They were, according to Professor Baggio's excellent definition, associations of persons in a city or district, and sometimes outside, who possessed some right, voice and activity in government[214] and, we need to add, offered one another guarantees of security, justice and tranquillity. In the beginning, they were more aristocratic than democratic; the distinction, found in many cities, between greater and lesser consuls,[215] the hereditary nature of certain respons-

---

[213] 'Whatever the previous municipal organisation, it was brought into a more general association in which the lesser vassals (soldiers), the good men, that is, nobles or freemen or foot-soldiers, and the artisans and common people, all entered. It was only in the more powerful cities I think, that the great vassals, or commanders-in-chief, shared in the pact' (Cibrario, *ibid.*, c. 4).

[214] *Monumenta hist. patriae. Leges municipales*, col. 257. — 'The names of the four consuls of Genoa in 1117 are preserved in a poem of praise about the tithes from fishing owed to the bishop of Genoa which was declaimed by them "in the presence of the good men", in the church of St. Laurence. They are Lanfranco Roca, Alberto Malo Ocello, Lamberto Gezo, Oglerio Capra. We note as a sign of advanced civilisation at Genoa that all the good men present at the judgment, or poem, had surnames. Amongst them are a Guido Spinola, an Abogrado, a Fornari and others "whose names", says the notary, "are difficult to write". This is from the contemporary parchment register entitled: "Praises by the consuls of the commune, and about their judgments".'

[215] 'A letter of 1115 from the Pisans to the citizens of Nice has the following address: "By the grace of Almighty God. Greetings to the venerable bishop

ibilities in determined families, or the rising of popular
sects against the tyranny of the nobles in the 12th century
seem to indicate this. For the rest, the consuls were chosen
from both the upper classes and the people. Otto of Freis-
ing writes in fact that there were three orders of persons in
the communes of Italy: the commanders-in-chief, the vassals and the people (the foot-soldiers may have been included amongst the vassals). He also says that such consuls
were chosen not from one order but from each of them to
suppress pride.[216]

2035. *5th stage. Civil societies were first formed to regulate a
part of the modality of rights, and then extended to universal
rule over this modality.*

Universality, that is, regulation of the entire modality of
citizens' rights (cf. 1621–1629), is a characteristic of fully established civil society. At the beginning, however, society was
formed to regulate only *a part of this modality*; later, it would
become perfect by embracing it all. This gradation is also evident in medieval history. The first *part of modality* which fell
under regulation was the *defence of rights*. It was in this area that
need, which serves as the impulse for association, was felt more
keenly.

> The communes, both immediate and mediate, could under
> some aspects be defined as *societies of mutual guarantee*. In
> the beginning, neighbours were the first to know if anyone
> broke the public peace, and they sought to calm the dis-
> cord. This can be seen in Anglo-Saxon laws, and more
> clearly in the statutes of Susa prior to 1148 where every
> misdeed is understood as known to neighbours, 'it will be
> decided by neighbours'. If something is done which pro-
> vokes protest, the public official will judge but impose
> different punishments on the upright, that is, the freemen,

of Nice, and to all the good and wise men of the same city, GREATER and LESS,
from the archbishop, consuls and viscounts with the whole people of Pisa,
who by divine Providence form the elements of the Pisans'" (Geoffrey, *Storia
dell'alpi marittime*, bk. 7).
    In 1126, the five consuls and the foot-soldiers of Mantua made a contract
with the abbot of Polirone. Here it seems that government of the municipality was left *de facto*, if not *de iure*, to the nobles and foot-soldiers alone.
    [216] Cibrario, *ibid.*, c. 4.

and the instigators or ring-leaders (*glittones*). Exception is made only for violent thieves, traitors and highwaymen over whom judgment has been reserved to his court by Amadeus III, *sub nostro velle sint*. We see from this that each citizen was considered a guarantor of the public peace, and that it was left to him to maintain it. With the exception of grave misdeeds, criminal action was not taken even in the case of murder if neighbours succeeded in settling the discord. However, as Roman law gradually came to prevail, such customs ceased to have any effect.[217]

In the statutes of the city of Soest, attributed to the first years of the 12th century, we read: 'Anyone who on impulse has renounced his city (citizenship) because he has injured a fellow-citizen in his person or his effects will renounce it finally.' The communes, therefore, could be defined as societies of persons sworn to uphold the public peace on their own authority and under mutual guarantee, whether they depended or not on a foreign lord.[218]

2036. *Civil societies* set up in medieval communes therefore underwent a process of formation similar to that of other societies or leagues with particular aims. In fact, the spirit of association manifested in the Middle Ages produced different special unions. One of these, whose primary aim was the guarantee or defence of rights, later took the name of civil society. This kind of society is not, therefore, something mysterious or *sui generis* to which the normal principles of other societies are inapplicable. It was the very similarity of nature which enabled other special societies either to be fused with civil society or to lord over it.[219]

---

[217] Cibrario, *ibid.*, c. 6. — Note here 1. how *civil society* undertook criminal justice *gradually*, not immediately. Part of the exercise of this justice was left to private persons, as we saw in *RI*, 149–155; 2. how the prevalence of Roman law, the law of more perfect civil society, removed the imperfection of criminal law left in great part to private individuals. The *Roman seed*, mortified but not altogether dead, is yet again that which slowly propagates itself in modern nations.

[218] Cibrario, *ibid.*, in a note.

[219] 'The spirit of association which, after trade, is the source of all greatness in the Middle Ages, was shown not only in the primitive organisation of the communes, but also later in the celebrated Lombard and Tuscan leagues, in the league between trade guilds (whatever the different names given to these

2037. These particular leagues of mutual guarantee were seeds of civil societies because they had as their aim the *modality of rights*, although only to the extent that this referred to the defence of their own rights (and even this often served as a pretext for invading the rights of others). This aim brought together all classes of persons whose interest lay in their own class, but especially the class formed by the principal or noble citizens.

> As far back as 1185, two years after the peace of Constance, Modena has records of rulers, *chiefs and vassals of the Mutiny*, whose ambition centred on a separate government. They were in fact forced to swear to support *the rulers of the city*, and to keep the peace among themselves.[220] In this and the following century, there are records in many other cities and lands about companies of patricians, under the name of families in charge of hospices or inns, baronies and military societies. But they were unable to hold out for long against the pressure and impetus of the people as a whole.[221]

2038. Separate governments were instituted in this way for different classes of citizens. Each government represented a small civil society set up on the same territory as others with which it had some kind of understanding.[222]

corporations of artisans), in the league formed for trade amongst the German Hanseatic cities, in the partial leagues, called Ganerbian, instituted between various chatelains of Germany for the sake of mutual security against the violence of more powerful lords, and in many similar facts. This spirit degenerated, however, and was the subject of abuse. It brought about the ruin of the cities in which *solemn commitments* and *oath-taking* were multiplied too easily. Often, as history tells us, a faction took over government, or two opposing factions usurped it in an impious, bitter struggle. Cohesion between the lesser vassals, freemen and people gave rise to the independence of the communes; the disintegration of these elements caused various difficulties which brought them to ruin' (Cibrario, *ibid.*, c. 5).

[220] *Antiq. ital.*, Diss. 51.

[221] Cibrario, *ibid.*, c. 5.

[222] 'When independence first came to the free cities, all the sections of government were ruled through consuls, divided in some places into major and minor consuls, that is, consuls from the nobility and from the people' (Cibrario, *ibid.*, c. 6).

[2037–2038]

2039. 6th stage. *Small civil societies unite and fuse into more extended civil societies to form the modern nations of Europe.*

The struggle between the *family* and *civil elements* is followed by the struggle between co-existing civil societies where we can distinguish: 1. the social (good) element; 2. the limited, restrictive (bad) element.

2040. Considered in itself, *limitation* of civil society is neither bad nor anti-social; it is simply extra-social. If people were perfectly virtuous, such an element would place different civil societies in a peaceful state by nature. The whole human race, although divided into various civil societies, would remain joined by the same bond of justice and religion, in other words, by the bond of *theocratic society*. It is extremely difficult, however, for the insufficiently enlightened human mind to conceive *civil society* as both divided and pure, that is, to conceive it for what it is, a special society. On the contrary, peoples and their legists always tend to include in their own civil society the entire concept of society, and to look to those outside the fatherland as totally disassociated and lacking every common right. This highly mistaken judgment is the result of *greed*, which restricts human desires and does not allow people to see beyond the narrow sphere of things illuminated by the false light of selfishness. Thus, the *limitation* of civil society is changed into an evil element that occasions disaster, discord and struggle between limited civil societies — and the smaller the societies, the greater the struggle.

The good obtained by Providence from these struggles is the fusion of lesser civil societies into greater. This is an improvement for mankind because it simultaneously removes *limitation*, the source of the evil.

2041. Let us consider the accidents which favour or hamper this providential work. First, the fusion of several small societies into greater civil societies is achieved more easily when a prevalent power is readily available to do this. As long as the discordant small societies are more or less equal, they continue to harm and buffet one another without ever uniting or fusing. Granted human wickedness, it is extremely difficult for small, quarrelsome societies to cast off their hatred and emulation promptly. They are not content to lose their own individuality by fusing into a common society through free pacts. Indeed, each society hopes to overcome the others; this is its ambition and its presumption, and it will not renounce this hope except through force. Nevertheless, gradual civilisation, of which Christianity is the source, and particular circumstances brought some societies into confederation. Without becoming a single nation under every respect, they had a federal government. This was the case in ancient Greece, although at an imperfect level; in Christian times, in Switzerland and the United States, at a more perfect level.

2042. If one civil society overcomes another and assimilates it, the resulting fusion is produced by virtue of the social force. This was the noble politic of the Romans who always preferred citizens rather than bond-servants amongst those they conquered. Citizens, who enlarged the republic, rendered it larger, more just and more civil.[223]

2043. A third way of fusion is present when *power*, unaccompanied by *sociality*, is then united to sociality. We need to consider this case more carefully because it is precisely what took place in the Middle Ages when flourishing nations were formed which now divide Europe.

2044. As we said, there was in the Middle Ages a *seigniorial element* alongside the *social element*. This seigniorial element was divided into two parts, which were found in: 1. feudatory houses; 2. sovereign houses. A double struggle ensued: the struggle of the social element with both feudatory houses and sovereign houses. The result of the twofold struggle was a priceless good: both social element and seigniorial element were checked and situated within just limits. Each tempered the other without destroying it. A wonderful conciliation took place, thanks to the principles of Christian justice, which led to a state of particular perfection and growth amongst family and civil societies.

We need however to explain this happy outcome of such a long, obstinate conflict. To do this, and understand how collision, humiliation and consequent pacification of two proud elements could simultaneously offer extreme advantage to *civil* and *family societies*, we must recall some principles.

[223] *SP*, 37–47.

[2042–2044]

2045. The defect of civil society totally unaccompanied by any seigniorial element is weakness. We have seen that it is altogether necessary for the government of civil society to possess a *prevalent force* through which it can make its rule over the modality of rights overcome all possible opposition. This force is so necessary to the *de* facto and *de iure* existence of government that we did not hesitate to declare it one of the characteristics of society itself (cf. 1640–1642).

2046. The defect of seigniory totally unaccompanied by civil society is oppressive force and tyranny. We have seen that the nature of mere seigniory implies that the master alone is *end*, and that all his bond-servants are *means* to his will. If, therefore, *seigniory* stands totally alone, without any social element, it is the most unjust, inhuman thing on earth.

2047. The obvious conclusion is that each of these elements will confer what is lacking to the other if some way can be found of bringing them together, joining and pacifying them, granted their division in the Middle Ages. It is also clear that *civil society* must receive from the union the *force* it needs, which is supplied by the seigniorial family; and that *family society* must receive from its entrance into civil association the justice and humanity it finds there.

This is indeed what took place in the Middle Ages. Through the mediation of Christianity, through its illumination and strict justice, through the bond of its charity, the separate elements of civilisation and family did not break under the tremendous pressure they exerted on one another; they mollified and befriended one another.

2048. Let us consider what actually happened in each of the two struggles. We have described the struggle of the communes with the feudatory families. The communes gained the advantage; the feudatories became citizens. Hence the regular organisation and power of those small civil societies. In this struggle the individual commune or individual city fought against several families with which it was in contact.

We still have to describe the struggle of the communes and cities with sovereign families. In this case, several communes and cities fought with individual houses that claimed seigniory over them; the sovereigns had the advantage. Hence the fusion of communes, cities and small republics into our great, modern nations.[224]

2049. The need of defence against the power of sovereign families first resulted in confederation amongst the communes. This, however, was not sufficient for fusion because a federal government is not properly speaking fusion of several communes in a nation. Moreover, such leagues lasted only as long as the danger did.[225]

2050. Nevertheless, the Lombard league made rulers grant them a greater degree of freedom than that available to subject cities not included in the league. As a result, the social element

---

[224] We need to consider that *feudatories* did not become citizens simply because forced to do so by *communes*. They were drawn to do so by the advantages that ascription to communes presented, and by the evils they feared through non-ascription. *Communes* never conquered lords directly by force of arms, but indirectly, through circumstances which made communes useful to lords and strengthened them against sovereign houses. It remains true, therefore, that the communes' power is due to the lords who entered them. This explains why wars fought by the people on their own against the lords never succeeded, at least not in the long term. 'Not one of these revolts, generally stained with atrocious cruelty, attained the aim desired by the rebels. The condition of the peasants in Jutland, Sienis and Frisia was practically free. The word "Frisian" was combined in a popular proverb with the epithets "noble" and "free". The wars these people undertook so unsuccessfully did not indeed remove, but weakened these prerogatives. In other countries, however, and in France in particular, the condition of the serfs remained miserable in the extreme. It would have been worse if Beaumanoir's opinion were strictly true. He writes that bond-servants are so subject to their master that he can take for himself all that they have in death or life, and imprison them corporally whenever he pleases, rightly or wrongly, without accounting for this to anyone except God (*Coutume de Bauvoisis*)' (Cibrario., *ibid.*, c. 4).

[225] 'The free communes of Lombardy, which united against the emperor Barbarossa formed a kind of federal republic as long as the league endured. If the league had succeeded in outlasting its own triumph, in suppressing the hatred of one city for another, in uniting all spirits in a common bond, at least for common defence, freedom would not have collapsed so soon under the command of the tyrants. The execrable names Ezzolino and Malatesta would not have blackened the pages of our history. In Germany, where ability and wealth were not so great and passions not so violent or evil, the Hanseatic league and the confederation of Rhenish cities later showed what great power could be forged through harmony amongst the weak, and what degree of prosperity could be attained in this way' (Cibrario, *ibid.*, c. 4).

[2049–2050]

increased through the spontaneous desire of the lords who already recognised their inability to preserve the seigniory they possessed unless they tempered it with society.

When the famous confederation of the cities of northern Italy, the Lombard league, was finally victorious in the long, ferocious war against Barbarossa, it obliged the emperor to recognise its independence solemnly in the treaties of the peace of Constance (1183 AD). At the time, it was feared that other fortified, populous cities, subjects of various rulers, would be drawn to follow the example of the league. To obviate this danger, the rulers had from the beginning of the century begun to permit some of the better cities to swear community allegiance (*comuniam iurare*), that is, to take the form of municipalities and municipal government with territory and jurisdiction.[226] Their aim was to obtain the considerable help of the cities and their bishops against the barons.[227] It was not long before the same kind of generosity was practised towards territories of minor importance: their good, ancient customs were recognised and allowed to be put into writing; personal enfranchisement was given to the inhabitants; and a single code of law, which was a book of privileges, a rural, civil, criminal, political code, and organic legislation, was provided for each territory on the basis of that which free cities had set up for themselves. The aim was to endow these territories with further privileges in the shape of immunities and other kinds of enfranchisement in order to forestall their envy of free communes and to eliminate any desire for troubled independence in preference to a quiet life.[228] This in turn was inevitably imitated by the barons

---

[226] 'L'Oisel, *Mèmoires de Beuvais et Beuvoisis*, p. 271. A charter of Louis VII, 1144 AD, reads: "The people of Beauvais have enjoyed from our father, Louis, for a long time, community allegiance as it was established and sworn, together with similar customs. We, therefore, grant and confirm these things to them provided they preserve their fidelity to us".'

[227] '*Ordenicus Vitalis*, bk. 2. — Sugenius, *in vita Ludovici VI*, c. 7.'

[228] 'The statutes given by Amadeus III to the city of Susa are, I believe, amongst the most ancient. He died in 1148. Cf. Cibrario, *Storia di Chieri*, t. 1, appendix, where the author has printed the confirmation and extension of these statutes under Thomas I in 1238; and *Historiae patriae monumenta, leges municipales*, col. 6. The statutes of Aosta are dated 1188, those of

themselves in the territories they still controlled either by
agreement or through force.[229]

2051. The absolute freedom obtained through force by the
communes of the Lombard league would seem to have delayed
the time needed for their fusion into a single nation. In fact, the
opposite occurred. Those independent communes or tiny States
experienced the absolute need for a superior force which would
bring an end on the one hand to the visceral discord between the
seigniorial and social elements, and on the other to the discord
and external, murderous wars that arose between the communes
themselves. Cibrario describes these internal and external dissensions:

> The civil wars fought between one territory and another,
> and between one house and another began in Florence in
> 1170. The names Ghibelline (imperial) and Guelf (popular)
> were a mantel covering private ambition.[230] The first
> people, that is, the first company of the people with given
> ranks, functionaries and standard-bearers, was formed in
> 1250 to resist the intolerable oppression of the Ghibellines.
> But when the people, that is, the Guelfs, prevailed definit-
> ively, their tyranny was worse than that of the Ghibellines,
> although it was said, and to an extent was true, that the
> Guelfs were the foundation and rock of freedom in Italy.
> The same thing happened at more or less the same time in
> other Italian communes. The rulers favoured the Guelfs
> from whom they hoped to have, and in many places ac-
> tually did have seigniory over the State. This was partly
> due to the disorders which always accompany popular
> governments, which are the worse tyrants and cannot last;
> and partly due to the dislike of popular governments for

Chambery 1232. Both are published in *Documenta, monete, sigilli raccolti in
Savoja, in Isvizzera e in Francia, per ordine del re Carlo Alberto*, by Luigi
Cibrario and Domenico Promis, pp. 82, 126. The statutes of Fribourg in
Bleisgau given by Duke Bertold of Zoehringen, are dated 1120.'

[229] 'D'Achery, *Spicilegium*, t. 2: 362; and 13: 330. — Brussels, *De usu
feudorum*, 1: 167, 176. — Perard, *Pièces rares pour servir à l'hist. de Bour-
gogne*, 274, 311, 412, 430 *et alibi*.'

[230] 'These names were recently recognised in the very places where they
were born seven centuries before. At Wurtemberg those who vote with the
ministry are called Ghibelline (*waiblinger*); Guelfs are the members of the
opposition.'

[2051]

the grandees which impelled the former to consign the State to a foreigner rather than allow it to return to those who had been driven away from it.[231]

It is clear from the obligation already undertaken by the chiefs and vassals of Modena in 1183 to maintain reciprocal peace that seeds of discord could without difficulty germinate between men equally desirous of command. The Gualandelli and Aginoni disrupted and bloodied the territory from the end of the 12th century; the Lambertazzi and Geremei, and later the Scacchesi and Maltraversi did the same at Bologna; the Sanguini and Rotondi at Novara; the Pergalini and Raspanti at Pisa; the Mascherati and Rampini at Genoa; the Bianchi and Neri at Siena and Florence. The members of each faction took care to differentiate themselves from the others in what they wore, in their colours and sometimes even in the way they folded their napkins. They had no scruple about shedding the blood of their consorts and kin, and often pushed their hatred to the extremes of bestiality. They tore their enemies limb from limb when they had sufficient power to kill them leisurely. Sometimes they took care to let them die without confession, and took pleasure in barbarously imagining their eternal suffering.[232]

2052. These desperate, brutal struggles could not be brought to an end without some superior force. Civil society always needs a prevalent force, proportioned to its greatness, and this force could be found only in the unity of the sovereign houses. The inevitable happened:

1. Sometimes the citizens of the free cities themselves submitted to the sovereign houses as their only hope of salvation.

2. Sometimes the losing faction, not all the citizens, appealed to a foreign tyrant.[233]

---

[231] Cibrario, *ibid.*, c. 6.

[232] Cibrario, *ibid.*, c. 5.

[233] Cibrario, speaking of the artisans' guilds in certain cities, which formed part of the government and were ruled by priors, or consuls, or one or more standard-bearers, says: 'It was these societies which in the end, when they saw matters turning in favour of the nobles, preferred to call upon a foreign tyrant than serve their fellow-citizens. The societies thought that they gained a final, lasting victory when they constrained the others to serve at the very moment when they were about to reclaim command' (Cibrario, *ibid.*, c. 5).

3. Sometimes, the sovereign houses, profiting by the discord amongst small civil societies, imposed themselves as protectors, peace-makers, and rulers. In their eyes, this was a great favour.
2053. Indeed

> to people unaccustomed to freedom who served a multiplicity of masters under the cloak of freedom, it must, generally speaking, have appeared more peaceful to serve a single ruler than the will of many whose seigniory was continually subject to change. People were disturbed at regular intervals by the frightening sound of bells calling to arms and the tumults of the lower orders; they had to drag inside the house whatever was outside, bolt their doors, fill their rooms with stones and slings and endeavour to defend themselves; they never knew when the enemy would prevail or they themselves would be ruined or suffer death or at least be sent into exile, leaving their house to be burnt and pillaged by the enemy.[234] Ordinary folk saw a commander-in-chief or *podestà* called to provide justice who turned on them and cut off their heads for some crime, but did not dare do the same with the grandees. Sometimes a mob of artisans would come armed to court and threaten to turn the city upside down unless certain persons were condemned to death; others of the lower classes took control of the judiciary, cited citizens to appear before them, and imprisoned, condemned to death or executed their enemies under some legal pretext. One faction would make a pact with robbers or with armed foreigners for the sake of freedom to shed blood and pillage for days on end in their own country.[235] It is clear that in such circumstances, the rule of an individual, though hard, must have appeared attractive, provided it was strong and just.[236]

2054. *Social government*, therefore, lacked *force*. The whole of society was looking for force, as well as peace, and it was easily found in the sovereign houses which, taught by evident circumstances, recognised their noble mission. They took the oppor-

---

[234] Cibrario, *Storia di Chieri*, bks. 3 and 4.

[235] 'There are frequent examples of all these disorders in the chronicles of Siena, Florence, Orvieto, Rimini, Bologna and other cities in Italy. They have been printed by Muratori.'

[236] Cibrario, *ibid.*, c. 5.

tunity of reigning in glory over societies, ruling them civilly rather than destroying them. To do this, however, they had to modify the concept of their seigniory with the concept of civil society. *Seigniorial families* thus received in themselves the good element they lacked; the spirit of civil society broke dynastic selfishness. These families beheld their greater interest, which extended magnificently beyond the walls and the palisades of their paternal castles and palaces. It was impossible for them to ignore the empire destined for them by Providence. This empire was more desirable than the one they had exercised over bond-servants and soldiers; it was an empire over freemen, that is, over citizens.[237] Civil societies called out to them for help, but for help as from *protectors*. These societies wanted to retain all their private rights, yet at the same time find the firm, strong regulation of the *modality* of their rights which was lacking. Reigning houses answered this desire.

According to Cibrario:

> Many of these cities had to submit themselves in the 12th and 14th centuries to the obedience of sovereigns within whose State their own limited territory was situated. However, the cities retained in the form of privilege their municipal institutions together with the possibility of proposing for selection by the ruler the noble they had chosen as *podestà*. In subject-territories this person took the title of 'vicar'. This was, we may say, the original, legal organisation of the communes. In fact, the prevalence of the guilds of artisans, the organised violence of popular societies, and of baronial and noble societies, caused great alteration, disturbance and distortion in those unhappy medieval republics. The only communes to attain and maintain great seigniory for a long period were those which ruled the seas. They sacrificed their freedom in the

---

[237] Sovereign houses, which already exercised a broad, liberal rule over the many seigniorial houses subject to them, were more suitable for understanding and accepting the social element than noble houses of lesser rank. They were already practising a kind of civil government. Moreover, the greater *extension* of their seigniory must have assured them of a greater quantity of the understanding needed for government. For the way to measure the degree of this understanding, cf. *SP*, 345–370.

interest of trade, and often used their considerable wealth
to save themselves from difficult steps.[238]

2055. Trade also explains why a considerable portion of social
freedom had to be granted by sovereigns to communes subject
to them.

> Rights in favour of trade were the privileges which they
> [the communes] held most dear, and which they enjoyed
> longest after they had lost their freedom. Thus, for
> example, the 'burden', as it was called, which each had to
> contribute annually, was fixed and could not be changed
> without their consent. Also fixed was the annual period of
> time they had to devote to war, and the distance war could
> take them from their own country. It was established that
> no one could be imprisoned if he were ready to provide
> bail (the only exception was capital crimes). For the same
> reason, fixed financial penalties existed for even grave de-
> meanours. Loss of a foot, hand, ear or eye was inflicted
> only in the lack of payment. Moreover, people could not
> be taken to court outside their own territory. Finally, mer-
> chants belonging to a privileged territory were free of
> customs either throughout the entire State of the ruler or
> in some part of it.[239]

2056. Sovereign houses therefore found themselves in an
enviable position. They could easily undertake to protect the
rights of all, and could exercise that immense complex of
benefits included in the magnificent motto: *recta tueri* [to protect what is right]; they could defend individuals against the
masses; commonalties against seigniorial houses; seigniorial
houses against one another and against popular factions; the
Church against impiety and blind passion; they could form an
alliance with each of these elements and thus strengthen themselves against others who might try to prevail; they could use
different parties and interests against each other whenever
necessary and opportune. They were thus in a position to ensure
a continual increase of their own domination. They were led to
do all this much more by the very force of things, by the
inevitable events guided from on high, than by their own

[238] *Ibid.*, c. 6.
[239] *Ibid.*, c. 7.

[2055–2056]

counsel. Our great civil societies, these wonderful European nations destined to bring extremely just and lasting civilisation to the whole world, arose in this way.

V. *The internal struggle to produce perfect civil society in nations already founded*

2057. The foundation of nations is posited when many small civil communities unite under a sovereign.[240] It is not true, however, that the perfection of great civil societies was attained in a single step. Nothing is done by leaps. The elements inherent to multitudes are not changed by a treaty, a decree, a battle or any instantaneous event whatsoever. Opinions, habits and in great part real forces remain what they were. Many seeds of discord endured, therefore, in small civil societies gathered together under a sceptre. There did indeed exist a higher hand capable of overpowering, diminishing and pacifying them, but this took time, constancy and endless conflict.

2058. The first condition of our modern nations is thus described by Cibrario.

> We have to imagine a State divided by as many minor States as there were dominant feudal castles and free or privileged territories. In other words, the monarchy was planted, as it were, with tiny tyrants, tiny aristocracies, tiny democracies. Monarchy was constrained to favour the popular principle in order to free itself from the impact of feudal bonds and baronial pride. We have to imagine a State made up of many, well-populated territories, each envious of the others, at enmity with one another, and anxious about their own interests which they were unable to transform into a common interest. Consequently, they were incapable of fully developing their greatness. This

---

[240] Sovereigns existed at the time of the barbarian invasions, but not properly speaking legally constituted *civil societies*. Sovereigns commanded individuals, subjects, bond-servants, but nothing more. True civil societies took root with the establishment of *communes* which were then united in provinces without being destroyed; provinces were then united in nations without being destroyed. These are the organs of the great civil commonalties of which we are speaking.

State was sprinkled, as it were, with fortresses which made
it weak rather than strong; it was rutted with bad roads,
independent of the lie of the land and of easier commun-
ications, which wandered up hill and down dale to the
gates of every miserable village for the sake of the dues
which could be imposed there. Imagine these bad roads
ruined by just wars on the part of the rulers or by private
violence, and you will have some idea of the scene that we
have tried to depict. Imagine also, and this was common in
Germany, that such violence remained unpunished. Lack
of public perfection, regular justice and government was
supplied by associated factions, as for instance in
Westphalia where justice was organised in a hidden, violent
and ineluctable way by vengeful tribunals whose sentences
of condemnation first came to the knowledge of those they
judged at the moment of execution.[241]

2059. In such a mixture of contrary elements, the great obstacle faced by sovereign families in their endeavour to lead and
preside over civil society was noble, powerful families. Force
always resides in these families. On the one hand they aspired
to independence; on the other they tended to seigniorial domination over the people, whom they wanted to see subject to
servitude and amongst whom they abhorred the thought of
citizenship. A highly enlightened policy on the part of sovereign
houses led them to become protectors of the people, that is, of
civil commonalties against the lords. They used the people
under their guidance to temper seigniorial spirits and to force
minor lords to equality with the citizens.

2060. Nevertheless, such a sound, universally advantageous
policy could not be understood immediately by sovereign
houses themselves. The obstacle was the seigniorial spirit which
had prevailed for so long in them, and drew its origin from their
very existence as families. Ancient prejudices, the traditional
manner of thought and feeling, could not be changed overnight.
New, liberal attitudes could not be attained as these families
stepped out of their caste, as a modern writer says.[242] Once the

---

[241] Cibrario, *ibid.*, c. 7.

[242] 'Kings were nothing more than noble chieftains who abandoned their
caste to create for themselves a special fortune by relying on foreign allies.'
Lerminier, *Philosophie du Droit*, bk. 3, c. 2.

communes had been subjected to their rule, intestinal strife broke out and continued, although less ferociously than before. According to Cibrario:

> The life of citizens, although quieter and freer than that of others, granted the misery of the times, was nonetheless difficult. Rulers short of money often came down on them with demands for help or subventions. It is true that they did this as though asking for a special favour, but they were often unsatisfied when communes granted two florins instead of the three requested. If payment was delayed, they had the whole treasury arrested and sealed the doors of the counsellors until the matter was settled. Moreover, despite the communes' privilege of providing only a certain number of soldiers for a time and within the limits of a determined territory, the ruler, under threat of imminent attack from some powerful neighbour, often commanded the council to assemble the entire general army at a certain time and place. If anyone capable of bearing arms was missing, the punishment was a fine of one hundred gold florins and perpetual displeasure.[243] There was almost continuous irritation between rulers and communes. The great lord commanded ambassadors to be sent to him with full powers to conclude business he himself proposed. Communes called them 'ambassadors *ad referendum*'. The ruler, for example, required a subsidy of two thousand florins. The commune found out how much other territories of equal standing had granted, and then offered a third or half of that sum. The ruler declared a general war; the commune sent a troop of twenty-five knights under their protection, and ambassadors[244] to detail the miseries of the people.[245]

2061. Sovereigns took a long time to accustom themselves to people already organised in civil communities; they had to understand that their own greatest force would be found in these civil organisations. The great lords would certainly have overcome sovereigns who chose to depend upon overbearing power. Consequently, the natural position of these sovereigns

---

243 *Lib. consil. civit., Taur.*, 1377.
244 *Lib. consil. civit., Taur.*, 1372, 1373.
245 Cibrario, *ibid.*, c. 7.

had to be that of defenders of justice, protectors of every right, guardians of the multitude of weak persons against the few who were strong. Rulers did indeed attain a suitable understanding with popular civilisation. From then on, the two sides communicated rationally, discussed rights, and dealt openly and loyally with one another. Bloody wars on the battlefield gave way to legal-political wars in assemblies. In turn political assemblies, following the example of Church Councils and composed to a great extent of bishops, were schools in which sovereign houses were enlightened about their true interests and finally became true civil heads of nations.

2062. The history of this great step along the road to civilisation, that is, of the first political unions, is described by the author of *Economia politica del medio evo* in the following words:

> When some provision had to be made about business that impinged on universal interest, it was the custom, even before the 14th century, to call a general parliament of nobles and deputies of the communes for the sake of their counsel and help. This was the case in Piedmont and Savoy for sumptuary laws, or the distribution of provisions, or fear of invasion by the great companies which infested Italy and France.[246] It was the first step towards national unity against the gradual division and disintegration caused by feudalism. Towards the end of the 13th century, regular assemblies of the three estates, that is, of ecclesiastics, nobles and commons, began in England. In 1302, Philip the Fair called these assemblies in France for the sake of help in his tyrannical plans against the pope and his own people. He flattered public opinion in order to strengthen royal authority. At that time, the estates had no political authority. The king called them together to ask some extraordinary subsidy from them; they consented, but at the same time begged the king to confirm and maintain their ancient franchises, and to reform some abuse (principally in the administration of justice or the bestowal of ecclesiastical benefices). The king either consented or denied the requests, and referred to laws which

---

[246] *Lib. consil. civit.*, Taur., 1328 AD and following. — *Conto del tesoriere generale di Savoia*, 1391, 1393 AD.

[2062]

already dealt with the matter. For the rest, the estates were subservient when the king was strong, and demanding in times of calamity, as for example after the unfortunate battle of Poitiers (1356). As Guizot judiciously said, these assemblies were either consultative or contractual. They began in Spain in 1350. Under the monarchy of Savoy, subsidies were requested in place after place for the whole of the 14th century by officials deputed by the ruler. The first general assembly of the estates was called by Amadeus VIII for Tonon, 13th October 1439; the second at Geneva on 8th December of the same year after Amadeus' election as Pope.[247] In the 15th century, when sovereign authority had been much reduced by civil wars and desperate times, the estates played a considerable part in political manoeuvring.[248]

2063. The next steps were those taken by Louis XI, Charles V, Louis XIV, and later by all the monarchs, to lower the nobility from their seigniorial level to that of citizens. This also was an immense advance, and extremely necessary to perfect our great, modern civil societies. Diminution of the excessive seigniorial and family element increased the civil element. Peaceful fusion of the two elements was made easier, or rather possible; the existence, peace and prosperity of civil commonalties, always under threat from violent, family selfishness, was assured. At the same time, the intellectual and moral state of the powerful families was improved as they came under pressure to respect and accept internally the element of civil justice.[249]

---

[247] '*Conto di Giovanni Lyobard, tesoriere generale*, from 31st August, 1439, to 7th March, 1440, fol. 242. Before that time, we find subsidies requested place by place from each commune, baron and prelate.'

[248] Cibrario, *ibid.*, c. 7.

[249] This step towards the civilisation of modern societies was also assisted in an incredible way by Christianity, which always contributes to the production of all the great benefits of mankind. There is some truth in what a recent author said: 'The stubborn insubordination of the barons against the throne was rendered forever powerless by the religious sanction granted to the hereditary monarchy. One example is the miraculous vigour experienced by Joan of Arc when she needed it to save from ruin the fairest kingdom of the world and its boy king. When Richelieu and Louis XIV finally succeeded in entirely overpowering the ancient aristocracy, and outlined their plan for unity and concentration (which was afterwards put into effect and perfected

I have no wish to describe this great work here. It was brought about by great foresight and by force, by just and unjust means, and has been fully and masterfully examined by many authors. It will help instead if we concentrate on outlining the truly beautiful *ideal* of civil society. This ideal remains the aim of civil society which still struggles to attain it, and will go on struggling until it has both eliminated every element inimical to the ideal, and fully conquered, digested and assimilated all the elements not truly inimical to it but disassociated from it.

The ideal concept that we intend to study and outline will, I think, allow us to understand the natural, irresistible, providential movement of civil association either as it progresses peacefully and harmoniously to the ideal, provided it is not held back and impeded on its way, or as it progresses convulsively and precipitously to the ideal, if it has to break free from constraints. I would almost say that in this fatal movement of civil society, as it tends to realise its idea, we have to look for the profound reasons of every social revolution, ancient and modern. This impetuous movement also explains those epochs in which civil society turns on itself in harmful fury, epochs which are more than suitable for convincing wise rulers that they can do everything by seconding the laws of social movement, and nothing by rashly and obstinately opposing them.

by the French revolution), it was thought that the violence and despotism they exercised against the nobles would be harmful to the royal power. Instead, it was favourable because the royal power was at the time the representative of divine right and still protected by people's faith. In addition, the onslaught of the royal power against the proud subjects overshadowing it was directed solely against the representatives of the brutal force hidden under the vain show of titles' (Laurent de l'Ardeche, *Storia di Napoleone*, c. 16).

[2063]

CHAPTER 4

The final form to which modern civil societies tend

Article 1.
The ideal of civil society

2064. Modern civil societies have a tendency to draw ever closer to their ideal, which we can summarise as follows:
Civil society will have attained its most perfect form when
1. Laws and governmental acts make no ordinances affecting the value of any *rational right* but regulate only the modality of all rational rights pertaining either to individuals or societies. In this way, *maximum rational freedom* is preserved.
2. All members of civil societies have *perfect equality* before these laws.[250]
3. The norms of rational Right are fully observed in respect of persons outside civil society.
2065. Granted this perfect form, the following goods are the immediate consequence:
1. The guarantee of all rights together with prompt, effective justice, equal for all.
2. Concurrence for all social and other goods, open equally to all, whether collective or individual persons. Hence:
3. The facility to improve one's fortune by rising through social levels and offices in proportion to one's greater suitability.[251]

[250] It would be totally worthless to have all the citizens equal before the social laws if these were evil. — For this reason, I have made *equality before the law* second to the principle that civil society should not touch the *value of the rights* of the citizens but only regulate the modality of their rights. This is the great principle which produces good laws and prevents bad.

[251] Is society obliged to choose the most suitable officials? I distinguish. If the society (the associated fathers) chooses on its own account, it has no jural obligation to do this, In reality, the choice usually falls on those known to be the most suitable, because society is moved to this choice for its own advantage. If however the choice is made by others in the name of or in place of society (for example, by its government, etc.), there is a strictly jural obligation.

4. The progressive development of every industry, of every kind of study, of intelligence, etc., and consequently:

5. The best possible moral-economic condition of the largest number of citizens who will certainly not lack the means to satisfy their primary needs.

6. A population balanced by production.

7. The maximum national force against external enemies.

8. The flourishing state of religion and of beneficent institutes which cater for any poor who might be deprived of the above-mentioned means.

2066. Careful consideration and unbiased discernment will show, I think, how these eight general goods follow, like necessary effects from their causes, the three laws of social justice in which we contemplate the ideal of civil society. This whole book explains this. Nevertheless I would like to add an observation about the connection between those goods and the three laws of the ideal civil system.

2067. First, we note that the three laws bring about civil society free from every seigniorial and family element. We respect these elements as a complex of rights, but not as a foundation of civil government.

2068. In fact, the first law, which allows civil government to dispose solely of the *modality*, not the *value*, of citizens' rights, is the opposite of the notion of *seigniory*, which disposes of the rights (of their value) over which seigniory extends.

2069. The second law, by indicating the equality before the law of all members of civil society, shows that an equal right has equal protection. This is the opposite of the notion of seigniory, which introduces the relationship of end and means between master and bond-servant, and demands privileges for the former which give him advantages over the latter. We must also note that demanding privileges in face of civil law pertains, properly speaking, not to the notion of seigniory but to the abuse and selfish spirit of seigniory.

2070. The third law, which requires that the norms of rational right be observed in respect of persons outside civil society, establishes the equality of all human beings before rational law. This is opposed more to unjust tyranny of all kinds than to just seigniory.

2071. Granted this, we see how the eight general goods, which must constitute the best civil state, proceed as necessary effects from the three laws or principles of the civil ideal.

If social government regulates properly the modality of all rights, all rights are guaranteed (the first general good), because defence of rights is the first purpose of regulation.

2072. If government regulates only the modality of rights without disposing of their value, all citizens enjoy *concurrence for all* social and extra-social goods, because their right of *relative freedom* (*RI*, 80–83, 273–281, 1667, 1673–1677) is maintained and guaranteed in all its extension (2nd general good).

2073. If no one is denied either *active concurrence* for a private concern or *passive concurrence* for public employment, the means for improving one's state are open to all. In the matter of private concerns and public employment, everyone is responsible for his own advancement by use of intelligence and diligence. Unless actual unsuitability is evident, the law excludes no one through bias. It is clear that society remains free to choose the most suitable of its citizens, whose choice is of concern to society.

2074. This concern to choose for office the most *suitable* citizens, independent of any other qualification, must suggest to society the appropriate means for discovering the *actual suitability* of the citizens to be chosen. Hence, the preservation of the full, relative-jural freedom of all citizens, and their equality before the law, brings in its wake the maximum facility, open to all, for improving their fortune (3rd general good).

2075. The *relative freedom* of everyone must be acknowledged as an intangible right that allows everyone completely free concurrence for every kind of work. Only an actual lack of real suitability can exclude a person from social responsibilities, not unfair laws or suitability presumed or invented by the law. Granted these conditions, it is clear that the result will inevitably be the *most natural, extensive* development of every good beginning, enterprise, branch of study and every talent.[252] In these conditions, a society's concern, and the recognition of its duty

---

[252] Time and the wisdom of civil governments are required for determining the best and most secure means for acknowledging this *prevalent suitability* without *prejudice* to any citizen; no citizen can be *precluded*.

[2072–2075]

to choose officials, urges it to choose for office those citizens who are in fact most suitable (4th general good).

2076. The result of this universal free concurrence for every unoccupied good, in conformity with activity and merit, is the best possible economic-moral situation at least for the greatest number if not all of the citizens (5th general good).

2077. As a result of their morality and foresight, population is balanced by production, the former growing in proportion to the latter (6th general good).

2078. The three principles of such a society, obviously seen as useful to all, must produce *political uniformity* of thought (with consequent annihilation of *political parties)* and the *greatest defensive force* against external assailants (7th general good).

2079. There can be no doubt that in a society as equable, moral and prosperous as this, any unfortunate person, even a foreigner, who turns to it, must find abundant refuge and aid (8th general good).

Article 2.
In the movement of 1789, the SOCIAL ELEMENT attempted to destroy the SEIGNIORIAL ELEMENT

2080. In France, after 1789, the struggle between *family* and *civil society* became fearful, sinister and bloody.

Some clear-thinking people have noted that the progress of civil society towards its ideal had at that time been obstructed by arbitrary ordinances, and that consequently society, needing to sever its fetters and move forward, had turned violent [*App.*, no. 6]. This may be true but does not affect the truth of the following observations.

2081. The *social element* reacted beyond the limits of justice; it attempted to invade the *seigniorial element* and, out of hatred and vengeance, destroy it. Indeed, having resolved to reign alone, it invaded the whole of *individual Right* under the pretext that there could be no Right except *social* Right. This claim was a natural consequence of its ferocious persecution of the seigniorial element, which pertains to individual Right where every individual right is a power, a principle of seigniory.[253] In such a state of things, civil society tyrannised individuals and smaller societies *(RI*, 1652–1654).

We need to take careful note of this fact; an investigation of this important period of struggle between *civil* and *family elements* does more for the progress of the philosophy of Right than a mountain of speculations. Hence we must pause to see how the aroused social element came to tyrannise over the seigniorial element. An impressive document which summarises the thought of the time is the *Declaration of the rights of man and the citizen* (1789). I will discuss a few articles from it — sufficient to show how the puffed-up social element tore the family, seigniorial element apart.

2082. 'Article I. Human beings are born and remain free and equal in rights. The sole foundation of social differences is common utility.'

1. 'Human beings are born free'. — In so far as they have personal dignity, they have personal freedom *(RI*, 48–52), but they are born in a *family*, this is, under paternal dominion (*RI*, 781-790). The Article totally forgets *Right in the family*.

2. 'Human beings are born equal in rights'. — This is true only in the case of those rights that are founded on human nature possessed equally by all human beings. Again, however, human beings are born in the *family* where parents and children are certainly not equal in rights. Moreover, families are not equal either in number or in the quality of acquired rights. Not even a new member of the family, who possesses rights *in solido* (*RI*, 1271–1275), can always be considered equal in rights to the children of other families. Hence, to say that human beings are born equal in rights is to forget once again *family Right*.

3. 'Human beings remain free'. — If we mean essential freedom, human beings certainly remain free. But a relationship of seigniory and servitude, recognised by rational Right (*RI*, 531–553) also exists. Hence, the unconditional statement that human beings remain free cancels *seigniorial Right*.

4. 'Human beings remain equal in rights'. — They remain equal in connatural but not acquired rights. Here, *acquired*

253 *ER*, 54–89.

individual Right is forgotten, together with the whole of *family Right*.

5. 'The sole foundation of social differences is common utility'. — When the input of the members of a society is unequal, as in the case of *multi-quota* societies, the difference of input produces different social rights, for example, a varying quota of what is useful (*USR*, 141, 216–254, 334–341). In civil society the contribution and the quantity of all that is useful varies in proportion to the greater or lesser ownership of the members. This is a *social difference* founded not on common utility but on individual, family rights. Furthermore, anyone who enters civil society intends to preserve all his rights of jural seigniory, for example, paternity. These require a distinction between master and subject, a distinction which affects social rights. Thus, a son under paternal authority cannot, according to rational Right, be a member of the civil legislative assembly if the father does not make him his representative (*RF*, 1418–1430, 1455–1512). There are therefore *social differences* which have their origin in the varying quantity of seigniorial rights. Consequently, if we acknowledge only those rights which are founded on common utility, we remove from individual Right of ownership and seigniory, as well as from family Right, all the authority due to them in civil society.

6. Furthermore, the extension of *common utility*, being uncertain, is equivocal. What does *common utility* mean, and who judges whether a particular social difference is founded on it? If everybody judges, we are in a state of anarchy. Why draw up a Constitution?

2083. 'Article II. The purpose of every association is the preservation of natural and imprescriptible human rights. These rights are freedom, security, ownership and resistance to oppression.'

1. Here, 'every association' can only mean civil association. *Civil association* therefore replaces all other societies and drives them from this world. There is no worse tyranny.

2. In addition to 'natural and imprescriptible human rights', *acquired rights* must be preserved. The defence of only natural rights allows the plunder of all acquired individual and family Right. The Declaration, which makes no mention of acquired

individual and family Right, speaks only about the proud *human being* and *citizen* who protects the so-called *lesser man*.

3. An association whose sole end is *imprescriptible* rights could not proceed coherently, unless *prescription* were abolished from the code of its national assembly. But this would mean the loss of one of the foundations of rational Right, principally seigniorial Right.

4. Is external ownership always an imprescriptible right? Is it a *natural*, rather than an *acquired* right? Is there anything in nature other than the faculty to acquire ownership? Is there equality in rights of external ownership? Acknowledgement of *ownership* therefore contradicts both this and the first Article.[254]

2084. 'Article III. The source of all sovereignty resides essentially in the nation. No body of people, no individual can exercise authority which does not emanate expressly from the nation.'

1. What is *the nation*? Is it the whole of the French people, including women and children, or simply the majority? Is it the fathers of families or the majority of a few taxed fathers, or of taxed fathers who actually vote? — Unless all this is defined, the Declaration says nothing by affirming that the source of all sovereignty is resident in the nation. The word 'nation', having no definite meaning, is determined by the free decision of all the parties, who afterwards can always exercise tyranny in the name of the nation. — Furthermore, if the nation means the majority of those citizens, taxed or non-taxed, who actually vote (this is what the nation normally amounts to in the reality of popular governments), we are dealing with three million out of thirty million.

In this case the ruler is the will of a million and half plus one. These command and make ordinances affecting the other twenty-eight and a half million minus one, so that the latter have no authority which does not emanate from the former, who

---

[254] Here, rights of acquired ownership are under discussion, not fundamental ownership, which is the natural faculty to acquire. We see this in Article 17 which says: 'Because ownership is an inviolable, sacred right, no one can be deprived of it except for public necessity legally and clearly verified, and on condition of a just, prior indemnity.' This article destroys all the theory presented in the preceding articles.

become the source of all obligatory law (Art. V). — In the third place, an unorganised people is certainly not a nation. So, who will organise it, and how? The non-existent nation cannot help; we have to turn to those different ways of constructing civil society that I discussed. The Declaration of 1789, which wants to form society, begs the principle by presupposing it. To say that sovereignty comes from the nation presupposes the existence of a people organised into a nation. In such a people sovereignty is already formed. Why then try to form it? The real desire was the destruction of the existing sovereignty and the establishment of another, the removal of a monarch who exercised a centuries-old sovereignty like a master and family head, and the enrichment of the citizens, members of the society. This is simply war made by *society* on *seigniory*, the usurpation of *seigniorial and family Right* by *civil instinct*.

2. No body of people, no individual can exercise authority which does not emanate from the nation. — These fatuous words abolish all seigniory and societies, in fact all human rights, because every right implies an authority. Their material sense is that the nation (civil society) absorbs everything — ideas, expressed as badly as this, were certainly confused! This exaggerated statement was not simply written but put into practice at the time of the Terror. When people act according to what they write, they certainly write according to what they think. Benign interpretations have no place here.

2085. 'Article IV. Freedom consists in being able to do all that does not harm another. Consequently, the only limits to the exercise of all human natural rights are those which guarantee for the other members of society the enjoyment of these rights. These limits can be determined only by law.'

1. Freedom is spoken of as if the only freedom were civil freedom. Once again, civil society substitutes itself for morals and for God himself. It draws everything to itself.

2. There are certainly other limits in addition to those mentioned in the article; there are moral limits. But these have been forgotten in face of the barbaric invasion carried out against humanity by arrogant civil society. — Moreover, why restrict the limit of freedom solely to actions harmful to the other members of society and not harmful to all human beings?

[2085]

Clearly, the *pupil human being* is sacrificed to the *teacher citizen*.

3. The article certainly wishes to speak about *civil law*. But because it speaks of *law* absolutely, no other law is recognised. Here again we see a violent invasion by selfish social instinct.

4. To understand the strength of these observations we must note that the document under examination bears the title: *Declaration of the rights of man and the citizen*. The freedom, the law and the limits of rights mentioned in the declaration, however, are those of the citizen who absorbs and annihilates the human being.

2086. 'Article V. Law has the right to prohibit only actions harmful to society. No one may prevent what has not been prohibited by law, nor be forced to do what is not commanded by law.'

1. This article begins by giving a law to law. It says that law has the right to prohibit only actions harmful to *society*. But why to *society* and not to individuals? Do the latter possibly not exist? In any case, who imposes this limit to law? Doesn't the previous article say that only law determines harmful actions? We have then the greatest confusion of ideas, the most glaring vicious circle: only law determines which harmful actions limit freedom, but law can punish only harmful actions!!!

2. 'No one may prevent what has not been prohibited by law, nor be forced to do what is not commanded by law.' Thus, a father or master can no longer prevent his son or bond-servant from doing anything whatsoever, if not prohibited by civil law. The son and bond-servant can always reply to their father's and master's commands: 'You can only force me to do what you want by showing that the law of civil society commands it.' Again, civil society, by means of this article, abolishes the whole of *family* and *seigniorial Right*, or grounds these not in reason and nature but in itself, as their only source.

2087. Similar observations can be made about the other twelve articles of this memorable Declaration. The same spirit permeates them all: disturbed and demented civil society will recognise nothing in the world except itself, and will annihilate every other right. This is truly absurd; society is condemned for its temerity in contradicting itself in the very title of its scientific manifesto. Although the title is *Declaration of the rights* OF MAN *and the citizen*', the manifesto allows no other authority to exist on earth except that of civil society, and authorities stemming from it and existing through its good. It also speaks about *natural rights* but makes every authority and power originate from the nation. Does the nation create both natural and imprescriptible rights? If so, why call the proclamation 'Declaration' and not 'Constitution'? What wretched, illogical philosophy!

Article 3.
The confused ideas of authors at the time of the French revolution

2088. Where there is passion, there is confusion of ideas. The movement of 1789 was a movement of upheaval; civil society did not move forward peacefully but raged against seigniorial and family society. Ideas necessarily became horribly confused.

Now that the bloody experience has passed, and discussion of principles is exhausted, we can, I am sure, make a calm judgment about the event, and confidently agree that, in the abyss of evil, a good, salutary seed was at work.

2089. For a long time civil society had felt the need to move towards its ideal. If upright, religious people had lovingly tried to nurture this good social instinct and help society take the desired step, humanity, spared the horrors of the revolution, would have recognised their merit. Virtue would have been boosted and religion glorified. Unfortunately, upright, religious people understood neither the ardent longing and urgent need of their own society, nor their own vocation. This failure is the greatest misfortune of nations.

2090. And what are the consequences? There is among all the peoples of earth a restless portion, torn by its own vices, wicked, whom Scripture calls 'sons of men'. They are ceaselessly driven by a relentless need 1. to satisfy the immoderate demands of particular passions (hence party interests and naked robbery); 2. to satisfy the general internal desire for movement, confusion and wrong doing; 3. to give free rein to their intense anger against truth, religion, Christ. This rabble of a people was captained by the so-called philosophers and illogical thinkers of the eighteenth century, who availed themselves of civil society's real need for progress. They incited society to satisfy this threefold evil tendency, promising to guide it to the desired progress which it could not itself determine or execute in some external form. The rabble put their trust in the first and only leaders to come forward. Tragically, these leaders were sophists and wicked men, and the cause of progress was now horribly bound up with that of anarchic, atheistic, popular passions. A thousand, contrasting ideas were aired, and the resulting chaos passed sadly from concept to reality.

2091. The effects, like the cause, were inevitably mixed. Some effects corresponded to the true desire and need of society, others to strong passions occasioned by and under the pretext of social progress. The former, which were good but mixed with the latter, which were evil, were for a time almost hidden from view and beyond belief. Later they were recognised with difficulty, more in the form of a chrysalis than of a butterfly.

2092. The revolution produced a famous son, Napoleon, who blamed all the evils of the revolution on the *False philosophy of the time* and *Impiety*. His verdict, expressed to the Counsellors of State at the time of Mallet's conspiracy (1812), was:

> All the tragedies suffered by our sweet France must be attributed to ideology, to that sombre metaphysics which would base the legislation of peoples on the first laws that its astute investigation has discovered instead of adapting laws to the knowledge of the human heart and the lessons of history. It was errors like this that inevitably guided the government of men of blood, who proclaimed the principle of insurrection a duty, and flattered the people into accepting a sovereignty they could not exercise.

Having seen the evils of sensist philosophy, he could not speak about them in any other way. As early as 1800, in his address to the clergy of Milan, he spoke about the evils of the wicked philosophy he had seen:

> Modern philosophers have made every effort to persuade France that the Catholic religion is the implacable enemy of every democratic system whatsoever and of every republican government. This resulted in the cruel persecution carried out by the French republic against religion and

its ministers; that great mass of horrible evils which preyed
on the unfortunate people of France.

Article 4.
The imperfect mediation between the family and
the seigniorial elements

> ... two centuries,
> One armed against the other,
> Submissively turned to him
> As if awaiting destiny:
> He was silent, and as judge
> Sat in their midst.

2093. Just as seigniorial families in Europe were compelled by
the irresistible force of events to move closer towards civil
societies and embrace that element of civilisation which would
wonderfully ennoble and perfect them, so civil societies together with their representatives felt the need to draw closer to
seigniorial families after having being separated from them, and
to have them as their natural protectors.

2094. This movement of *civil societies* towards *seigniorial
families* is evident in France after the horrors of the Terror.
Having embroiled herself in this great agony, she felt ever more
urgently the need for a unique protective force of right.

2095. Napoleon, the true representative of France, underwent
a change in thought and feeling. His way of thinking and feeling
became perfectly harmonious with that of the society he eminently represented, and at the close of his life he correctly
presented himself as the mediator of the two worlds:

> I became the ark of the old and new covenants, the natural
> mediator between the ancient and new order of things. I
> possessed the principles and confidence of one, I had
> identified myself with the other. I belonged to both, and
> could in conscience have taken the side of either.

This *hurler of lightning bolts* of the 13th *vendémiaire* said on
St. Helena where he had been taken:

> Totally content and satisfied about these great points, and
> with the whole of Europe once more at peace, I would
> have had my own *congress* and *holy covenant*. These were

my thoughts, but I was robbed of them. In an assembly of all the monarchs, I would have dealt with OUR FAMILY INTERESTS, and fully justified my actions to the people.

2096. Why then did this mediation between the civil and the family elements not succeed? Or why did the mediator himself fall victim to his own mediation?

My answer would be: Because the only mediation possible between family and civil society is that which is spontaneously carried out by *truth, justice* and *religion*. I have already indicated that today the prevalent force in our Christian societies consists of these three elements; they are the *substance* of social order.[255] The uneducated mediator did not know this sufficiently.

2097. Napoleon, instead of putting his trust in *truth*, proclaimed *enthusiasm for pagan glory*, the glory of the great men of Greece and Rome,[256] and released a torrent of exaggerations. His vain enthusiasm ceaselessly deceived himself and continues to deceive others. Hence, changes to the truth, which popular manifestos abound in and in his own most solemn acts. Humanity was inevitably discontent, because it is made for truth.

Instead of trusting in *justice*, Napoleon thought he saw the destiny of the world and of himself in *force*. This was a direct consequence of the system of the utilitarians to whom, thinking himself justified, he so often appealed with wonderful simplicity. But force is an *accident*, not the *substance* of the great cause which moves humanity and gives it an unperishable law.

Instead of having faith in the omnipotence of the One who protects the Church, Napoleon considered the Church and its rights to be purely a matter of politics, or at least he acted as if he believed this. His acumen and his power were ensnared by the net of Pius VII's simplicity. It is clear that the great man did not sufficiently see where the real connection of power lay.

---

[255] *The Summary Cause for the Stability or Downfall of Human Societies*, 127–143.

[256] Benjamin Constant later wrote: 'Today we have forgotten that towards the end of the empire the French were opposed to and even distressed and tired of the victories which France was condemned to carry off.' This is the real weakness of glory and military campaigns in our Christian, civilised times.

Consequently, his mediation was bound to be imperfect: mediation destroyed the mediator.

Article 5.
How complete mediation between family and civil elements will be achieved

2098. Today, perfect mediation between *family* and *the City*, which must lead both family and civil society to the ideal of their perfection, can be carried out only by *truth*, *justice* and *Catholicism* (the one perfect form of Christianity). All who apply these three means to theory and to the realisation of civil order assume the office and dignity of mediators; their mediation will not oppress or destroy them.

2099. They will never be destroyed because, although truth, justice and Catholicism may have their implacable enemies, this hatred will not annihilate the work of such mediators, whose task has ended with the crown of martyrdom. In the measure that truth, justice and Catholicism increase in splendour and clarity every day, these three things will have less and less need of witnesses by blood. Society will no longer be the persecutor; only individuals, whom society will punish as murderers.

2100. But we need to explain how truth, justice and Catholicism are called to exercise so great an influence on the organisation of humanity and destined to accomplish such a sublime mediation.

To simplify the discussion, I will class these three great means under the single name 'justice'. It is reasonable to call truth justice because it is just that everyone possesses, expresses and uses truth as the rule of their actions. It is also reasonable that the most perfect justice be seen in Catholicism because, just as its theory is pure truth, its practice is the realisation of consummate justice raised to the supernatural order.

2101. *Justice* in this fuller sense, therefore, reconciles and perfects two opposite societies, domestic and civil, by influencing them and moderating their instincts. It does this in the following way:

    1. The theoretical and practical principle of all justice exists

in humanity. It was placed there by Christianity, which alone possesses the *theoretical principle* in the truth it teaches, and the *practical principle* in the grace with which it strengthens the will. — First stage.

2. The theoretical and practical principle of justice is applied to the two societies, domestic and civil, which it must perfect. From it are deduced the special laws of these societies, and the solution to their complex, difficult juridical cases. Centuries of effort are needed to deduce consequences and to struggle against error introduced with brute force, and sometimes under the guise of positive law. Error disturbs the great work of minds, and at certain times seems actually to pervert that work. — Second stage.

3. Finally, when the special laws of domestic and civil society have been deduced from the principle of justice, the third and most important step must be taken. The laws must become part of the people, put into every mind and imprinted on every persuasion. Only when everybody knows them and is persuaded of them, do they acquire a new light, an unexpected power and public observance, which no individual force or evil mind can oppose. — Third stage.

2102. When does *justice* really begin to show itself as a prevalent force in human affairs? At the third stage, when everybody begins to think in harmony with it, that is, when there is UNIFORMITY OF NATIONAL THOUGHT ABOUT THE LAWS OF SOCIAL JUSTICE. This is the irresistible force that enthrones justice. How magnificent it would be to have a people fully instructed about just, social maxims, completely uniform in its judgments about the prescriptions of both domestic and civil society. In its majesty and security, such a people would be a king, a lion at rest.

2103. Uniformity of thought in social justice has in fact already begun, and in some nations is well advanced (Ireland, for example). These nations offer an image of great human dignity whose like we would not find in all history. That is why I confidently said, 'Today we have begun to locate the strength of the social force, the very substance of society, in full justice' — government today is with and through justice.

2104. In the midst of the atrocious experiences sustained by France, errors and prejudices fell from people's minds, passions grew weary and became exhausted. Parties were destroyed or weakened; sensist philosophy became dumb, wickedness ashamed. Hence the inexplicable need felt by civil society for progress towards its ideal. Under this pretext it struck out at itself; it disencumbered and freed itself from many unfortunate elements in which it had lain confused and oppressed. The good seed, having escaped the hands of wickedness that held it prisoner, slowly developed. The people even began to agree to a few maxims of social justice. Such is the present strength of France and the cause of the peace we have enjoyed for thirty years.

Here, I must quote a few passages (if only they were more than passages!) from the speech given recently by Lamartine at the banquet of Mâcon (1843):

> The revolution of '89 produced among us commonality of political beliefs and ideas. Indeed, it is clear to any thinking person that in the midst of these apparent differences, of these various shades of seemingly contrary opinions, there was basically the same thought, a common political faith. Our present concern is simply to rid this political faith of the few prejudices which still darken it, and to make it shine irresistibly in all minds, binding them together in one, unanimous, all-powerful teaching.

Such was the beginning of the uniformity of thought about political justice; it was also, in that nation, the beginning of conscience, as the above words demonstrate.

2105. If however social justice is to become national opinion, and its maxims are to enter uniformly into every mind in the nation, a great deal of open, free discussion is needed. Without this, the individuals who compose a nation cannot understand each other. To accomplish it, they need to share their feelings continuously over a period of time and engage in earnest debate. Errors must be eradicated from people's minds and, when fully revealed, be completely refuted in all these forms. The imperfect ideas of individuals must be perfected by encounter with the ideas of all. The exchange of ideas must lead individuals to distinguish between the view which is accepted by all and receives immense authority from the support of all, and the view which is merely individual and easily abandoned as soon as those who hold it see they are alone in holding it. Finally

[2105]

continual dialogue must convince individuals that they already agree in many things without knowing it; the difference lies only in expressions and forms — deep down, thought is the same, so that frequently the only thing required for agreement is a common, uniform mode of speech. Human beings soon find a common mode of speech if they realise that this is the sole cause of division among them, particularly if dialogue urges everybody to learn everyone's mode of speech, which then becomes the same language for all.

2106. The harm done at certain times in political matters by *freedom of the press* is all too well known. But it cannot be denied that nations, once they have reached the third stage described above, rightly or wrongly demand freedom of the press because they feel the need to form a common, popular, national opinion about the principal maxims of social justice,.

In this case it is no longer a matter of knowing 'whether censorship prevents many evils' but 'whether censorship is possible', or even, 'whether the harm it averts is greater or less than the harm resulting from its suppression'.[257]

Napoleon, on his return from Elba, made the following declaration which was stimulated by the very force of events, not by some theory, and still less by any inclination to do so:

> I wanted to rule the world. To obtain this I needed a power, an authority free of all restrictions.[258] Perhaps a constitution will be better for governing France alone... Think what you want and do what is possible. Make your thoughts known to me. Do you want free elections, public discussions, ministers who stand surety for their acts? In a word, do you want freedom? I also want all this... Above

[257] It is purely a question of prudence, as was pointed out not long ago by one of those outstanding people who for the defence of the Church resisted napoleonic despotism. The immortal Cardinal Pacca wrote: 'Prudence requires toleration of this freedom as the lesser evil' (*Saggio sull'indifferenza*, etc.).

[258] Why did he want so much? For the good of the world. But this is madness; the good of the world is JUSTICE; it is contained in these four words: TO EACH HIS OWN. Napoleon believed in the system of the *utilitarians*, offspring of the sensist philosophy which under the name of *ideology* the great man hated. This system ruined his empire and himself because it rests on feet of clay.

[2106]

all, I am convinced that it would be absurd to forbid and strangle the freedom of the press.

Napoleon is aware that the nation he is addressing has reached the third stage. All his victories and glory could not make the nation return to the second or first stage. He declares his conviction that he must change the system. Necessity solves the most difficult social problems.

Article 6.
Harm caused by freedom of the press;
just ways of avoiding it

2107. We would really have to lack common sense to be ignorant of the immense harm produced by freedom of the press in political matters.

We must note however that freedom of the press in political matters, desired by the people, becomes less harmful in nations that have reached the third stage where the laws of social justice are sufficiently developed and need only be diffused. Public need for this freedom increases and harm from it diminishes in proportion to the degree that the power of public opinion favours justice. Freedom of the press is fatal for those whose opinions on questions of social justice are formed day by day solely by biased authors. The harm that prejudiced authors can do is in inverse proportion to the immense power of public opinion for good. Authors must respect this power and, kept in check by prevailing opinion, be guided along the right way. If they abandon it, the most severe, terrible *censorship* awaits them.

2108. But, as we said, the level of public opinion for good varies in relationship to the number of people in agreement, and the number of moral and jural maxims they accept. In fact, no people has reached such a stage of agreement that they are unharmed by freedom of the press. Indeed, every people feels the need to apply some restriction to the press and some co-active law to prevent abuses. The problem lies in finding the most just and equable ways to do this satisfactorily, considering the circumstances of different peoples.

2109. The ways proposed so far have been *prevention* and *repression*. The former always causes grave difficulties when applied by nations which have reached the third stage of opinion about social justice and are in the process of forming a common opinion about socio-jural principles. This kind of opinion has already begun to emerge in England, the United States, France, etc.

2110. It is not our business here to investigate whether prevention is possible, suitable or useful among these nations; this is a question for Political Science rather than Right. The little we have said is sufficient. However we cannot overlook the question of the justice of prevention; no author of socio-rational Right can remain silent on such an important jural point. Publicists have probably never treated the matter under this aspect. I simply want to offer to my readers' discernment a few thoughts which, like everything I write, are motivated by a spirit of reconciliation, equity and peace. Reconciliation and peace, I am sure, spring spontaneously from the depths of what is just.

2111. Prevention as a method of avoiding many abuses of the press consists in submitting authors, publishers, printers or editors to certain formalities prior to the publication of their works, for example, to an examination of their work, presentation of manuscripts in a certain form, delay in publication, etc.

2112. Granted that these formalities and modalities are carefully carried out and guided solely by wisdom, truth and honesty, they can undoubtedly prevent abuse by the press and defend society from the influence of harmful authors. I do not wish to investigate the degree of difficulty required to obtain this, or whether it is in fact possible. These are important questions but outside my purpose. I take for granted that the laws and officials responsible for applying these modalities are not defective. I limit my investigation to this question: 'Does civil society have the right to defend itself in this way from its adversaries?'

2113. First, I note the following: 1. if the modalities intended to prevent abuse by the press do not harm those subject to them; and 2. if the written material is such that the author or publisher is not worried about delay in publication, no one can complain when civil society obviously exercises a right proper to it by imposing modalities in self-defence. We have seen that not only civil society but private individuals can mutually impose modalities on the exercise of others' rights when such modalities do not diminish the value of the rights, that is, of the real good obtained by their exercise. One of the principal rules of moderation governing the exercise of a right is: 'Everyone must so exercise their right that it imposes the least possible limit to others in the exercise of their rights' (*RI*, 958).

2114. Moreover, these modalities often cause only slight inconvenience. In times of peace, for example, academic and scientific questions, and purely literary works unconcerned with important social issues, are normally published for pleasure, to impart harmless instruction or communicate scientific information to the world of culture. Even important questions about humanity itself are discussed abstractly without reference to the passions of the day. Publications could in fact be brought forward slightly or postponed without adverse consequences to publishers, authors or anyone else.

2115. On the other hand, writers and publishers may voluntarily submit their works to examination and delay in publication either because 1. this is the custom, or 2. everyone, including authors, feels the need for special, exceptional precautions in the absence of informed public opinion, or 3. writers themselves, having a love of public good in common with the government, are ready to make some particularly virtuous sacrifice of their own freedom without being obliged to this by strict, jural necessity. This is no dream. It has happened often and in many places, and does honour to peaceful people who, willingly united with their government, are prepared to make sacrifices in their constant movement towards public good. Lack of jural resentment in the face of censorship certainly gives government the right to profit by it and shows that the time is ripe for censorship.

2116. However, this does not entirely settle the question.

It is certainly not true that what is just in one place and time is just always and everywhere. We too often err in laying down universal rather than particular propositions when truth is found only in the latter, and in wanting to find abstract justice where we should be applying it to circumstances.

Let us suppose that: 1. circumstances are different from those described above, and the present question is raised in a nation which has formed a great commonality of thought regarding the mean principles of social Right and Morality; 2. literature is obliged to be the organ for perfecting this great public opinion; 3. the press, because of its deep involvement in all private and public interests, exerts a great influence on the happiness or unhappiness of many people; 4. in this nation, culture is widespread, intelligence active, everything expeditiously executed, and constant discussion is a natural and habitual need; 5. it is a nation where there is always a danger of one party taking exclusive possession of the press as a very powerful weapon for subjugating other parties whose voice they wish to silence, or rather, a party taking possession of censorship in order to silence truth and justice and overthrow emerging upright opinion. We are, in short, talking precisely about France as it was at a particular time. Moreover, in this nation, even good people and the most fervent friends of truth and holy religion have the greatest interest in freedom of the press. Because all can read and write, the circulation of written matter is extremely large, and the rapidity of its propagation has become an important means for obtaining the desired effect, on which all parties rely. In such a nation what will be the best solution to our question?

The least delay in the publication of material, the rise in costs and the increase in inconvenience cause real harm to those who are interested in the publication of written matter. The cause of truth, justice and religion (and religion has no other appeal than public opinion) is endangered. Can civil society inflict this harm on individuals under the pretext of the public good; can it arbitrarily prevent any appeal to universal justice?

According to the principles I have proposed, we must first decide whether perverse literature has increased and become pernicious to such an extent that we can reasonably fear it will replace society with anarchy, and whether any other means exists for avoiding such a danger. There is no doubt that society can defend itself with preventive law against abuse of the press. This is a political matter, and affects the interests not simply of the majority, but of all, even of those who suffer partial damage from such prevention. As we said, harm done by civil society to individuals is abundantly compensated by the benefit they receive. In this case, we presume first of all that government, acting in the name of society, is truthful and limits itself to preventing social anarchy.

2117. If, on the other hand, the danger of subversion of public order is remote or can be avoided by other means, censorship and all other preventive ordinances are intended either 1. to remove the evil feared for people who become victims of perverse literature, or 2. to prevent defamation and calumny to decent persons who are the target of malice. But here the good of only a few, not of all, is involved and, as we have seen, some cannot be made to suffer harm for the good of others.

2118. However, there is certainly some defence against the guilty, provided that the necessary ordinance is laid down only for them. The defect inherent in *preventing* abuses of the press lies precisely here: although people must be considered innocent until proved guilty, authors and publishers are harmed by preventive ordinances — in the circumstances we have described — before they are proved guilty, despite the fact that the ordinance is intended to examine their possible guilt. It may be objected that prevention *is not considered* a punishment but a caution, and that the delay it produces in publication together with all the inconvenience it causes is only an accidental consequence not intended by the legislator. But we have already shown that right is offended equally by direct and indirect acts, and that justice is always violated when harm is caused to another either directly or in consequence of our action (*RI*, 1700–1703, 1898–1900). Innocent and guilty are certainly harmed by prevention, not because this is intended to inflict harm or punishment, but because, in the circumstances, it actually does so, even contrary to the intention of its user.

2119. This would not be the case if prevention, instead of being general, were reserved solely for those already proved guilty. I have established that we can defend ourselves against probable injuries, even with harm to those who cause them, provided they are first known to be guilty. A person who has once been guilty gives others the right to fear him as a result of his guilt. If prevention were reserved solely for those already convicted and punished juridically for composing and diffusing perverse material it would contain no injustice. The harm suffered would be imputable solely to the perpetrators (*RI*, 1832–1838).

[2117–2119]

2120. *Repression*, however, knows no exceptions and is always a sacred right of society. It is the *right of defence* which society has for itself and its members against present injury; it is also the *right of compensation*. Through the right of defence, civil society can punish guilty literature with all the severity necessary to distance people from this crime because the degree of defence, as we have seen, extends as far as necessary for repelling harm. Through the right of compensation, society can establish punishment for the guilty that compensates both itself for the reasonably calculated harm it has suffered, and private citizens for their damaged reputation.[259]

Article 7.
Conclusion, concerning the SUBSTANTIAL POWER now being formed and destined to lead civil societies to their ideal

2121. We can now draw some conclusions from what has been said.

If societies were composed not of fallible human beings but of angels confirmed in grace, they would not need material force to make justice and virtue prevail. But because this is not the case (indeed, human beings bear within themselves a seed of infinite wickedness), civil society cannot survive unless the *judgments* of its tribunals and of its just *laws* are sanctioned by force.

This force however can be entrusted only to imperfect human beings, who are constantly tempted to abuse it in contradiction

---

[259] What we say about civil society cannot be applied to ecclesial society. The first purpose of civil society is defence of the rights of all individuals; no one may be sacrificed to it. On the other hand, the purpose of ecclesial society is to build up the kingdom of God, to increase on earth virtue and happiness, the supreme good of the human soul. Because this society directs all human beings to this supreme spiritual purpose, it can oblige them not only to justice but to mutual charity, to dedicating themselves, their goods and rights to a single end. All this is required by the greatest spiritual good and growth of the divine kingdom on earth; it can subject human beings to all those prescriptions that help the good of the Church, among which is prevention against abuses of the press.

of the justice they should defend. It is precisely here, as we have said, that the heart of the great social problem lies.[260]

We also investigated whether this great problem could be solved by one of the two political systems put forward by eminent statesmen, *social antagonism* and *absolutism*, but found both equally ineffective for solving this very complex difficulty.[261] We asked therefore whether the problem of social organisation were insoluble and whether we had to despair of ever being able to unite material force with the cause of justice in such a way that force could never serve any other cause. After examining all possible expedients, we had to conclude: 'The only solid foundation for the health of civil society is the probity and moral virtue in the individuals who compose it.' From this we deduced the consequence that the greatest and most beneficent aim of society is 'to plant early in the spirit of those who compose it, the knowledge, esteem and love of truth, justice and religion.'[262]

2122. This doctrine, propounded in *Society and its Purpose*, is further developed and perfected in this chapter.

My intention has been to show how in modern civil societies, granted the secret influence of Christianity, a *moral force* superior to every *material force* is slowly being produced and formed; a pure, incorruptible power destined by the eternal author of the human race to direct, dominate and save all other forces. This supreme power is 'the uniformity of thought of the masses concerning the principles of social justice and the special consequences of these principles.'

This is the ballast whose great weight must safeguard the social vessel and prevent it from capsizing. It is a wonderful invention of Providence, not of human beings. It is a new force, greater than steam, condensed air and magnetism, which will safely guide the great ship to the port for which it is heading despite all storms and hurricanes.

---

260 Cf. *SP*, 111–131.
261 *Ibid.*, 265–282.
262 *Ibid.*

[2122]

CHAPTER 5

How civil society gradually regulates modality of rights
ever more extensively

Article 1.
Epilogue. — The first step forward in civil society: it limits
itself to regulating modality of rights

2123. We need to recall what has been said, note where we are,
and see what remains to be done.

First of all, we saw the kind of stimuli or needs that moved
fathers of families to form civil society. These needs develop,
and their growth keeps pace with the development of the intellective and moral faculties of those who associate. This development and growth urges the fathers to perfect their civil
association by changing it from temporary, unstable association,
weakened through division and dispersion of energy, to strong,
stable and perpetual association through unity of power; the
fathers move from an association deficient in some organs to the
kind of association that possesses all its organs, limbs and civil
powers.

2124. We then considered the contrasting instincts of *domestic*
and *civil society*. We described the long, terrible but providential
struggle, past and present, that civil society had to sustain
against domestic society, and vice versa. We showed that without the mediation of *perfect theocratic society* this hostility
becomes fatal. Both societies, shaken and laid low by continual
vice, finally perish: the conquered through external violence, the
conqueror, now alone, through internal corruption.

We observed how the conciliation of family and civil elements
could not be achieved through fusion; they did not want to live
as one and lose their individuality. Conciliation could be
achieved only by reasonably tempering family instinct with civil
instinct so that, instead of wanting to rule blindly, both instincts
might accept the restraint of reason, of justice divinised by the
Gospel.[263] These two wild instincts, now tamed, agreed to

263 This discussion of *family* and *civil instincts* is very similar to the

respect and even help each other. Family and civil society lived together — the leopard lay down with the lamb, as a prophetic expression has it. The two societies do not fuse but preserve their individuality; although opposite in character, they harmonise and mutually help and perfect each other.

Nevertheless, despite this precious principle of harmonious co-existence and alliance, war does not cease instantly. The blind instincts of the two societies often shatter the peace treaty; every time one usurps something from the other, revenge is sought. But war does not endure because the principal mediator and guarantor of their individual existence is imperishable Christianity. Thus, after war, both societies are wiser and more perfect than before, more distinct in mutual relationships which have been determined with clarity and greater precision.

2125. Finally, we saw that one of the conditions by which civil society attains its ideal is awareness of its limits so that all danger of its entering the sphere of family society ceases. These limits must be determined by the object of civil society, that is, regulation of the modality of its members' rights. Hence the first law constituting the ideal of civil society is, according to us: 'civil society must abstain from disposing of the value of rights, and limit itself to regulation of their modality'. This was precisely the purpose of the final struggles we described, that is, 'the constitution of an independent civil society which does nothing more than regulate modality of rights.'

Article 2.
Second step forward of civil society: government is extended to the whole sphere of the modality of rights

2126. The step just described can be reduced to the following: 'Civil society, having separated from domestic society, subsists of itself with its own organisation. At the same time, it accepts

discussion we had elsewhere on *instinct of ownership*. We showed that *ownership as instinct* is raised to the dignity of right only when it is tempered by *moral reason* which commands it not to harm the same instinct present in others (*RI*, 921–959).

[2125–2126]

the equally independent subsistence of domestic society in harmony and friendship with itself.' This mutual recognition of and respect for each other's jural existence helps both by moderating respect for each other's rights. In other words, civil society is limited by this step to regulating the modality of rights. Having grown strong in this legitimate office, the exercise of its responsibility can no longer be torn from it by tyrannical domestic society.

2127. We must now move on to the next step, taken by civil society when exercising its proper office.

The phrase, 'modality of rights', which is the object of the office, applies to an infinite number of things. But in the beginning civil government does not see the breadth of this application, and limits itself (it cannot do otherwise) to regulating that part of the modality which it sees.

As we said, *civil society* is a particular society when first instituted, but later grows and gradually becomes universal (*RI*, 739–743).

2128. This growth is certainly due to the increase of stimuli and needs. As nations become more civilised, social governments become more aware of the necessity to add new, special and particular regulations to the modality of rights. Previously, this measure was not required.

At first it seems that civil society changes its end at different stages, and even changes into another society. In fact it is only extending its interests in service of the end itself, which is the regulation of the *modality* of rights. When Louis Haller recently maintained that States do not have a common end but only a complex of ends with greatly differing particular views, he was aware that governments act differently in different periods and social conditions, that is, they apply themselves to obtain certain partial aims which previously did not stimulate their attention. However, he was unable to make a generalisation which would gather all these ends into the one general end which determines exactly the essence of civil association. We have called this general end the regulation of the modality of rights.

We must discuss more carefully this second step towards the *ideal of society*, an ideal presupposing a society whose concept includes regulation, *according to needs*, of *the whole sphere* of the modality of rights.

[2127–2128]

Article 3.
Description of the sphere of complete regulation of
modality of rights

2129. When many persons with rights enter into a relationship, particularly when they live on the same land, the following
can happen:
1. One person maliciously attempts to invade the rights of
another.
2. One person believes he is exercising his rights innocently
but in fact is harming others; consequently disputes arise.
3. Many persons exercise their rights independently of each
other without exceeding the sphere of the rights. They impose
on themselves a mutual limitation greater than that which
would result from a harmonious agreement between them
about ways of exercising their rights, an exercise which would
give everyone greater freedom and obtain the greatest benefit.
For example, if owners of different neighbouring lands which
have no defined roadways agree to define them, they avoid
common harm by refusing arbitrary passage to owners or
workers with their carts, cattle and implements.
4. Many persons can obtain much more benefit by uniting
their forces and ownership to exercise certain rights in common
than they can by individually using their forces and ownership.
For example, if many unite to provide the wheat necessary for
their families, they will obtain better terms through the greater
quantity of goods they buy. If they agree to pay for a school-
master, they obtain for their children instruction which they
could not have if each family had to pay for a teacher of its own,
etc.
2130. The four parts of what we call the regulation of the
modality of rights are therefore: 1. to defend one's rights; 2. settle
disputes; 3 modify the exercise of the rights of individuals either
to prevent the harm threatened without such modification, or
4. to obtain a benefit which would be impossible if everyone
exercised their rights without regard for the rights of others.
2131. The phrase, 'modality of rights', which I use in opposition to *right, value* or *good of right*, is defined precisely as
'everything that can be done with or about a right without

[2129–2131]

diminishing the *good* contained in it; this good must pertain inviolably to the subject or owner of the right and either remain equal or be increased.'

Using this definition as guide we can determine the immense sphere of responsibility encompassed by complete, fully developed, civil society as we have ideally conceived it; in other words, encompassed by that society which we have defined as 'the supreme regulator of the modality of all the rights of its members'.

2132. The definition indicates that the responsibility of civil societies entails the exercise of four major functions:

1. Protection of all the rights of the members and of the free exercise of their rights.

2. Judgment and settlement of disputes.

3. Regulation of the exercise of rights so that every individual's or lesser society's use of their own rights will, without prejudice to them, leave others maximum freedom to exercise their own rights.

4. Amalgamation of private rights, when this is required to avoid a common evil or to obtain a common good.

A word about each of these four *general functions* of civil government will not be out of place.

§1. *First function of civil government: protection of all the rights of the members and of the free exercise of their rights*

2133. The protection of all the rights of the members and of their free exercise is obtained from civil society by two dynamics:

First dynamic: defence of the members and their rights against culpable attack from individual or collective persons, foreign to the society, — wars, diplomacy, etc.

Second dynamic: defence of the members and their rights against culpable attack by other members.

2134. Both these *dynamics* can be activated by civil society in various ways, by exercising:

a) The *right of prevention* in favour of the subjects. In the

City, this is normally done through ordinances concerning policing.

b) The *right of defence* in favour of the members. In the
City, the *right to punish*, preceded by *criminal judgments*, re-
lates to this right.

c) The *right to compensation* in favour of the members. In
the City, this is preceded either by *criminal* or *civil judgments*.

2135. Although the *protection of all rights* can be exercised in
part by authority, good-standing, eloquence and other indirect
ways, it can never be deprived of the support of *material force*.
For this reason, society, as we said, must be *strong*; it must have
at its disposition a force sufficient to repress the perverse, and
banish fear in the good.

One of the principal advantages obtainable by families from
their entry into civil association is the possibility of living without fear of each other. This makes possible mutual benevolence,
as well as trust, which replaces the fear which formerly divided
them. It is true that this *fear*, which formerly made families
mistrust each other, is now directed against the government,
which has force at its disposal, and thus places a very harmful
kind of division between citizens and government. But the fear
ceases when government gives citizens sufficient guarantees
against the abuse of its force, a provision called for by sound
politics. The greatest of these guarantees is the formation of an
upright, powerful public opinion which dominates material
force itself and against which nothing can be attempted with
hope of success.

2136. We must however clarify the steps taken by civil society
as it gradually embraces each of the four functions mentioned
above. *Protection of rights* (and properly speaking, of *their
defence*) is the first function to draw the attention of citizens and
governments because it is the most necessary (defence). It is so
necessary that it alone has the power to encourage families to
unite. Other civil functions, not so necessary as to call for the
institution of society, are useful accessories to already instituted
society.

This explains why so many publicists posited the end of civil
society solely in the *defence* of rights without adding other
functions. For this reason, it seems strange that the national

assembly of 1789 limited the end of civil association to the preservation of rights.[264]

2137. But although no civil association exists which does not propose at least the preservation and defence of rights, there is some development in this very first civil responsibility, precisely because the *right of defence* extends in step with the development of the human race (*RI*, 1901–1907), and because the social means of defence become more perfect.

2138. We must note again that, although those whom we have called *relative citizens* (children of families, and wives), are not *per se* charged with the common defence, they do have the *right of passive*, not *active defence*.

2139. Finally, we must also note that the protection of all rights necessarily includes the protection of all those societies that differ from civil society, and to which individuals have a right (*USR*, 426–445).

§2. Second function of civil government: deciding and settling disputes

2140. Civil society's first task is to defend associated families against the material force of external enemies, and to defend individual families against the material force of other families.

When the prevalent force in civil society prevents families from using violence against each other by blocking the use of force by private persons, individuals have time and ease to put their case peacefully. Civil society stands between them as mediator either *to judge* which individual is right, or *to arrange* an equable agreement in disputes where conclusions are so doubtful or shared that certainty is unobtainable (which is fairly common). In this case the parties have the right and obligation to come to some agreement (*RI*, 465, 1026).

Hence, this function of civil society is twofold; it has two *dynamics* because, in order to settle disputes peacefully between families, it must at different times exercise:

a) judgments about decisions;

---

[264] 'The end of every association is the preservation of the natural and imprescriptible rights of man' (*Déclaration des droits de l'homme et du citoyen*).

b) judgments about transactions.

2141. But all this must be done without invading the right that fathers of families have to reach agreement among themselves (*RF*, 1552–1553). Generally speaking therefore civil society must not intervene officially in family disputes, but limit itself to 1. preventing recourse to force by its members; 2. accepting calls for help from petitioners, or appeals from private arrangements and arbitrations which it either rectifies or executes, if they are just and equable; 3. putting an end to private disputes which involve hatred and which, if not brought before a tribunal in civil society, would go on for too long with harm to families, and more importantly, with harm to civil association itself.[265]

§3. *Third function of civil government: to regulate the exercise of private rights in such a way that they pose the least possible hindrance to others' freedom*

2142. This function implies the following social *dynamics*:

First dynamic: to remove everything that impedes free concurrence for all goods that can be objects of right, which I have already listed (*RI*, 1973), such as privileges, customs, prejudices, etc., contrary to free concurrence.

Second dynamic: to provide that, when a person exercises his rights, his actions impose the least possible limitation to others' *inoffensive freedom*. This determines the ways in which each person can exercise his right.

Third dynamic: to change the form of individual rights, while preserving for the possessor all the good they contain. This is done to obtain a common benefit without harm to anyone; it determines the forms most useful to everyone in which rights must be vested.

2143. The benefit which is the object of the *third dynamic* can be *public* or *private*. Private good, however, must not be procured through a form of privilege so that it is restricted to certain persons or particular classes to the exclusion of others. It must

[265] The institution of private judges is not therefore a usurpation of a right of civil society. If however private individuals begin to sanction such judgments with *external force*, both responsibility and right exclusively proper to the City would be usurped.

be open to all citizens, granted they are in similar circumstances from which they cannot be excluded by any arbitrary governmental act.

2144. For example: fathers of families, or whoever takes their place, could agree to establish the following law: 'Whenever the purchase of part of a neighbour's farm or house is necessary or very helpful to a farmer or house-owner for regularising his own farm or home, adapting it for various uses, or greatly improving it, and whenever his neighbour obviously has little or no interest in maintaining the property in question, the neighbour will be obliged to sell it to the farmer or house-owner for a just and equable price.' Such a law changes the form but not the value of private rights. In fact, I think a time will come when laws of expropriation for a private good will be made, just as laws of expropriation for a public good have already been passed.

2145. This third function of civil society comes to light or develops later than the first two. Even when civil society finally understands that it is called to exercise it, it needs to make still more progress before it discovers the many extra, new, complicated and delicate ways in which it is called to exercise the function.

§4. Fourth function: to amalgamate private rights when a common evil has to be avoided, or an opportunity arises to procure a common good

2146. The end of civil society can also be promoted by placing some rights in common. This *amalgamation of rights* would seem basically to be the same as a change in the form of rights, the third force of the previous function, because rights can be associated only if their owners suffer no harm or are compensated for all losses either by the avoidance of a greater evil or by the acquisition of a greater good. The third function however is concerned with change in the form of *single rights* without amalgamation, while our present function concerns the placing of rights in common, in society.

2147. This fourth function divides into the following *dynamics*:

First dynamic: organisation of the government of society, that is, the power to establish, and nominate to, all military and civil offices.

Second dynamic: administration of the common goods of the State

Third dynamic: imposition of taxes which, with the common goods of the State, are sufficient to maintain and conduct social government. This is the first use of *common goods* — necessary expenditure for government.

Fourth dynamic: undertaking those enterprises of *public* good which cannot be assumed by individuals or particular societies. If the enterprise procures a good that is not only *public* but truly *common* (that is, for all), civil society can assume it even in concurrence with private individuals or private societies, when it believes it can achieve a greater common good. This is the second use of *common goods* — useful *enterprises*.

Fifth dynamic: stimulation of moral-intellective-industrial progress by means of rewards for free concurrence: the third use of *common goods* — rewards for benefactors of public good.

2148. Civil societies that have existed for a very long time exercise all these five dynamics or divisions of the regulation of the modality of rights. Each division is an immense field for civil progress, by means of which society comes to manage and exercise its energies with increased 1. suitable extension; 2. distributive justice; 3. ease (overcoming obstacles and avoiding distress for the citizens), and 4. effective aid.

2149. These four qualities, which must be present in the exercise of the fourth function, and of the other functions as well, are duties of *active civil society*.

2150. Supreme civil power, autocracy, has the responsibility to see that its representatives and all who are working for it do not fail in these duties (*ius supremae inspectionis* [right of overall inspection]).

It will be helpful if I add a few observations about each of the five dynamics mentioned above.

A.

First dynamic: organising the government of society

2151. Those who exercise autocracy must organise social

government in such a way that a society realises its ideal, according to their vision of the ideal.

2152. It is clear that *autocracy*, if it is to attain this end, has the right to establish organs and social responsibilities, to nominate to these, and to choose means it considers best. To do this it can establish a set of means, procedures and subordinate powers with which to determine all responsibilities and nominate the people most suitable for them.

2153. Note that in the matter of establishing responsibilities, which are real burdens despite their benefits, they must, like burdens and benefits, be shared out according to the most strict distributive justice. This is a jural obligation of autocracy. Let me take *military service* as an example.

2154. Conscription, introduced by the emperor Napoleon, is certainly a very burdensome law for citizens. Not content to govern the society over which he presided, Napoleon aspired to conquer the world and used this law improperly. However, conscription in itself was, apart from popular prejudices, a huge step taken in these times by civil-distributive justice. I personally consider it the richest legacy and greatest benefit left us by that great commander-in-chief. If every social good is due to distributive justice, we should not be surprised to find the present power of European nations attributed chiefly to the law of conscription. Thanks principally to this law, they have acquired an insuperable domination over the other larger continents of the earth. Among themselves their dynastic struggles and outbursts of pique have been replaced by a dignified respect which assures peace. Such are the effects of an outstanding law, the kind of good that follows every step taken by society towards *distributive justice*.[266]

2155 Generally speaking, social *autocracy* has the right and

---

[266] It could be asked: 'According to rational Right, must citizens contribute to the army in proportion to their social contribution?' The answer, it seems, must be 'Yes'. How then is the burden of conscription distributed equably? I reply: in civil society, every material effort and danger can be calculated in money. A soldier's value can be given in terms of money. Granted the law of conscription, therefore, families who are not involved ought to contribute financially to compensate other families who, in addition to their contribution to society, send their sons into the army.

responsibility to establish the form of government and determine the civil constitution.[267]

B.
Second dynamic: administering the goods of society

2156. Civil society can own (*USR*, 446–449), like all other societies that do not renounce this right. But it can own only by the same titles as an individual person, and with the same limits (*RI*, 1663–1665). Its sole means therefore for preventing occupancy of unoccupied things is not an arbitrary decree but pre-occupancy or some necessary measure for defence.[268]

2157. The kinds of good that civil society enjoys are distinguished into two classes:

1. *Every good common* to every individual (*res communes vel publicae*), such as air, light, roads, rivers, sea with certain limits, etc. Government is responsible for the defence of these goods, for keeping them common to all and in good condition, and for improving them.

2. *Every good of the social body* (*patrimonium reipublicae*). These must be administered by the government with just economy, and their product applied to cover expenses *necessary* for the good of government and for the proportional benefit of member families.

C.
Third dynamic: the imposition of taxes or social contribution

2158. From the moment fathers are united in civil society, they have accepted the obligation of contributing to the necessary expenses of the society in proportion to their possessions and to

---

[267] Note carefully that *autocracy* is not, in my opinion, a form of government but the radical power, or *merely-social* or *invested* power (*USR*, 312–313), which gives rise to different forms of government. *Autocracy* is present in every form of government because the first and radical power, from which the form itself of government receives jural authority, has to be present somewhere in every form of government. For this reason Heeren's division of the forms of government into *despotism*, *autocracy* and *republic*, would seem to be very mistaken.

[268] Certain authors attribute to civil society the right to prevent foreigners occupying unoccupied land in the society's territory. In my opinion it can do this only if it occupies it in reality or by a just title of defence. Cf. *RI*, 514.

[2156–2158]

the help they receive from the society. Hence government, responsible for social administration, has the right to impose these taxes.

2159. Today the most learned publicists have more or less the same notions about the matter, relative to the general principles. Pietro Baroli says:

> If a civil society has public goods, their product is the first income of the State. If these goods are lacking or are insufficient, the citizens have the duty to supply from their private goods.
>
> Contributions must be calculated exactly according to expenses, which in turn must be calculated according to the real needs of the State. To require a contribution over and above this amount would be a culpable abuse of the right and an unjust despoliation [*App.*, no. 7].
>
> Similarly contributions are always proportionate to the goods possessed by the citizens.[269]

2160. The right to impose ordinary and extraordinary taxes pertains to the so-called *eminent domain_* which society has over the goods of every individual.[270]

But, as Samuel Coccejo excellently observes, we should reject the word 'domain' when dealing with society's right to use for its own end a part of the goods of private individuals.[271] The word contains the concept of arbitrary use which the person who has dominion (ownership) can make of his goods. Govern-

---

[269] *Diritto naturale pubblico interno*, §193.

[270] Some authors distinguish between the right to *impose taxes* and *eminent domain*. They say that by the former, society disposes of a part of the incomes of private individuals; by the latter, of the *substance* itself. This is a frivolous distinction. The citizen who pays taxes can calculate the amount on the income or substance of his goods, which does not change the nature of the right of the society imposing the taxes. The so-called *eminent domain* is the society's faculty to dispose of that part of the goods of individuals which is necessary for its end, whether this is a part of the income or of the substance itself of property. If 'tax' means an ordinary, regular contribution, it is in this case a special act of what is incorrectly called *eminent domain*.

[271] 'The voice of the master is not well used in commands' (H. Grot., bk. 3, c. 20, §7). Grotius also writes: 'Nor do they [government] have any right, other than that of rule, over their subjects' money,' and Coccejo comments: 'which consists in the right to defend, not destroy the subjects' goods' (*ibid.*, Grot., *loc. cit.*).

ment however is simply the collector and administrator of the common *contributions* for the end of society.

The principle gives rise to the following two limits of the right to collect taxes, which we have already mentioned:[272]

1. The contributions must not exceed the need of the social end.

2. They must be equably distributed in proportion to the citizens' abilities.

2161. Consequently (and this is admitted by publicists), if the governing society, in immediate need of means, has no time to distribute the portions according to ability to pay, it must remedy this misfortune as soon as possible.

2162. For example, the harm inflicted on the citizens by a government pursuing a just war must be distributed among the citizens as soon as possible, and restitution made for those who contributed in excess of their obligation, taking into calculation also the consequent harm.[273]

2163. Furthermore, modern societies are still very far from solving the difficult problem 'of the equable distribution of social responsibilities. They do not consider the distribution of responsibilities a *jural*, but a *political or economical problem*. We may well ask: 'Which distribution of social responsibilities helps a government most in its administration, or makes the responsibilities felt less by the majority of the citizens, or by the most powerful citizens, so that no one complains? Which distribution is more conducive to the production of wealth?' But before all these questions, we should ask another which is certainly more

---

[272] By 'tax' I understand whatever private *good* social government is required to use for the end of the society.

[273] Grotius teaches that 'the City is obliged to indemnify from the public purse the harm done to those who have lost their possessions. Both the public itself, and the person who has suffered harm should, if necessary, contribute. The City is not relieved of this responsibility if at a given moment it cannot pay the money. Whenever resources are at hand, a kind of dormant obligation awakes' (*De iure B. et P.*, bk. 3, c. 20, §7). Henry Coccejo explains: 'One citizen must not be more burdened than another, because all are equally obliged to defend the State. The extra burden imposed on a citizen must be paid back from the treasury or by public contribution' (*loc. cit.*). Nevertheless we must not confuse harm caused by enemies with that caused by the government through the necessity of war. The latter harm, not the former, should be distributed by social government.

[2161–2163]

humble, but much more profound, sacred and helpful to society: 'Which distribution of social responsibilities is more just?' Justice, poor neglected justice, is precisely what statesmen often disdain to face. They do not oppose it; they simply understand it differently, take it for granted and ignore it. It contains however the secret of the best way to govern and of all public prosperity, as the long history of the world already begins to reveal.

2164. Many nations prefer *indirect taxation*. The reason is clear: taxpayers are less aware of what they contribute; governments rely on people's ignorance to make them pay. Here, I must admit, the political problem fulfils one of its conditions, but the jural problem becomes more and more complex, even perhaps insoluble. It is probably impossible to regulate indirect taxation in such a way that it is ultimately distributed according to the norm of distributive justice, that is, according to the citizens' abilities. A people, well instructed about its interests, would not want greater indirect taxation, because it would at least want to know whether taxation were equably distributed, which indirect taxation would never allow. On the other hand, the people would not refuse to contribute directly what they saw was necessary and obviously distributed according to strict justice.

2165. In Right we can and must ask: 'Does taxation have to be shared in proportion to the capital or income of the citizens?'

I am of the opinion that annual taxation must be inflicted on income. This is certainly more difficult, but we are not free to substitute one problem with another, simply because one is easier and the other more difficult. My opinion rests on the necessary presupposition that annual taxation is paid with a portion of income and not with capital.

The case of *forced loans* or other extraordinary taxation is different. These, it seems, would have to be paid from capital.

D.
Fourth dynamic: the undertaking of certain enterprises for the common good

2166. Civil society was not instituted to undertake some particular utility but, as we said, to regulate the modality of rights.

The protection and facilitation of all the enterprises of the citizens and of other societies are directed to this end.

2167. Hence civil government acts contrary to its mandate when it competes with its citizens or with the societies they form to procure some particular utility, and even more when it reserves to itself the monopoly of enterprises which it forbids to individuals or their societies.

2168. On the contrary, the more civil societies relinquish enterprises and leave them to private activity, which they must protect and encourage, the more closely they approach their ideal. We can safely assert that in this matter at least, greater progress in civilisation is made by a government that procures more public good through the spontaneous action of individuals and of the private societies it protects, and distances itself from leadership in such enterprises.

2169. Nevertheless civil society has the authority to undertake of itself the useful enterprises which could not in any way be successfully attempted by individuals or private societies. This is the only case where civil society can properly undertake such enterprises without exceeding the sphere of the modality of rights. In doing so, it is not removing or obstructing the freedom of individuals and the possibility of concurrence, that is, it is not depriving them of any valuable right. Citizens, who have instituted civil society as a necessity, not a superfluity, want government to do only what they themselves cannot do.

2170. A hope that individuals or private societies undertake certain useful enterprises, may be vain, not because the *nature* of the enterprises makes such undertaking impossible, but because individuals and private societies do not attain the level of ideas, ability and activity necessary for these enterprises. If this is true, civil society (the government) will take care to increase in the citizens the abilities they still lack. It can *provisionally* initiate some private enterprises, for example, provided they cede them as soon as individuals should themselves be ready to undertake them.

E.

Fifth dynamic: the stimulation of moral, intellectual and industrial progress by means of rewards for free concurrence

2171. This is a supremely civil duty. It unites the citizens better, and is universally profitable at the least cost, that is, the cost of the rewards.

2172. I note, relative to this duty, that a deplorable confusion of ideas and a manifest injustice would result if the rewards consisted in honours and privileges which facilitated the acquisition of social posts by those who had won them without becoming more suitable for them. For example, to offer a ministry of State as a reward to a person who had killed his enemy would expose the society to having a murderer as minister.

Article 4.
Conclusion

2173. The sphere of activity of civil government is large, but does not embrace all responsibilities at the initial stages of its institution; some responsibilities become known as the centuries pass. As civilisation develops, public opinion invites civil government to concern itself with ever new and greater things, but always within the sphere of the modality of rights.

Civil societies pursue the road of progress in regulating this modality by recognising the continually new demands it makes on them and the new responsibilities necessary for bringing such regulation to perfection. Necessity and public demand require more and more assistance and activity from governments.

2174. This progress has in some way an opposite effect to the kind described in the previous chapter, where we saw how progress of civil societies towards their ideal continually keeps their action within the sphere of modality. In this chapter, we have seen progress that continually extends their action from one object to another, from one responsibility to another, within the same sphere of modality of rights. This sphere is narrow for primitive societies, but immense for societies that have attained great perfection.

SECTION TWO

RIGHT IN ALREADY CONSTITUTED CIVIL SOCIETY

[INTRODUCTION]

2175. So far we have explained the concept of civil society (cf. 1564–1731) and its *Right* (cf. 1732–1741). We have also shown how the *concept*, conceived by the mind, could be *realised* factually among human beings, and we discussed the origin of such a society (cf. 1742–1895).

In order to know this origin without being misled by imagination, we had to look at history and see how civil society, at the very beginning of nations, established itself in different ways in different regions. After we had classified these ways, reduced them to their ultimate species, supplied where necessary what was lacking and perfected them by philosophical reflection, we drew from them the *theory of the origins of civil society*.

We saw that the concept, the model of civil society, was expressed factually at various stages. To determine the different levels at which civil society in its institution expresses its nature, we felt the need first of a better general concept of society. Then, by clothing this concept with its various conditions and bringing it into reality with its own special elements, we had to take it to the point where it expressed perfect civil society. We thus discovered the *archetype*, the ideal, of civil society (cf. 2064–2079).

We also had to note the historical steps by which society progressed to maturity, and indicate the stimuli which goaded human beings on in this work. In short, we had to deal with the *successive formation of the City*, that is, with its progress towards that perfect state in which, purified of every heterogeneous element, *it no longer assumes responsibilities not contained in its concept* but does assume every office present in that concept. For centuries, struggling against the obstacles it meets, the City follows these two ways of progress. And because it has not yet completed this task, we saw what remains to be done and will be done.

2176. All this pertains to philosophical Right in civil society as civil society *is in the process of being constituted*, not with the Right of *already constituted* civil society. In this last sense, the part of Right we have explained so far concerns individual Right, or rather that part which unites individual Right with social Right and concerns the acts of individuals when they wish to associate civilly.

2177. In any case, the theory of society has the nature of Right. In its jural concept, society is simply an aggregate of rights and obligations arising from acts of association (*USR*, 1–20).

2178. Under another aspect, Right which presides over *civil society in the process of being constituted* (discussed in the previous section) can certainly be considered a part of *civil-social Right*. Even after constitution, civil society needs to move forward. Hence, all the acts it does after its constitution, or are done for it by its government, influence either its better constitution or the preservation of the level of formation already obtained, or even its deterioration and destruction. These acts can become unjust simply by altering the nature of society instead of continually improving and completing it.

2179. Our task therefore is to explain the *Right of constituted civil society*. We say at once that such society must first do everything in keeping with its essence and natural constitution, as we have described them. This fruitful principle gives rise to that part of Right to which this Section is dedicated. I will divide the Section as follows.

2180. *Seigniorial Right* relative to civil-social right was dealt with sufficiently when we discussed the nature and formation of the City. We showed how seigniory can in reality be mingled with society.

The other two parts of civil-social Right, *communal* and *governmental* (*USR*, 145–153), are better not divided, I think, but treated together. We need to continually compare the proper rights of government with the common rights of citizens, and to consider their mutual help and mutual guarantee. Because our purpose is to express in the clearest light possible what is just, I think it better to consider first what is unjust, in the way that the dark areas of a painting make the light areas stand out. We can then come down to particular organs and limbs by which the civil body moves, noting their ramifications and upright, equable movement. Finally, after considering civil society *according to the bonds* that constitute it, and *the organs* of its action, we will investigate the relationship between *social-prudence* and *social justice*, and conclude: 'Granted the meticulous observance and fulfilment of the prescriptions of Right, the natural constitution and action of civil society is that which continually orders and adapts it according to the norms of prudence' (cf. 316–317, 346–366). In this way, the *Philosophy of civil-social Right* is joined with the *Philosophy of Politics*. Although these two disciplines must never be confused, a golden link unites them so tightly that the second begins where the first ends.

This section will therefore have three parts:

PART 1. Possible elements of injustice in
civil society

„   2. The organs of civil society

„   3. The *just* and *prudent* constitution
of civil society

PART ONE

POSSIBLE ELEMENTS OF INJUSTICE IN CIVIL SOCIETY CONSIDERED AS SUCH

2181. In individual Right we considered civil society as a *collective person*, jurally equal to *individual persons*, and we indicated the eleven kinds of injustice it can commit (cf. 1647–1688). My intention in this part is to discuss, as I said I would, those proper marks which distinguish it from every other jural person (cf. 1659). I begin by demonstrating clearly how civil society is a jural person equal to but distinct from every other person.

CHAPTER 1

Two equalities: JURAL and CONSTITUTIVE

2182. Civil society considered under the aspect of an already formed collective person, is simply a subject of rights and duties, equal to every other subject. I call this 'jural equality'.

But if, in addition to this general characteristic of jural person, we consider the special prerogatives of civil society, that is, the marks proper to it which distinguish it from every other jural person, civil society becomes *unequal* to all other jural persons. It therefore lacks the second kind of equality, which must not be confused with the first and can be called 'constitutive' or 'jural-constitutive equality'. Civil society is therefore a collective person which has *jural* but not *constitutive equality* with all other persons.

We said the same about the family, and the same can be said about every other person. Each has some equality and some inequality with all the others: equality in so far as it is a jural person, a subject of rights; inequality in so far as it is a person constituted in its own specific way.

2183. The importance of this distinction can be seen by

applying it to possible difficulties about rights. Let us see how the jurist sometimes considers one person as equal with others and sometimes in their constitutive inequality.

In the case of a right contested by two persons, the judge must consider them perfectly *equal*. He must simply weigh the reasons on both sides, ignoring everything whatsoever that distinguishes the two persons or is proper to them. The reason is clear: the judgment in this case concerns solely the relationship between the contested right and each person. All that they may have and possess through other titles does not enter into the judgment, which can be pronounced even if the judge knows the plaintiff and the accused only under false names.

On the other hand, if a right is not in dispute, but juridically decreed or held in peaceful possession, the problem concerns respect for the right. In this case both persons, the one who has the right and the one who has the duty to respect it, stand before the judge as unequal, because one possesses what the other does not. Any right whatsoever, held by a person, causes inequality in others because it causes duty in them. Right and duty are contrary relationships and therefore unequal, that is, they lack *constitutive equality*.

2184. Hence all doctrines concerning rights can be reduced to two simple formulas: the first considers persons as equal, the second as unequal. The first states: 'Attribute right to the person to whom it belongs, whoever the person may be, because all persons are considered equal.' The second states: 'Respect each person in proportion to the rights he possesses', or 'Respect all rights in every person.'

2185. Jural equality is the foundation of *commutative justice*; constitutive inequality, of *distributive justice*.[274]

---

[274] Leibniz, in his dissertation *De actorum publicorum usu*, which is the preface to the *Codice diplomatico*, etc. (§12), distinguishes three levels in natural Right: 1. *Strict Right*, which he makes consist in commutative justice; 2. *Equity*, which he makes consist in distributive justice; 3. *Piety* or *Probity*, which he posits in universal justice. He says, 'At the lowest level of right (for Leibniz, this lowest level of Right is commutative justice), human differences are not recognised apart from those arising from the matter in hand; and everybody is considered equal. At this higher level (that is, of distributive justice), merits are taken into account with the result that privileges, rewards and punishments are present. Furthermore, even the *distributive justice* of

2186. *Jural equality* requires civil society to recognise and respect others' rights just as it requires that its own rights be respected. *Constitutive inequality* attributes to civil society certain proper rights which must be respected in it.

2187. To attempt to destroy either *jural equality* or *constitutive inequality* is therefore a violation of right, because *constitutive inequality* is also jural, that is, authenticated by rational right.

CHAPTER 2

The four sources of injustices in the civil body

2188. I will not deal with the obligations of civil society considered as a jural person equal to all others. These have been discussed. Instead, I will briefly explain the injustices that violate those duties of the social body which arise from its constitutive inequality. The four sources of these injustices are:

2189. Civil *society*, *government*, the *form* of government, and *individual persons* connected with this form.

2190. These four matters, although distinct, are often confused because one cannot exist without the other: government determines civil society; form determines government; persons determine form. Persons activate the *form* of government; the form activates government, and government activates society.

2191. Hence, there are errors, injustices and evils proper to civil society. Some pertain directly to government, but not to society; others, properly speaking, are inherent in the form of government, but not in government itself. Finally some originate neither from society, nor government nor the form of government, but solely from persons in whom the governmental form resides and from whom it emanates.

2192. The injustices and evils of *society* come from ignorance of its purpose. For example, we may think that civil society can dispose of everything as it likes, and that everything must be

civil government is *rigorous justice*, at least when the autocracy of the fathers has passed into other hands' (cf. 2065).

sacrificed to it; we do not see clearly that civil society must limit itself to regulating the modality of rights without ever exceeding this limit, and that consequently it cannot dispose of the rights of individuals as such, etc. In this case we would have *tyranny by society*, no matter what government or form of government exists, and no matter who rules.

2193. The evils of *government* come from 1. ignorance of the full range of means available for fulfilling the purpose of civil society; 2. failure to recognise the jural equality between government and citizens, and 3. false opinions about government, etc. Hence, *tyranny* (and sometimes *indolence*) *by government*.

2194. The evils of the *form of government* arise 1. when the form is not the most suitable and prudent possible (*USR*, 346–466), according to circumstances; and 2. when erroneous, exclusive theories are held about which form is the best, declaring one form absolutely better than the others for all time and in every place. Hence, *impotence*, *uncertainty*, or even *tyranny by the form of government*.

2195. The evils due to *individual* persons who are part of the form of government arise from arbitrary decisions, abuse of power and the distribution of public offices to satisfy passions, caprice, pettiness and particular interests. Other injustices and evils arise from lack of protection against false theories concerning the nature of society, of government and of the form of government. And even when these three things are in good order, the collective or individual person exercising civil authority can be a tyrant, although in a more limited way. This is *tyranny* or *indolence* by persons.

2196. In civil matters therefore there can be three kinds of offended entities and four kinds of offenders. Those offended are individuals, the public and the commune; those who offend are society, government, the form of government and officials. Among the offenders, erroneous theories and occasions of injustices are found only among officials because they alone are complete entities; the other three are abstract entities. Although, in the last analysis, civil injustices can be committed only by individual persons, this does not invalidate the mental distinction of four sources of civil injustices. To apply the remedy to an evil the causes of the evil must be known.

[2193–2196]

CHAPTER 3

Injustices against real and ideal right by persons holding civil power

2197. In the case of persons, we must recall the distinction between *real* and pure or *ideal Right*.[275] The distinction yields two kinds of questions about persons who hold social office, that is, about *specific* or *individual and real persons*.

2198. Relative to *individual* persons we can ask, 'Do they make ideal Right real? If they do, there is no injustice; if not, there is injustice. The test must be based on real facts. These cases therefore do not pertain to the *theory* of right but form its practice and must be decided by competent, real judges.

2199. Relative to *specific* persons we can ask:

1. 'Have they been legitimately invested with the kind of power they have?' — The question concerns the existence of *titles* by which they assert their investiture with a social power.

2. 'Do they exercise this legitimate power without abuse?' — This question concerns the relationship between their acts and the concept of the special power they claim to have; the former must correspond exactly to the latter.

The theory of Right deals with both kinds of question.

CHAPTER 4

Injustices in the form of government

2200. The first question concerning specific persons ('Have they been legitimately invested with the kind of power they have?') presupposes another: 'Does this particular civil power exist in society?' If it does not, the first question cannot be asked.

Let us say the power concerns the *judiciary*. The first time a

[275] *ER*, 76.

tribune appears on the social scene, we must ask whether such a magistrature was legitimately introduced into society, or fashioned by someone without authority. This jural question concerns the form of government, and can be asked more generally: 'Is this form of civil power legitimate, that is, instituted by someone who can jurally institute it?'

The question concerns only the form of the power, and clearly prescinds from real persons who might be invested with that form. Consequently, it precedes the other question about individual or specific persons.

Although every question of social injustice can, as we said, be referred to those who commit the injustice, there are always two classes of questions about these persons:

First Class: Have individuals been illegitimately invested with a particular civil power because *titles* were lacking?

Second Class: Have they been illegitimately invested with the power because the power was not *legitimately instituted* in the society?

2201. The second class of questions can be resolved only by first settling the question, 'What authority can *legitimately* determine the form of government?'

2202. The reply is obvious: that authority which is the source of *government*. In other words, government, and the form of government with it, which is the distribution of governmental powers, comes from *autocracy*.

We described *autocracy* (*USR*, 311–312),[276] and explained its origin when discussing the origin of civil society (cf. 1792–1804). We also saw that it can be alienated (*USR*, 293). Autocracy is the basic power, the foundation of all social powers, their source, and the reason of their legitimacy.

---

[276] Autocracy can be divided into several powers, but not every particular power, although autocratic, can determine the form of government. The faculty to determine this form cannot be absent from the complex of all the powers that taken together form full, unlimited autocracy.

CHAPTER 5

Injustices in government

2203. Persons who usurp a social post can fulfil the office with complete justice. When this happens, the injustice is in the persons, not in their governmental acts.

Persons who illegitimately introduce a new form of power can nevertheless fulfil the natural office annexed to the new form and direct it to the true end of the City. This is the case where, as we said, the injustice is in the institution of the form, not in governmental acts.

Viceversa, the form of governmental power can be legitimate, but persons legitimately invested with it can abuse the power, exceed its limits, neglect its exercise and direct it to an end different from that proper to the society they govern. Here, injustice is in government, in its acts.

2204. Government can sin against *extra-social Right*. In this case, we once more encounter injustices which violate jural equality and commutative justice, discussed in individual Right.

Government can sin against *social Right*. If it does, its injustices violate the constitutive laws of society and exceed the limits derived from these laws.

CHAPTER 6

Injustices in society

2205. Finally, injustice can be in society itself, not in its government, nor the forms of its government nor the persons who have usurped power; it is present during the formation of society, in the pacts and laws that posit society in being.

2206. It tarnishes the relationship between the *social body* and *individuals*, whether members or not.

2207. An example of an injustice by society towards non-members would be refusal of membership to certain individuals in order to oppress them by an unjust seigniory[277] — legalisation of the state of slavery.

An example of an injustice towards members would be authentication of an illegitimate seigniory among the members — legalisation of the state of excessive servitude.

2208. The first example pertains to extra-social Right; the second, to social Right and, properly speaking, to the part we have called *communal right* (*USR*, 151).

I will discuss these examples of injustice at greater length because they are also violations of *individual freedom*, but I think I have said enough in various places of this work [*The Philosophy of Right*] about civil society's violations of the *right of ownership*.

Article 1.
Slavery

2209. The conclusion of Caligula's argument, drawn from the analogy between shepherds and princes, was that either kings must be gods, or people beasts. This conclusion contains two monstrous errors proper to pagan societies: 1. human beings can possess other human beings in the way a shepherd possesses a sheep; 2. governors of civil society have this right.

The first error shows the extreme degradation to which the human race had fallen; man had mentally rejected his own dignity. The second comes from the first, provided we add to it the incapacity of minds, unenlightened by the Gospel, to distinguish between *right* and its *modality*. This distinction requires great development of the faculty of abstraction. Because this development was lacking prior to Christianity, people necessarily confused *just* with *unjust servitude* (more commonly called

[277] By its nature, civil society, like any other society, can refuse membership to anyone it likes, but it may not do so in order to exercise an illegal seigniory over whomsoever it likes. On the other hand, individuals who are able to contribute can claim to be accepted as members of civil society whenever their right of guarantee and jural claim requires this. Similarly, civil society itself can claim that individuals become members when it can invoke its right of guarantee and jural claim.

slavery),[278] and slavery with *subjection*. They applied their false ideas about servitude in domestic society to subjection in civil society: subjects were slaves, the ruler was head of the house, and any evil he forwent was attributed to his mercy. Without any opposition, he granted himself divine honours, going further than Caligula's alternative, whose two members, he maintained, were simultaneously human beings made beasts and rulers made gods.[279]

2210. These absurdities will not surprise anyone who knows the nature of humanity apart from the Gospel. What is more surprising is that even in modern times servitude has been confused with subjection. Rousseau's principle, 'Human beings are born free, and are everywhere in chains', shows this. Grotius himself did not clearly see the distinction between civil government and domestic seigniory, thus preparing the way for Rousseau to refute it. If civil government involves slavery, or even simply legitimate servitude, it can easily be demonstrated that the social contract is the only just way to form civil society, because the servitude of adults never exists outside the family without a contract (*RI*, 554–557). Like Hobbes before him, Rousseau, who had formed a similar concept of civil society by drawing it from a classical prejudice, could not avoid his social contract. Poor Grotius, who had agreed with the concept of society, was mistaken in allowing some other possible origin. Everything shows that Rousseau did not see the distinction between *power over rights* and *power over the modality of*

---

[278] I have already shown that the *right of seigniory* and the *duty of servitude* exist. False philosophers vainly try to destroy them under the pretext that a bond-servant is an inferior being. They have little idea of what human dignity is. The true greatness of human beings is moral, and lies in the exercise of the virtues proper to their state. The fidelity of an incorruptible bond-servant, to whom the master can entrust the most delicate business in complete safety, or of a bond-servant who endangers his own life to save his master's, is the greatest and most moving virtue. Such a man is a treasure. In the state of bond-servant he retains and increases all human dignity. Sophists, by reducing all states to a single state, successively destroy the different kinds of moral virtues.

[279] For the title of gods usurped by ancient rulers, cf. Pietro Gregorio, *De Republica*, bk. 6, c. 12.

[2210]

rights; he finds no difference between a father's power over his family[280] and that of a head of civil society over the people.

2211. This false principle is the cause of the contemporary mania for republics. Certainly, if civil society had power over citizens' rights, the only tolerable governments would be republican; indeed, extreme democracy would be the only just form of government,[281] and this fact alone would render governmental power inalienable. Expressed simply, civil society would not be possible; the human race would have to remain in the state of nature.

Article 2.
The pure right of command

2212. Similarly, it is absurd that human beings have a pure right of command, totally independent of any other right. The

[280] When Rousseau realised that this principle implied the greatest despotism, his remedy was to change the nature of the family by restricting *patria potestas*: 'Children are bound to their father only as long as necessary for their preservation. Once this need has ceased, the natural tie is dissolved. The children, freed from the obedience they owe to their father on the one hand, and the father, freed from the care owed to his children on the other, equally gain independence. If they continue to remain united, they no longer do so *naturally* but *willingly*, and the family itself is maintained by pact' (*Contr. Soc.*, bk. 1, c. 2). Rousseau is right, if we grant that what human beings do *willingly* is opposed to what they do *naturally*. The bonds he is speaking about can only be physical; if they were moral, they would be voluntary, which, according to Rousseau, excludes them from being natural. But I understand right as a moral bond, not merely a physical bond; it therefore subsists between father and son all their life. Rousseau's concept of pact is also false. According to him, everything done willingly is a pact. 'The social order does not come from nature. It is therefore founded on pacts' (c. 1). This conclusion is hasty. There are moral bonds which are *willed* precisely because moral. However they arise not from pacts but from an act of the will which recognises its obligation, despite the lack of previous pacts.

[281] This is demonstrated by the observation, which Rousseau himself recognises in his system, that not only a majority but all citizens without a single exception must form part of the social contract. He says, 'The law of the majority vote in itself establishes a contract and supposes unanimity on at least one occasion' (*Contr. Soc.*, bk. 1, c. 5).

right of command, as such, is proper to God alone,[282] and supposes a different nature for superior and inferior. Relative to human beings, to command solely for the sake of commanding would be stupid, and would serve no useful purpose. Only in God can a command, as such, be just and wise, because in him it is an end in itself, and obedience is a real good for the person who obeys (*RGC*, 540–631).

2213. Hence, the defect through lack of precision in the words of a well-known author: 'Every society is founded on the right to command, and on the duty to obey. Remove these, and you have destroyed the very idea of government.'[283] The ambiguity of these words is destructive if the purpose of the command is not added. The human right to command comes from other rights. I will explain this more clearly.

The moral foundation we have laid for human rights is the primitive law, which is independent of human beings and intimated equally to us all from the first moment our reason develops. It states simply and forcefully: 'Do harm to no one.' This is promulgated universally by reason without regard for the circumstances of any particular human being: 'Do harm to no one, even if you have to suffer evil for it or lose some good. Evil may not be done to others whatever the benefit hoped for.' Hence, the intangibility of rights (*RI*, 1641–1703). To remove from human beings what is joined to them through the bond of ownership is to harm them; their ownership and rights must be left intact. But if these rights are to remain intact, human beings must submit to certain ordinances enacted by other human beings. For example, the only limit to our right to freedom should be that which is necessary for others to exercise their rights. This limit means that many must submit to a single will (social will) so that freedom neither expands nor shrinks capriciously. Hence the obligation we all have to allow a single mind to regulate the modality of our rights for the greatest common good, and also the duty to obey, with the corresponding right to regulate and command.

---

[282] It is therefore also proper to those to whom God said, 'He who hears you, hears me' (Lk 10: 16).

[283] Lamennais, *Mélanges relig. et philos.*, vol. 1, *Influence des doctrines philosophiques sur la société*.

This duty of obeying one's fellows is the duty of imposing on oneself that submission to others which is necessary for effecting the respect due to their rights. It is the duty of imposing a burden (if it is a burden) on self, even of suffering something, whenever necessary, for the preservation of others' rights.

Hence, on the one hand we have the right to use our own goods and regulate the modality of others' rights, and on the other, to allow others to use their goods and regulate the modality of our rights. In civil society, this is the right to command and the duty to obey reduced to its basic form.

2214. This duty of persons to obey, which is necessary if other persons are to have free use of their rights, is not founded in other persons but in the rational law, which is in God. Hence, both the natural duty to obey and the natural right to command come from God.

2215. The absolute right to command, which pertains to God and to those he has sent, differs from the civil-social right to command, which properly speaking is simply the right to use one's own goods and to regulate the modality of others' rights. The difference can be better understood by noting that the right to command is by its nature positive, whereas the right to use one's own goods is by its nature negative. The right to use one's own goods is relative to things; our attention is not directly on persons relative to whom we are, as it were, in a state of inaction. The absolute right to command, however, concerns persons directly and pays no attention to things, which are not the formal object of this right.

For example, a government promulgates health orders to preserve the country from a contagious disease that has invaded foreign soil. Obedience is obviously necessary. The right to command therefore is acknowledged in the government, provided it is distinguished from the pure right to command. The government has the right to declare what is of common benefit, safeguarding the rights of all. Such a declaration must be respected because 1. rational law teaches that rights must be fully respected; 2. there must be someone to declare how they are to be respected; and 3. this is the person (individual or collective) who legitimately occupies this office, that is, those authorised by the government.

In civil government, therefore, the right to command can be

reduced to the right to declare what kind of modality of rights is more suitable for the good of all; it can be reduced to the right to obey the duty — which in fact exists prior to society — to follow that modality of our rights which better suits the good of our fellow beings. When human beings pass from the state of nature to that of civil society, the difference undergone by this duty is merely accidental. In the state of nature human beings have to observe that modality of their rights which they judge more suitable. In the state of civil society they have to observe the modality which social government judges more suitable. This judgment therefore takes the form of a command; the duty to follow the more suitable modality takes the form of obedience — only the form is changed, not the substance.

Obedience to the natural law, which commands respect for others' rights, is therefore always imposed upon human beings. The civil right to command is simply the right to impose respect for this law. It is not contradictory but necessary for natural law to have fixed interpreters among human beings. Interpreters become, as it were, a talking law, according to one definition of civil heads of nations.

2216. Those who positively denied the existence of a supreme being would certainly direct their attacks against the natural law which shines in all minds and is the foundation of civil power. But those who lacked only an explicit knowledge of a God could know and feel the obligatory force of the natural law, which would never cease to reveal itself in their hearts. Finally, those who thought that knowledge of the rational law is knowledge of God himself would be victims of the platonism which spawned so many heresies in the Church, and still insinuates itself today in the writings of good, meticulous, but short-sighted authors. The rational law is divine light indeed, like the form of truth itself, but human beings need something more to conceive an infinite, supreme, real being — he who sees the light does not always see the sun.

[2216]

Article 3.
Legitimate hard servitude

2217. Having rejected *slavery* and the *pure right to command*. I will say a few words about *legitimate servitude*.

We need to distinguish between *hard* and *gentle servitude*. Subjection, servitude, slavery and subjugation of any kind are frequently confused concepts. Let us separate them from each other.

2218. When the human race presumptuously exalted itself, it did two things: it put itself in place of 1. the rational law, and 2. God. Both kinds of self-exaltation resulted in undue, illegitimate subjection.

2219. The strict notion of legitimate servitude is the right of one human being over the *actions* of another.

2220. This kind of servitude is limited by the law of moderation which must govern the use of one's right: 'Human beings must use the thing over which they have right solely in conformity with the end to which the thing is ordered by its nature.'

2221. According to this law:

1. The actions of a bond-servant can never be directed to an evil end. A master cannot command unlawful actions of a bond-servant.

2. The actions of a bond-servant can be directed only to the preservation of human nature, not to its destruction or harm. A master cannot command his servant something seriously harmful to bodily health, and must allow what is necessary to preserve it.

A human being in the servile state suffers no positive evil, but is impeded from that greater good which he could gain by his own actions if able to direct them to his own advantage.

2222. Human beings however are not always able, nor wish, to make good use of their actions. Hence servitude is a real good for those who through ignorance or malice might use their actions evilly, and is indifferent for those who would not know what to do with their freedom. Perry says: 'Muscovites readily sell themselves. Montesquieu adds that he knows the reason: their freedom is worthless.'[284]

[284] *Essai des Lois*, 15, 6.

[2217–2222]

This is true not only for a nation but generally for all barbarians, who have little sense of their freedom. The Anglo-Saxons willingly sold themselves and their children throughout their history.

2223. Barbarians, who did not really value freedom which had little worth for them, needed an appreciable time to value it in those for whom it was worthwhile. The Goths who took Rome under Alaric did not know what to do with their prisoners and sold them at a very moderate price. Later however they were better able to assess bond-servants taken in war and sell them according to the value of their abilities or even retain them for their own service.

2224. It would be very desirable if all human beings were able and wanted to make good use of their actions; if they did, their freedom would acquire great value. This is one of the steps forward that the world is taking, and it is a supremely beneficent action to urge all people to it. But we must not deceive ourselves and think that freedom is truly an equal good for all, or even a good. The author of Christianity pointed out the way to all freedom in the axiom: 'The truth will make you free.'[285] This short statement expresses the art of making human beings free. Let them receive the truth whole and entire; let their minds be enlightened and their hearts set at rest; then they are capable of governing themselves. At this point freedom is very precious; now all human beings have a right to it.

Voltaire says,[286] 'If there is disagreement about some human condition, people in that condition must decide which state they prefer' *(RI*, 610); in judging others, it is a great mistake to apply one's own thoughts and desires to them. There have in fact always been people who preferred servitude to freedom, who felt moderate servitude to be a good, not an evil. For this reason, the Hebrew law foresees the possibility of bond-servants, after seven years service, refusing the freedom offered by the law. If servitude were equally burdensome for all, the world would not have swarmed with bond-servants; they would not have shown love nor the heroism of fidelity and sacrifice for their masters,

---

[285] Jn 8: [32].
[286] *Dictionn. philosoph.*, Art. *Esclaves.*

nor would masters have shown the greatest affection for their bond-servants.[287]

2225. While the incapacity for using one's freedom can make servitude opportune, wanted and desired, vice can sometimes justify seigniory. A famous author said rather harshly: 'The human being is too perverse to be free.'[288] Recourse to the vices of oppressors is certainly not enough to explain the servitude under which a great part of the human race laboured before Christ; we have to take account also of vice on the part of the oppressed. Unfortunately the majority of the human race had to be kept in chains so that humanity would not destroy itself. Social organisation was hard and rigid; iron stays held together a building that was threatened by ruin and had many times been torn apart.

2226. The ignorance and wickedness of bond-servants make *hard* servitude legitimate. If they had ability, obedience and intelligence, the master would not be forced to use such a strict discipline. But his hardness cannot be arbitrary; it must be determined by the most exact, necessary justice.

2227. Servitude is also hard when it is perpetual. The hard

---

[287] It is helpful to note, against the sceptics, that people make the same principal, fundamental judgments; any discrepancy is only apparent, or concerns remote applications. For instance, we can maintain that everyone always believed, and still believes, that *personal dignity* cannot be considered a simple means. Nevertheless the expression, 'to buy and sell human beings' would seem to indicate the opposite. But this is not so; we need to get to the basic meaning of the thought expressed so badly by this phrase. The 'human being', who is bought and sold, refers to his material part, not to *personship*, We have difficulty in fixing our attention on the latter, and it was more difficult to do so in ancient times. This observation will reduce the distaste produced by the formula with which the Gauls normally sold themselves, something which they did frequently and easily: 'You are permitted to impose on me whatever discipline you choose; you can sell me or do whatever you like with me' (*Marculf. Formul.*, bk. 2, 28). It is impossible to understand this last phrase to its fullest extent; we have to modify it mentally by adding a little clause: 'provided the laws of uprightness and morality are respected.' The clause was not expressed because human attention had not yet been directed to it, and therefore the imperative formula to express it exactly had not been found. Cf. *Storia comparativa de' sistemi morali* concerning this silence of antiquity, ch. 5, a. 7.

[288] De Maistre, *Du Pape*, bk. 3.

characteristics are therefore: 1. strictness of discipline in order to keep bond-servants to their duty; 2. perpetuity of service.

2228. Christianity was unable to abolish hard servitude at once because bond-servants were as wicked as freemen. Its first occupation was to improve them.

2229. The Hebrews distinguished two kinds of servitude: hard and light. But care was taken that neither should exceed the laws of justice and humanity — the institution of the sabbath particularly favoured bond-servants. God often reminded the Israelite people about the slavery suffered, and permitted, in Egypt so that they might understand from their own experience how burdensome it was to be oppressed by work.

Servitude was hard or light depending on whether bond-servants were Hebrews or foreigners.

Hebrew bond-servants, who were more instructed in the divine law, more affectionate towards their brethren among whom they served and more apt for freedom, did not need rigorous discipline. Consequently, their servitude could be less hard. The law prescribed that if a Hebrew, forced by poverty, sold himself to another Hebrew, that is, sold his labour, the purchaser must not treat him as a bond-servant but as a mercenary and settler, and must in the jubilee year free him and his children, and let him recover the possessions of his ancestors.[289] Furthermore, it was forbidden to send him away empty; the master had to provide him lovingly and fraternally with flocks, wheat and wine.[290]

Hebrews however could keep foreign male and female bond-servants in perpetuity and hand them on by heredity. Gentleness was not prescribed for these, perhaps because it was impossible to exercise it, granted their lower morality.

2230. Punishment by imprisonment can be reduced to the concept of hard servitude. Indeed, houses of forced labour and prisons for those justly condemned to life imprisonment are simply places where bond-servants are subjected to the hardest servitude. The difference between this and hard servitude is simply the title: instead of a title of sale, let us say, the title is that of crime committed, a title that makes the servitude harder

[289] Lev 25: [39–41].
[290] Deut 15: [13–14].

without changing its nature. The guilty are real bond-servants of society, which has a just title to govern, bind and apply their activity to some particular work (*RI*, 1995–1999).

2231. Except for the servitude to which some individuals are personally subject, long standing Christian nations no longer need servitude. After eleven centuries, those who were bond-servants were capable of freedom. In 1167, religion, by means of Pope Alexander III, promulgated the decree 'that all Christians must be free from servitude.'[291] Note carefully, this decree is not speaking about intrinsically unjust *slavery*, but *hard servitude*, which in certain circumstances is just. Intrinsically unjust slavery was abolished at the first proclamation of the Gospel and fraternal love.

2232. Hard servitude however was treated differently. Christianity maintained bond-servants in the humility of their state, inviting them to be content with being *freedmen of Christ*.[292] But after great numbers of them had been baptised and sufficiently educated to freedom, the Head of the Church solemnly

---

[291] Voltaire, in *Saggio sui costumi* (ch. 83), says: 'Finally, in 1167, Pope Alexander III declared in the name of the Council that all Christians must be free from servitude. This law alone must make his memory dear to all peoples, just as his efforts to maintain the freedom of Italy must make his name precious to Italians. Much later, by virtue of this law, king Louis Hutin declared that all remaining bond-servants in France had to be freed.' In this quotation the historian confuses *hard servitude* with *vassallage*. According to the testimony of Bartolo (who was alive in 1300), bond-servants as such no longer existed at his time; by virtue of Christian laws, he says, human beings were no longer sold. On the other hand, at the beginning of the 13th century, there were still bond-servants in Italy, as we learn from papal decrees. Hence, concludes Bodin, we can accept the total cessation of bond-servants in Italy by the middle of the 13th century; he then adds: 'History tells us that Louis Hutin, who became king in 1313 (the time when Bartolo lived), paid for the freedom of all slaves who wanted freedom, in order to defray the cost of war. But we must understand this relative to those who are enfeoffed and subject to emphyteusis, whom we, even in these days, see freed by royal letters,' (bk, 1, c. 5).

[292] 'Were you a slave when called? Never mind. But if you can gain your freedom, avail yourself of the opportunity. For he who was called in the Lord as a slave is A FREEDMAN OF THE LORD' (1 Cor 7: [21–22]). Christ made bond-servants his freedmen by changing the nature of servitude; he abolished all that was injust and inhuman in it, and gave bond-servants who believed in him a most noble moral freedom.

[2231–2232]

announced that the time had come for *hard servitude* itself to be abolished among the children of the same heavenly Father.

2233. Its abolition now became obligatory for Christian masters. The task was undertaken universally, although the odd exception remained, just as cases of servile wickedness remained. But, during the previous eleven centuries, hard servitude had been the general case and liberation the exception.

Although it is now seven centuries since the Head of the Church forbade *hard servitude* among Christians — and in fact abolished it — it has raised its head again and endures in the colonies. But this is due principally to the unbelief of masters and governments, which has made people return to the pagan world, their ears closed to the voice of the Church, their hearts blocked to the voice of humanity.

2234. Servitude in the colonies is not only hard, but often an immanent, wicked, inexcusable slavery. Christian governments are bound to punish its practice severely. Governments and masters are also obliged to abolish the hard servitude which the Church has rejected for ever.

2235. It is true that if Blacks were ready for full freedom, they would help themselves, but the unbelief of masters, enchaining both their bodies and their souls, prevents their attaining it. Simultaneously, and through a similar lack of faith, the half-learned who exert influence in governments preach freedom but do not know how to bring bond-servants to appreciate and use the gift willingly offered them.

A well-known writer, speaking of today's serfs in Russia, says:

> If one day they are given freedom, they must be prepared for it over a long period. In the state of ignorance and stupidity in which they are sunk, they could make only very sad use of it. They would murder their masters, or cut each other's throat. I myself once believed, trusting our fashionable philosophers, that it would be so easy to make them a present of their freedom. But today I simply find it a ridiculous and impracticable idea.

2236. Certainly, a too rapid transition of a multitude from powerlessness to power, from total servitude to total freedom, is extremely dangerous. People who pass rapidly from a lowly state to great fortune suffer a kind of vertigo; much more so when a whole race, after long servitude, passes to the level of freedom.

2237. The slaves granted manumission by the Romans did not suddenly pass to the state of full freedom but remained at the level of freedmen, a state midway between slavery and full freedom. In this state they maintained a relationship of gratitude, subservience and even some legal bond with their master; for example, if a freedman died intestate and without children, a third of the inheritance went to his master. Rules existed concerning the age and number of those who could be freed, and formalities were necessary for this. Justinian, a Christian ruler, finding the world improved by the Gospel, was able to remove many encumbrances from the free manumission of slaves, and also from the middle state of freedmen.[293]

2238. When I say 'the world improved', I mean the lower, greater part of the world. Although the corruption of morals under the emperors, which caused the gangrene in the empire, reached its zenith in the upper classes of Roman society, we can safely assert that the morality of the lower classes, where religion found the least obstacles to its influence, notably improved. Consequently, the increased ability of bond-servants gave them greater value, and made them worthy of many favourable ordinances. It was they who, almost exclusively, exercised the liberal arts and the sciences. They were granted a kind of ownership, at least relative to their families. In fact we have a great number of inscriptions drawn up by slaves in favour of their wives, children, companions and masters. Hadrian and the Antonines made new laws to protect the lives and safety of bond-servants against the cruelty of their masters.

2239. But the very corruption of the Roman masters, the majority of whom were strangers to Christianity, contributed indirectly to the rapid improvement of the slave population.

---

[293] 'But the influence of government and religion continued to diminish the harshness of this dependent state, and the pride of a master ceased to be inflated by his absolute dominion over the life and happiness of his slave' (Gibbon, *Storia della decad. dell' Imp. Rom.*, c. 44). Prior to this passage, the author had spoken censoriously of Justinian's ordinances in favour of slaves, having failed to reflect on the preparation which Christian bond-servants would have partly received.

[2237–2239]

This corruption also rendered them incapable of governing by themselves, and after falling victim to the fury of enraged factions which decimated them, they decided to alienate their own sovereignty and place it in a single citizen.

The only way that Roman ruling authority, when constituted, could preserve itself against the Roman citizens' habit of commanding, was by a tacit alliance between itself and the servile part of the nation against the body of citizens. The emperor, having everything to fear from the great families, thought he had nothing to fear from the slaves. He thus considered it in his interest to exalt the people at the bottom of society and make them his creatures, while casting down those at the top and removing from them the force to harm him. The result was a real revolution and the overthrow of society.

2240. Gallienus (253–268 AD) forbade the senators military service.[294] Serfs, with the assent of their masters, were admitted to military service, and veterans could no longer be recalled by their master.[295]

The extermination of the most outstanding senatorial families causes horror as we follow its traces: from the proscriptions of Silla to the abhorrently wicked Maximian, butcheries of the Roman nobility were repeated, with the result that Goths and Lombards found little noble blood to spill [*App.*, no. 8].

Everything lowly in the Roman republic was elevated, and everything superior, humiliated. The free inhabitants of Rome were first made to descend to the level of the most barbaric provincials. Later, after Rome was abandoned, the emperors gave preference to the cities and provinces where they themselves dwelt. Septimius Severus filled the senate with eloquent slaves; between the battle of Actium and the reign of Vespasian it was filled with new families.[296]

The lowest people, the slaves, particularly the eunuchs,

---

[294] 'The affluent, soft Romans,' says Gibbon (ch. 10), 'fell back on their natural character and accepted this dishonourable exemption from military service as a favour. As long as they were able to enjoy their theatres, baths and villas, they put the most dangerous responsibilities of the empire into the rough hands of peasants and soldiers.'

[295] *Cod. G.*, t. 62, c. 11, l. 4.

[296] *Annal*, bk. 3, c. 55.

became the favourites of rulers and their ministers. Servile clans soon began to contribute emperors to the Roman throne.[297]

2241. The evils resulting in the empire were extreme, but just, natural and conformed to the justice of the supreme Being.

When slaves attained the highest power after their liberation, they had the characteristics proper to the exercise of tyranny. Arrogant with power, they exercised it in the only way they knew — by making people unhappy: in their eyes, the misery they produced in their fellows was the measure of their greatness. Indeed, freedom on its own, for which they were not ready, made them aspire to dominion. We have an ancient example: the Volsci lost their freedom through the rebellion of their emancipated bond-servants.[298]

Inept at exercising great power, the slaves who had been so suddenly freed, very soon attained the art of accumulating wealth. Avarice became their characteristic vice, as so many favoured freedmen demonstrate. Activity is more easily used for evil than good: if those who have been freed so rapidly have no opportunity to practise *cruelty* or *avarice*, the danger of rapid emancipation is the accumulation of layabouts and beggars. Thus at the time of Constantine we see previously unknown hordes of beggars, to whom that great ruler responded by providing institutions of Christian beneficence.

2242. We can conclude that:

1. first of all, gentleness must be preached to masters, obedience to bond-servants; both must be enlightened so that the latter become capable of using their freedom, the former of using their seigniory uprightly;

2. as bond-servants make progress, the burden of legitimate servitude must be reduced until finally abolished.

2243. Politics is infamous and criminal:

1. when it makes or keeps human beings ignorant and corrupt so that it can hold them in subjection or servitude; and

[297] Macrinus' servile clan was the object of his enemies' reproaches. Diocletian's parents had been slaves in the house of the Roman senator, Anulinus.

[298] Florus tells us: 'The Volsci, the last of the Italians and richest of the Etruscans, gained confidence and begged help against their former slaves who, having taken advantage of the freedom given them by their lords, had usurped power over the republic and ruled' (bk. 1, c. 21).

[2241–2243]

2. when it keeps in the most burdensome and intolerable servitude those who have become enlightened and capable of honest activity.

Article 4.
Serfdom among the Romans

2244. We have seen the kind of wound slavery inflicted on domestic society (*RF*, 1402–1417). Decadence among the free population turned the wound gangrenous; the attempt to remedy it was usually too late.

2245. The decline of Roman families, the reduced population of freemen and abandonment of agriculture[299] were new reasons inducing the lords of the world to draw greater profit from the slave population and make freemen bond-servants. They tied to the earth a part of the slave population, prisoners of war, the poor,[300] insolvent debtors and those who offered themselves for such work. Hence, *servi glebae* [servants of the glebe] or serfs.[301]

2246. When a class becomes more useful or necessary to the masters who make the laws, it immediately improves its state and at least has sufficient protection for its preservation. Serfs, although assigned to perpetual, fixed service, enjoyed the state

[299] The law which tied agricultural workers to the land was not, properly speaking, drawn up to protect agriculture but to ensure for the treasury the exaction of property tax, thus depriving the owner of the excuse that it was difficult to obtain labour.

[300] A law of Gratian, Valentinian and Theodosius (382 AD) subjected beggars to serfdom in favour of those who denounced them.

[301] Opinions vary about the origin of serfdom. Géraud attributes it to Greek origin; Carlo Troya to Germanic origin. Cibrario, who mentions these opinions, says that 'serfdom began at the time of Diocletian, who transported entire populations from Asia to France to cultivate the land. This example was imitated in the west by Maximian who set the conquered Franks to cultivate the wild country of the Neni and Treviri' (*Dell' E. P. del medio evo*, bk. 1, c. 2, ed. 1842). It seems however that this kind of service among the Romans must be dated from the first laws forbidding landowners to separate from the land those who worked it, because the proper characteristic of serfdom was the *adherence of the labourers to the land*. I do not know if these laws go back to the year 359, which is the year of a Law of Constantius mentioned in the Justinian Code (*De agricolis et censitis, leg. 2*).

of *free human beings*. Thus, properly speaking, their state no longer pertained to slavery, but to legitimate servitude, as I have called it.

2247. The fact that laws bound them to the soil conformed with the concept Roman legislators had of artisans who, although free, were considered perpetually assigned to public service (*servi ministeriales*) and had to live and die working at the craft they had chosen.[302] Among the Romans, colleges of crafts were an extension of eastern castes.

2248. *Servitude of serfs* was the same as *servitude of artisans*. They were called freemen; they were not slaves, but real bond-servants because their work was bound by laws, or rather by the power of the City. This explains the Romans' aversion to the profession of crafts as base and servile. And every educated human being knows how harmful this was to Rome.[303]

2249. Laws sometimes aggravated, sometimes lightened the state of serfs. Finally, Christianity removed the fetters from their activity, gave them back all the rights of domestic society[304] and made them apt to become citizens.

[302] A law of Arcadius and Honorius (498 AD) ordains that armourers be marked on their arm to prevent their escaping. Here society is becoming tyrannical. Artisans were necessary to society, which naturally became dependent on them; when they did not work, they could constrain society to enter into pacts. Stronger societies declared artisans its *servi ministeriali*, obliged them to work and, in order to control them better, forbade them to change occupation. These laws of a political nature violate natural freedom and are reprehensible, unless initially justified by some jural title.

[303] 'Roman citizens, although extremely poor, disdained the exercise of a craft. Clothed in rags, they lived off two coppers a day, spent the day in the forum and slept under a portico near the Trigeminan gate, or on straw under a tree in the woods of Aricia; they scraped a living doing nothing. Consequently, not only locksmiths, dyers, carpenters and masons were slaves and foreigners, but architects, readers, librarians, scribes and teachers. The law aided this base opinion and treated the craftsmen as slaves' (Cibrario, *ibid.*, c. 2). It was in fact the laws of despotic civil society that debased opinion: by binding the craftsman to his craft, they really made him a bond-servant, which prevented Roman citizens from ever taking up the practice of a craft.

[304] Justinian ordered that if one of the parents were a serf and the other, free, the son was to take his mother's condition. He applied the principle that *partus sequitur ventrem* [offspring follow the womb]. This enactment was doubly unjust: it was made for illegitimate children, which was not the case

Legitimate servitude can be just if founded on a just title. But in the case of artisans we see no just title among the Romans, unless *consent* were given for the sake of the privileges and protection granted to their guilds.

2250. In the case of serfs, the following can constitute just titles for ascription to serfdom, provided service is limited to the life of individuals and not extended to clans: 1. spontaneous inscription among their number (*adscriptitii*), 2. legitimate, just conquest, 3. commuted capital punishment, 4. indolent poverty, proven to be *habitually depraved*, 5. occupancy of uneducated persons incapable of using their activity, without jural resentment on their part.

2251. In the case of clans, a master can never violate the serf's right to marriage and domestic society in all its extension. Furthermore, in keeping with the development of the offspring's moral and intellectual faculties, he must relax restraint and leave them free if they wish; if not, he violates rational Right.

Article 5.
Military bond-service

2252. Legitimate servitude is *hard* when total and life-long or accompanied by the harsh discipline necessary for obtaining the work due, for directing boorish behaviour and for restraining the perversity of a bond-servant. It is *gentle* when temporary and free of harsh discipline.

2253. Sometimes servitude, which considered in itself is *hard*, is not hard for those subject to it. Barbarians, as individuals, scarcely feel the burden of domestic servitude, but as a body, show an incredible enthusiasm for their rough, indisciplined

when one spouse was a serf and the other free; and the application even to illegitimate children is opposed to rational law (*RI*, 1541–1546). If both spouses were serfs but of two masters, a third of the children were assigned to the mother's ownership, according to a law of the Theodosian Code, *De inquilinis*. Justinian made a different division: a decree exists assigning all offspring to the master of the mother, contrary to *rational Right of domestic society*. This right must be respected by civil legislators, which was not the case before Christianity.

[2250–2253]

freedom and independence. Because they are inept at understanding and respecting a general organisation, they are inept at civil government and suited only to domestic organisation, to understanding and obeying the individual directions of a master. The indomitable Germans, who submitted solely to a commander-in-chief chosen by them, and only for as long as they liked, set so little store by their individual, private freedom that, as Tacitus says, they gambled with it.[305] In short, what they found burdensome was not the corporal effort nor the harshness of mechanical service, but the acceptance of an organised, regulated life whose value they did not appreciate; for them, this was the heaviest burden.

When Valens allowed the Goths to cross the Danube and gave them provinces in which to settle he was unable to subject them to imperial law, but only to tribute and a partial servitude ('military servitude', as I call it). Hence the first idea of feudal government.

2254. Medieval feudalism, or feudalism of any other time, from the greatest feudal lords to the least vassals, did in fact bring in its wake hard, servile burdens, such as military service.

Barbarian peoples readily submitted to similar hard conditions, but not to complex civil law, although submission to law is less burdensome than gentle servitude; it is not even servitude (cf. 1723–1727). On the death of Athalaric, the Visigoths spontaneously enrolled themselves under the imperial standards, drawn by the friendship that the emperor Theodosius had shown their kings. In the same way, many half-savage peoples like the Buriats, Tartars, Bulgars, Turcomans, Aralians, Kara-Kalpaks, Kirghizes, Bashkirs, Nogais, the inhabitants of the Causcasus, the Circassians, Kalmucks, etc., are at present subject to Russia. Properly speaking they are not subject to a civil government but to military conditions, which are characteristics of what I call 'hard servitude'. Some of them have submitted spontaneously: many families of the Kirghises, imitating their brethren, requested subjection to the emperor Alexander who visited their territory in 1823.

2255. But the most complete example of military serfdom is

[305] *De morib. germ.*

that conceived by Count Arakcheyev for Russia and executed by Alexander himself for 80,000 troops of the line.

If we briefly consider the two or three hundred villages established in this way, we see that they began by constituting themselves in a state of *hard servitude* in the full sense of the term. This was far from moving towards their freedom in accord with nearly all the other European countries' natural progress from vassallage to civil subjection. Under a rigorous, totally military regime, their heavy duties have been divided throughout the day. They hardly own their own children, who are subjected to the common discipline from the age of eight. Nevertheless this harsh, burdensome servitude becomes easier through habit, and offers a particular advantage in contrast with every other kind of servitude. The military discipline and methodical duties to which they are subject are not directed simply to the benefit of the master, as in other kinds of servitude, but are a real, strict education, even though servile.

Through this education they acquire 1. an increase of physical strength, which is a natural consequence of an austere, hard-working life, where the disorders of dissoluteness are unknown; and 2. an increase of moral strength, because regularity of life together with moderate education inculcates ideas of order which they come to love as a result of long and constant habit. These two outstanding benefits can eventually compensate greatly for the harshness of servitude which was perhaps necessary for such an uneducated people.

2256. Indeed, is it unreasonable to fear that a people educated in this way and growing to a possible six million may develop such tremendous physical strength, sustained by sufficient moral force, that their strength will far outstrip that of the rest of the population of the empire and become the real arbiter of the latter's destiny?

2257. Such a danger could be avoided by natural emancipation according to the requirement of rational Right. The degree of freedom thus granted would balance the feeling and need for freedom, a balance, which if greatly disturbed, would endanger public peace.

Article 6.
Mercenary servitude or domestic service

2258. Gentle servitude, as I have called it, is neither perpetual
nor subject to hard discipline, although it has degrees: it can
extend to all the saleable actions of a bond-servant, or simply to
a few determined by agreements or the nature of the service.

The servitude of mercenaries who agree to a determined kind
of service for a daily, monthly or annual wage, or for any other
period of time, is gentle servitude, not unknown to Christian
nations.

Article 7.
Administration

2259. *Administration*, or social office, must not be confused
with servitude. I have explained its distinguishing characteristics.[306]

Article 8.
Subjection

2260. Subjection is a mixed concept, originating in medieval
times when *seigniory* intermingled with *government*. Civil dependence was mixed with a servile element, and in this sense
meant *dependence on civil government*, a dependence associated
with a greater or lesser degree of servitude.

Article 9.
Civil dependence or subjection

2261. Dependence on civil government, today normally called
subjection, is in itself totally different from servitude because

[306] *SP*, 111–131.

the word 'subjection' seems to have changed from its original meaning.

2262. Not even the highly commendable Haller is free from the very serious error of confusing civil *subjection* with *servitude*. He wrongly believes that the distinctive mark of a monarch is that of being the only *free* person in the State, which supposes that all the other members of civil society are subject to a kind of servitude.

2263. 'Free human being', 'owner' and 'civil governor' express three totally different ideas, and must never be confused.

Free human beings are neither owners of external goods nor governors; their actions are not subject to anyone's dominion but directed solely by their own will.

2264. Owners are neither free nor governors. For example, people who are employed in the gentle servitude practised today, possess something but serve masters, and do not govern.

Governors are neither owners nor entirely free. Properly speaking, intelligence alone is required for governing a body of human beings, and even a whole nation. Even if a wise person owned nothing, he could govern, nor would it be absurd if he were bound by some tie of servitude, not necessarily to the nation he governs but to a third party, a parent, for example.

2265. Subjection therefore, understood as simple civil dependence, does not necessarily involve the concept of servitude. Servitude means some other person's right over individual actions, whereas subjection is another person's right over the modality of individual actions and even over the modality of all other rights.

2266. Although the ancients very frequently confused civil dependence with servitude, they sometimes showed signs of sensing the difference. For a long time the Roman people could not accept the emperor's assuming the title of lord (*dominus*) because this word presupposed servitude rather than civil dependence. Plato gave the supreme magistrate of his republic the title of *protector*. This shows clearly that he had no part whatsoever in others' rights or goods but was charged with protecting them; in other words, his office concerned only the modality of rights and goods. We also see the distinction between the states of servitude and civil dependence in the embarrassment of the Roman jurisconsults who, by confusing them, made the emperor a despot over the life and goods of his subjects. Having made him master of everything with the usual adulation of jurists, they had to explain how and why he could not make use of such great authority. They said that all the subjects of the empire enjoyed their possessions and their very lives through the *clemency* of the emperor. But this legal opinion was incomprehensible to anyone who could still use a little reason; it revealed the falsity of a principle that entailed such evil consequences. On the other hand, the jurisconsults made pronouncements opposed to the principle, when, for example, they said that civil laws could not alter blood relationships and rights.[307]

Chapter 7

The principle of free concurrence, applied according to the prescriptions of rational Right, saves civil society from all the injustices listed above.

2267. So far we have tried to unravel civil Right and identify many of its threads. We must now bring these together and, if possible, make them one continuous thread. For this purpose we need to recall that I reduced the duties of civil society to two general duties: 1. civil society must not extend its action beyond the regulation of the modality of rights, but 2. must extend it to all the parts involved in the regulation of the modality.

The usual cause preventing civil society from extending its action to all the parts involved in its proximate end (defined as 'the most equable, useful regulation of the modality of rights'), is its own poor development and that of its members. This is an imperfection, not an injustice. On the other hand, civil society commits a manifest injustice every time it fails in its first duty

---

[307] The rule of Roman Right, 'Blood rights cannot be removed by any civil law' (*Dig.*, bk. 50, t. 17, l. 8) is truly a fine rule, but the dictate of nature and reason was soon contradicted and suppressed by corruption, which can always accompany legal forms. Thus, slavery and distance made a mother no longer a mother! Cf. *Dig.*, bk. 38, t. 17, l. 2, §2.

by crossing the limit of the modality entrusted to its regulation and entering the rights of individual and collective persons.

2268. All the injustices proper to society and its government therefore (but not those of persons and form, nor those which society as a jural person can have in common with all other jural persons) can be reduced to this formula: 'Crossing the line of modality'.

2269. If civil society, and government in its name, do not cross this limit, all citizens, including foreigners, maintain in full their *jural freedom*.

2270. I call this freedom *civil freedom*, in so far as it is preserved in society and protected by its laws. Hence, wherever the *whole of civil freedom* is preserved and protected by government, there is no injustice of any kind on the part of society and its government. The very rights of ownership are reduced to *jural freedom* which bears in itself all human rights (*RI*, 65–66, 84, 290; *ER*, 340).

2271. I think it is possible to find a simple formula that would express the unique principle or universal means which, applied correctly, renders civil society immune from every injustice. I would propose the following:

'If civil society maintains inviolate the principle of universal free concurrence, according to rational Right, it will avoid every injustice.'

2272. The formula can be explained in this way: rational Right allows all individual and collective persons to acquire equally any right whatsoever, provided the *modes of acquisition* are just. Granted that *politico-positive Right* does not use arbitrary ordinances to reduce the sphere of a jural person's freedom, the concurrence under discussion is preserved.

2273. I say 'arbitrary ordinances' because there is in Right itself a mode of limiting another's freedom which consists in *preoccupancy*, in our ownership, in the use of our rights of ownership and their functions, for example, the function of defence and guarantee.

I will now discuss particular cases of concurrence.

Article 1.
Concurrence for citizenship

2274. Civil society is not obliged to receive an outsider as one of its members unless forced do so by right of guarantee. In this case, granted that the applicant has all the qualities necessary for membership,[308] admission must be allowed. Requirement, by positive ordinance, of arbitrary qualities before admission denies the natural, universal concurrence under discussion.

2275. It is true that an aspirant's right of guarantee to civil association can have no value when a society needs to exclude him for its own defence or guarantee. This would be the case if the outsider's customs were reprehensible and opposed to those of the society. The society would justly fear a change to the morals and the upright, religious beliefs of its citizens, which is the seat of uniformity of social thought, the overall force of society.

2276. If there are no causes justifying exclusion from citizenship, an outsider must be admitted if he requests this, or the right of guarantee authorises him to make the claim.

2277. This however refers only to pure civil society unmixed with seigniorial elements, that is, to the ideal of pure civil society. For this reason, outsiders were not accepted into ancient civil societies, even though the applicants possessed, according to rational Right, all the qualities proper to the state of citizen. In those societies the *state of citizen* did not mean simply 'member of civil society', but 'a group of rights that were part social, part seigniorial'. Dissolving this group is the work of social progress.

2278. So far, jurists have not investigated the meaning of the word 'citizen' among different peoples. Because the word expresses a group of extremely variable rights, it cannot be given a fixed definition, as if it had always kept the same inalterable meaning. A fixed definition would prevent any equable judgment on the constitutions and civil laws of different peoples.

2279. Civilisation spread by means of colonies[309] founded by

---

[308] Hence civil society is not obliged to admit the poor; on the contrary, if they do not pay any tax (capitation), they must be excluded from citizenship.

[309] Cf. *SP*, 371–391.

the most famous states. From the beginning only the conquerors were *citizens* of these cities, uniting two qualities: *citizens*
among themselves, *masters* relative to the conquered people —
they were both citizen and lord. Under these conditions,
citizenship cannot be further extended without activation of the
jural modes which allow others to be admitted independently of
seigniory. The Helots in Sparta will serve as an example. They
were a conquered people,[310] subject to moderate servitude. An
historian notes:

> It must be said that their condition was more that of State
> bond-servant than of private individual. They could not be
> put to death or emancipated except by public decree. The
> government itself, bound by an ancient pact, could not sell
> them outside the country.[311]

Spartan *citizens* were therefore simultaneously *lords*, and their
government a seigniory: a person made a citizen was also made
a lord.

Granting citizenship in these societies was necessarily the
same as performing an act of free beneficence:

> All the roads to freedom however were not closed for the
> Helots. First of all, those who had done useful service
> during war were very often freed. Secondly, the Spartans
> quite often took as companions for their sons Helots who
> came to share not only in civil discipline but in freedom,
> and sometimes even obtained citizenship. Again, in the
> second Messenian war, we are told that, because the State
> lacked citizens, Helots, called επευναχτοι, were given as
> husbands to the widows and granted both freedom and
> citizenship.[312]

2280. In ancient civil societies, founded for the most part by
seigniorial power but also by simple heads of families, the
inclusion of a seigniorial element in citizenship was common.

---

[310] According to the more probable opinion, the word 'Helot' comes from
ελος, a city of Laconia conquered by the Dorians. Later it came to refer to
condition, not origin.

[311] C. Cantù, *Legislazione*, n. 2, §3.

[312] *Ibid.*

Here we have the explanation of tribes in all ancient cities; from the beginning, tribes divided according to their ancestry:

> In Argos and elsewhere there were three tribes of Dorians: the Hylleis, Dymanes and Pamphyli, together with a non-Dorian Irnezian tribe. In Sicyonia, three Dorian and one Aegialian; in Cyzicus, four Ionian, two of another lineage; in Ephesus, five of different lineage.[313]

2281. Furthermore, in many ancient States only citizens possessed land because it had been given to them at the time of the conquest. Adding new citizens was the same as donating wealth to the persons who were made citizens. Here again, acceptance of a foreigner into citizenship is an act of arbitrary beneficence.

2282. The existence of communal or social goods also confers some real rights on citizens who thus become owners as well. Granting citizenship to foreigners becomes more difficult in these conditions.

2283. In modern times we have often seen old-established citizens or sharers in communal rights hold themselves aloof from new citizens or sharers in communal rights. The former reserve fields for themselves, or the right to collect wood, or to enjoy the fruits of common land. Disagreements arise between them and new claimants to the same right because of their quality as citizens or sharers in communal rights.

This case could be resolved equably, I think, in the following way. If the new citizens have been admitted by law or order of a higher governmental authority without the agreement of those already citizens, the latter would be right to hold on to the exclusive enjoyment of communal goods. But, through the laws of free concurrence, the new citizens should be allowed the faculty to purchase at an equable price the right of co-ownership of communal goods.

2284. This explains why citizenship was bought for a substantial sum — it was not only citizenship that was purchased, but the real, seigniorial rights attached to it.

2285. We also see how civil legislators violate principles of justice when they think they are free to extend citizenship or a share in communal rights by means of new laws without any

<hr>

313 *Ibid.*

regard for the real and seigniorial rights inherent in citizenship, and without obliging new citizens to compensate those who are already citizens or to request their unanimous consent. Arbitrary laws of this kind, which dispose of the goods and rights of the ancient sharers in communal rights, exceed the sphere of civil power, which applies solely to the regulation of modality.[314]

2286. Whenever other rights, such as real and seigniorial rights, are attached to citizenship, the right to vote in public deliberations cannot be universal. The regulation of the modality of rights in assemblies is not the sole topic of discussion; some masters and owners discuss their own interests, and in this regard they are similar to a private family gathering. This is the origin of aristocracies. We will take Greek aristocracies as an example.

2287.

> Citizens of full right discussed public matters in their gatherings, tribunals and courts. Gatherings called γερ–ουσιαι, and sometimes βουλη, were of a fixed number of created or hereditary nobles. At Corinth there were two hundred, all Bacchiadae; among the Eleans, nine hundred perpetual members, drawn from particular families; among the Cnidians, sixty (αμνημονες), some of whom were perpetual and some chosen from the nobles; among the Epidaurians, a hundred and eighty, who chose from among themselves a few αρτυνους as a small council; among the Massalians, six hundred (τιμουχοι), chosen from the nobles, of whom fifteen and three presidents constituted the small council. In some cities there was a

[314] This imperfection of the law must be classed among those caused, as we saw, by poor development of the faculty of abstraction (cf. *SP*, 830–838). As I have said, the imperfection can be avoided simply by analysing the meaning of the word 'citizenship'. On the one hand, we have its pure concept, which is that of 'member of civil society', and on the other the rights of ownership and seigniory joined *de facto* and *per accidens* to the quality of citizen. Pure citizenship pertains to the modality of rights. Consequently it is the government's responsibility to confer it, provided only that new citizens pay the contribution. The real and seigniorial rights joined accidentally to citizenship do not pertain to modality but are nevertheless true rights. Government therefore cannot take a part of these rights from the old owners to give it freely to others without the consent of the owners, or without an evident benefit sufficient to compensate their loss.

[2286–2287]

kind of middle state between the few members of the senate and the universal assembly. These specially chosen citizens (συγκλητοι) formed their own assembly.[315]

If the sole matter discussed in these gatherings dealt with the regulation of the modality of rights, it would certainly have been equable for all members who paid the contribution[316] to take part. But this becomes unjust when discussion concerns not only modality but also the means for making some people's rights both prevail and increase against the rights of others who are compulsorily excluded from the gatherings.

2288. What we have said explains the origin of *aristocracies* and of all the political differences between the various classes of citizens, as well as the origin of different degrees of citizen. These inequalities necessarily arise in all civil societies where the *seigniorial* and *family* element is still unseparated from the *civil.* When civil society has been purified and become an institution existing of itself, as its *ideal* requires, these forms will naturally come to an end because they become unjust, useless, harmful.

2289. For this kind of progress, the faculty of analysis and abstraction needs to be greatly developed. Clearly, *social Right*, when confused with seigniorial Right, can only suffer continuously from the confusion; a single solution cannot satisfy the

---

315 C. Cantù, *Legislazione*, 2, 1.

316 One of the indications that civil society is disturbed and even absorbed by the seigniorial element is exemption from public taxes in favour of certain classes of citizens. This right can only be *seigniorial.* This is even more true if the social burdens are carried by non-citizens while citizens remain unburdened. In Greece, 'noble descendancy was distinct from plebeian; plebians were not even considered as citizens. A few of them however were free to possess provided they paid a tax; others were bond-servants of the glebe.' The Perioeci, 'who in Sparta were excluded from every right of citizenship, had no vote, were not admitted to responsibilities, and were not allowed to marry; they simply paid tax and supplied a stipulated number of soldiers with armour and light arms.' In Athens 'slaves apparently had to pay annually three obols each; family heads among rent-payers had to pay twelve drachmas, widows six, and freedmen three obols extra. The annual total of all taxes can be put at more than fifty talents. We are ignorant of taxes on crafts and business, of whatever kind or quantity. but we know that citizens were exempt.' We see here how much the *seigniorial element* was involved in ancient *civil societies.*

[2288–2289]

demands of two Rights. Social Right, if not purified of seigniorial Right, is obstructed and as it were paralysed.

Article 2.
Concurrence for the state of freedom

2290. In a purely *civil* society not mingled with seigniory, rational Right requires that the process for becoming a citizen be open to foreigners when 1. these have the qualities required by the simple notion of citizen, 2. they ask for citizenship and in particular can base their request on the right of guarantee. This is *free jural concurrence* for the state of citizenship. But there is also a bond-servant's *free jural concurrence* for the *state of freedman.*[317]

2291. We have seen that

1. No law (excluding penal law) can prevent a bond-servant from possessing and becoming the subject of any right whatsoever not opposed to the prestation of the labour owed to the master (*USR*, 178–180).

2. The prestation of labour can always be calculated in money or some other way.

3. A bond-servant's master cannot deny emancipation when the bond-servant himself, or others on his behalf, gives him a value equivalent to the bond-servant's labour (*USR*, 181).[318]

2292. It follows therefore that:

1. The master who denies emancipation in this case commits an injustice and must not be supported by civil law.

2. The bond-servant has the right to use all the means in his

---

[317] I am not speaking about illegitimate servitude (slavery), an unjust state which, as I have said, must be immediately and totally abolished in fact, precisely because it does not exist by right.

[318] In Athens '(slaves) not infrequently agreed a price with their master and bought their freedom with their own funds' (Dione, *Crisost. Orat.*, 15, p. 241; Petit, *Legg. Att.*, p. 259). 'As Hermann notes (*Ant. Gr.*, §114, 11), we cannot deduce with certainty from Plautus' *Casina* that, in spite of their masters, slaves could redeem themselves without such a pact' (C. Cantù, *Legislazione*, n. 3, §16).

power, apart from the prestation of labour due to his master, to obtain his emancipation (*USR*, 182).

3. The bond-servant in perpetual servitude can reasonably claim that a master whom he finds hard and unjust sell him to another master. This does not affect the master's right; it is simply a change of modality.[319]

4. A civil society would injure a bond-servant's rights if it 1. denied these forms of emancipation, according to rational Right; 2. applied impediments, or 3. claimed that emancipation was not an act of individual Right pertaining to commutative justice but an act of its authority.

5. Civil society must expressly protect a bond-servant's rights, even if he is not a citizen. Otherwise, in the case of a master's injustice, it would have to allow bond-servants to obtain justice of themselves. This could expose the masters' families, and civil society itself, to many problems.

2293. There is according to rational Right, therefore, concurrence of a bond-servant for the state of freedom, independently of the authority of civil society which is obliged by justice not to harm but prudently protect the concurrence.

Article 3.
The concurrence of citizens for all social goods and offices

2294. In modern times, hatred of every kind of monopoly clearly indicates the progress of civilisation and the prevalence in modern societies of the civil element over the seigniorial element.

2295. Another indication of progress is the repugnance — increasingly evident in public opinion — for all laws and ordinances which incapacitate a whole class of persons or, under the title of testing suitability, demand arbitrary, excessive and over-cautious qualifications before people can be admitted to certain posts or are suitable for exercising certain offices, particularly in the case of private occupations, such as arts and crafts

---

[319] The Athenians recognised this right of a cruelly treated bond-servant to require that he be sold.

2296. Nevertheless it is absolutely certain that a wise government can and must require guarantees from those seeking public offices, and tests which can assure the government and the public of the aspirant's suitability. But we still need to answer the great problem: 'What guarantees and tests must be required of aspirants to public posts, so that 1. society is assured of their suitability and, where the choice concerns several suitable competitors, which has the *greater suitability*, and 2. the *least possible restriction* is placed on universal concurrence?'

2297. This is one of those difficult problems whose solution is gradually obtained over the centuries. Experience and political reflection can indicate ways to continually reduce those obstacles to concurrence presented through qualifications or other necessary guarantees and tests, without diminishing the probability of choosing a suitable aspirant, and among suitable aspirants the most suitable.

2298. It is sufficient for me to have proposed the problem, which still needs direct study. I will make a few general comments about it.

First of all, the obstacles to *jural concurrence*[320] would, it seems to me, be completely annulled, if the condition of greater suitability could be fulfilled. The suitability would have to be ascertained by tests directly demonstrating it, excluding all indirect tests which generally relate more to the *means* by which the suitability is supposedly obtained than to the suitability itself.

2299. *Direct* tests of suitability are:

1. *Public opinion* which attests the aspirant's suitability. — But we still need a solution for the question: 'What are the means for knowing public opinion with the least danger of error, and for not taking private, incomplete information as public opinion?'

2. *Previous relevant facts* about the aspirant, particularly public facts which exhibit his suitability; published works, to ascertain his knowledge,.

3. *Strict examination* at a time *close* to the choice.

---

[320] By *jural concurrence* I mean *concurrence by right, concurrence protected by rational Right*. Note carefully, I never speak about a truly unlimited concurrence; the only concurrence I support is that limited by rational Right alone.

4. *Practical tests* in which temporary responsibilities of minor importance are entrusted to him. Hence, a *formal*, not *material* gradation of posts, calculated not only by years of service, but by ability and prudence during service.

2300. There may indeed be advantages in committing the appointment and proposal of employees stably and exclusively to the body of people of which the new employee will be a member, but there are also drawbacks, and one very notable drawback: the body of people that makes appointments and proposals soon changes into a faction, intent on exploiting this power for its greatest private profit. It is a fact (which will certainly be known to political prudence) that when a faculty, right or public power has become *fixed* in a certain class of persons, they eventually learn how to make it productive for their own private advantage. Time sharpens minds, which discover a thousand clever ways of accomplishing this. Such people gradually form corresponding practices which pass as legitimate and equable; they consent and conspire in an extraordinarily instinctive way for the same end, and through habitual behaviour that passes for a tacit pact. Hence, to avoid forming FACTIONS whose choice of the most suitable people is limited to a very small number of adherents, no time must be left for jiggery-pokery; and proposals for posts must never depend in a fixed and stable way on these factions. What then is to be done?

An autocrat could authorise a reputable, upright person, who would act on only *one occasion*, to propose those who are to be given *important* posts. I say one person rather than many because his honour would be involved and he would want to succeed in the task entrusted to him. In certain Italian universities, the magistrate responsible for studies did precisely this: the person commissioned to find a worthy professor for some seat was particularly careful to gather very accurate information about the most outstanding academics of the time, with the result that an eminent subject was always proposed. It is true that in the case of social posts, many qualities and special merits must be considered, but these are to be weighed, as I said, by a *tribunal of distributive justice*, by a kind of jury which is never fixed but chosen for each occasion, whether or not the composition of the tribunal is regulated by fixed laws or maxims.

[2300]

CHAPTER 8
The sanction of civil rights

Article 1.
The sanction of civil rights is found in two supreme forces

2301. In civil society two supreme forces constitute the sanction of all social rights: 1. material force, and 2. prevalent public opinion.

2302. The *supreme material force* must be in the hands of the governors of society (cf. 1640–1642); otherwise, government of society would be impossible.

2303. *Public opinion* constitutes the sanction of the rights proper to the governed.

Article 2.
Civilisation increases in proportion to the growth of the two supreme forces which sanction civil rights

2304. Civil society's growth in perfection keeps pace with the growth of the two forces. Justice becomes more secure and civilisation continually makes greater progress.

2305. In Europe both forces have undergone extraordinary growth: the *material force* of the State through the outstanding Napoleonic law of conscription; the force of *public opinion*, through the press, popular discussions and movements, and through the holy Alliance where we see the principle of *justice* battling against the evil principle of *utility*. These causes united many scattered, divergent opinions, and undertook the great task of uniforming the opinion of the modern masses about social justice, a task that is making rapid, unpreventable progress.[321] Uniformity of opinion in political matters is, as we have seen, the legitimate force of the people.

---

[321] A symptom of this progress is 1. the contemporary need for religious and jural *convictions*; 2. the proclamation of the moral duty to *make known*

2306. Political policy which prevents the people from acquiring uniformity of opinion about political justice is blameworthy and false because:

1. *Uniformity* of opinion leads civil societies to their highest perfection.

2. The governed have an inalienable right to use all means conducive to this purpose.

3. Obstructing the means for attaining this desirable uniformity can never be the task of society, which essentially desires and tends to it. Obstruction would be the work of a *party* seeking to dominate society with tyranny, or of a *master* ignorant of his duties. But uniformity of opinion reconciles all interests and brings peace; to oppose it is to foment war and renounce the peaceful settlement of quarrels, a duty incumbent on all (*RI*, 462, 501, 1026).

4. Such *uniformity* cannot arouse fear or reasonable suspicion on the part of *social government*; on the contrary, it alone offers definite norms which government can follow unerringly in its dispositions (*RI*, 1672, 1687–1688).

2307. Nevertheless government, which leaves free for the governed all the means able to guide them to uniform thinking in the matter of civil justice, can and must use the same freedom. It can and must use its influence to rectify public opinion, particularly and perhaps solely by informing the people of public facts and their circumstances, by telling them the reasons for its dispositions, and thus by interesting them in its ends of common or public usefulness. Finally it can and must punish *severely* all those who 'can be convicted of having spread *false facts* among the public with the intention of misleading public opinion' or, even without this precise intention, with malice or excessive irresponsibility. Public opinion is always misled by lies about facts. When malicious diffusion of false facts is declared a crime officially by public magistrates, the probity needed in forming public opinion is sufficiently safeguarded.

one's convictions, a duty which has been so supremely and recently expressed by the Gospel as the work of faith. In this regard, I think the work of Vinet, *Essai sur la manifestation des convictions religieuses etc.*, Paris, 1842, is symptomatic and worth noting.

[2306–2307]

Article 3.
Agreement between the two forces produces the most stable public peace and prosperity

2308. Government can and must desire in all its citizens the formation of uniformity of thought about questions of social Right: hence, 1. it must not obstruct the means or suppress the speech of those who wish to discuss these questions freely; 2. it must promote and protect the means, and 3. use its own means to obtain this uniformity. These, as we have said, lead to clear, full knowledge of public facts (without the government assuming the office of teacher, which is not its function) and suppress all publicly disseminated, malicious, falsified facts.

This last duty of government seems to me so important that I consider it requires its own very extensive law, drawn up in such a way as to be effective. The time will come when we will feel the importance of such a law. The nation which first undertakes to formulate it will show how its advance in civilisation outstrips that of the other nations.

2309. When this precious uniformity, the maximum power of nations, has been procured, a new, very felicitous duty is initiated for governments, which guarantees public tranquillity and the greatest possible development of national prosperity. This great duty consists in always maintaining perfect agreement between the two supreme forces of society, the *material* force (which must be in the hands of government) and *public opinion* (in the hands of the governed). In other words: 'It will be the sacred, supreme duty of government to rule civil society according to prevalent public opinion, not according to particular theories.'

2310. A government acting in this way is secure and very strong, and can do everything for good. Society cannot be disturbed because every dangerous disturbance always arises from the real or imagined opposition between the *material force* and the *force of public opinion*. When these two forces work together, no other power can offer the least resistance.

2311. I say 'real or imagined opposition' because the public can for a short time be deceived. Demagogues of any party can make them believe that government, contrary to fact, is against public opinion. But if trouble-makers are not supported by real governmental errors, their words are completely empty. We have said however that government must take care to rectify public opinion, repel the calumnies with which parties burden it, and present in full, public light the truth of the facts, its own intentions and the reasons for its actions. In short, it must continually, frankly, intimately and trustingly communicate its feelings to the masses it governs. If the masses are kept fully informed of the government's wisdom, they will be steadfastly affectionate and obedient, and love the government more than their own life.

2312. But if public opinion is unknown, how can a government regulate its dispositions to fully reflect public opinion? And how can it know public opinion whose manifestation it prevents?

Obviously a wise, non-partisan government which truly wishes to be guided in practice by public opinion must allow such opinion ample opportunity to manifest itself. It has nothing to fear from revelations it truly desires to follow. One of its duties, therefore, is its jural, prudent responsibility of allowing the masses to freely manifest their opinion, which it then uses as a basis for its own wise, beneficent action.

2313. This doctrine will, I hope, appear so obviously true to anyone unfettered by narrow theories that he may wonder whether it is even possible for 'a non-partisan civil government ever to want to act against prevalent public opinion.'

The query does in fact merit an answer, as follows. As I said, *civil autocracy* is not a naturally inalienable right, as political sophists have claimed. It can in fact be alienated like any other man-made right and conferred on either a collective person (pure aristocracy) or an individual person (pure monarchy) (*USR*, 312–314). Thus, two cases must be considered: in the first, *civil autocracy* remains in the hands of the fathers; in the second, it is conferred on an individual or collective person.

In the first case, the fathers can govern by themselves (pure democracy), although this cannot be realised except perhaps in a very small civil society; or they can set up a delegated or ministerial government (*USR*, 312–214).

Only when the fathers retain *autocracy* and exercise civil government is there no collision between the material force and formed public opinion;[322] in this case public opinion is the very opinion of the fathers who govern.

In all the other cases, government, whether autocratic or administrative, is not directly guided by public opinion, and can collide with public opinion, by ignoring it or making private, dynastic aims prevail over social-civil aims.

Article 4.
A wise civil government never lacks a way to sanction all civil rights

2314. We must bear in mind that, once uniformity of opinion has been sufficiently formed among the masses, a wise government never lacks the force to protect all its own civil rights and those of the people it governs.

Such a government can be correctly called all-powerful for good when it ceaselessly strives 1. to increase uniformity of thought in all about the maxims of public justice, and 2. to apply its enactments impartially and flexibly in accord with prevalent public opinion, rather than accommodate *a priori* systems or partisan suggestions, or the limited calculations of a few particular counsellors. In this way it avails itself of the two supreme forces of society, its material force and the support of prevalent opinion.

2315. This kind of government is in a position to repress any injustice whatsoever against public order or private rights; it is a government that completely protects all rights.

2316. Such a government need work now only for unity of organisation in which authority and material force are sufficiently centralised. This condition is fully verified in monarchies.

[322] Note, I speak about *already formed public opinion*, that is, more or less uniform opinion. The profound defect of purely democratic governments lies in the great difficulty they have in bringing about this uniformity. Parties usually tear this kind of government apart, and the subsequent division makes it impossible for government administration to agree with prevalent public opinion. This is not because, granted prevalent public opinion, government could not agree with it, but simply because the opinion is either lacking or too imperfectly formed, or always undecided.

[2314–2316]

For example, if the *autocracy* of a certain society is in the hands of a single individual, and all its material force is bound to the autocracy (as it must be), the individual autocrat can freely repress even the injustices perpetrated by magistrates or ministers of the society who, precisely because they do not share in the autocracy, cannot easily exempt themselves from due punishment. The masses, pleased at seeing crime punished everywhere, have nothing more to do or desire than praise their very just ruler.

Article 5.
The sanction of civil rights when a government fails in its obligations

2317. But what if government, and autocracy itself, abandon this safe line of conduct? What if a government's dispositions oppose public opinion about right, or the masses see all rights harmed rather than protected by government blindness or malice? Do the citizens themselves have a legitimate sanction for rights violated by social power or in its name; and if so, what is this sanction? This most delicate and difficult question of social Right, cannot be avoided (*RI*, 459). I will therefore propose the opinion which seems to me to conform with truth and justice, although I am ready to change it as soon as I am shown something better.

§1. *Principles, taken from individual Right, to be kept foremost in mind in this discussion*

2318. Defence and restitution is a function connected with all rights (*ER*, 246–251). The *exercise* of this function can be very difficult to carry out without exceeding its limits. This is precisely the situation of those citizens who intend to defend or restore rights of their own injured by civil authority or, more accurately, in its name or under its pretext.

2319. Before beginning such a difficult discussion, I must

[2317–2319]

present the principles which direct the exercise of the right of defence, or more generally, of sanction. I will draw these principles from various parts of individual Right and from the two books that precede it [*ER*], where I discussed them.

First principle regulating the exercise of the right of coercion. The coercion present in every right is *personal force* (*ER*, 246–251). Because right is essentially moral, this force must be exercised *morally* (*RI*, 383, 400, 923). Hence whenever the exercise of coercion is morally tainted, it ceases to be right. This is the first and most important limit to the right of coercion.

Second principle regulating the exercise of the right of coercion. Consequently, the exercise of coercion, when involving violence which harms the person over whom it is exercised, can be and is totally forbidden by morality. This is the case of a son who can never strike or injure his father to enforce respect of his rights. Immorality is always involved in an act of this nature (*RI*, 843, 1792). The same is true for a wife relative to her husband (*RF*, 1431–1443).

Nevertheless, although the exercise of a violent and injurious defence may never take place in certain cases, we cannot conclude that true right is absent. The essence of right does not require the force which guarantees it to be continually in act, as we said in the case of a father enfeebled by old age (*RI*, 858).

2320. *Third principle regulating the exercise of the right of coercion.* I cannot defend myself by inflicting harm on another unless the culpability of the person who prejudices my right is certain. The prejudice itself however need not be certain (*RI*, 1747, 1823, 1830).

2321. *Fourth principle regulating the exercise of the right of coercion.* In cases of doubt, we must accept there is no culpability in the person who acts, according to the saying: 'Everyone is presumed good until proved evil' (*RI*, 1840–1847).

Note that every administrator or governor has the duty and right to administer and govern according to his view of things and to do all he considers helpful to his government. When he has done this, he is no longer responsible to those he governs for his human errors, nor for the greater good he could obtain for them but does not because of his limited faculties and abilities, that is, because of his invincible powerlessness. The governor of a society is the *competent judge* of the mode of governing.

Although the governed have the right to place before him what they believe necessary for his office, they cannot blame him if he omits what they see as better. On the contrary, they must accept the consequences of the institution of government, just as they must accept the decision of a competent judge (*RI*, 610–612, 631, 713).

2322. This does not prevent us from being judges of our own good and evil (*RI*, 630, 713). In our case, the greatest good of each of the governed is certainly that of being governed, although in every human government imperfections and defects play a part. If each of the governed claimed to direct the government, government would be impossible on earth. Even if this were possible, imperfections and defects would still be present, because every person governed would cause other imperfections and defects inherent in the manner of government he thought best and most preferable. To avoid this great weakness a *unique social-mind* was created to direct and govern civil society. Moreover, the good a social government can effect and the evil it can remove is neither a good nor a right of the governed. On the contrary, the object of their right is solely the good effectively and really procured for them by the government. A distinction must be made therefore between *social gain*, and *ownership and individual rights*:

a) *Social gain*, which is produced by governmental administration, consists in the evils avoided and the good acquired. The government is the *competent judge* of the manner of this administration. The governed must be content with the large or small gain they obtain from it, even if convinced that other ordinances would have resulted in a larger gain. They only have a right *ad rem* to the social gain, and do not determine its quantity, which depends on the degree of perfection of administration over which the government has the right.

b) In the case of *ownership and of rights of the individual*, a government may lay its hands on goods which are the object of these rights. It can do this either by providing equable indemnity and compensation (given or promised), which is a governmental act of which the government is the sole competent judge; or by seizing goods without promise of compensation or any social title, which is an act of injustice committed in the name of the government, and an abuse of authority. Here, the *competent*

[2322]

judge is the person harmed, who has the same right relative to those invested with power as to others because society and government are jurally equal to every other subject of Right (cf. 2181–2187).

2323. *Fifth principle regulating the exercise of the right of coercion.* The right of coercion must be used only when it can obtain its effect, and even then not always, but opportunely.

A person whose right has been injured causes greater harm only to himself whenever he wants to use his insufficient force for self-vindication. He is thus obliged not to use his right of coercion because the *occasion* is lacking, which is a *jural* condition for exercising one's rights.

It cannot be objected that right in this case depends on the accident of force, contrary to what we have said elsewhere (*ER*, 246–251). We must distinguish between *right* and its *exercise*. *Right* remains unchanged as a *faculty*. For the faculty to be *actuated*, it must always find in reality certain conditions which render its act reasonable in all respects. This complex of conditions I call 'a favourable occasion for exercise'. It is possible for right to have the occasion to exercise some of its functions but not others. As long as the latter lack an occasion, they remain suspended, and the desire to exercise them is contrary to reason, that is, to jural law. Good sense acknowledges this when it judges an undertaking correct from its successful outcome. It would judge differently if it had not succeeded. Thus common sense recognises the condition for justice present in the prudence of those who have brought an undertaking to a happy conclusion. A weak person who, although in the right, wishes to sustain an unequal struggle in which he loses profitlessly, is not justified, is not really exercising a right. His duty is to surrender and commend the defence of his rights to divine Providence.

2324. *Sixth principle regulating the exercise of the right of coercion.* Force may not be used in defence of one's rights if harm is done to the innocent (*RI*, 1747–1757).

2325. *Seventh principle regulating the exercise of the right of coercion.* Force may not be used to defend one's rights when the harm done to the guilty assailant is far greater than the value of the violated rights (*RI*, 1803–1819).

2326. *Eighth principle regulating the exercise of the right of*

[2323–2326]

coercion. The harm done to the guilty must be necessary for defence. If we can safeguard our rights without harm to the guilty we must do so (*RI*, 1793-1802, 1989–1993).

We must choose the least harm possible to the guilty. Hence material force may be used only when peaceful ways of obtaining the same purpose are precluded.

2327. *Ninth principle regulating the exercise of the right of coercion.* This follows from the previous principle. If someone culpably attacks our right by misuse of his own, we must be content to prevent the misuse without despoiling him of his rights (*USR*, 382).

2328. *Tenth principle regulating the exercise of the right of coercion.* Consequently, we distinguish the *offending subject* as *offender* from all the innocent persons united to him, together with all his other accidents, qualities or rights which are not related to the offence. As far as possible, we preserve everything connected with him which does not form part of the efficient cause of the offence itself.

2329. *Eleventh principle regulating the exercise of the right of coercion.* Finally, no one may use the right of coercion except in legal and jural ways. If his right still has no defence, he must impute this to his ignorance alone.

§2. *Opinions of authors*

2330. Discussing the opinions of authors, we find they are divided on this very difficult question, just as they are on other questions. Some grant to the governed the right of coercion relative to those governing; others deny this.

2331. This disparity of opinion seems to arise because some authors consider the matter in the abstract, others in the concrete.

2332. The former are evidently satisfied to establish the existence of unquestionable, reciprocal rights and duties between the governed and those governing. They can therefore conclude that both sides must possess coercion, the function accompanying all rights.

This is the opinion of Grotius, Pufendorf, Horn, Burlamachi,

Vattel, Rousseau, Berkeley, Höpfner, Fichte, Meister, Blackstone, Locke, Scheidemandel, C. L. Haller and others. However they strive hard to restrict the use of such a dangerous right to a varying number of conditions; some in fact grant it only to the majority of a nation.

2333. Those who deny the right base themselves mostly on one or other of the following arguments:

A. The duties of civil authority are solely *ethical*, not *jural*;[323] such duties have no corresponding right of coercion. — We have seen however that the nature of jural duty consists in respecting the right of others (*ER*, 268) by not entering the sphere of their ownership (*ER*, 341). We would therefore either have to deny all rights of the governed relative to those governing — an absurdity never professed by anyone of balanced judgment — or grant that the duties of those governing are truly jural. And if we claimed to define jural duty as that which has no corresponding right of coercion, the argument would be a vicious circle.

2334. B. A doctrine that grants the right of coercion to the governed is dangerous. — Those who disagree reply, 'It is indeed dangerous if proposed purely in itself, but if kept within its limits, it becomes extremely helpful both for the governed and for the preservation of the authority of those who govern. On the other hand, jural questions are not about whether particular opinions are dangerous because they can be easily misused, but whether they are true in themselves without relationship to abuse (*RI*, 459).

2335. C. Supreme civil authority comes from God. — Not

---

[323] Baroli maintains that the duties of sovereigns towards their subjects are purely *ethical*, not *jural*. Elsewhere he says that the duties of sovereigns are imposed by *jural natural law* (*Diritto naturale pubblico interno*, §215). He also says that the duties of sovereigns have corresponding true *rights* in the subjects: 'The *rights* of the subjects, as such, correspond exactly to the ruler's duties towards the State' (*ibid.*, §217). But it seems to me that just as duties imposed by *ethical law* must be called *ethical*, so the duties imposed by *jural law* must be called *jural*. Similarly, merely ethical duties are those to which there are no corresponding rights in others. Hence, when persons have true rights which are objects of duties, the duties must be called *jural*. This word, which comes from *ius* (*right*), means simply either the source of the duties (jural law) or the corresponding right in others by whom they are observed.

[2333–2335]

only civil authority but every right, authority and power, even pure *de facto* power, comes from God, according to the well-known axiom, *omnis potestas a Deo* [all power is from God]. In other words, legitimate power, and right of any kind, come from God through jural law. Consequently, if rational jural law grants a right of sanction to the governed, which is our quest, it also comes from God. The question is not solved by the divine source of authority but by consulting the proximate source of rights, that is, *jural reason*; only this can tell us whether the right of coercion under discussion exists. And granted that jural reason really admits the right of coercion, we are at once in a position to argue that this right, like all other rights, comes from God.

2336. D. The governed are unable to judge whether civil authority acts well or badly, because only those who govern can judge how civil society is to be governed and directed. — This argument, unlike the previous ones, cannot be answered briefly. I need to put forward as thoroughly as possible the reasons of those who maintain the contrary opinion, so that full light may be thrown on the matter and all doubt removed.

We must first do away with the superficial distinction made by some authors between *judging* the acts of civil authority *as such* and *judging their effectiveness*. They allow the former but not the latter. But I understand 'judging their effectiveness' means judging them, and on the basis of this judgment, being able to redress the wrongs received from the use of material force. In this case, the distinction, resting on the solution given to the previous problem, is useless for solving the present problem. Leaving aside therefore such an inept distinction, let us see whether the argument based on the principle that the governed have no right to judge those who govern, can in effect remove the right of coercion from the governed.

In the first place, the principle that the governed are not competent judges of governmental acts is true only within certain limits. In fact the following are cases where the governed are undoubtedly competent judges of the acts of civil authority, not directly but indirectly:

1st. case: the judgments of the governed concern their own *moral duties* and only indirectly the acts of civil authority; for example, if civil authority were to force them to do an intrinsically evil action. Baroli says:

> In this case, he (the subject) does not judge the king's enactments but the action he himself would have to carry out. If this action is absolutely contrary to his perfectly determined ethico-religious duty, he must consider it morally (ethically and jurally) impossible. Hence, because he does not judge the sovereign's commands but the morality and justice of his own action, he in no way violates his duty of passive obedience.[324] The fact is that if I judge what I am commanded as unlawful and unjust, I indirectly judge the command itself as evil and unjust.

2337. *2nd. case*: the governed make judgments concerning certain *moral duties of others*. If I can and must judge that an action (for example, an assassination or perjury) is something intrinsically evil, I can and must also judge that it is evil as much for others as for myself, and that the authority imposing it acts unjustly whether it imposes it on me or on others.

2338. *3rd. case*: the judgment concerns the harm done to the ownership and other rights of an individual without corresponding compensation. Here, the offended individual is the competent judge of the violation of his right and of the harm done him (*RI*, 610, 631, 713).

2339. *4th. case*: the judgment concerns a person's ethical duty to help or defend either others when the governor is trying either to draw them to commit evil or to harm relative rights of ownership; for example, the obligations of fathers to defend the chastity of their children, or even their possessions. In this case the competent judge is the subject of the moral duty, according to the established principle that 'everyone is competent judge of his moral duties' (*RI*, 195).

In these four cases at least, the competence of the governed to judge is verified.

2340. On the other hand, those who govern are certainly the competent judges about how government should be directed; their judgment is competent when they choose one rather than another among possible governmental ordinances, provided

---

[324] *Diritto naturale pubblico interno*, 220, *2.

that all, *considered in themselves*, are legal and just. It does not matter whether the ordinances bring greater or less good to the governed, or protect them more or less effectively; those who are governed must submit rather than use coercive means, even if they think they know better, have more effective means, or consider other means imprudent.

This principle seems so evident that without it a society could neither subsist nor obtain its end. It simply demonstrates that coercion by the governed cannot be applied in doubtful cases; presumption must always be in favour of those who govern. However, the principle does not demonstrate the absolute exclusion of coercion in certain cases. The sentence of a competent judge loses all authority against the evidence, because no human being can ever cease to be reasonable, as God made him (*RI*, 610–612, 631, 713).

2341. It is true that in very special cases, such as that under discussion, the degree of evidence necessary for resisting this kind of competent judgment must be greater than in ordinary cases. But this does not mean that such evidence can never be obtained.

2342. E. It is not possible for the governed to use their right of coercion without producing a greater harm than that which they wish to avoid. Hence they have no right to posit coercion in act because of the principle mentioned above in principles regulating the exercise of the right. — Bossuet makes much of this argument. He says that the reason forbidding peoples to exercise the right of sanction in any case whatsoever is similar to the reason which

> obliged even freer peoples, when war was inevitable, to renounce their freedom and concede to their generals an absolute power over them. It was considered better to run the risk of perishing even unjustly through the general's orders than to face certain defeat through lack of union at the hands of more united enemies. — For similar reasons, a people that has experienced the evils, confusion and horrors of anarchy, gives up everything to escape them.[325]

[325] Mons. Marchetti notes that Bossuet begins with the false supposition that only *anarchy* existed in the world before the institution of governments. Moreover he correctly censures Bossuet's concept of the state of nature, a

Furthermore, since a people has no power over itself which it cannot direct against itself, it sometimes prefers to risk maltreatment by a sovereign than find itself having to suffer its own fury as a result of reserving powers to itself.[326]

2343. These words of Bossuet generate many observations by those who hold the contrary opinion:

1. They deny that any use whatever of coercion by the governed must inevitably promote anarchy and its accompanying horrors. The denial gains much more force when the doubt is applied to nations well on the way to civilisation. In these nations, discussion, the wisdom of the leaders and people, the justice of the cause, and uprightness of intention exercise a great influence. Bossuet's adversaries say that the exercise of coercion is certainly dangerous and blameworthy when exercised by an unbridled, corrupt multitude, as happened in France. But the same cannot necessarily be said about a people long instructed in the most moral and religious feelings, exhibiting that great unanimity in principles of social justice which keeps even the most powerful masses in order.

2344. 2. Is it true that coercion applied by the governed does greater public harm than good? Can this be easily calculated, particularly when it is a not a question of redressing an accidental and inconsequential wrong, but of restoring public order, which is the necessary basis for a nation to progress century by century to its greatest maturity? Monsignor Marchetti, a very Catholic author, further reflects that this kind of specious reasoning lacks sufficient force for quelling the multitude. He says:

The learned author of *De deux puissances* etc. invokes the

state described by the eloquent prelate as that in which 'we must suppose everyone to be independent of everyone else and also of the multitude' (*Avertiss.* 5, n. 55–64). Marchetti says: 'Here Bossuet considers the human being as born free and in anarchy. This idea is not far removed from that which later became common among publicists of the Revolution' (*ibid.*, sect. 2, 67). We see indeed how ancient the roots of error were; they penetrated even the best heads, among whom was undoubtedly the famous bishop of Meaux.

[326] *Avertiss. 5 sur les Lettr. de M. Jurieu*, n. 55.

natural principle of *greater harm.* This principle, which always causes disturbance to good order, may indeed provide strong reasons for restraining a people, but none for persuading them. If they understood that revolt would be worse for them, no one would need tell them not to rise; they would automatically refrain. The problem lies in the people's calculations of the evil that is harassing them today rather than tomorrow's book which they can hardly read.[327]

The truth is that *common sense* (not *popular passion*) can read tomorrow's book better than today's. It can sacrifice the passing present good for a long-term, enduring good. Sometimes, a sublime, immortal, providential feeling thrusts an entire generation down into the abyss, bringing about the salvation of many generations who, after making progress and being rejuvenated, live lovingly and peacefully in their own country.

2345. 3. Relative to Bossuet's example of military government, Mons. Marchetti makes the following observation:

> I do not see how a rational interpretation drawn from the state of war, which is a particular circumstance and violent to human nature, can supply us with a general rule upon which to base both the stable order of the City and the ordinary extension of supreme power. This would be going too far. It seems clear to me that we would have *military*, not common, jural-natural law as our derivative basis for government. It is odd, surely, for us to reason to the right of a commander-in-chief to do what he likes with his army, even in the strangest case, as the argument seems to maintain? No, obedience can be asserted for doubtful cases, but it can never be upheld in face of evident, profitless destruction.[328]

2346. 4. Bossuet himself, however, had no intention of including all cases in his theory. The minister, Jurieu, proposed the case of a ruler who commanded half his subjects to slaughter the other half. Bossuet replied that a purely hypothetical case had no place in the argument. Mons. Marchetti makes the following reflection:

[327] *Della Chiesa quanto allo stato politico della Città*, Conf. 9, sect. 2, 65.
[328] *Ibid.*, n. 68.

According to reason, a rule is not obliged to provide for *impossible* cases. But if it does not extend in reality to every *possible* case, it is clearly defective. In natural law we could propose a hundred cases of this kind, stronger even than Jurieu's.[329]

Bossuet's solution, although certainly good, concerns only cases outside the question; the most difficult and complex cases, covered by the question, are not dealt with. This is a facile way to reply to serious difficulties, but philosophers cannot be satisfied with it, still less the people.

§3. The inviolability of the sovereign's person according to socio-rational Right

2347. Although the authors' observations mentioned above are indeed wise, they do not completely settle the question concerning the right of the governed to use coercion. We need to go gradually deeper into the matter, trying first to determine certain particular propositions which will make the general solution much easier.

I first affirm that through socio-rational Right the sovereign's person must in every case be inviolable.

2348. I mean of course the sovereign in monarchies, because the proposition is not so evident in democracies and aristocracies. In these forms of government no individual person enjoys sovereignty, which lies solely in the social body. Consequently every individual is partly subject to the ruling collective person, so that *sovereign inviolability* would refer to an abstract person. But this is not the case in monarchies. In these, the sovereign, a *real* individual, is not subject to other individuals or to the nation itself.

2349. It would be possible to demonstrate the personal inviolability of an individual sovereign with moral arguments similar to those I used to demonstrate that a son cannot use his right of coercion against his father to the point of bodily injury (*RI*,

[329] *Ibid.*, n. 62, fn.

[2347–2349]

842–843). But the quality proper to sovereigns results from a special cause which protects it from harm.

2350. Sovereignty, considered independently of every seigniorial right that may be joined to it, and solely as *a person's own right to govern civil society*, indicates an *office* different from the concept of *member of civil society*.[330] Thus, whenever a citizen is raised to the rank of sovereign, he ceases to be a citizen; instead, he becomes head of the citizens. This needs to be carefully understood. A lawmaker, in his quality as lawmaker, cannot be subject to the laws; he exercises an office whose concept is outside society; he is above society. Society is that for which laws are made, that which wants to be governed and submits itself to common regulations in order to obtain the resulting common advantages. The sovereign however is the person who gives laws to the members and sees that they are carried out. As such, therefore, he is outside civil society.

2351. It is true that many sovereigns wished to be considered citizens relative to their temporal goods, making these subject to the same modality as the members' goods, and paying taxes into the treasury.

2352. But their person itself could not be placed in society and made subject to the penal laws common to the citizens because of the clear contradiction between making a law and receiving it. People may object that there is no absurdity in the sovereign's freely willed submission to such laws, but that would, in my opinion, destroy the hypothesis which posits an individual exercising a social autocracy which he does not abdicate. If he is responsible for judging everybody, who could judge him?

If there were someone in the society able to judge the sovereign *in virtue of social Right*, such a judge would share supreme authority with the sovereign. There would no longer be an absolute monarchy, which contradicts the hypothesis, but government by two individuals, each of whom judged the other.

2353. In civil society therefore no power exists that can judge the sovereign person. *Penal social right* does not exist for him. His person is correctly said to be inviolable.[331]

---

[330] Cf. *SP*, 111–131.

[331] The sacrilegious parricide of Louis XVI was carried out under legal forms in the name of civil society! This shows just how ignorant, false and

2354. Finally, the inviolability of sovereigns is given a more majestic characteristic by the Catholic Church's consecration of their person.[332]

§4. *No one has the right to dethrone an absolute sovereign*

2355. The royal right of inviolability is valid for individual sovereigns whether they have received unconditional or conditional sovereignty, provided the conditions of the latter do not remove autocracy.

2356. But the individual invested with unconditional autocracy has another royal right: he cannot be deposed from the throne.

2357. One of the principal reasons for this right is that while

wayward was the knowledge of *social Right* among those demagogues. The question that some ancient authors proposed, 'whether for self defence, sufficient for safety, you can kill the unjust aggressor even if he is a sovereign', pertains to *extra-social Right*, from which we prescind, and does not exhibit the French sophists' crass ignorance of the principles of social Right. The same must be said about the other question concerning the defence of innate rights, which we have discussed in *RI*, 84–127, 141–238.

[332] I wish to give honourable testimony to Ab. Gioberti by quoting a passage from his recent work, *Del primato morale e civile degli Italiani*, where he condemns as crime all violent social revolution: 'Catholicism gives special strength to political institutes in so far as it consecrates and deifies sovereign right, which it declares inviolable, and condemns all rebellion of subjects against it. This teaching is deeply philosophical because its contrary confuses and essentially nullifies the ideas of sovereignty of subjection. In every case, the opposite teaching severs, or at least endangers the nerves of power, which it sometimes considers violable. Nor does it matter that in certain cases rebellion may be helpful, and even seem necessary. The goodness of moral laws must on the one hand be measured by their more usual effects and on the other be absolute. Every exception mutilates and nullifies them. According to rational and Gospel ethics, every action which is generally and naturally harmful must be considered forbidden even in those few cases where it can be productive. If this were not the case, the moral rule would be subject to the narrow understanding and decision of the individual. Violent revolutions inevitably take place when they are necessary, which justifies Providence, which permits them in virtue of the good they cause in such occurrences. But this does not excuse their authors, because evil means can never be sanctified by the goodness and uprightness of the end.'

[2354–2357]

we can defend ourselves against others' abuse of their rights and even suspend the exercise of their rights, we can never despoil them of their rights. In reality there is never a need to go to such an extreme, because the governed always have other more moderate means for protecting their rights.

2358. A still greater injustice would be to deprive an entire royal family of sovereignty because of abuse by one or two individuals. It is a strange contradiction that, while some political sophists denounce as barbaric and cruel the confiscation of goods and similar penal laws on the grounds that this punishes the children for the fathers' crimes, they do not scruple to punish reigning families by depriving them of the throne.

§5. *No one has the right to profess anarchic teachings or to promote anarchy even indirectly and as a means to a better social state*

2359. This proposition is self-evident. Anarchy is the greatest of all social evils, the complex of all disorders. Any teaching therefore that promotes it is clearly the negation of every right, and persons whose actions directly or indirectly encourage it are guilty at one and the same time of all social crimes.[333]

2360. There are however today well-intentioned but deluded authors who justify anarchy as a temporary state on the way to a better organisation of civil society.[334] Unfortunately they have forgotten the first words of morality which forbid us to do evil that good may come, and also the first words of Right which forbid us to infringe any right whatsoever of others, even when we expect the greatest utility from it (*RI*, 1696–1703).

---

[333] The reigning supreme pontiff, Gregory XVI, most reasonably complains that 'freedom of every kind is proclaimed under the desire for novelty and promoting rebellion. Disturbances are fostered in civil and sacred matters; all sacred authority is rent asunder' (*Epistola Enciclica, etc*, 18 Kalend, Sept. 1832.

[334] Cf. the second letter of Ab. De Lamennais in *Apologetica*, p. 440.

§6. *In unconditional autocratic governments, it is never licit,*
according to social Right, for the governed to use the right of
violent coercion against the monarch

2361. We can see from all that has been said that legitimate
means for the governed to guarantee their own rights vary
according to different forms of government.

My intention is to discuss first of all the means which social
Right authorises for use in the most absolute, unconditional
monarchies. In this I will principally follow C. L. Haller, who is
also followed by Baroli.

I shall show that in this form of government the governed
never lack the most effective means for guaranteeing their
rights, that they have no need to use the right of coercion, and
that consequently the use of coercion is always illicit and unjust
(*RI*, 1764–1768).

A.
The peaceful means with which the governed can sufficiently
guarantee their rights in the most absolute monarchies

2362. The means I shall list presuppose above all that the
governed have solid grounds for appeal against social authority.

The first duty of the governed is to be completely certain that
grounds for appeal exist; in case of doubt, presumption is in
favour of those who govern, as we have seen. Whenever a people
is alert to this, has no preoccupations about it, and does not let
its imagination run wild or its passions be enflamed by rabble-
rousers, many causes for complaint vanish of themselves. Baroli
says:

> If subjects distrust their ruler, and are quick to accuse him
> in everything he does, to calumniate him even in the most
> innocent and just things, to view him as an enemy of his
> people, a despotic, evil potentate, they destroy the possib-
> ility of every bond of love and trust. They cause him to be
> suspicious, overbearing, strict, fearful of everything, and to

exercise his authority with an iron hand, often repaying injustices done to him with other injustices.[335]

2363. We also saw that the governed have the moral-jural duty not to claim the best of all government administrations as such, but simply a government that strives for the *relative best*, that is, strives for all it can procure with the means that it possesses and can use in good faith.

Furthermore, it must be borne in mind that the good behaviour of citizens can preclude and forestall any call for appeal.

1st. means. The first and best means of defence is the moral goodness of the governed. Coercive laws that restrict freedom and impose heavy burdens on the people to their great harm are in most cases provoked by the immorality of the people themselves.[336] Revolutionary doctrines in particular, sown in the minds of the masses, have a tremendous influence rendering government oppressive, and indeed force it to be so. Baroli describes these pernicious doctrines as follows:

> On the one hand, we have sovereignty that is suspicious of its subjects, always ready to misinterpret everything they present, inclined to severe coercive measures and on the brink of despotism. On the other, subjects are mistrustful of the supreme power, embittered critics of its every act and inclined to oppose it. The result is a difference of views, feelings and ends, a collision of interests, rancour, hatred, passive and active opposition to authoritative commands, secret societies, plots, conspiracies, proscriptions, civil wars, bloodshed, desolate families, revolution, anarchy, and in the end despotism. These are the sad consequences of the false teaching that subjects can legitimately exercise positive resistance to the ruler's prescriptions. Burke, in his reflections on the French revolution, wisely observed that when prudence makes tyrants of kings, principles make rebels of subjects.[337]

If evils result from the immorality of the governed, they no

---

[335] *Diritto nat. pubb. int.*, §222.

[336] Cf. *SP*, 432–448 for a discussion on laws provoked by the corruption of the masses.

[337] *Diritto nat. pubb. int.*, §222.

longer have a right to apply coercion. They must remove the causes of the evils by changing themselves for the better.

2364. *2nd. means*: the diffusion of knowledge of socio-rational Right; the ceaseless proclamation of its inviolability and usefulness. This means is most effective. It leads to the formation of that *uniformity* of social thought in the masses which is the most powerful guarantee of public order and all human rights. It shines resplendently in nations, once they have come to a certain level of civilisation. Baroli writes:

> If real, internal, public, natural right together with the wise modifications it undergoes in different States (positive, internal, public right) were better known and more deeply impressed in human minds, the practice of injustice would encounter insuperable difficulties. Upright principles of public, natural right, when diffused, dominate the hearts of both rulers and subjects, and are barriers to the execution of evil, both in the person who meditates evil and seeks to actuate it, and in individuals who are prevailed upon to carry it out.[338]

2365. Although diffused knowledge of the principles of rational social Right must be the basis for that uniform opinion which is the greatest guarantee of civil nations, it is helpful if positive-social right and its history are diffused as well. This knowledge draws the hearts of both the people and the sovereign back to ancient national practice, weaning their spirit away from harmful new practices. Haller says:

> History shows that wherever a people is interested in past events and in knowing all the vicissitudes of their country, and wherever they celebrate the glorious events which established, increased and consolidated the civil bond of the State, citizens' rights are very secure, injustices very rare, and the abuse of power encounters insuperable obstacles. Better still, such abuse is unknown in this kind of civil society. The fairly common study and knowledge of public right in Germany contributed greatly to the enduring preservation of the German empire, to the freedom of the States that composed it, and to the guarantee of the private rights proper to the inhabitants of that vast

[338] *Ibid.*

country. And we know the effects produced in England by the fairly widespread knowledge of the political history of that country, and of the royal promises which brought to an end long, bitter and intestine dissensions.[339]

3rd. means: religious influence. Uniformity of faith in religious belief is simultaneously the extremely solid foundation and keystone of that very powerful uniformity of opinion in moral and jural principles which, as I said, is destined to give immovable solidity to civil order in Catholic nations.

Napoleon's statement, 'I see the mystery of social order in religion. It is grafted on heaven by an idea of equality which restrains the poor from slaying the rich', can be very fittingly applied to subject and sovereigns. Religion in subjects forms the power of rulers, because subjects, without any conscience to subject them, are stronger than rulers. Religion in rulers is the best guarantee of the subjects' rights. Vattel proclaims:

> Masters of the earth, you acknowledge no superiors here below! What surety can we have about your intentions if we do not believe you are filled with respect for the common Father and Lord of mankind, and inspired by the desire to please him?'[340]

Atheistic philosophers are no sane choice as governors compared with religious rulers!

2366. *4th. means*: persuasive influence exercised on the monarch. Although the monarch is endowed with free will, it would be a great mistake to think that the members of the civil society he governs have no influence whatsoever on his conduct. We will leave aside his family on the worst possible supposition that the only kind of dynastic tradition it can offer is arrogant despotism. But outside his family, the members of the society he governs, considered as a whole, have an immense influence on the formation of his character and in the direction of his governance. Some are responsible for his education; others are his counsellors; others, ministers and officials, in other words, those who carry out his ordinances. The education he receives, the opinions in which he is formed, the counsels, suggestions and

---

[339] *Ibid.*, *1.
[340] *Droit des Gens*, t. 1, ch. 12, §125.

[2366]

co-operation given him in the execution of his wishes: all these come from citizens, and are the real cause of the good or harmful effects of his governance. This observation has the following important consequences:

2367. *a*) The citizens as a whole can never have the right to use violent coercion against their supreme governor. Some of them will necessarily be accomplices of his injustice and consequently have in their power a peaceful means for eradicating it. They can cease to co-operate.

2368. *b*) Those closest to rulers are themselves influenced by other people, who contribute to their education, form their character and refine their passions, etc. These people depend in turn on the influence of others, and so on. Clearly, therefore, all civil society is an interconnection of reciprocal influences; not a single human being is without influence on others. Not even the majority of citizens, therefore, can ever have a just title to exercise the right of coercion. In the absence of other peaceful means of defence, only pure necessity can justify coercion. But this is never verified in reality in public matters, where an immediate emendation of the government would take place if the reciprocal influences of the citizens were changed from bad to good. Anyone who considers the complex of influential causes must see that governments are precisely what people make them, and that corrupt rulers come from corrupt people; in other words, the people have the ruler they want. If justice, morality, order, diligence, strength prevail in the complex conduct of the mass of citizens, the result must be a just, moral, ordered and strong government.

2369. *c*) The effective injustice of a government's acts are in effect the result of a combination of very small cases involving citizens' unjust, lascivious, conniving and immoral acts. Even if this could justify (which it cannot) violent coercion, the coercion should never reach the ruler. Rather it should be directed against the executors of his unjust decisions. Even if it is supposed that all the decisions were entirely his alone and not inspired or suggested by perverse citizens or the contaminated atmosphere of a corrupt society, it is a principle of right that coercion is not exercised against unjust thoughts but against their external realisation by wicked, cowardly citizens (*RI*, 1770–1778).

[2367–2369]

2370. This is the jural reason why ministers, but never the sovereign, bear responsibility in constitutional States.

2371. *d*) It may be objected that, if the false way pursued by a government shows the wickedness of the complex of reciprocal social influences, this does not alter the fact that in societies some citizens are upright and totally innocent. They cannot be forced to suffer injury to their rights which is neither an indirect nor a direct effect of their perversity. — I reply: Who can be certain of total innocence in the social situation we are discussing? Who can be completely certain of not having been infected by the fetid atmosphere of the society in which he has been born, educated and lived? Who can be sure of never having committed any base act, spoken falsely, spread pernicious prejudices, even under the pretext of good? And finally, who is so perfectly good that he dares to condemn the mass of citizens, considering himself one of the few untouched by social corruption, of which we are frequently ignorant and from which we cannot escape? Even if we could be certain about all these things, it is a principle of right that coercion cannot be exercised unless a prevalent force can be used with inevitable effect and without doing further harm. In such a society the small number of the elect, granted they could be brought together, will never be in this situation. Even if they were, ought they to sacrifice the overwhelming majority for themselves?

2372. *e*) Even in these situations, particular or special societies can often obtain redress for their wrongs through commendable prudence and wisdom rather than through violence. Haller says:

> We can help ourselves by using our own intelligence and skill, by a docile, conciliatory conduct, without violating duty. Just as we can take refuge from a storm, or make use of a contrary wind and change the force that threatens harm into a beneficial power, so we can escape violence. The ruler has friends, counsellors, those in whom he places his trust. We can look to them for support; we can try to persuade them that injustice has been committed and, through them, bring the ruler to follow the path of justice and equity.[341]

341 Baroli, *Diritto nat. pubb. int.*, §222.

[2370–2372]

2373. *f)* Finally, good people can counter injustice with heroic meekness. This is not only a moral means of perfection and of divine merit in this life, or at least, in the next; it is abundant compensation for all wrongs received from others and, although slow, it is also a most effective means of persuasion, gently influencing the wills of rulers.[342] It serves as an example, as instruction for the people and a medicine for corrupt, violent society. Throughout history this moral, divine cure was applied by Christ and his disciples to healing an unjust, violent, cruel world. Its secret power effected the humanity of the present generation, the attractiveness of our manners and the desire for peace embedded in all Christian peoples, for whom violence is becoming more and more repugnant. In short, it has brought about *European civilisation* whose prosperity we enjoy and whose future shows great promise.

2374. *5th. means*: passive resistance. Whenever these means of persuasion do not obtain redress for wrongs, human beings must take comfort from the thought that no power can divest them of their true and absolute good, which is their essential right and the seat of all human dignity. No force exists that can constrain us to act contrary to moral laws and stain ourselves with sin. Whenever we are commanded something unlawful, we have the *right of passive resistance*, that is, not to obey. We are required by justice to hold uprightness and virtue in such high regard that we find in them and in God an entirely sufficient reward for our suffering, and in our suffering a pledge of immortal glory. To value them less is a moral defect, baseness. There have always been sublime human beings, armed with this moral feeling, who have preferred to die rather than kill. These are perfect Christians, who often showed this sublime cause of their patience before tyrants, and like lambs let themselves be dismembered by wolves.[343]

[342] 'This commendable conduct of subjects must succeed as a valid impediment to the continuation of the abuse of power. Meekness, patience, resignation are virtues that calm even the most enflamed anger and the most obstinate, mad desire for revenge, which is certainly not true of the case under discussion. In the eternal order of things, great evils and injustices do not last long. Likewise, nothing violent endures' (Baroli, *ibid.*).

[343] St. Eucherius' words about Maurice are well-known. When the emperor Maximian was trying to force the Christian Theban legion to sacrifice to

2375. Matters however seldom come to such an extreme, and civilisation grows in proportion to the rarity of such cases. In most instances, passive resistance, while remaining firm, can be exercised with such attractiveness and prudence that it becomes less displeasing to the person commanding an injustice. Haller writes:

> Without refusing obedience, it is possible to soften, temper and defer the execution of wicked, unjust commands, and often totally block them. The ruler, as a human being, cannot be entirely consistent in evil. Unforeseen difficulties are continually encountered; the execution of one imposed injustice requires another hundred injustices, which are neither desired nor commanded. Finally the evil in itself is neither proposed nor seen as an end; it is considered a means for obtaining a purpose. In such circumstances, those who must carry out the action have the right and duty to request further instructions, to point out the obstacles and indicate other expedients which may be more acceptable. Further reflection takes place perhaps, and the execution of the evil is deferred. Often the unjust measures are revoked by the person who prescribed them, or become useless due to a change of circumstances. Means of delay such as these and wise moderation are rarely impossible. Those who act in this way do not lose the ruler's esteem and trust; on the contrary, he generally trusts them more.[344]

2376. *6th. means*: the exercise of the right to express one's feelings in the correct way, to tell the truth (*RI*, 101–121) and to make the necessary suggestions to the ruler for emending legislation (*ER*, 1–20; *RI*, 1672, 1687–1688). The exercise of these rights has been sufficiently discussed elsewhere.

2377. *7th. means*: the exercise of the right of remonstrance and petition. Baroli argues as follows:

---

idols, Maurice, who was head of the legion, answered: 'Emperor, we are your soldiers, but freely confess that we are servants of God. — Life, our final need, has not forced us into rebellion. We have our weapons yet do not resist, for WE PREFER TO DIE THAN KILL' (*Apud Ruinart., Act. SS. MM., de ss. Maurit. et Soc.*, n. 4).

[344] Baroli, *Diritto naturale pubblico interno*, §222.

A ruler is a human being, a limited, free, reasoning being, subject to delusion and error. As such he needs people who can advise, support and aid him with their insight, experience and knowledge. In this way he can prudently avoid what may be prejudicial to the State and guide it to its goal with greater ease and certainty. It is the ruler's subjects who have the greatest interest in teaching him the way and the means to the end, all the impediments opposed to it and the dangers to be encountered. He needs to be taught about the conflicts caused by such situations, and the measures to be taken to overcome, avert and remove them. All this advice, when founded on upright knowledge of natural law (ethical and jural), of the laws in force in the City, and of the condition of the City, makes a truly valid bulwark against the abuse of supreme power. This defence does not offend or harm the rights constituting the supreme power nor the person who possesses it; on the contrary, it induces him to exercise the power legitimately.[345]

2378. In absolute monarchies the *right of remonstrance and petition* is the most precious right of all. When given total freedom, such a right is sufficient to render useless, and consequently illegitimate and criminal, the coercive methods of the governed.[346]

2379. To exercise this right most effectively and in its rational-jural integrity the following is necessary:

1. Every collective or individual person who has rights to defend must be able to exercise it; every citizen, every lawful society, a group of citizens, the majority, the whole body (all of whom are different subjects of social right) must be able to petition and remonstrate (*USR*, 367).

2. The remonstrances must be well thought out and weighed. Petitioners must be allowed sufficient discussion to agree upon wise and fully mature remonstrances which they can submit to the ruler.

3. The remonstrances need not be secret; indeed it is helpful if they are public, at least when this is the wish of those making

---

[345] *Ibid.*

[346] Rulers and ministers who look upon numerous petitions as a nuisance and hindrance to their office, and use indirect means to reduce their frequency and bluntness, are greatly mistaken.

them. In this way, if they concern matters that cannot be granted, impartial public opinion will uphold the ruler's refusal.

2380. These conditions make the right of remonstrance and petition a very effective safeguard for the rights of the governed. Exercised with maturity and wisdom, the right is a means of informing the sovereign clearly about the justice of the cause. If, however, the petition were to contain defects of form, the cause would lose its force; false counsellors could base a negative answer on it, or interested parties with influence over the sovereign could make bad use of it.

Furthermore, the right can often sincerely and faithfully express public opinion, which is the best rule for good government and, when uniform, an irresistible, persuasive, moral force. Any wise government therefore would want to know and acknowledge this opinion as its sole infallible guide and most faithful counsellor.

2381. *8th. means*: the right of pact. In my opinion, a people has no right to limit sovereign authority, nor the right to forcefully impose constitutions which limit it. I accept Baroli's opinion that

> To be legitimate, such limitations must come from sovereignty itself, because only the one who has a right can jurally dispose of and limit it.[347]

Note however that no authority can be said to be limited when determined exactly according to the law of reason, provided no arbitrary decision dictates the determinations, which must be formal, not material. Here, I refer the reader to what I said in general about *Right of jural claim* (*USR*, 160–167, 182, 196–197, 207–208, 212, 220, 232, *App.* no. 2), Right of *guarantee*, and of *pact* (*RI*, 524, 1703, 1837, 1863–1881).

2382. *9th. means*: the exercise of the right of emigration I have already discussed emigration (cf. 1632–1639). Haller notes:

> Emigration can certainly be regarded as a doleful benefit (*flebile beneficium*), a sad expedient and a fertile cause of bitterness and grief. Nevertheless, it is a means of guarantee against oppression and for obtaining peace. Thanks be

[347] *Diritto naturale pubblico interno*, §222.

to God, there are other States, countries and lands on which the sun shines beneficently, where it is possible to find the peace and safety sadly not granted on one's native soil. Unlike the polyps, a human being is not attached to the spot where he was born. The great stretch of our globe, inhabited by so many different peoples, offers a secure refuge to downtrodden justice, persecuted virtue and, in addition, honours, distinctions and compensations which the blind, ungrateful homeland has changed into oppression and proscription.[348]

In any case (as C. L. Haller observes), one need not always emigrate in fact. Often a short distance is more than sufficient to avoid contact with a prejudiced power and enjoy once again lost peace and security. Changing one's situation, choosing another occupation and abode, limiting needs as much as possible, renouncing one's claims to distinctions and dignities, even abandoning those already possessed, and having no further thought for benefits that produce unbearable burdens, are the natural, obvious means that every human being has for escaping from an oppressive power.[349]

B.
Objections

2383. Today, this teaching should be universally known. It should be taught to the peoples at large, and firmly impressed on their minds. Total sincerity and openness is required, however, if people are to be persuaded of its truth. We must also be convinced that today nothing can be kept hidden from the consideration of entire nations. Whatever monopoly of knowledge and information existed in the past has vanished today. For civilised nations, underhand social teaching has become petty, hateful, impossible trickery.

People also need to know the objections that may be made against solid maxims. Difficulties should be set out, expounded vigorously and completely, and answered with impeccable

[348] *Ibid.*
[349] *Ibid.*

logic. Only then can we hope to persuade minds and hearts. Objections passed over in silence by official teachers gain greater force in all minds; objections dismissed as insignificant develop forcefully; reticence counselled by false prudence provides a pretext for discrediting the best maxims in the world, which then remain entirely undefended.

I would be avoiding my own responsibility if I omitted anything that has been said or could be said by way of objection. I hope that my replies will be fully satisfactory.

2384. As far as I can see, there are two cogent, possible objections against the teaching on peaceful means:[350]

1st. Objection. The masses have great difficulty in coming to know these peaceful means. They find it difficult to understand the order of their distribution, or how to use them effectively, to foresee their results and wait patiently for the outcome. Even a wise, self-controlled person can hardly do this. The civilisation of nations may have begun but ignorance and its consequent recklessness of action are characteristics of the majority of the masses. This has been the situation of the European nations for centuries. Surely, undeveloped nations can exercise their right of coercion, when their ignorance of other ways makes violent coercion absolutely necessary for the defence and guarantee of their rights?

2nd. Objection. By supposing that the nine peaceful means mentioned above are practicable, we have done what Bossuet did. When the minister Jurieu proposed the case of extreme tyranny, Bossuet replied that it was a hypothetical case, outside the scope of theories. In fact, for the most upright, moderate publicists, the question whether the right of coercion can be exercised against unconditional autocracy is only an extreme case concerning the worst of governments. If government is the

[350] Note, it is not my intention to repeat the objections of those who consider the social contract as the only jural origin of civil society. Among these are radicals, communists, jurists of the French revolution, etc. As I have already refuted their system, I consider their objections void. I will confine myself to discussing those objections which I consider the most important, brought forward by people of good sense, unrestricted by ultra-liberal systems. In my reply, I hope to satisfy their expectations, especially as they are upright people of good faith who acknowledge intrinsically respectable principles of justice, without any reference whatsoever to their utility.

worst, as the hypothesis says, its despotism would undoubtedly prevent citizens from using any of the peaceful, persuasive means they might possess to give lawful value to their argument. The means you indicated apply to another case, therefore, not to the one under discussion.

Furthermore, an autocratic, unconditional government has a thousand ways of suppressing the most legitimate freedom, particularly if the government combines force with cunning.

For example, you propose the diffusion of knowledge of the principles of social rational Right. But this is precisely what a misguided government prevents by great cunning united with force. It bans discussion of these principles, and in the schools only tolerates teaching that excuses its conduct. In a word, it ensures ignorance, nurtures prejudice, teaches errors; above all, it is afraid that those whom it governs might form a uniform opinion about the principles of justice, which would raise an insuperable barrier against the abuse of its power.

Religious influence also would be of no avail if the government held religion in bondage, claiming authority over it and honouring it only on condition that it co-operates with and ministers to its despotism.

Again, the exercise of the right to express one's feelings, to speak the truth and to suggest ideas necessary for the emendation of legislation by the supreme power is of no avail if the people have been silenced. A great number of speakers and authors would be so corrupted by money that they would justify the most enormous arbitrary decisions invested with legal form. A depraved government would have no difficulty enacting minute, complex, voluminous legislation, and thus blocking all honest public and private criticism. When the critics' silence caused offence, they would be condemned as lacking respect, as enemies of the government; seriously suspected of conspiracy, they would already be considered as rebels. And all this of course would be done in the name of law, after the government had deprived their opponents of all possible concurrence for posts of employment and social honours (considered solely as sovereign favours), caused them widespread trouble, and handed them over to the police (if not worse). All this would follow upon frequent paternal warnings or convictions for breaking the sovereign laws. Who knows what the final outcome would be?

You speak about the right of remonstrance and petition, but you cannot be taken seriously. Nothing could be easier for a degraded government than to abolish this right or, if that is hypocritical (which it is in the majority of cases), render it useless and a pretext for greater oppression. Initially, the government will grant the right in writing precisely to hide its despotism better. Later, by requiring innumerable formalities which cannot be fulfilled, they render the right ineffective. Initially the right will be limited to private concerns, but the government will consider it a serious evil if remonstrances multiply, or many citizens support them, with the result that the right becomes more and more the organ of public opinion. The government will then obstruct the means which the remonstrating citizens can use to draw up a respectful petition that has been carefully prepared, contains only what has been well tested and cannot be reasonably rejected. In order to draw up the remonstrance, wide consultation and long discussion of all its articles, of its phrasing and of individual words, is necessary, but the government, which is afraid of everything and only seeks motives and pretexts for rejecting the remonstrance, will be suspicious of such discussion and prohibit it. History has shown time and time again how a petition containing a very just appeal has been rejected, and in fact regarded as criminal evidence because it contained expressions less than respectful, or spoke the truth without flattery. When the request has been substantially irrefutable according to right, a way has frequently been found to reject it by insisting on some accessory point, overlooked through insufficient consideration, in which the petitioners were wrong. In the years immediately prior to 1790, many petitions of this kind were presented to European sovereigns with the most deplorable outcome, simply because they were defective in their composition and in minor points, although their main argument was well grounded.

2385. Finally, the right of emigration can easily be abolished by positive law. In which case, flight, even that described by Christ, 'When you are persecuted in one town, flee to another', can be declared a crime against the State!

If therefore you intend to keep to the particular case of a

[2385]

people subject to the worst and most cunning government imaginable, your suggested means are valueless.

C.
Replies

2386. In reply to the first objection I say that the right of defence can be exercised only within the limits proper to the right (*RI*, 1769–1819). Under the given conditions, it is not possible for a primitive people (the kind in question) to have the ability, insight and tranquillity of soul necessary for using the right. The case is similar to a person who has a doubt about the lawfulness of an action but is unable to use a reflective principle to solve the doubt. We have already shown that in such a case the person is obliged to follow the safe way, a way which does not expose him to the danger of injuring uprightness and justice. This explains why moral teachers in primitive, undeveloped peoples are consistently tutiorists. Because they can find no other way of avoiding the danger of sin, tutiorism becomes obligatory.[351]

The same argument applies to a people whose intellective faculties are undeveloped. Heroic patience in bearing the evils of an unconditional, legitimate but despotic monarchy becomes a strict obligation for them, precisely because they are unable to evade the obligation in the right way and without sin. This was the path followed by the first Christians. Many fine moralists have taught the same system, a system which was just because necessary at the time they wrote.

2387. To the second objection I reply that a government may obstruct some but not all of the above-mentioned means: the first, fourth and fifth means are always available. Nor can it obstruct the others entirely, but only render necessary greater skill and virtue in their implementation. For example, the influence of religion, particularly in Catholic nations, cannot fail totally. Jesus Christ established pastors in his Church, imposing on them the strict obligation to lay down their lives for their

---

[351] *Conscience*, 799–801.

sheep. They are also obliged to take care of the soul of the sovereign and make him feel his subjection to the supreme Being, no matter what harm they suffer. This heroic ministry is especially the responsibility of the Head of the Church.

In the same situation, every citizen can make use of the sixth means. Speaking the truth is sometimes a strict obligation which must be fulfilled even at the cost of life, especially when the horrors of revolution have to be avoided. In this case, good citizens sacrifice themselves for their country.

2388. Relative to the fourth means, anyone who examines the argument attentively will see that the objections carry no weight. Such a person will be convinced that the sole cause of the wickedness and incompetence of such an oppressive government is the wickedness of the governed themselves. If the people reform themselves, they will reform the government.

§7. Conditional monarchies

2389. Both the civil head and the citizens are obliged by the pacts they make, and by the conditions stated or certainly understood.

If this reciprocally binding contract is broken by the civil head, the offended side can certainly use its right to free itself from the conditions of the contract. The reader can find sufficient teaching about the use of this right and about the religious-moral cautions to be observed in its application in the various places where I have discussed such rights. A longer explanation, relative to Catholic States, will be found in *Conferenze di ragion pubblica* to which I refer the reader for the sake of avoiding repetition.[352]

[352] The question is dealt with in the third part (Rimini, 1824, printed by Mansoner and Grandi). — The work is certainly badly written; it is prolix, caustic and sometimes partial. Nevertheless it contains very beautiful truths illustrated with considerable learning and acumen. A good Catholic writer who could reduce the three thick volumes to a single large one would be doing something useful for the progress of Catholic-social ideas.

§8. *Democracies and aristocracies*

2390. These forms of government normally have legal means, laid down by their constitutions, through which citizens can obtain redress for wrongs suffered. These means must be added to those proper to absolute monarchies.

2391. Granted a pure democracy, violent coercion would clearly be eliminated and could never be exercised against supreme authority. Because every citizen is a part of sovereignty, sovereignty is present if the citizens all agree, with the result that no one will make war on it. If they disagree, their dissension must be judged with the principles of extra-social Right. This kind of war is made by partial, independent societies.

2392. The same must be said about a pure aristocracy whenever discord arises among the nobility. As far as the people are concerned, who have no part in the sovereignty, we must apply to them what was said to be licit for those who are governed without being simultaneously governors.

PART TWO

THE ORGANS OF CIVIL SOCIETY AND THE SOCIAL FUNCTIONS DETERMINING THEM

CHAPTER 1

The organs of civil society pertain to the science of Right in so far as their existence depends on jural titles

2393. The description of the organs of civil society pertains to *Right* to the extent that every organ must be constituted in a just mode, and that individuals representing organs and exercising their relative functions be chosen in just modes. *Ideal Right*, the theory of Right, determines both the jural modes through which different organs develop to give life and action in civil societies, and the modes through which officials are nominated; *real Right*, the application of right, determines the positive titles through which a given real person represents a given organ, that is, exercises a social function (*ER*, 54–89).

2394. An organ of society exists with a just title when it originates from the very nature of society or is constituted by a competent authority.

These are the two general titles which give legitimacy to the existence of the organs possessed by society.

CHAPTER 2

The relationship of organs with the nature of civil society, with its end, and with its different functions and dynamics

2395. Social organs are to some extent equal in all civil societies, and to some extent different in different societies.

2396. Organs which emanate from the essence of society are

[2393–2396]

equal. Because this essence is equal, organs actuating it are also equal.

2397. Organs constituted by competent authority are varied. This depends not so much on arbitrary choice, although this normally has some influence on their choice and formation, as on social needs and arrangements which vary according to accidental circumstances, such as the development and general tendency of a society. These decide the choice of competent authority in providing one kind of organisation for society rather than another.

2398. As we saw, different circumstances in civil society, different development, different needs, natural and man-made, and different tendencies determine the *real end* of society in very varied ways.

Indeed, the end of civil society has something stable and unchangeable, that is, the regulation of the modality of all rights (cf. 2128) in all civil societies alike. It also has something changeable. In other words, the end is conceived and developed, or *analysed*, in various ways in the collective mind of society. There is no doubt that the various *elements* composing the complex social end, which is always the perfect regulation of the modality of rights, are always better known and distinguished in societies further advanced along the road to civilisation.

2399. The end conceived in general, that is, synthetically, is common to all civil societies; it is a constitutive of their nature. As an identical nature determines the equality of certain organs, so an identical end determines the uniformity of this part of the organisation. But in so far as the end, conceived by the social mind, is analysed and distinct in its elements, so too the organs are found to be more or less developed, multiplied and distinct in different societies.

Indeed, granted that the social end is analysed and developed in a determined degree and manner, the functions of society are found to be determined in a corresponding degree and manner. These functions are simply a complex of the specific actions with which society endeavours to obtain its proper end relative to all the elements in which it has been able to conceive the end as distinct. Society, however, cannot execute its functions without different organs and actions. Consequently, organs are put into existence by social functions. When society moves to execute one of its functions, it immediately creates the organs necessary for this. The effort which society makes to act is the cause of its successive organisation. The organisation is perfected, therefore, according to the degree and mode of social activity, to the extent and measure that society undertakes to fulfil its functions.

2400. Nevertheless, the *same function* can also be assumed by society with different degrees of effort, and according to the stage of synthesis or analysis found in the concept of society. These are further elements which influence and vary the production of its organs. A different degree of effort produces stronger and more perfect organs; a more analytic concept of the desired function produces more distinct and multiple organs. A complicated organisation is not *per se* a defect in society. In fact, it must necessarily be found in all perfect, civil societies. It was always found in long-lasting societies such as the Venetian republic. Too simple an organisation is a defect of nascent societies or of those whose constitution was dictated by inexperienced persons tied to philosophical theories. These societies soon disappear unless social instinct intervenes opportunely with new decrees for their conservation.

CHAPTER 3

The relationship between the organs and actions of society

2401. I have distinguished governmental *functions* and the different *dynamics* into which they are divided according to the *aims* which government intends to attain with them. These aims of functions are the elementary parts of the complex end of society. As the end of civil society is the regulation of the modality of rights, so the end of a social function can only be a part of this regulation.

2402. Society, however, has to perform several actions to obtain the end of a given social function. The aim is not reached by a single action, but by several actions together.

2403. This happens partly through the nature of the acting *subject*, and partly through the nature of the *object* to which the subject's action tends. Relative to the *subject*, the human being and to a greater extent society, composed of human beings, is an entity of several parts. Consequently, they obtain what they want only by performing several actions and bringing into play several organs. For example, anyone who wishes to eat, or do anything else, has to carry out at least three actions: 1. conceive *intellectually* what he wishes to do; 2. decide to do it with an act of *will*; 3. carry it out with *locomotive forces*.

2404. Relative to the *object*, the good desired is often unattainable without several simultaneous or successive actions, granted the limitation of the actions themselves and the subject who carries them out. For example, if I want to eat some bread, I have to: 1. sow the wheat; 2. harvest it; 3. mill it; 4. make dough with the flour; 5. cook the dough; 6. eat it.

2405. Thus *the functions of society* are distinguished according to the elementary aims making up the social end. Similarly the *actions* of society are distinguished according to the law of social activity resulting from the nature both of the subject and the object. Again, the multiplicity of these actions multiplies the organs of society which must carry them out.

CHAPTER 4

Description of jural activity in civil society as this activity appears in its different powers and activities

2406. I do not think it necessary to say anything further about the nature and quality of social organs. However, I do think it would be very opportune to outline here subdivisions of jural activities in civil society, whose developed existence I take for granted. These subdivisions indicate the organs needed.

Article 1.
Autocracy and social action

2407. All jural activity in civil society, as in all societies, is first divided into two kinds: *autocracy* and *action*.

2408. Autocracy is the radical governmental power of society; action is all that autocracy does, directly and indirectly. Autocracy is government in *potency*; action is government in *act*.

2409. Act supposes potency. Every government, therefore, of any form or nature, supposes some *autocracy*, that is, some power of its own, some primitive right to govern. However, although autocracy is present whenever we find society, it is modified in different ways in different societies.

Article 2.
Different modes of civil autocracy

2410. 1. *Autocracy* is limited by the end of society because social power is not extended outside the confines of the end to which society is ordered. The *autocracy* of civil society is, therefore, the first and radical power for regulating the modality of rights.

2411. 2. *Autocracy* can be possessed by any subject with a direct, natural title, or with an indirect, conventional title, or with a mixed title (*USR*, 311–314). In civil society, as in all other societies, autocracy depends on a direct, natural title found in the hands of persons who associate; and on an indirect, conventional or mixed title found in the hands of one or more persons to whom it has been ceded by the associated persons.

2412. 3. *Autocracy* either remains *united* or is *divided*. It is united when all the powers contained in it are allocated to a single person (individual or collective); it is divided when different persons (individual or collective) possess it separately.

2413. If civil autocracy is united in a *collective person*, the person results either from all the associated individuals and is called *democratic autocracy*, or only from some of them, or even from several individuals who are not members of the society. In this case, we have *aristocratic* or *oligarchic autocracy* or, more generally speaking, *polycratic autocracy*.

If civil autocracy is united in an *individual person* (member or non-member of society), we have *monarchic autocracy*.

2414. Sometimes, however, civil autocracy is divided into several parts consigned to different persons (individual or collective). In this case, we have those forms of government in which various separate governmental powers reciprocally limit one another, or are limited by pacts, conventions, fundamental laws, customs, constitutions. In these governments, unity of thought and action is obtained through the voluntary *concord* of the different individuals, or different bodies, amongst whom the powers are divided. Society lives and works through this concord which is brought about partly through ways previously established in the social constitution, and partly in *ad hoc* ways.

Article 3.
Social action is exercised by means of
MENTAL CONCEPTION and EXECUTION

2415. Autocracy, which is merely (jural) potency for government, gives rise, when activated, to *social action*.

Social action, like the human being from whom it proceeds, is normally twofold. In other words, it is both intellectual and operative action. Autocratic action must, therefore, be found first under the form of *conception* and then of *execution*. The human being as such can effect nothing with the body without first mentally conceiving the action.

2416. The mind behind autocratic power is a *social mind*, and must be regarded as such by all members of society. Hence the first characteristic of the autocrat is that of being 'the sole competent judge (the supreme judge) of everything related to the government of society.'

Article 4.
The execution of the notion conceived by the autocratic mind;
how this activity subdivides

2417. The autocrat can carry out his governmental conceptions either *per se* or by means of ministers.

2418. Hence, the executive acts of governmental conceptions undertaken by autocratic power are divided into two classes:

[2415–2418]

1. Acts which the autocratic power carries out of itself.
2. Acts which the autocratic power carries out by means of ministers of its choice.

§1.
Governmental acts which autocratic power carries out itself

2419. Specifically different acts, which autocratic power can carry out itself are distinguished into seven classes. We shall say a word about each of them.

A.
Material operations *which serve to carry out the conceptions proper to autocratic power*

2420. It is clear that anyone with an absolute right to govern can carry out whatever he mentally conceives, if that is what he wants to do. Indeed, he cannot do otherwise in certain respects. Nevertheless, this ability diminishes as civil society extends and grows more perfect. The first rulers, for example, carried out the sentence of death with their own hands. It is clear that a head of civilised society has executives to relieve him of this and many lesser burdens.

B.
Commands *given either to members or to ministers, that is, to organs of power*

2421. In civilised nations, commands given to members diminish almost to the point of extinction because members' obligations are expressed and imposed by means of general laws. The same is true of commands given to ministers or organs of power. Normally, the direction they receive is provided by stable laws and regulations rather than through arbitrary, momentary precepts. However, this last kind of command can never be rendered totally useless even in more advanced civil societies.

[2419–2421]

C.
Judgments

2422. The right of judgment over everything regarding society pertains in the first and last instance to autocratic power. These judgments can be of two kinds: *obligatory* and *free*.

2423. Judges can moreover pronounce effective decisions necessary for the good of social society, that is, its end, or in purely private cases. The first kind of decisions must be undertaken on account of the social power of their office; the second solely at the instance of private persons who have the right to settle their disagreements peacefully on their own account, if this is what they want to do. Government has no reason to interfere with them unless their disagreement leads to violence. Only in this case does its intervention become 'necessary for the end of society, and a part of its social responsibility.'

2424. According to Baroli:

> The right of judicial power contains in itself other rights, that is, necessary means for its exercise. These derived rights are: *a*) the *right to investigate*, or to know the legal state of the question and to investigate the jural connotations of a given action; *b*) the *right of decision*, that is, the right to declare whether legal presumptions have been verified and equally whether legal consequences must therefore take place. Here we are dealing with the right to apply the law of the City to cases in question and simultaneously to determine the effects deriving from this right; *c*) the *right of notification*, that is, the right to intimate and make known to parties the decision arrived at, and to hold them to their duty; *d*) the *right of coercion*, that is, the right to have the legitimate, intimated and notified decision carried out forcefully. Without this subordinate right, judiciary power itself would for the most part be useless.[353]

2425. *Obligatory judgments* are divided into *civil* and *criminal*. The former are decisions intended to prevent litigants from coming to violence amongst themselves, the latter to punish actual violence or the infraction of laws and commands from powers that be.

---

[353] *Diritto naturale pubblico interno*, §144.

D.
Legislation

2426. The importance of the right to legislate requires a more extensive treatment than we have given to the preceding rights.

I.
Civil society must be directed by laws rather than precepts

2427. The substitution of *laws* for *precepts*[354] in a civil society is an immense progress. The autocrat's precept is instantaneous and easily abused by arbitrariness, passions and ignorance on the part of human beings in general or of those human beings who possess and exercise autocracy. Momentary circumstances influence the autocrat; they lead him to enunciate precepts mingled with his own human, individual interests and his heart's affections. Often he has neither time nor inclination to improve upon these instantaneous commands. The law, on the contrary,

---

[354] The word *law* takes on various meanings in normal speech. Sometimes it is understood as any *principle* whatsoever *of obligation*. In this sense it embraces both natural reason and the obligatory will of a superior expressed either in *precepts* or in *laws* (strictly so-called). In this wide meaning, *law* is defined as: 'A notion of the mind used for making judgments about the morality of actions, which must be guided by it' (cf. *Principles of Ethics*, 1). Sometimes law is understood in a more restricted way; for example, as the obligatory, manifested will of a superior. In this case, it does not express every principle of obligation, but a single determined source, that is, the will we have mentioned. Authors who maintain that knowledge about the superior who intimates the law is necessary to constitute a law, understand law in this sense. In fact, not even *natural reason* is a law in this sense until people know that God exists and wants human beings to live according to natural reason. But in the first meaning, *sic et simpliciter*, of *obligatory principle*, natural reason is law *per se*. Human beings feel themselves obliged to conform their life to the dictate of reason simply by perceiving the principle of obligation, without reflecting on the positive *will* of any totally eminent being (God). — In the third place, *law* is understood not as every manifest will of a superior, but as obligatory will manifested to a community. In this sense, *precept* is distinguished from *law*. — In the fourth and last place, *laws* are called *signs* manifesting the superior's will. In this figurative sense we say, for example, that the civil Code contains the civil laws because it contains the written words which indicate, for those who can read, the will of the legislator.

is made for all; it is made for an entire class of cases. These cases are not real and actual, but possible; they are the objects of abstract contemplation. Accidental interests and passions play a smaller part here. This is to the advantage of the law which is normally the fruit of mature judgment and lengthy consideration.

2428. Moreover:

1. Government acting through precepts rather than law prevents prior knowledge of duties on the part of members who cannot prepare themselves to carry them out — precepts are usually instantaneous.

2. The autocrat cannot provide sufficient precepts for social regulation in the case of an extended society — the law, however, takes account of innumerable cases.

3. The autocrat cannot maintain *social equality*, to which members have a right, on the basis of precepts — it is almost impossible, either through forgetfulness or some other human weakness, to be consistent in all precepts.

4. Regulation through precepts, which is scarcely conceivable when autocracy is in the hands of a single individual, excludes all forms of government where the autocrat is a collective person — these forms absolutely require stable laws.

5. Finally, *precepts* do not express any general plan of conduct in the eyes of the members to whom they are given — members remain uncertain of the future, ignorant of the aims of government and incapable of co-operating helpfully in government.

II.
Extension of the right to legislate

2429. There are two principal limits to the right to legislate:

1. Laws must be directed to obtain the end of society without regard for matters alien to this end.

2. Laws must contain nothing contrary to the moral law. According to Baroli:

> Everything that does not influence the end of the State lies outside the legal sphere of the right of which we have spoken. In the same way, everything unjust of its nature is

[2428-2429]

excluded from this legal sphere. — Consequently, reason establishes the irrefutable maxim that the right to legislate is limited.[355]

a) *The competent judge of the first limit*

2430. Nevertheless it is certainly the responsibility of the autocratic power itself to pass judgment on the first limit to legislation. All that remains for members is the 'right of evidence', which alone is valid against the competent judge (*RI*, 611–612).

Once again we must remember that the *master* and the *autocrat* (the radical power of civil society) are different. The *master* governs *per se* in virtue of *seigniorial Right*; the *autocrat* governs for the social good. The *master* is the judge competent to decide 'whether his government is useful for him or not' because each person is the competent judge relative to what is good or bad for himself (*RI*, 610, 615). Bond-servants governed by a master, although they can demand non-interference in their inalienable rights or in any rights which they still possess, have no right to claim that the government of their master should serve their good. It is sufficient that he should not harm them unjustly.

Civil autocrats are in a different position. They govern to obtain the social-civil end. In this case, the right of judging the competent judge which, when evidence is present against him, remains with members of civil society, is extended beyond knowing 'if harm has been done to them unjustly' (a judgment that even bond-servants can make), to knowing 'if the benefit they can claim from good government has not been done to them' (*RI*, 735–737).

b) *The competent judge of the second limit*

2431. Each individual is the competent judge of what is good or bad for himself. *A fortiori*, therefore, each one is competent judge of his own moral good or evil. Each person has the right to know what is morally good or evil (and consequently what pertains to right and what does not[356]); he is also *obliged* to know

---

[355] *Diritto naturale pubblico interno*, §109.
[356] Cf. *ER*, 256–268.

this. Judgment about uprightness is given to all; it is not exclusive to civil government (*RI*, 144–166).

2432. Each individual is independent of the power of authority in others when dealing with judgments about upright actions (granted, of course, that individuals are obliged to consult those who know more than they do, at least in doubtful matters). Nevertheless, this does not mean that the individual is independent of God in judgments about morality and the natural law. He must use the divine law to understand and interpret the natural law, and must submit his judgment to the power of the authority which God has delegated on earth by establishing men who in his place pass judgment on sins. This supreme judgment proper to divine competence pertains to the theocratic society founded on earth by God's messenger, God-Incarnate (*RGC*, 745–757).

III.
Is the autocrat subject to laws?

2433. The civil autocrat's right to legislate is limited by the end of society (political limitation) and by natural law (moral limitation). He is therefore subject to a double law, of which he is not the author: the law consequent on the end and nature of civil society, and the moral law in all its extension. The question, 'Is the civil autocrat subject to laws?' can only apply, therefore, to laws that he himself has made.

2434. The laws made by the autocrat come from rational Right and from his own particular, willed decision.[357] The question,

---

[357] St. Thomas states: 'Every law posited in a human fashion contains the notion of law in so far as it is derived from the law of nature' (*ST*, II–II, q. 91, art. 2). Properly understood, this does not exclude *positive laws and particular willed decisions*. Certainly, all laws made by a legislator must have their explanation in the end of society, that is, he must conceive them as useful means to this end. From this point of view, they are deduced from *rational Right* which requires the legislator to act in such a way 'that all laws are useful for the said end.' Nevertheless, there can be many expedients which seem equally suited to attaining the end, and the legislator who chooses one rather than another rightly make his own decision. From this point of view, the law

therefore, is this: 'Does rational Right and just, willed decisions (which indicate social laws to him) have as its object both his own person and those governed, or only those governed?' My answer is: 'The laws that rule a civil society regulate the modality of all the rights of the associates; they apply therefore only to members of the society.'

Of its nature, governmental power is extraneous to the community of members. Indeed, the governor of a civil society, and even the autocrat-governor, can be a foreigner. The concept of *member* and that of *governor* do not necessarily include one another.[358] The autocrat as such is not subject, therefore, to his own laws because, as such, he is not included in the community of persons for whom the laws have been made. This is the justification for Ulpian's statement: 'The ruler is not bound by the laws.'[359]

2435. In this case, the relationships between the autocrat in his quality as human being and other individuals must be determined by *extra-social Right*.

2436. However, nothing prevents the person invested with autocratic power from possessing a double quality as autocrat and as member of the civil society over which he rules. We have already shown how this is possible.[360]

2437. In this case, the quality of member must not detract from rights he possesses as autocrat (the right of inviolability, etc.). It is necessary, therefore, for this relationship to be regulated by means of equable, prudent conventions [*App.*, no. 9] between him and his co-members who will certainly have to renounce the exercise of certain rights they have in his regard. This is required by the quality of autocrat with which he is

is a *willed decision* in so far as it was preferred in the mind of the legislator to some other equivalent law. Thus, *willed decisions* in the formation of laws, although they cannot be excluded, are reduced to insignificance. Nor does this prevent the law as willed decision from being derived from rational Right relative to the end to which it is directed.

358 *SP,* 111–131.

359 *Dig.* I, 3: 31. — Note that in the Roman empire, the quality of *head of civil society* was confused with that of *master* (*dominus*). The latter quality excludes all subjection to laws; a master cannot be subject, and cannot, therefore, submit to laws made solely for subjects.

360 *SP,* 111–131.

invested, a quality which impedes the exercise of these rights. The other members may, however, be compensated for this.

2438. But not all reciprocal rights between members of civil society are incompatible with the quality of civil autocrat, that is, with the head invested with civil government. For example, the autocrat as owner[361] can, like all other owners, be subjected to laws regarding ownership without any harm resulting to the fullness of his autocracy. It may be objected that as supreme judge he will if necessary judge his own cause. This is true, but he still has the same obligation to judge justly, according to the laws that he himself has promulgated for all the members. Fittingness and decorum require even more from him: they require him to leave the judgment in such cases to other tribunals free from his intervention. This is not a jural obligation, however, unless some convention has previously been made about the matter.[362]

2439. Here we must note that there are publicists unwilling to recognise the autocrat as a possible subject of civil laws — this depends, as we said, on his being a member or not — because they think it unbecoming to his majesty. This, however, is a clear manifestation of their poorly developed *faculty of abstraction* (cf. *USR*, 259–260).[363] They still cannot separate the two person-

---

[361] Note that perhaps all the places in Roman legislation where the ruler submits himself to the law are concerned with questions of ownership. Paul, for example, says: 'It is not fitting for the Emperor to vindicate his right to matters established or entrusted in an imperfect testament. It is proper for such majesty to observe the laws from which he appears to be free.' (*Digest.*, bk. 32, t. 3: 23. Cf. also *Cod.*, bk. 6, t. 23: 3, 20, t. 1: 4. — *Instit.*, bk. 2, t. 17, §8.

[362] The Roman emperors had been released from the *formalities and solemn undertakings* of the law by a positive act of the people. This at least is how *fideicommissa* was conceived by the Roman jurisconsults, as we can see in a rescript of the emperor Alexander, 233 AD. 'Although THE LAW OF THE EMPIRE (the royal law made by the Roman people) has released the emperor from THE SOLEMN UNDERTAKINGS OF THE LAW there is nothing more proper to the power of command than to live according to the laws.' (*Cod.*, bk. 6, t. 23: 3). These final words show how moral and jural feeling combined to amend an imprudent convention or law such as that which released the ruler from *all the solemn undertakings* of the law (*USR*, 346–355).

[363] Cf. *SP*, 839–843, for reflections on the *faculty of abstraction*, which serves as a thermometer indicating degrees of civilisation.

[2438–2439]

ages, *autocrat* and *member*, despite the facility and lack of damage to either with which this can easily be done,[364] especially if possible collisions have been foreseen by wise conventions. Indeed, the personages are so separable that the autocrat as member can delegate a proxy to represent his interests without any personal intervention on his own part except for drawing up a mandate of proxy. This is possible through the right possessed by every member to be represented by others (cf. *USR*, 255–258).

2440. Whether the civil autocrat becomes a member or not of civil society depends upon his will. He cannot be compelled to do so if he has not agreed to this. No society can constrain an outsider to enter unless this is the only way of putting the *right of guarantee* into effect. Nor does it seem that the civil autocrat can be refused entry as a member of the society he directs. At most, the society can desire equable, wise conventions that determine, to mutual advantage and peace, the exemptions from social duties incompatible with autocratic dignity. The society will, of course, be compensated in some way for the damage it suffers.

2441. The good sense of antiquity found it highly commendable and very useful for the autocrat to receive spontaneously the quality of membership in civil society; no harm was suffered to the authority of the society by such a step. As a member, the autocrat was subject to the laws promulgated for all members. We read, for example, in the Roman code these admirable words of the emperors Theodosius and Valentinian: 'It is highly suitable to the majesty of the Ruler that he proffer himself as bound by the laws. Our authority depends on the authority of the law. And indeed it is more fitting for overall rule that the ruling power submit to the laws.'[365] A century later (455 AD) it was still expressly declared: 'All are bound by the laws, even if they belong to the divine household.'[366] Note that the Roman

---

[364] It is easy to see these two qualities as separable if we consider those forms of government in which autocracy is divided between several persons, or even bodies. In these forms it is necessary for sharers in autocracy to be citizens; in fact, it is almost impossible for them not to be citizens.

[365] *Cod.*, bk. 1, t. 14: 4.

[366] *Ibid.*, 10.

emperor did not consider himself absolved from the formalities of the laws as a necessary consequence of his dignity, but as a result of a special law and convention between himself and the Roman people.[367] Conventions of this kind, which were however too broad and indeterminate, came to be restricted by moral, jural, common sense, and later by *custom* which, as a tacit expression of public opinion, was considered in the Roman system to have the force of law.[368]

2442. Christianity exercised great influence in this matter because of the two tendencies it constantly shows:

1. The tendency to free human beings from arbitrary, human laws by bringing men and women to the knowledge and observance of rational and divine law.

2. The tendency to associate human beings prudently.

Through this second tendency, Christianity invited persons invested with civil autocracy to desire at the same time to be members of its society and hence subject to its laws. St. Ambrose expressed this feeling when he wrote to Valentinian: 'What you have prescribed for others, you have prescribed for yourself also. The emperor makes the laws and should be the first to observe them.'[369] Canon law lost no time in publishing as an excellent rule what St. Augustine and St. Isidore had written: 'It is right that the ruler should obey his own laws. — Their voice has just authority if what they forbid to their people is also taken as forbidden to themselves.'[370] The Code of Canon Law had no hesitation in registering as Christian the decision of Cato: *bear the law which you yourself imposed.*[371] Such teaching

---

[367] *Cod.*, bk. 6, t. 23: 3.

[368] 'Ancient custom is rightly observed as the equivalent of law. — Laws oblige us only because they have been accepted by the judgment of the people. As a result, unwritten laws approved by the people are obligatory for everyone. It is of little interest whether the people express their will by voting or by what they actually do' (*Digest.*, bk. 1, t. 3: 32).

[369] St. Ambrose, *Ep. 3 ad Valentin.*

[370] *Decret.*, p. 1, distinct. 9, c. 2.

[371] *Decret. Gregor. IX*, bk. 1, t. 2, c. 6. 'We command that when anyone establishes a law for another person, he himself should use it. Wise authority declares: *bear the law which you yourself imposed. Etc.*' This persuasion shown in the sayings of the Fathers and in ecclesiastical laws that the legislator himself should obey his own law obviously arises from the supposition that

shows that the autocrat, when accepting the quality and condition of member of civil commonalty and becoming 'recitizenised', is acting in accordance with the societal spirit proper to the Catholic religion.

IV.
The compilation of laws

2443. The autocrat has the *authority* to make laws which, however, cannot and must not be made by *authority* alone; *wisdom* must also play its part. The person (individual or collective) invested with the right to legislate has the duty to form laws with the greatest possible wisdom. In other words, he must use every means suitable for attaining all possible light in the prevailing circumstances and formulating the best laws. This explains why the most celebrated definitions of civil laws given by the ancient sages indicated not only the *authority* from which the laws sprang, but also the *wisdom* of the learned who had assisted authority in their composition. Papinian's definition states as an attribute of law that it is *the decision of prudent men*;[372] Demosthenes' definition, embraced by the jurisconsult, Marcian, states in the same way that the law must be 'a decree of prudent men'.[373]

'the political law declares what is just'. In other words, it is an expression of rational law. Here it is clear that the person making the law should also observe it. Nevertheless, it cannot be denied that there is, as we said, an arbitrary element in the body of positive, civil laws.

[372] 'The law is a common precept, a DECISION OF PRUDENT MEN, pressure brought to bear on crimes which are contracted either spontaneously or through ignorance, a formal promise made by the republic' (*Digest.*, bk. 1, t. 3: 1). The final expression, 'a formal promise made by the republic', shows that the ancients considered a law to contain a kind of pact between the citizens who, by uniting to form a society and providing laws for themselves, also promised to observe them reciprocally.

[373] 'Law is that which all must obey for many reasons but principally because every law while springing from the insight and gift of God' (the best of the ancient philosophers recognised a divine element in reason and saw law

[2443]

2444. We may ask, however, whether the civil autocrat's duty to use all possible enlightenment, even from others, is *jural* or simply *moral*.

It is undoubtedly *jural* because the duty of governing well is jural. Nevertheless, we should note that the autocratic ruler is the *competent judge* of what he can do, and that those governed must presume that he acts competently, as we said.

2445. We also have to reflect that no Christian ruler today presumes to make laws without consulting many wise people. Indeed, even when the Roman republic in its decadence gave to the world the principle, 'that which pleases the ruler has the force of law',[374] there was no attempt in such improper words to maintain that the *wisdom* on the basis of which valid laws have to be conceived was concentrated entirely in the ruler. The words were to be understood in the sense that *authority*, one of the two effective elements of law but invalid if unaccompanied by the other element, *wisdom*, was concentrated in the ruler. The poor development of the faculty of abstraction explains the insufficient expression of a principle which flattery was swift to seize upon to the harm of rulers and peoples.[375] Christianity had to work hard to illumine people's minds; new laws emanating from Councils of bishops made known to the restored world, which benefited from them, that although legislative *authority* could be brought together in one person, legislative *wisdom* could not. Authority must seek counsel and sure direction.[376]

as the insight and gift of God because it sprang from the eternal rule, BEING, which shines before the human intelligence) 'IS ALSO THE DECREE OF PRUDENT MEN. It is pressure brought to bear on those who offend either spontaneously or through ignorance, a formal promise made by the City, a prescription according to which all present in the republic must lead their lives' (*Digest.*, bk. 1, t. 3: 2.

[374] *Dig.*, bk. 1, t. 4: 1.

[375] To tell a ruler that he can make any law he likes is base, cruel flattery. Right, morality and wisdom are by that very fact sacrificed to his authority and power. To tell a ruler that he has the necessary wisdom to make laws by himself is also flattery, but less tragic. Here, one at least admits that wisdom is needed to make law, which safeguards the principle. Even great men made use of this second kind of flattery when they had to praise great rulers. Pliny, for example, said to Trajan: 'We are ruled by you, and subject to you as we are to the laws' (*Paneg.*).

[376] The *inviolability* of sovereigns appeared at its most marked in the world

2446. In fact, legislatures face immense difficulties. The law must be directed to obtain its end not only relative to its *object*, but also to its *form, promulgation, interpretation,*[377] *application* and *execution*.

2447. Let me say one word about form. Granted the qualities of jural equality and of certainty, law is perfect to the extent that

a) it remains closer to individual Right, and creates fewer new rights;

b) it uses fewer legal fictions;

c) it expresses rights in fewer forms, especially if these forms multiply entities unnecessarily — for example, a contract which remains basically the same may change nature simply as a result of positive expressions or forms;

d) the legislator shows himself less absolute and less immutably determined — in other words, he should not forget Justinian's maxim: 'We always try to discover something which is both consonant with nature and capable of correcting previous things.'[378]

as a result of the moral light shed by Christianity. Count Giuseppe de Maistre has already noted, with his usual clear-sightedness, that Christianity brought about the elevation of sovereign majesty after having persuaded rulers to relinquish the power of judgment in their own cause and entrust it to tribunals. The same can be said about the power to conceive and compile laws.

[377] Obligatory interpretation of law is proper to the legislator. In doubtful cases, therefore, an executive body must never be granted permission to interpret law according to its own understanding and advantage. This deplorable eventuality would be present if, for example, revenue officers could interpret finance laws at will. The tax office could take action, but at its own responsibility and with a possibility of appeal to the sovereign when taxpayers were evidently splitting hairs to avoid payment rather than bringing forward real doubts of interpretation. Appeal to the sovereign is sufficient in this case where the tax-office is limited in its faculty to interpret law. If, however, interpretation is handed over in its entirety to the revenue, appeals would be insufficient. They would be too frequent, and too costly and troublesome for tax-payers.

[378] Nov. 18, *praef.* — This excellent maxim was written into the Justinian Code when the function of free, but non-Roman, bond-servants was abolished. The dignified way in which it was expressed may be seen in the following quotation: 'Freedom without Roman citizenship will no longer be allowed to trouble our republic; it is totally abolished because we realise that it is no longer in use and is bandied about as an empty name expressing this

[2446–2447]

e) finally law is expressed more clearly, laws are better classified and the reasons for laws are more obvious.[379]

V.
Classification of civil laws

2448. The laws of civil society can be classified in various ways according to the *concept* chosen as the basis for classification.

2449. We shall say a word about two classifications according to the two concepts of *obligation* which they produce, and of the *aim* (of social good) which they intend to produce.

a) *Classification of civil laws according to the different mode and degree in which they oblige*

2450. The question of the moral obligation of civil laws is often discussed; some authors have even gone so far as to deny it.

2451. Some of these, it would seem, have been brought to such an absurd error by noticing that some special laws do not oblige in conscience those to whom they are applied. These authors have drawn a general conclusion from particular cases.

2452. The question must be divided into three parts, which are:

1. Can the civil legislator make laws which oblige in conscience?

2. Does the legislator intend to make all his laws oblige in the same way?

3. Do obligatory civil laws always oblige when applied, or are they open to exception? This final question is reduced to another form as follows: What are the conditions under which a civil law of an obligatory nature puts in act its obligatory force?

2453. The first question must be answered affirmatively. A legislator unable to oblige in conscience with his laws, could not

kind of freedom. WE WHO VENERATE THE TRUTH DESIRE IN OUR LAWS ONLY THOSE THINGS WHICH THE LAWS CAN IN FACT OBTAIN' (*Cod.*, bk. 7, t. 5).

[379] Roman laws almost always express their reason. This is wisdom.

be mentally conceived as a legislator. His laws would be mere non-jural facts, not laws.

2454. The second question must be answered negatively. In other words, we must say that the intention of the legislator is to be understood solely from the nature of the law, not from his mere will. He cannot, in fact, intend that all the laws he makes should oblige in the same way.

This different mode of obligation of civil laws is the basis for the classification under discussion. I say 'this different mode' because some kind of obligation is necessary if law is to be law. However, obligation is sometimes indirect; at other times, it obliges not those for whom it is made but others, who for instance have to apply it. We shall see this better later on.

2455. The third question has been amply dealt with by authors treating of laws in general. I shall simply add a few special observations which, although not omitted altogether in normal works on the subject, are not perhaps expressed with all the universality and clear-sightedness of which they are capable.

2456. Civil laws cannot be other than general. In other words, the legislator discovers through experience that a certain difficulty happens frequently in given circumstances, and decides to put the matter right.[380] However, the difficulty does not always arise in these circumstances, and to that extent the law in this particular case has no purpose. Civil law can, therefore, cease to oblige morally on condition that leaving it unfulfilled does not produce disorder in society, and above all that this does not require violence. If magistrates use force to bring about the fulfilment of the law, for instance, they cannot be opposed. Each person must fulfil the law even in the case where the law has no purpose. In this case, the persons responsible have the right to ensure the observance of the law because public authority must be regulated in its judicial and executive ordinances according to the letter of the law only.

What has been said about laws directed to removing certain difficulties is also to be applied to every other law whose aim is known unhesitatingly and fully: if the purpose ceases, the moral

---

[380] According to Theophrastus, 'laws have to be instituted in those matters which occur with maximum frequency (επι τον πλειστον), not those which occur casually (εκ παραλοχου)' (*Dig.*, bk. 1, t. 3: 3 — *ibid.*, 4–6).

obligation to observe the law ceases, although the legal, external, penal obligation continues and must be respected even in conscience in the way described. No one has the right to break the law even when minimum violence or scandal is involved.[381]

2457. We can now expound the classification of civil laws according to the mode and degree of obligation which they induce.

2458. 1st class. *Merely penal ordinances.* — Some authors, who deny that merely penal ordinances should be called laws, maintain that in fact they are not such. They are right about the name. An ordinance which does not determine any moral state in the person who observes or transgresses it, and does not induce obligation in anyone, even indirectly, cannot be called 'law'; law indicates something jural and moral (cf. *ER*, 293–317). This, however, is a question of words which we can avoid by calling such public arrangements in the City *ordinances* rather than *laws*.

2459. On the other hand, it cannot be demonstrated that there is anything intrinsically absurd in the concept of merely penal ordinances. It cannot be seen as absurd that 1. the civil autocrat be content to procure, through the force with which he is furnished and the fear of punishment rather than the bond of moral obligation, some public good that public opinion either refuses to accept as such or considers very doubtful; and 2. the community of members understands his ordinance in precisely this way and consequently does not consider itself obliged in conscience. These two circumstances are reasons which enable many respectable moralists to affirm the existence of merely penal ordinances.[382]

---

[381] Judges, who have to give their decisions on the basis of external data, cannot take into account internal, unknown elements which also concur to produce moral obligation. For example, according to St. Alphonsus: 'Privileges onerous to third parties, such as not paying tithes and similar matters, are prescribed through contrary use, even in the case of privative non-use (not only negative non-use). For example, the privileged person, conscious of his privilege, has not spontaneously wanted to use it when he had the opportunity. This is understood of the external forum. The person who has no intention of renouncing the privilege does not lose it in conscience' (*Istruzione e pratica per li confessori*, c. 20, n. 14).

[382] St. Alphonsus Liguori, the most renowned moralist of the last century,

2460. But while it may not be absurd for an autocrat to make merely penal ordinances, are they useful for civil societies? The moral reason in favour of these ordinances runs as follows. Good morality on the part of members is more easily attainable if members are less tied by moral obligations in the case of uncertain public good. This is particularly the case when obligations are minute and difficult to observe and, at the same time, divide social burdens more by chance than with strict, clear equity. Customs' duties and financial restrictions are cases in point. This is a very strong reason which inclines certain learned men to favour these ordinances.

2461. On the other hand, the following reasons are opposed to penal ordinances.

1. Merely penal ordinances impede the unanimity of members and government in their tendency to work together for the social end. Consequently, they render citizens less adapted to the duty, incumbent on all, of co-operating willingly with government for the proximate as well as the remote end of society (cf. *USR*, 377–378). If members are not obliged, for example, to pay customs on goods, their sole thought is to avoid these taxes and thus oppose the end for which they were imposed.

2. Strife is aroused between members and government. Government has to use forceful means and penalties in such cases to obtain the end it has in mind. As a result, persuasive, moral means are abandoned. This is against the principle of Right which requires persuasive, moral means to be used first; force is to be used only in extreme necessity (cf. 1827–1828).

3. Strife of this kind induces immoral feelings in the spirits of members when they see themselves oppressed by brute

---

is one of these. He teaches that a merely penal ordinance is to be distinguished from an expression of law indicating the mind of the legislator. He says: 'Another is the purely penal law which provides no command. For example, "Anyone who does this will be penalised". This does not oblige in conscience whatever the gravity of the penalty, as the theologians of Salamanca maintain (c. 21, n. 53), with Navarra, Palao, Tapia, Reginio and others.' He recalls the custom, that is, the opinion of the community, according to which it is not obliged in conscience to observe such ordinances. He adds: 'Hence, municipal laws which forbid under penalty the cutting of wood or herbs, or fishing and hunting, do not oblige under fault because THIS IS THE CUSTOM' (*Th. M.*, bk. 1, n. 145).

violence, and punished for matters in which they believe their consciences are clear. They go on to persuade themselves falsely that they can lawfully defend themselves against public force. This is nothing more, they think, than protecting their own right.[383] Serious physical and moral evils arise from such strife.

4. Moreover, if members are persuaded that such ordinances are merely penal, smuggling is encouraged. Many people undertake this kind of life which is full of lies, fraud, immorality, violence. Entire families are ruined by it and often become little more than assassins.

5. Some authors maintain that laws on tariffs are merely penal or at least that anyone breaking them is not obliged to restitution. The damage suffered by the State, they say, from those who do not pay, is made up by the State through penalties.[384] But even if this were the case, another disadvantage, totally opposed to justice, would follow: the person who pays a penalty, pays more than the tariff. Burdens, therefore, would sometimes be nil, and sometimes extremely onerous to families who suffered in this fashion. Everything would depend upon chance, or on degrees of astuteness or even wickedness amongst those who succeeded in foxing the government. In the end, good people would pay what was owed by the wicked.

2462. All these reasons prove that merely penal ordinances,

---

[383] Some authors maintain that people caught not paying their customs and tolls must in conscience undergo the penalty because 'this law seems conditional, or disjunctive, that is, you either pay customs or the penalty' (St. Alphonsus, *Th. M.*, bk. 3, n. 616). This would be a very odd law, if indeed it were a law. People would not easily understand how they were obliged to suffer a penalty for having avoided the tax without fault, as they are told. It would be much easier to convince them that they are in fact obliged to pay tariffs.

[384] St. Alphonsus expounds this reason not as his own, but as taken from others: 'The subjects' obligation to pay customs to the ruler is compensated, when they escape tax, by the obligation of suffering the penalty to which subjects are liable. It seems that rulers would be satisfied if a fine were imposed on those avoiding customs. *A fortiori* if (as a more learned author maintains) the customs' revenue would exceed the needs of rulers were subjects to pay customs in their entirety' (*Th. M.*, bk. 3, n. 616). According to me, this last reason can be turned on its head in this way: if it is true that customs paid in full would exceed the need, it is also true that customs would be decreased if they were paid fully and willingly.

generally speaking, are neither useful nor suitable for civil society. We now have to see if they can be useful as a lesser evil in certain particular circumstances, or even if they can always be avoided by the autocrat.

2463. I shall offer only a few comments on this important question.

First comment. — Peoples are found in two different states:

1. In the state of minors who are governed and allow themselves to be governed without their giving any thought to social government. In this state, they have no thought in common with government; their thoughts are wholly elsewhere, like those of young children under parental government who have no consideration for their father's foresight and fatigue in nourishing and wisely educating them. Their aims are not his, nor does he share them with his children who are incapable of giving him help and advice. In this state, their virtue consists in blind obedience and submission; their defect lies in complaining about the lack of an outing, a doll, a sticky bun, or about lessons being too long and similar things. They do not complain about their parent's lack of wisdom in governing them. In other words, they pay no attention to universal, complex good, but restrict themselves to individual wishes, and to instantaneous, feelable good.

2. Or in the state of grown-up children who help their parents with advice, and work for good government in the home. They share their father's views, and are conscious of the importance of the total result of government which they use as a standard for measuring its goodness or defect. In addition, they are able to sacrifice partial, accidental good to the greater good they expect from government. In this state, the civil virtue of peoples is formed simultaneously by obedience and counsel. They work together with the government for the social end. The vice of such peoples is found in factions and in the violence ensuing from factions.

2464. We say that when these two states of peoples have been distinguished, merely penal ordinances can assist the morality of those in the first state. Such individuals, who do not share in governmental views, are not stimulated in their observance of laws by anything aimed at the public good, to which they pay no attention. Consequently they often offend against it. It is

[2463–2464]

better, therefore, not to expose them to formal sin. The person who commits formal sin degrades himself; at the same time awareness of his fault depresses and discourages him.

The matter is different for those who understand the necessity and end of governmental ordinances. Their civil virtue is stronger, they themselves are more developed, and it is much harder for them even to think that they could act against the civic end without doing wrong. Certainly, exonerating them from fault in breaking the law would only have the appalling result of weakening their commitment and their eagerness to work together with government for the public good by faithfully fulfilling governmental enactments. Such developed peoples, who are far advanced in civilisation, also know that defrauding customs and excise does nothing to reduce public burdens. On the contrary, customs duties have to be increased to compensate the losses through fraud which, without lightening the public burden, simply cause difficulty by upsetting the equable distribution of taxes. It is a theft against other individuals, if not against government, who have to make up for what has been cunningly left unpaid. In any case, it is immoral. Advanced peoples will never be in favour of moral teaching which favours merely penal ordinances. On the contrary, they will consider them ignoble, uncivilised, lax and corrupt.

2465. *Second comment.* — Penal laws (ordinances) are generally reckoned those dealing with customs and excise, that is, indirect taxation. It is certain that there is a jural-moral obligation on the part of every member of civil society to pay the quota of tax required by his capital and income.[385] If, therefore, we presume that all social burdens have been distributed equably, no one can avoid paying his contribution without committing a sin of theft against society. We could ask, however, if indirect impositions produce an equable division of the burden. It is impossible, even for government, to calculate whether these impositions ensure that all members pay what they should in proportion to their substance and their annual incomes. The simple statement of this doubt immediately makes us think of a single tax which could easily be proportioned to

---

[385] We are still a long way from putting this principle of public justice into practice!

income, and easily be shown to be well proportioned for all. It is clear that such an arrangement would remove a great pretext used to justify contraband, as well as all the other ways in which members try to avoid payment of these taxes.[386]

2466. *Third comment.* — Finally, we must note that truly penal laws are those used by civil society to threaten and impose punishments on crime with the aim of restraining the criminal drive.

2467. Certainly, the criminal has a moral obligation

1. to repent of his crime, to amend and to avoid further criminality;

2. to compensate people for the damage caused them, as far as this is possible;

3. to make up for the scandal by which he induced or disposed others to imitate him.

Besides this, can it be said that he has an obligation to submit spontaneously to the temporal-civil penalty? I do not think so. But if there is no obligation, the penalty seems nothing more for him than a merely penal law. To this extent, I would agree substantially with C. L. Haller, who considers that penalties imposed on criminals by society (to be carefully distinguished from compensation, which is obligatory, as we said) are nothing more than dispositions made by an autocrat to regulate the sanction of laws and to restrain criminal drive.

2468. Such dispositions are truly obligatory for judges, granted the institution of criminal courts, who are obliged to use them as norms for their decisions. They are not, however, obligatory for the guilty who are truly disposed to satisfy society, as far as they can, for their crime.[387]

2469. Nevertheless, they are obligatory for criminals who cannot avoid them without using violence against the public force which applies them. Public justice acts justly in applying

---

[386] Cf. Liguori, *Th. M.*, bk. 3, n. 615–617.

[387] Foreigners who commit crimes are, therefore, subject to the punishment established by the laws of the place where the crime is committed, despite their not being obliged by other local laws. As the jurists say, they 'become subjects by reason of their crime'. This does not mean that they are naturally obliged to undergo punishment which they can avoid without external disorder, but that the City has the right to force them to undergo punishment by making them, in this regard, its subjects (*RI*, 1995–1999).

them to the criminal, and no one has a right to oppose them forcefully. This perhaps is what is meant by writers who affirm that penal laws do not oblige in conscience 'prior to a judge's decision'.[388]

2470. 2nd. class. *Permissive laws.* — These laws declare licit something previously forbidden by positive law (cf. *ER*, 289–292). 'Permissive law' is also the name given to laws which expressly declare some action juridically lawful.

2471. What is the obligation of these laws (as we said, there is no law without obligation)? The obligation of permissive laws does not affect those who wish to posit a lawful action within their power. It does affect all others who, as a consequence of the law, are forbidden to use violence to prevent any third parties from positing the action which, having been declared legal, is taken under the protection of the law.

2472. An action lawful before the law, but not affected by positive declaration, would indeed be protected as a right by civil society. However, there would be no permissive law in its regard.

2473. 3rd class. *Facultative laws.* — Civil society intervenes to regulate the modality of rights only when

1. families, or individuals composing them, cannot regulate themselves, or

2. do not want to do so.

Civil society promulgates *facultative laws* in cases where families are capable of regulating the modality of their rights, but do not want to do so. Families may have recourse to such laws, or not, as they please. Laws of this nature are all those which aim at eliminating or settling litigation through the intervention of judges. Litigants who succeed in settling the matter themselves are not obliged by these laws. If they do not succeed, and one of the parties cites another before a public court, or both parties refer the matter to a judge's decision, these laws become obligatory.

2474. The obligation of such laws consists therefore in this:

1. One of the parties can be obliged by the other to appear before a judge.

---

[388] Cf. Suarez, *De Legibus*, bk. 3, c. 23, n. 9.

2. When the parties appear before a judge they must follow established procedure and carry out the decision unless they have come to some new agreement amongst themselves.[389]

2475. *Immediately obligatory laws.* — These laws command or prohibit some action. Having all the requisites of law, they are morally obligatory for the persons for whom they are made, except for the case of which we have spoken.

2476. I have no doubt that legislative perfection requires that in every law the legislator's mind about the *manner in which the law obliges* should have been clearly delineated. This aspect of law still leaves much to be desired.

b) *Classification of civil laws according to their different purposes, that is, according to the different social good at which they are aimed*

i) *Civil-jural laws and civil-political laws*

2477. We have already said that there are, in every society, *socio-jural and socio-political* laws. This division depends on the good at which the laws are aimed (*USR*, 417–424). In civil society these two classes can fittingly be called *civil-jural laws and civil-political laws.*[390]

---

[389] The expenses of litigation are to be decided as follows. — The plaintiff pays *all* the expenses if he loses. The defendant is free of all legal expenses, including those owed to his lawyers or others. If, moreover, the case was not even doubtfully in favour of the plaintiff, but due to malice on his part, he should be condemned to pay restitution for the trouble caused to the defendant. If the plaintiff wins the case, the total expenses of both parties should be paid *pro rata dubii*. In other words, if the case was evidently in the plaintiff's favour, and the defendant was renitent, the latter should pay the expenses plus a fine for the trouble caused; if the defendant is not guilty of renitence, there should be no fine. If there is doubt on both sides, expenses are divided *pro rata dubii*, as we said. These dispositions will help to diminish litigation to the extent that they conform to justice.

[390] Certain political laws preceded merely jural laws in the formation of legislation. Cf. the first statutes of the Italian communes which contain practically nothing except regulations about the duties of public functionaries and some enactments about policing. It is indeed necessary for the State to be constituted before it can begin to operate, to judge litigation between citizens and to support its decisions with sanctions.

[2475–2477]

2478. We must note, however, that even civil-political laws are truly *jural*. In other words, they spring from jural reason applied to society, and induce obligation. As we have seen, *de facto* society modifies rights anterior to society, and produces new rights (*RI*, 1020–1024). It follows that laws of civil society, although they have a single end (regulation of the modality of rights), have two subordinate aims which serve as two means for obtaining such regulation. Laws determine:

1. *individual rights* to the extent necessary for obviating disagreements between families and individuals;

2. *social means* for the increase of the good of all.

2479. These are the two great sources of civil laws. They can be expressed in the following way:

The *first source* of civil laws is *jural reason* applied to determine (individual) rights pertaining to human beings even in the state of nature.

The *second source* of civil laws is *jural reason* applied to determine social organisation and the obligations of officials and single members of society, with the aim of enhancing co-operation for the attainment of the social end.

ii) *How social, civil Right modifies individual right*

2480. This second source gives rise to modification of individual rights, and to totally new, social rights.

2481. Hence, the legislator can act as follows as a consequence of the end of society, for the sake of which all are obliged to co-operate. He can

1. suspend or prohibit members from exercising any activity proper to rights possessed independently of society — for example, *de facto* activity directed to maintaining their own rights;

2482. 2. determine the rights which, according to simply individual Right, remain doubtful either absolutely or in relationship to the limited capacity of the human mind — a limitation which prevents agreement about the solution of some specific case.

3. Civil law can render obligatory (provided this is necessary or useful for the social end) that which, according to individual-jural law, would be only morally or fittingly obligatory. This

end, already obligatory of itself, is the supreme genus of social obligations. Potentially it includes more special obligations (the obligation to use means for an end) which the legislator determines and expresses in jussive or prohibitive commands.[391]

4. At this point, we have to decide once more if a legislator can give, take away or transfer rights.

There is no doubt that civil legislators can give new rights to members. They give the rights, determined by law, which arise from the *de facto* existence of society (social rights).

Equally, there is no doubt that legislators can also take away rights from members. They remove rights corresponding to the burdens members assume on entering civil society (social obligations, burdens), which legislators determine according to the laws.

Legislators cannot however change or transfer individual rights *directly* because their authority does not extend further than the modality of rights. They can do so *indirectly* and *per accidens* when they are obliged to determine in general, with fixed laws, what remains indeterminate in the state of nature. In this case, they determine what is uncertain by fixing their attention on that which normally happens. Things do not always occur, however, in accordance with legislators' suppositions. In

---

[391] Certain limits placed by the civil law on the use of ownership can be reduced to these ordinances. These limits are intended to ensure that use is totally human and moral and thus acquire the dignity of full right (*RI*, 921–959). Article 592 of the French procedural code is an example. In speaking of the loss of goods, it says: 'The following cannot be placed under distraint: 1. objects which the law declares real estate; 2. the accommodation necessary for people under distraint, and for their children living with them; the clothes in which people under distraint are dressed and wrapped; 3. books relative to the profession of those under distraint, to the sum of three hundred francs at the choice of the distrained person; 4. machines and instruments for the teaching, practice or exercise of sciences and arts, to the same sum, and at the choice of the distrained person; 5. military equipment, according to enactment and rank; 6. artisans' tools, necessary for their personal occupations; 7. flour and small commodities necessary to feed the distrained person and his family for a month; 8. finally, a cow or three sheep or two goats, at the choice of the distrained person, with the necessary straw, forage and grain for litter and feed for the said animals for one month.' Article 530 of the French commercial code, which prescribes the assistance to be given by his creditors to a bankrupt, pertains to the same kind of ordinance.

this case, the law alters individual rights without cause for complaint by the members, who have to cede their right for the sake of the common good which is the end of society. These accidental losses or changes of rights, which gradually adjust themselves, are social burdens and obligations precisely because they are necessary for the end that society has in view, and because each member is compensated to his own advantage by the good he gains from society itself. In fact, there is no real loss, but a highly useful change of modality. We have occasionally given examples of this accidental effect of laws. One of them is that of a child who has to be content to remain a ward or minor even though his precocious development could, in the state of nature, provide some right to free disposal of himself and of what he owns (*RI*, 720–771).

2483. It may be objected that although society has indeed the right to make laws founded on presumption of some occurrence, and to enforce their execution because it can only use wise presumption when truth is unattainable, members are not obliged to conform to these laws in all cases in which they know that the presumption serving as a foundation for the law is not verified. This would be in accord with the rule indicated earlier: 'truth is preferred to presumption'.

This conclusion is, however, too general and, therefore, inexact. It should be distinguished as follows:

1. The legislator's authority contributes an essential element to the validity of certain acts. If the law declares, therefore, that in certain circumstances the legislator's authority does not intend to intervene to make an act valid, such an act is null in all those cases where these circumstances prevail. This is so whatever the legislator's end in denying his assent, and even if it were true that this end has no place in a particular case. The necessary concurrence of power, denied in general to that act, is lacking. Examples of this are the conditions which a civil legislator attaches to the privileges he grants.[392] If the conditions are not

---

[392] This is found most often in ecclesiastical laws. For example, the Church does not recognise the religious profession of a person who is not yet sixteen years of age, nor the marriage of a girl under twelve years of age or a boy under fourteen. Although the person who makes religious profession or who marries before the fixed age may have all the other qualities necessary (eccle-

verified, the privileges cease even if the conditions are founded on a presumption that in certain cases contradicts the truth.

2484. 2. Moreover, mistakes are sometimes made through believing that law is founded on a presumption of fact when this is not the case.[393] Indeed, laws very often aim at removing some danger of harm to society. The harm does not always occur, but there is always a danger that it could. In these cases, the law is not properly speaking founded on the presumption that a fact will occur, but on the truth that danger will not be lacking.[394]

2485. It may still be objected that if no wrong occurs in a particular case the end of the law ceases. If so, the law serves no purpose and is not obligatory. — I reply:

1. This objection would have some weight if the harm that the law intended to avoid were *private*, not *public*. In such a case, the *private* individual can judge whether something is going to do him harm. If he thinks not, he can renounce any help from the law, which is usually facultative in these cases. But the private individual is incompetent to judge in cases when the law aims at suppressing *public harm*; only society, or whoever represents society, can be the competent judge in this matter.

---

siastical law presumes they are lacking) for the validity of such acts, these acts would be invalid because their validity requires the consent and co-operation of legislative power.

[393] This kind of mistake, of which we shall give a single example here (although many others are possible), is very easy to make. The ends the legislator had in view in making the law do not always come together with complete security. For example, some would maintain that the law which obliges a person accepting probate of an inheritance, without first making an inventory, to pay the debts exceeding the total inherited is founded on the presumption that the heir intends to defraud the creditors in some way. In fact, there are other reasons why the heir in this case must pay more than what he receives: 1. because of the additional reasons for making the inventory, which is a reasonable formality intended to safeguard creditors, who can require such formalities or modalities by the right of guarantee; 2. because the law has stated expressly that if the heir accepts without an inventory, he has entered into a tacit convention to pay the creditors. This convention has been implicitly prescribed and sanctioned by the law itself (*USR*, 337, 345, 421–423).

[394] Hence Suarez says: 'Properly speaking, fear of that danger is not dependent on presumption, but on a true, certain judgment' (*De Legibus*, bk. 3, c. 23, n. 9).

[2484–2485]

Normally speaking, therefore, the individual has to follow the law.[395]

2486. 2. If such laws are observed equally by all, burdens and social rights will be distributed equably. If some individuals do not observe them, equality amongst the citizens could be disturbed. Nevertheless, the civil law should not be followed if, in an individual case where the harm feared by the law does not occur, a prohibited action were rendered ethically obligatory or a commanded action were rendered unlawful.[396]

Sometimes a law is not founded in presumption, as appears at first sight, but in legal *fiction*. Here it intends to oblige in every case, as we have noted elsewhere (*RI*, 1372–1376). Its function is to determine what has been left undetermined by individual Right, or to raise to the status of obligation what is only fitting or equable in individual Right.

2487. 3. The law however may be founded not upon danger of public harm, which is never lacking, granted the circumstances indicated by the law, nor in some legal fiction, but in presumption about an individual fact viewed by the law as its object. In this case, obligation ceases in all cases where the supposed fact is not verified. This is the sole meaning of the rule: 'presumption cedes to truth', or the other: 'truth is preferred to presumption'.

2488. 4. Finally, we should note that everything obligatory according to rational justice and not positively and justly modified by the civil legislator, remains obligatory even if not sanctioned by the civil legislator. Hence, duties of justice for Catholics in regard to the Church or theocratic society remain intact even when the civil power does not protect these duties

---

[395] In the final analysis, society has the right to know if the law has been carried out by everyone, and to punish transgressors. If individuals use their private judgment to act independently of the law, they undoubtedly incur just punishment, as we said.

[396] This is Suarez' comment. He justly teaches that the law must not be carried out 'whenever there is a presumption contrary to the truth necessary for the uprightness of the act' (*De Leg.*, bk. 4, c. 23, n. 2). If, for example, a spouse, who cannot show the existence of any diriment impediment but knows nevertheless that consent was lacking, is obliged by law to use marriage, that spouse must abstain. The truth of consent, contrary to the presumption of the law, is necessary if the act is to be upright.

with some external sanction. For example, before Licinius granted freedom to Christianity and recognised Christianity's right of ownership,[397] the Catholic Church could not be despoiled of her temporal goods, even under the pagan emperors. This is in accord with the natural right of ownership possessed by every society (*USR*, 446–449). Pious legacies in favour of the Church were equally obligatory for Catholics under the same pagan emperors even before Constantine decreed their validity (325 AD). The same was true for all legacies to pious causes or charity prior to their sanction.[398] Degenerate Christians could have considered these legacies as non-existent without blame from civil law which protected the theft negatively by refusing recourse at law to those offended — who were also deprived of the opportunity of private coercion which had been excluded by the state of civil society.

The same can be said about certain formalities required by civil law for an act (*RI*, 14–16). The act, even without the formalities, can be valid in conscience for those who know that nothing is lacking in the act relative to the requirements of rational Right. Those who are ignorant of this can without fault adhere to the letter of the law. Here, presumption, not destroyed by truth, is in favour of the law.

iii) *Laws of civil society, and laws of theocratic society received or acknowledged by civil society*

2489. Individual Right receives certain modifications from the Right of civil society in so far as individuals who unite in civil society oblige themselves spontaneously to sustain the burdens necessary to attain the end of civil society. In the same way, civil-social Right receives certain modifications when people

---

[397] Licinius' edict is found in *De mortibus persecutorum*, 48. The emperor does not speak in the edict as though he gave Christian society the right to possess for the first time, but shows that he recognises a previous right and is restoring what has been violated: 'The same Christians, ACCORDING TO THEIR OWN CORPORATE CHURCH LAW, ARE KNOWN TO HAVE POSSESSED not only the places where they used to meet, but other buildings also, none of which belonged to individuals. By the law which we have indicated above, you will order all these things TO BE RETURNED, without ambiguity or controversy, to these same Christians, that is, to their CORPORATE BODY and to their CONVENTICLES.

[398] *Cod.*, bk. 1, t. 2: 26; t. 3: 24, 26, 28, 49. — *Nov.* 131, c. 12.

[2489]

enter theocratic society. By the very fact of entering (and they have an inalienable right to this) they will to accept the obligations springing from its end. These obligations necessarily limit and temper their individual and civil rights.

2490. Indeed, the end of theocratic society is the highest of all ends (*RGC*, 661, 767–797) and as such requires that other ends, even the civil end, become means, not obstacles, to itself. They would be obstacles if, for example, the end of civil society were considered in isolation from and independent of the end of theocratic society. This is a common mistake nowadays when people affirm that civil law should be *godless*.[399]

2491. We shall speak, however, only about perfect theocratic society (*RGC*, 671–712). In what kind and number of ways does the Catholic Church emend civil legislation?

First, it does not accept anything in human law which it finds contrary to divine revelation, to justice and morality, and generally to its own end. However, because the Church is the *City of peace*, as it is called in Scripture, it imposes on its members a *peaceful* obligation to reject evil elements. In other words, the obligation lacks forceful sanctions, although its observance is a condition of membership and of participation in the Church's goods. Moral-religious obligation in contrast with the enactments of the City is the means used by the Catholic Church to emend whatever is unjust, wicked and impious in civil law.

2492. It must also be noted that the Church has its own way of promoting this reformation. I like to call this a 'creative' way because it resembles that used by the Almighty in the reformation and regeneration of mankind. The Almighty regenerates human beings by infusing them with a new principle of supernatural life.[400] This principle, infused in the soul, eliminates the

---

[399] Some have maintained this *impiously*, some through *abuse of abstraction*. The former are in a certain way coherent with their own principles, the latter are not. Indeed, if people who unite in civil society believe at least in a God who lays down laws, and rewards good and evil, they must consequently ensure that the civil laws they make do not offend divine laws. This is even more the case if they believe in revelation, in Christianity, in Catholicism. There can be no greater absurdity than imagining that because people come together in civil society, they can shake off the will of God, granted that they recognise and believe it is manifested to human beings, as all Christians do.

[400] Cf. *Dottrina del peccato originale*, 91–118.

sinful principle by raising up the human person and rendering him immune from the sinful principle. So the Church, unable directly to abrogate or correct pagan civil laws containing injustice, sets up against them its own new legislation. It does not even mention pagan laws. This is how it drew Christians away from the extreme injustice present in pagan legislation.

Two legislations, theocratic and civil, thus confronted one another; the former was destined to conquer the latter. St. Jerome, describing this double legislation, says:

> Caesar's laws are one thing, Christ's another; Papinian commands one thing, Paul another.

He gives an example of these opposing laws:

> For pagans, the brake on male licentiousness is very lax. Only rape and adultery are condemned. Lust is permitted in brothels and with servant-girls as though fault depended on dignity rather than will. For us, what is unlawful for women is equally unlawful for men; and it is the same for slaves.[401]

When Christian youth, obedient to the Church, brought its influence to bear on civil society, it emended civil legislation in accord with the contrary model of Christian legislation.

2493. We should also notice that civil laws which err against justice, morality and religion, are for the most part *facultative* and *permissive*. The Church normally attends to their reform simply by forbidding her children whatever is permitted but not commanded by these laws. One example of this are the laws which permitted concubinage for a year before valid matrimony. These were corrected by the Church in 1286–1288. Another example are the inhuman laws depriving children born of incestuous marriages of their right to nourishment.[402] These, too, were proscribed by the Church.[403]

We need to reflect, however, that even a simple *facultative civil law*, if founded on injustice, normally induces and protects unjust facts. It is facultative only when the interested parties

---

[401] *Ad Ocean.*
[402] *C.*, bk. 5, tit. 5: 6. — *Nov.* 89, tit. 1, c. 15.
[403] *Decretal.*, bk. 4, tit. 7, c. 5.

[2493]

agree not to use it. If one of them wishes to hold to the law for his own advantage, he is protected and upheld by civil authority. We have an example in any civil law which requires many formalities for the validity of a will (*RI*, 1416). It is certain that public power puts no obstacle to the validity of a will if all the interested parties are happy to consider it valid despite its lack of legal form. Validity according to rational law is sufficient.[404] Public power merely places no obstacle to this; the law is simply facultative. The picture changes if one of the parties wants to invalidate the will. Civil authority upholds this party and obliges the other to submit to the law. The law itself then becomes obligatory or, better, penal. The same can be said about Roman laws which declared invalid any marriage contracted by a child of a family without the consent of the parents,[405] or marriage between a step-father and the widow of his step-son.[406] These marriages were declared valid by the Church.[407] Civil laws certainly do not oblige the contracting parties to separate if neither of them complains. In this sense, the law is facultative. If, however, one of the parties does complain, separation is enforced by public authority.

2494. Finally, the Church declared that certain punishments imposed by Christian, civil society were unjust; others, not imposed, should according to justice be imposed. Christians whose duty it is to make such laws, hear and obey the Church if they are her devout children.[408] Parity of punishment for man

---

[404] I have shown that the faculty for making a will is present in natural Right. It is not created by civil laws (*RI*, 1377–1393).

[405] *Instit.*, bk. 1, tit. 10. — *Digest.*, bk. 23, tit. 2: 2.

[406] *Ibid.*, 15.

[407] *C. Trid.*, Sess. 24, c. 1, *De Reform. Matr.*

[408] The Church worked for the perfection of civil legislation not only as Church, but also as a *body with political rights*. In this condition she was called to take a direct part in the formation of laws and, in a word, to share in civil autocracy. Everyone knows how the clergy were the first estate in all the nations of Europe. The *Bibliothèque de l'homme publique* (t. 3, p. 51), a publication highly unfavourable to the clergy, says in speaking of the Franks and Burgundians: 'Ecclesiastics, the only educated people, almost all of Roman origin, became the interpreters of law which they made more acceptable and human than barbarian law. They had the largest share in the capitularies of our kings, and in our first and second rank of aristocracy, which formed the Code at that time. One section of these capitularies is the work of

and woman was restored in the case of adultery; Roman laws had favoured the male.[409] Women were no longer subject to punishment if they remarried within a year of their bereavement.[410] These punishments were not only deficient from the point of view of equity and justice; they also tended to set men unduly over women. It was men who made the law and, unjust as they were, made it for themselves. The Church also reformed the law that allowed a husband to kill an adulterer found with his wife,[411] and a father to kill his daughter caught in adultery.[412] These laws authenticated acts of anger and revenge; they did not decree justice and exemplary punishment.[413]

2495. The Catholic Church, as we said, recognises laws of civil society as obliging in conscience.[414] In the same way, Catholic Christians who make up civil society or possess autocracy and the faculty of making laws are obliged in conscience to accept the reform and emendation of civil laws when this springs from the Church's opposition to injustices in these laws. Catholics are also obliged to order civil laws in such a way that they never prejudice, but assist the attainment of the more noble end of theocratic society, and harmonise fully with its just laws.

iv) *Sub-classification of politico-civil laws*

2496. Politico-civil laws are those which spring from 'jural

the Councils which were adopted and confirmed by the king and the nation; the other was the work of the ancient parliaments. — As far as the nobles were concerned, disagreements were terminated by war. Vassals, extending their rights as they pleased, or on the occasion of some particular offence, fought against their sovereigns. It was the clergy who acted as mediators for most of these conflicts, and opposed private wars and violence with the maxims of the Gospel, rational right and the threat of excommunication. Their mediation consistently enriched them and brought them ever greater consideration.'

[409] *Decretal.*, bk. 5, tit. 16.

[410] *C.*, bk. 5, tit. 9: 1. — *Decretal.*, bk. 4, tit. 21, c. 4: 5.

[411] *Dig.*, bk. 48, tit. 5: 24, 25; *C.*, bk. 9, tit. 9: 4; *Nov.*, 117, c. 15.

[412] *Dig.*, bk. 48, tit. 5: 23, 29.

[413] Cf. M. Troplong, *De l'influence du Christianisme sur le Droit civil des Romains*, Paris, 1840, for a recent work on this subject.

[414] 'Laws do not distain to imitate the sacred canons. At the same time, the enactments of the sacred canons are helped by the decisions of rulers' (*Decree of Gregory IX*, bk. 5, t. 32, c. 1); 'Indeed, holy Church does not reject service under secular laws which reflect equity and justice' (*ibid.*, t. 33, c. 28).

[2495–2496]

reason applied for determining social organisation, or the obligations of officials and all members for the sake of co-operation in attaining the end of a society.' These laws can be subdivided into State constitutions and political laws properly so-called.

2497. I.) *Constitutions*. — Baroli, speaking about so-called fundamental laws, writes:

> The sovereign has the right, and is indeed obliged to establish all laws, of any kind whatsoever, which are required for the end of the State, and for present and future social good. These laws must be required by natural, jural law if they are to take on the characteristics of real necessity and utility for the City (it is only from such characteristics that they draw both their legitimate origin and their justification). This requirement will be absolute if related to the essential conditions of the City, or relative if related to the accidental, particular situation and circumstances in which civil society finds itself. If situation and circumstances call for the publication of fundamental laws, the sovereign has the right and the duty to promulgate them. Not doing so, he violates his own obligations and injures the rights of his subjects. A twofold advantage flows from such formation of fundamental laws. First, they have a legitimate origin because they spring from the person who has the exclusive right to make and promulgate them. Second, they bring true, salutary benefits to the people because they are prepared and required in accordance with the needs of the time (they are required by the circumstances in which the State finds itself). As such, they are extremely useful for the people. Moreover, they are not momentary, like lightning, but long-lasting, stable and perennial springs providing constant prosperity. They are, without doubt, consonant with the character, situation and needs of subjects. Their promulgation, fervently desired by the people, does not cause divisions, discontent and resistance, but brings an enthusiastic blessing on those who drew them up.[415]

These words show clearly that the author is speaking about fundamental laws which emanate from an already constituted legislator in society. Properly speaking, these laws should be called *organic*, rather than *fundamental*.

---

[415] *Diritto naturale pubblico interno*, §114, *1.

2498. It is equally true, however, that a legislator cannot conceive the formation of true laws before he comes into being. These 'laws' should therefore be called more suitably conventions. They may be tacitly admitted, or written. In an absolute monarchy, for example, it is tacitly admitted by the entire society that the monarch is absolute.[416] If this should come to be written down, it would be a truly fundamental constitution, placing in existence the legislative power of the monarch.

2499. The same is true of the act by which autocracy is transmitted and divided amongst several subjects.[417] This would

[416] Seigniory has no need of tacit convention, but there is no doubt that the right to govern a civil society autocratically, placed in the hand of a single individual and separated from seigniorial right, does need some tacit convention. This is the general opinion of all Catholic authors. St. Alphonsus is one example. He writes: 'It is certain that the power of making laws has been put in the hands of mankind. This power relative to civil laws does not pertain to anyone by nature except to the community of mankind which transfers it to the single individual or group of persons by whom the community is ruled' (*Th. M.*, bk. 1, n. 104). This conclusion, although fundamentally right, is inappropriately expressed: 1. properly speaking, the power of making *civil laws* is not given to mankind *by nature* (only fathers have the power to make laws for their families); nature provides only the power of making *conventions*. There is, moreover, the power to constitute *legislative authority* by means of conventions between human beings; 2. it is not true properly speaking that legislative power passes from the community of mankind (unless this has been organised in a democratic government) to one or two individuals. Rather, the community of mankind which has no power to make laws sets up this power in one or more individuals through *conventions* by which all oblige themselves to obey one or more persons whom it elects by way of contract as its head and governor.

[417] This was the Roman view. According to their conception, legislative power passed from the people, who possessed it in the already constituted republic, to the emperor alone. This concept undoubtedly served as a basis for all imperial authority. When mentioned in the *Digest* by the jurisconsults it was called the 'royal law'. 'What pleases the ruler has the force of law. By means of the royal law on which the ruler's power of command rests, the PEOPLE HAVE CONFERRED ALL ITS OWN POWER OF COMMAND TO HIM AND UPON HIM (*Dig.*, bk. 1, t. 4: 1). Justinian put this law in his *Institutions* (bk. 1, t. 2, §6) as the foundation of his authority. We have to remember that the same royal law, which is presumed to be given by the Roman people to the individual who assumed supreme power, could not have been a law, but only a *convention*. It became law, however, for members of the Roman commonalty because it was agreed both by the people who ceded their legislative right and by the individual who acquired and retained it as his very own.

be the case if a democracy, by choosing a ruler, changed itself into a constitutional monarchy. True conventions are formed between the various subjects who are each invested with a part of the autocracy, that is, between the people, the chosen king and the nobility (the house of hereditary peers). The complex of these conventions, when possessing the force of law, are normally called 'constitutions'.

2500. Laws of this kind, once agreed, cannot be undone except by the holder of the autocracy as a whole. If conventions have been made between the different powers making up the autocracy, they cannot be undone or changed without agreement amongst the parties themselves.

2501. The matter of these constitutions cannot be accurately determined. They may include various levels of organic arrangements which differ from mere organic laws solely through the different obligation they induce, through the nature of the conventions which bring about their formation, and through their greater stability.

2502. Nevertheless, it could be said that the appropriate *material* of civil constitutions must be the precise determination of rights and political obligations of the seven subjects to be found in all societies, but especially in civil society (*USR*, 367–383).

2503. II.) *Political laws, strictly speaking.* — These are the laws established by an already constituted legislative power. They are directed at organising the *social executive*, the *tribunal* and the *force* in everything not provided for in the State constitution. They also prescribe rules of procedure enabling these three powers to act in the way best suited for attaining their end.

2504. These laws can be called organising or *organic laws* to the extent that they *organise* the three powers. They become *laws of political procedure, economic* or *administrative laws*, and *police laws*, etc., to the extent that they prescribe directives for some already organised social executive. Finally they are *laws of procedure, laws determining the political rights of members brought before competent tribunals*,[418] and *criminal laws* to the

---

[418] Civil codes are bodies of laws of various kinds. Sometimes they determine individual rights, according to natural reason; sometimes they establish rights or modifications of rights in view of the social or political end. I want to insist that the perfection of codes of law requires a precise distinction

extent that they prescribe directives for already organised tribunals. They are *military laws*, divided according to the branches of the armed forces to which they are regularly directed, to the extent that they prescribe norms for force.

2505. We put criminal laws amongst politico-civil laws.[419] As we said, their end is not the punishment of crime, but restraint of the criminal drive. Such restraint forms part of the social end (*RI*, 1819). We have spoken already about the Right of defence against probable attacks on rights which human beings possess in the state of nature (*RI*, 1820–1994). Here we shall add a few comments about the exercise of penal right in civil society.

v) *Penal right of civil society*

2506. *The reason for punishment inflicted by civil society on delinquents.* — Restraint of the criminal drive by means of exemplary penalties, that is, through fear brought about by the threat and infliction of punishment.[420]

2507. *The absolute measure of punishment.* — We have to distinguish *compensation for harm* from *punishment*. *Compensation* should be ample, that is, sufficient to compensate certainly and fully any harm deliberately caused.[421] *Punishment*,

between the various modes of law.

[419] Consequently, civil society can proceed *ex officio* to search out and punish even private crimes, as Romagnosi very aptly maintains in his *Osservazioni sulla dissertazione 'Della legislazione criminale' del Sign. avv. Massa di Mentone* (*Biblioteca Italiana*, nn. 114–115, 4th and 5th questions).

[420] This truth was well known in antiquity, as we can see in affirmations of Plato (*De Legib.*, 9, and *Gorgias*) quoted by Seneca (*De Clem.*, 1: 15) and A. Gellius. (*Noct. Actt.*, 6: 14); and in Aristotle (*Politic.*, 7: 13) and Cicero (*De Off.*).

[421] The subtleties of certain authors lead them to claim that the moral obligation to compensate harm depends upon 1. the will to damage a specific person; 2. fault. For example, they say that a person who burns John Smith's hayrick in the belief that it belongs to David Jones is not obliged to compensate John Smith because there was no intention of damaging his property. — The answer to this most subtle of subtleties seems to be this. The intention of harming David Jones contained two dispositions: 1. that of harming human nature in an individual; 2. that of harming David Jones, a determined individual. Granted that there is no obligation to compensate John Smith, who was not the intended victim, there still remains the obligation of compensating human nature which is the same in John Smith and David Jones, and which

however, must be the *minimum* required for the end in view, that is, restraint of the criminal drive (*RI*, 1684).[422] Establishing this minimum requires the observance of certain matters.

2508. First, exemplary punishment will never obtain total restraint of the criminal drive. How far, then, should punishment go?

My general answer is that the rigour of penal law can be taken to the point where further application would cause more harm than good. It should not be taken further even though it does not achieve total restraint of the criminal drive. This means that the rigour of penal law must be confined to that degree which brings *maximum* good. This *maximum* is calculated by subtracting the evil,[423] which in part is always connected with the rigour of penal law.

the arsonist intended to damage. If he is not obliged to make restitution to David Smith, he is obliged to restore the hayrick, the object he set on fire. The owner will then re-possess it for himself and use it.

[422] According to Gioia (*Dell'ingiuria e dei danni*, etc., bk. 3, sect. 1, c. 1: 3), 'if there is no satisfaction, the public feels alarm proportioned to the uncompensated damage. Punishment alone is not sufficient to destroy the alarm caused by crime. It will indeed reduce the number of delinquents, but they will never be a zero number of criminals. Examples of crimes committed more or less publicly arouse a proportionate fear; each person sees that he could suffer in the same way. This fear ceases when crime is constantly followed by satisfaction and by punishment. Crime followed by punishment but not by satisfaction would simply show that the number of guilty who were punished equalled the number of ineffective punishments. Corresponding alarm would be produced in public morale (Bentham, *Traités de législation*, tom. 2)'.

[423] The evil connected with penal law is not so much the punishment inflicted on delinquents as the suffering caused to good people. Every delinquent has innocent relatives and friends. The harm that he suffers through punishment falls on entire families and on others indirectly affected by the rigour of the law. Damage is also caused by the inevitable consequences of penal legislation, such as criminal laws, tribunals, enquiries, armed police, spies, and so on. This can only be adequately compensated by the greater good one expects from it. Nevertheless, when considering the many *evils* necessarily brought about by penal justice, some weight should be given to the suffering of the guilty whose health, credit, and so on, deteriorate. They may even be deprived of life, which could have helped them to reform and do some good for themselves and the social body. This last consideration should be added to all the others which make it desirable to restrict the death penalty as far as possible. I am certainly not amongst those who, like the Avv. Carlo

[2508]

2509. This *maximum* can be calculated only approximately by expert, perspicacious minds who can see to some extent the effects of different degrees of harshness. The calculation is complicated, and to be carried out with complete prudence rather than rational analysis.

One element in this calculation is the drop in crime. This can diminish to the point where the few crimes that occur bear no relationship with the punishment. In other words, they happen simply through human fallibility and corruption, and could not be avoided whatever the increase in the rigour of public punishment. This is the greatest possible reduction in crime in *any given civil society*.[424] To attempt to obtain more would result in abandoning the *maximum* good to be desired from penal laws. Moreover, this kind of reduction is often unrealisable. To want to obtain it by constant increase of rigour would result in the loss of the maximum good that penal laws must serve. The maximum good, therefore, is not properly speaking the reduction in crime to the extreme proposed, although the rarity of crime is one of the elements which form part of the calculation of that maximum [*App.*, no. 10].

2510. *The relative measure of punishment.* — There is no doubt that the measure of punishment must vary in different civil societies according to the *intensity* of the criminal drive to be suppressed, and according to the *insensitivity* to exemplary punishment which serves as a counter to criminal drive.

2511. In other words, *punishment* should be decreased in a nation in so far as its average criminal drive is less *intense* and the people are more *sensitive*[425] to similar punishments. The

Lucas (cf. *Du système pénal.*, etc., Paris, 1827 — a work which won prizes at Paris and Geneva), maintain that the death penalty is always unjust, but I do hope that certain civil, Christian societies will cease to make use of it in the not too distant future.

[424] 'In any given society' because this final *rarity of crime*, which will always remain whatever penal rigour is in place, varies in different civil societies according to the degree of their evil tendencies and habits.

[425] Sensitivity varies in degree according to race, the social age in which a people is found, dominant opinions, and so on. It is said that the peoples in Suripatan decided to undertake only defensive wars, and to cut off the enemies' noses rather than kill them. This worked wonders (cf. Saint-Foix, *Oeuvres*, t. 4). But would this kind of defence be equally successful against a

absolute measure of punishment will be fulfilled by lesser punishment in a very sensitive people amongst whom *crime* is *rare* and the desired good is at its *maximum*.

2512. The degree of intensity of the criminal drive depends on a people's *wickedness* and its innate and acquired tendencies to evil. The degree of *sensitivity* to exemplary punishment depends on the *greater degree* of activity, and of indolence and habit, in inflicting punishment, as well as the level of self-respect. It also depends on the level of foresight and culture, or torpor and barbarism. A temperament inclined to torpor and barbarism does not easily reflect on possible punishment or on the danger of incurring it. The more *corrupt* and *barbarous* a people is, the greater its need of more severe punishment.

2513. We noted that antiquity is divided into two great cycles relative to moral and intellectual progress. The first begins with a state of moral goodness accompanied by a healthy, perspicacious, natural understanding, and gradually descends to a state of barbarism. The second rises from this final state of barbarism to that of civilisation. Greek traditions begin the history of the human race with the second cycle, and describe progressive civilisation. There is no trace of the more ancient course of history. Consequently Greek and Roman penal laws are at first extremely severe and bloody. One example are the Draconian laws, written as they say in blood. But as peoples develop and improve, penal laws become milder. Finally, the Romans arrive and bring civil society to its apex in the ancient world. Their boast is to have formulated milder penal laws than any other nation: *gloriari licet nulli gentium mitiores placuisse poenas.*[426]

2514. If, however, we go back beyond the time in which Greek and Latin authors describe penal laws in all their crudeness and severity (the penal laws pertaining to the first legislations known to these authors), we find milder punishment. Indeed,

European nation? — Nor do I think that the remedy used to prevent Milesian girls from killing themselves would be effective at all times and everywhere.

[426] This was said *à propos* the death penalty inflicted on Metius Fuffetius. 'This was the first and last death penalty amongst the Romans on a par with other laws of humanity. It is a matter for pride that punishment on other occasions was milder than that inflicted by other nations' (Liv., bk. 1). Cf. Rollin's comments, t. 3, on the mildness of Roman punishment in reference to the execution of Metius Fuffetius.

the death penalty was excluded at the beginning of the world because, I think, it was not necessary at the time [*App*., no. 11]. When Plato described penal legislation, he regretted the impossibility of providing the mild punishment he desired. According to him, very ancient legislators had been able to do this because the first of them were children of the gods and had legislated for heroes, themselves children of the gods. Plato himself, however, lived in an inferior, human age, and had to legislate for human beings:

> There could well be some citizens with an indomitable, obstinate nature — like vegetables which, when struck by lightning, cannot be softened even when cooked in the fire of the severest laws.[427]

These ancient legislations mentioned by Plato must have belonged to the first cycle. The second cycle began with what the Greeks called 'the age of men', before which they had only fables about gods and heroes. Thucydides' words hinting at the progress from mild to rigid punishment should therefore be referred to the first cycle:

> It is possible that in the old days light punishment was applied even for serious crime. Such punishment came to be despised, however, and in time the death penalty came into force.[428]

2515. The *relative measure* of punishment has to be calculated from the jural, moral condition of a given people. As far as we are concerned, this jural, moral condition is the *median quantity* and the *quality* of the criminal drive. The counter-thrust provided by punishment must be proportioned and harmonised with this quantity and quality, as Romagnosi admirably points out:

> The way of adapting the penal counter-thrust to the criminal drive consists in countering it with the threat of punishment analogous to the presumed *nature* of the criminal drive, and proportioned to the presumed *degree* of energy possessed by this criminal drive.[429]

[427] *De Leg.*, 9.
[428] Bk. 3, §45.
[429] *Genesi del Diritto penale*, §1504.

However, we want to speak only about the *relative quantity*, not the quality of punishment.[430]

2516. The following comments have to be made on this point. The separation of penal legislation from other means used by government to bring society to its end is a serious abuse of abstraction. Penal legislation cannot be perfect unless it is accompanied by all other moral and intellectual means intended to diminish crime. Civil government has the same obligation as each individual 'not to use violent methods to obtain what is just until all peaceful means have been found useless' (*RI*, 505, 1796–1799). These peaceful methods intended to prevent crime and eliminate the criminal drive are reduced to promoting everything that enhances people: virtue, religion and education. According to G. D. Romagnosi:

> Before employing painful sanctions, those who exercise penal power are required to prevent crime by the use of all suitable, effective and harmless means. Recourse to punishment is to be the final remedy only.[431]

---

[430] Note the distinction we make between the absolute and relative quantity of punishment. The *absolute quantity* is determined in theory by a general formula equally applicable to all civil societies, sound or corrupt. To determine this quantity we had recourse to two effectual limits caused presumptively by penal legislation. These limits are: 1. the *rarity of crime*, which has reached such a low level that greater rigour in the law would be unable to diminish crime any further; 2. the *incidental evils* accompanying penal laws, and every degree of rigour used by them, which increase to the point that the *maximum*, refined good brought about by penal legislation begins to diminish. The perspicacity of politicians must subtract these evils from the sum of good brought about by the penal law, and consider the sum of refined good which remains. The degree of rigour must not increase to such an extent that the maximum of refined good is made to decrease. As we said, the *absolute measure*, that is, the degree of rigour of punishment in *every civil society* is that which diminishes crime as far as possible and no further, without causing *per accidens* other evils which detract from the refined, maximum good effected by penal laws. To obtain the *relative measure* of punishment, we have to see how punishment must be increased or lessened in different nations or civil societies of different jural-moral condition in order to achieve in some particular nation an *absolute measure* of punishment. Here success depends, I repeat, on the *degree* of the criminal drive in a given nation, or class of persons in the nation, and on the *characteristics* of this drive. From these two elements, we must calculate the *relative measure* of the punishment we seek.

[431] *Genesi del diritto penale*, §421, 55, 163.

He goes on, noting that this is a *jural duty* for civil society:

> It has been said many times that it is better to prevent than to punish crime. Expressed in this way, the principle is simply a maxim of political expediency. I would go further, however, and insist that punishing crime when it could be prevented would be cruelty and INJUSTICE. Here we see that something first proposed only as useful becomes a rule of rigorous right.

This is the standard with which to judge civil governments so neglectful of many suitable, persuasive means 1. for removing the occasion for crime, 2. for destroying the tendency to crime by bettering the wills of the citizens and 3. for suppressing the first signs of crime before it has a chance to develop. The execution and torment rendered necessary through their neglect or wickedness is nothing more than infraction of right, social offence and public assassination.[432]

2517. The legislator must therefore establish only necessary penal laws. Prior to this, he must use all his skill to ensure that necessary punishment is reduced to the minimum. He will achieve this, as we said, by

    1. encouraging moral virtue with every means in his power;

    2. removing all occasions of crime with wise vigilance and care, without offending the rights of anyone or unduly restricting inoffensive freedom;

---

[432] Plato speaks of penal laws after the institution of every moral virtue in his City. His introduction to the discussion on penal right should be placed at the head of the criminal code by every legislator. 'It could seem out of place to provide laws for the things of which we are now about to speak (that is, crime) because we are dealing, in fact, with a City which we consider admirably disposed for the acquisition of virtue. Surely, it must seem strange to everyone to suppose that a wicked man could be born in a well-educated City, just as he could elsewhere. Do we really need the threat of laws to prevent someone from becoming a criminal or committing such things? Do we need laws to punish crime that has been committed? In other words, do we expect to find such wicked people in our republic? We, however, do not formulate laws as though we were the first legislators, the children of God. Their laws were intended for heroes, born like the legislators from the gods...' Truly just penal laws are those which the legislator prescribes for civil society after he has educated and established it with all the wisdom of which he is capable.

[2517]

3. ensuring that the threat of punishment is clear to all, and that fear of punishment is the maximum to be derived from the nature of the punishment. The same punishment can, in fact, be threatened and carried out so as to induce fear more effectively — and more effectively even than greater punishment.

2518. Several aspects of public justice coalesce to produce this last effect. They are all jurally obligatory as corollaries of the general obligation which governments have to reduce, with means proper to themselves, the necessity of punishment to the minimum level. In other words, they have to make the least punishment as effective as possible. These aspects are:

1. the *greatest* public *vigilance* in apprehending the guilty;

2. *incorrupt force* which ensures unalterable, speedy process of prosecution of the guilty;

3. *wise, cautious procedure* which takes account of the crime without confusing innocent parties with the guilty;[433] the procedure should also be *brief* and *loyal;*

4. *determined, immediate, inevitable punishment, adapted to the manner and characteristics of the criminal drive;*

5. *exemplary execution* of the punishment, that is, it should

---

[433] It is extremely difficult to determine judicial proofs which are simultaneously *alert* and *cautious*. It is extremely difficult to determine the weight to be given to the judge's *intimate conviction*, which cannot be entirely ignored. In fact, codes which wisely determine *precise*, ascertained facts of a crime do not go on to determine *ascertained facts* from *ascertained facts*, but leave this to the judge's discretion. For example, it may establish as ascertained that such and such a weapon or instrument was used to commit a crime, but it will not be established that this weapon was already owned by the accused person at the time of the crime. This proof will depend on the judge's logic. A bloody table knife is found near the body of a deceased person; a corresponding fork is found in the house of the accused. The judge may consider this coincidence sufficient proof that the knife really belonged to the accused. The Austrian Code, which does not determine such proof from the ascertained fact, leaves the conclusion to the judge; it does however determine the ascertained fact. On the one hand, finding signs of the presence of the accused, such as marks of his shoes near the body, is not considered proof because this indication is not enumerated by law; on the other, finding signs or clues of the knife, such as the fork mentioned above, is sufficient proof of the ascertained fact because the signs or proofs of ascertained facts are not determined by law, but left to the critical assessment of the judge.

[2518]

be *public*, suitable for arousing terror, *moral* and *respectful of human dignity* [*App.*, no. 12].

2519. Let us grant that civil government neglects no peaceful means useful to society for diminishing crime and reducing the criminal drive; let us also grant that it has put into force to the best of its ability the *minimum, relative measure* of punishment needed to suppress the criminal drive in any given civil society committed to its care. Two questions now arise: how can government recognise the effective extent of this *relative measure?* and if, as we said, this measure is relative to the criminal drive, how will government be able to recognise the degree and characteristics of this drive in a given nation?

2520. First, we should note what Romagnosi has to say on the subject:

> If the preventative action of this (penal) teaching is to be *general* and lasting, it obviously has to be directed against the criminal drive present in an entire people and *normally capable* (granted certain circumstances) of breaking out and disturbing social order. The criminal drive in question is not the *real*, individual, criminal drive understood by educators, moral philosophers and directors of conscience. On the contrary, it is the drive which, granted the circumstances, can *normally* break out among a people and upset the social order.[434]

2521. Second, we note that the laws of the human heart are common to all. If we wished to discover from these laws the degree and characteristics of the criminal drive, we would have only a general, abstract result, applicable to every society. We would never know the degree and characteristics of the criminal drive in a given civil society. For example, the laws of the human heart enable us to establish in general that the criminal drive will be greater in those individuals who 1. have greater *power to harm*, 2. *occasions for doing harm*, 3. *lust for possessions*, 4. take *pride in domineering*, 5. have other passions and vices, 6. *boldness*, 7. *lack of moral restraint*, 8. *hope to succeed* and *go unpunished*, and 9. have *no fear of discredit*. Similar circumstances or moral qualities of individuals can be added to this list. None of

[434] *Genesi del D. P.*, §1391, 1345, 337.

this, however, enables us to know the measure of the criminal drive which really exists in a given nation. It is simply a rule which, when applied to positive data, leads us to discover that measure.

2522. Third, as we said, certain qualities and dispositions are found in the human heart which can serve as a rule for knowing the quantity and characteristics of the criminal drive in individuals. The same is true for civil societies, each of which possesses certain conditions of its own enabling us to indicate with probability the degree and characteristics of its criminal drive, provided that the factual conditions on which the calculation is based are known exactly. These conditions and social qualities refer equally to the state of the people and to that of government at various levels of its perfection.

2523. These observations show that theoretical principles and rules are not sufficient to provide knowledge of the measure of the criminal drive in any given society. Compilations of facts are required in which we see actuated the symptoms and indications present in the theoretical rules. The abundance of diligently compiled, symptomatic facts enables us to reduce them to a single general fact, an average fact which expresses the frequency of the case and consequently the probability that it will be repeated. The degree of this probability is the measure of the criminal drive.

Where are we to find such a classification of facts? So far, they do not exist anywhere, although they should be registered in the *moral statistics* of which we spoke elsewhere. They are poorly developed despite their urgent necessity.[435] A time will come when these statistics will be recognised as the eye of politics, and especially of criminal legislation. Deciding punishment without them will seem to be gambling with the sorrows and torments of human beings. Collecting accurate statistics of this kind and periodically renewing them is therefore a condition for public justice; it is a jural duty of the civil legislator.

2524. *Equality of punishment.* — There is no doubt that punishment threatened by society should be equal for all. We must not be misled about this equality, however. We are dealing

---

[435] *SP*, 853–858.

with jural equality, that is, equality before the law.[436] Relative to penal legislation, this equality can be formulated as follows: 'Every member of civil society, finding himself in the same circumstances and committing the same crime, will be tried in the same way and receive the same punishment.'

2525. This *penal-jural equality* does not, however, remove two other inequalities. Indeed, it cannot be preserved unless the legislator takes account of the two inequalities we wish to indicate.

These arise from variations in the *circumstances* indicated in the formula: from the *delinquent*'s circumstances, and from the circumstances of the *person offended*. In other words, both the delinquent and the person offended can be unequal; both can exist in unequal circumstances, which have to be calculated for the punishment to be equal.

2526. We note however that not every inequality in the delinquent, and not every circumstance of person offended requires consideration. Attention must be confined to whatever is necessary to temper the punishment in such a way that it is maintained at an equal level for all.

2527. We ask first: 'What are the circumstances of the person offended which must be kept in mind by the criminal legislator?' — 'Only those which change the *species* or the *gravity* of the crime.'

Punishment would not have penal-jural equality if it were the same for different species and different degrees of gravity of crime. This *species*, and *gravity* in the same species, if it is affected by the circumstances and qualities of the person offended, must be calculated according to these *circumstances* and qualities. This does not mean that the legislator takes account of the person offended. He is considering the crime which he wishes to punish justly. If it is more serious, penal teaching requires that society be protected more rigorously. Legislations which, for fear of offending penal-social equality, feel themselves obliged to punish a crime without regard to the qualities of the person offended,[437] have misunderstood penal-social

---

[436] *SP*, 214–215.

[437] Gioia, speaking about the statutes of the Italian republics, claims to have noticed 'that in the midst of political disputes, civil legislation took several

equality. I am speaking, of course, about those qualities which render a crime more serious.[438]

2528. We have to pass now to the conditions of the delinquent: 'What are the conditions of the delinquent which have to be kept in mind by the penal legislator?' There is no doubt that conditions relative to the delinquent which change the species or aggravate the crime must also be considered. They come to form part of his penal-jural responsibility (*RI*, 1779–1791).

2529. In addition, legislative wisdom will note all the circumstances of the delinquent which are of assistance in discovering the most *effective* and at the same time *mildest* punishment as a counter-thrust to the criminal drive of other individuals in the same circumstances.

2530. This, too, will be done haphazardly and imperfectly if the moral statistics of which we have spoken are not compiled.

retrograde steps and violated EQUALITY WHILE PREACHING IT (*Dell'ingiuria etc.*, p. 2, sect. 2, c. 3, §1). He also says: 'If we compare the laws of barbarian peoples between the 5th and 12th centuries with those established by the Italian republics which appeared from the 12th century onwards, we find that punishment for injuries done to ecclesiastics in the first period was three times the ordinary punishment. In the second period, the former punishment was lowered and made equal to the ordinary punishment. Greater punishment remained as a guarantee for civil authority alone' (*Delle injurie etc.*, p. 1, bk. 1, c. 5, a. 1, §2). Again: 'The laws of medieval Italian republics, directed BY A CONFUSED IDEA OF SOCIAL EQUALITY, took no account of distinction in injuries which could be committed against women as well as men. Equal punishment was inflicted for these injuries. This is criminal injustice. Women are more susceptible to contempt, more easily alarmed, and weaker physically' (*Dell'ingiuria etc.*, p. 2, bk. 2, sect. 1, a. 2, c.1, §2).

[438] One of the qualities of the offended person which does not render the crime more serious is, for example, his wealth. A law of Ina, king of Wessex, quoted in Canciani (*Leges Barbarorum*, etc., t. 4, p. 239) was, therefore, unjust, and today seems laughable. The crime was measured, according to a very apt phrase of Gioia, in acres. It increased relative to the amount of land possessed by the person offended. The calculation was made as follows:
   If Wallus has a hide of land, his value will be 120 units
   If he has half a hide, 80 units
   If neither, 60 units
A similar law attributed to Alfred the Great is also cited by Canciani (*ibid.*, p. 250). These laws remind us of the way normally used in England to indicate a man's wealth: 'He's worth so many pounds'. Only Gioia's tortuous, petty spirit could maintain that crime should be measured relative also to the wealth of the person offended.

[2528–2530]

These statistics should contain the classification of delinquents for various periods of time according to their age, sex, profession and other social distinctions. This will show which crimes are normally committed by one class rather than another.

2531. The tenor of punishment should be examined on the basis of these factual matters to discover the most efficacious and mildest punishment for each class of persons. Punishment will then be established according to the *characteristics* and degree of *intensity* which achieve the effect intended by penal teaching. This, as we have seen, is directed 'to reducing the frequency of crime to the two limits constituting the absolute measure of punishment.'

2532. *Characteristics of punishment.* — Granted the various *characteristics* and the *degree* of the criminal drive in different classes of citizens and foreigners (civil society has to defend itself against foreigners according to the same principles of equity), it is not contrary to the principle of social equality that punishment, the counter-thrust to the criminal drive, should take different forms and impose different burdens. If these differences are calculated not arbitrarily, but on the basis of *moral statistics* made known to the public, they will not be considered in any way unjust. They would, however, be seen as unjust if the legislator maintained rigid equality of punishment for the various classes of people that he had in mind. Moreover, variation in punishment is not only the way to achieve penal justice; it will also be praised for its humanity as the only way to mitigate, as far as possible, the rigour of punishment.

2533. We must speak now of the various, particular kinds of punishment.

Punishment by disgrace. — Every publicly known punishment brings with it a degree of disgrace corresponding to the degree of punishment. Disgrace is simply public disapproval of the crime. Disgrace, therefore, forms part of natural justice; as punishment, it follows inevitably upon crime. This just punishment cannot be inflicted for fault, however, except by upright, public opinion which forms a just estimate of fault. And it will be better inflicted in so far as public opinion is more uniform. But one of the most important duties of civil government is to use means peculiar to itself to rectify and enlighten public opinion, not to falsify it (cf. 2305–2307). Disgrace, therefore, must not be confined to certain crimes; it is a part of punishment attached by nature and reason to all crimes without exception. It must be inflicted by the public, not by government. Considerations of this kind make me wish that civilised people would completely remove humiliating punishments from criminal codes and be content with having the crime denounced to the public who alone are the competent ministers of justice in this matter and, as such, capable of inflicting merited shame.

2534. Acting in any other way produces various difficulties which, instead of serving justice, alter its balance, distort upright public opinion and foment immorality. The reasons for this are as follows.

1. If government wishes to distribute disgrace, it either wants to do this *according to justice* or believes it can arbitrarily increase disgrace for certain crimes to the degree required as a counter-thrust to the criminal drive. In the former case, government would have to assign a certain portion of disgrace to all crimes, which it cannot usefully do. Well-formed public opinion already does this of its own accord; others cannot do it in place of public opinion. In the latter case, government necessarily *injures truth* and *justice*, and *wants to accomplish the impossible*.

It *injures justice* because disgrace has only one measure, determined not at will but by the measure itself of the crime. Disgrace is not, therefore, amongst those punishments which can be increased and decreased according to the degree of the criminal drive. Consequently, it does not appertain to punitive power.

It *wants to accomplish the impossible* because what it desires is necessarily in opposition to public opinion which alone decrees the true blame to be placed on faults. Such opposition brings government into disrepute.

2535. 2. Because legislation's arbitrary use of humiliating punishment falsifies public opinion in some way, government automatically falls short in its sacred duties and ruins public morality.

2536. 3. Increasing the degrees of disgrace due to crime means sowing the seed of ill will; it is a true act of hatred against the delinquent. Such a sad effect amongst the public simply means that a wicked passion displaces tranquil, just disapproval in the mind. The great need of humanity is not an increase of hatred, but of benevolence in the heart.

2537. 4. Even stronger, I think, is the case against chastisement that exposes the delinquent to public derision, and abandons him to wicked mockery and torment by the crowd[439] and by children (who as a result soon develop bad habits). It is desirable rather that the people conceive feelings of commiseration for the guilty. I mean moral commiseration, which first leads people to desire the emendation of the criminal and then the end of his punishment.

2538. 5. Man-made *disgrace*, augmented by public demonstrations and declarations, becomes even more unjust after the delinquent's reform. He suffers longer than is necessary, and the stain, which perhaps cannot be wiped out, gives rise to feelings of indignation, hate, despair and impudence. Initially, this makes emendment difficult, and then impedes its stability.

2539. *Fines and corporal punishment.* — It seems clear to me that a delinquent who inflicts damage on the public purse (for example, by damaging a public road) should always compensate society for the damage caused. If this fine, which is compensatory of its nature, is not sufficient to suppress the criminal drive, some suitable punishment should be added.[440] However, I do not think that this principle of compensation can be applied with total consistency. According to the principle, expenses sustained by the State in maintaining criminal justice should be fully compensated by fines inflicted on the criminals who cause

---

[439] I refer to the chastisement that the uneducated rabble tends to prefer. Governments who second this deplorable desire are making a serious mistake. 'In the case of adultery committed by a wife with the assent of her husband, the statute of Ferrara condemns him to be taken through the public streets on a cart, the front of which is decorated with two horns of a goat or a bull' (*Statutorum*, bk. 3, c. 103). What is really odd is to find a recent author proclaiming this as a glory of our poor Italy! Melchior Gioia, the author in question, adds the following serious comment to the words we have quoted: 'This emblematic sign (of the horns) and others found in our Statutes — show that several ideas, presented as original by Bentham, may be new in England. They are not new in Italy' (*Dell'ingiuria*, etc., p. 2, bk. 1, sect. 2, art. 2, c. 3, §1).

[440] People unable to pay should compensate with work. If family obligations make this impossible, and the family itself is innocent and not to be involved in the chastisement due to the guilty party, sufficient corporal punishment should be inflicted to restrain the criminal drive, as our principles showed.

[2537–2539]

them,[441] just as the expenses sustained in the administration of civil-private justice should be compensated by those who litigate maliciously, or are in the wrong (cf. 2474). Why should harmless, peaceful citizens, who give no trouble to courts, be burdened in this way?

2540. At this point, we need to compare fines and corporal punishment. Which penalty is the better?

Wherever possible, fines should be used. They debase people less and respect their dignity more. As a consequence they are milder.

2541. Moreover, fines allow for precise gradations.

2542. The suitability of this kind of punishment was recognised in the Middle Ages,[442] when almost all crime[443] was

[441] However, the portion of the expenses which guilty people cannot pay must be sustained by society. These expenses should not be imposed on people guilty of other crimes.

[442] According to Bentham, financial punishment is suitable when the damage caused by the delinquent, or the advantage he gains, is of its nature financial, or such that it can be valued financially. When the injury is of its nature extraneous to finance, compensation cannot be measured exactly relative to the loss incurred. In this case, fines are not appropriate (*Traités de Législation*, t. 2). This, however, is obviously wrong. Bentham 1. confuses *satisfaction* with *punishment*; 2. forgets that punishment is not measured by the crime, but only by the criminal drive that needs to be restrained; 3. does not realise that even the most diverse good and evil are simultaneously measured very well by the effect they produce in the human spirit, as I noted in *SP*, 581–585.

[443] In many medieval legislations, punishment imposed for murder was paid by a fine. This reflected the mildness of primitive legislation, and of the legislation which Plato established in his book on laws. So, for example, the Salic law (t. 43) decrees: 'If a freeman kills a Frank or a male barbarian who lives under the Salic law, he will be judged guilty and held to pay 8,000 denarii, that is, 200 coins (gold coins, equivalent to 40 silver denarii). If a freeman kills a Roman male, a table companion of the King, he will be judged at 12,000 denarii, 300 gold coins.' — The law of the Alemanni (t. 44) states: 'If anyone kills a male, he will be fined 9 wergeld (wergeld is a form of fine); if a woman, 18 wergeld. — The law of the Bavarians (t. 3, n. 13): 'If anyone kills a freeman, he will pay his parents if they are still alive; if not, he shall pay his patron, or the person on whom he depended while he lived, twice 80 gold coins. The fine is doubled if anything happens to a woman.' The law of the Ripuarians: 'If any freeman kills a Ripuarian freeman, he will be judged guilty at 200 gold coins.' The Saxon law: 'Anyone who kills a noble will pay 1,440 gold coins.' — English law: 'If anyone kills a noble (men were divided into

punished by a monetary tariff, and in remote antiquity almost as soon as money was invented.[444]

2543. It may be objected that in this case the rich will be advantaged over the poor who cannot pay and will have to undergo corporal punishment. But this kind of objection shows that the purpose of punishment imposed by civil society has not been well understood. It is not a question of punishing crime with a just standard, but of restraining the criminal drive. If, therefore, society restrains crime amongst the rich with fines alone, it has achieved the end of punishment, and all its other rights in the matter cease. Society has an equal right to restrain the criminal drive amongst the poor, but it cannot do this through fines. It must use the means available, that is, corporal punishment. We are not dealing with a distinction between rich and poor, but the exercise of a right which civil society has towards both classes. This right is also a duty. We are dealing with the attainment of a public good, that is, the defence of all citizens against any crime which could break out.

2544. But how can you measure such totally different matters as fines and corporal punishment, which have no common unity? — The same mistake! The measure of the two punishments is exactly the same provided they obtain the same effect, the restraint of the criminal drive. Each punishment must be

nobles, freemen and bond-servants), he will be fined 600 gold coins; for a freeman, 200; for a bond-servant, 30.' Frisian law: 'If a noble kills a noble, he will pay 70 gold coins; if a noble kills a freeman, 54 gold coins and one denarius; if a freeman kills a noble, 80 gold coins.' Lombard law (bk. 1, t. 9): 'If anyone secretly kills a baron, a freeman, a bond-servant or a handmaid, but only one or two were responsible for the murder itself, they must pay 800 gold coins.'

[444] According to Servius, the Latin expressions, *luere, persolvere poenas*, etc., recall the very ancient custom of paying for crimes with fines. He comments on Vergil (bk. 1, v. 136): '*Luetis, persolvetis. Et hic sermo a pecunia descendit: ANTIQUORUM ENIM POENAE OMNES PECUNIARIAE FUERUNT* [You will expiate, you will pay. Here the word refers to money: FOR THE ANCIENTS, ALL PUNISHMENT WAS PECUNIARY].' Fines go back to the time when money was weighed on a scales. Servius again says (in his commentary on the *Aeniad*, bk. 2, v. 229): '*Expendere* is derived from the use of money. The ancients always punished financially, as we see. Even in very early times, when MONEY WAS WEIGHED, it was used instead of capital punishment.' He makes the same comment about the word *pendere* (bk. 6, v. 20).

[2543–2544]

brought to the level where it obtains its effect without consideration of other punishments, or without need for comparison with them. We are not dealing with distributive justice here, or, if we are, it is already fulfilled when an equal check has been placed on both classes, rich and poor.[445]

2545. Other questions could be raised about fines and painful, physical punishments. Let us begin with fines.

First question: Must fines be measured by the degree of a person's wealth?

Answer: — No. The more normal cause of delinquency is cupidity. The criminal drive is therefore usually in proportion to this. If we suppose that there is less cupidity amongst the rich, the criminal drive amongst them will be less and require less counter-thrust. On the other hand, the degree of cupidity is also the measure of the pain caused by the fine. Hence where cupidity is greater, whether in the rich or poor person, the fine itself becomes more painful and pungent. There should, therefore, be perfect equality in fines.[446]

2546. Second question: which goods should be subject to fines? In other words, granted that a fine has been inflicted, and that the guilty person has a debt towards society, on which goods should the fine be levied?

Answer: — *a*) First, not on the chattels which in France are called 'goods considered stable by law.' These are the goods necessary for subsistence, such as the bed belonging to the guilty person, the beds of his wife and children, necessary clothes, tools of one's trade, and so on. According to Roman law, these

---

[445] Melchior Gioia shows his ignorance of penal teaching when he endeavours to criticise the statute of Tortona which substituted the loss of an eye for a fine of 200 lire which a man had to pay for violating a consenting virgin, and the loss of a nose for a fine of 100 lire which the consenting virgin had to pay. He reasons as follows: 'There is no need to point out that loss of one's nose is infinitely more deforming than loss of an eye. On the other hand, we should not forget the difference of the sexes. The old codes are full of similar *proportional* mistakes between punishments' (*Dell'ingiuria etc.*, p. 2, bk. 2, sect. 2, art. 1, c. 2). This decree of the Tortona statute, and many others in the ancient codes, are certainly barbarous and deplorable, but not because of their *lack of proportion*, as Gioia maintains.

[446] This is also G. D. Romagnosi's opinion. Cf. *Genesi del D. P.* §1569–1576.

goods should be respected even when other creditors demand their rights.

b) Second, the law has to punish only the guilty and, as far as possible, prevent punishment from falling even indirectly on the innocent. At the same time, families and their well-being, not individuals, are the special, proper aim of civil society (*RI*, 735–737). The fine should not therefore affect that share of goods necessary to a family if it is to go on living and progressing without falling into misery. The fine should be levied with due regard to the age and health of the wife and children, and the number of children. These are matters to be fixed by wise laws, and not left to the discretion of judges or bailiffs.

2547. *c*) Finally, the share of goods determined by the constitutive law of civil society as necessary patrimony for the status of citizen (cf. 1690–1693) should be left intact. The family of the guilty person pays the necessary poll-tax from these goods.

2548. Here I cannot omit an excellent passage from Plato which touches on almost all these points simultaneously. He begins by recognising the preservation of the entire society as the sole reason for capital punishment. Society cannot in fact be preserved if incorrigible citizens go unpunished as they rebel against divine, domestic or even civil society. He goes on immediately to speak with admirable wisdom about fines. He says:

> It may be that a citizen has committed some heinous crime against the gods, or his parents, or against his homeland, and has no intention of changing his attitude. The judge, if he sees that this person, although well instructed and educated from his youth, has not abstained from crime, will judge him irreformable. The penalty for this is death, the least of evils. Rather than suffer vituperation, let him be executed — something which is out of the ordinary — as an example to others.[447] HIS CHILDREN, however, AND ALL HIS DESCENDANTS should be honoured and praised if they show great attachment to virtue, and abandon their father's way of life, despite being the offspring of a wicked person.[448] The republic should be careful not TO CONFIS-

447 What a great similarity this has to Hebrew laws!

448 What a beautifully delicate law this is! An innocent family has inevitably

CATE any wealth belonging to these people. The conditions of families must always remain the same, always equal, in the republic.

These conditions correspond precisely to what we have called the *political patrimony* mentioned by ancient writers (*RI*, 1401–1404).

> But if anyone has committed a crime punishable by a fine, this will be levied against the goods which he possesses over and above the family-holding (the 'political patrimony' as we call it) which must remain intact. The guardians of the law will accurately inform the judges about this extraneous wealth which shall be deleted from the note in the list of taxable goods. In this way no one will be deprived of his holding if he has fallen on bad times.[449]

2549. Third question: What stipulations should be attached to corporal punishment?

Answer: — All punishments (except capital punishment) could be taxed as fines. Corporal punishment could then be imposed as a substitute for fines if the guilty person were unable to pay. This substitution should be established beforehand in the criminal code, and mentioned in the decision.

2550. Flogging and in general every sharp, but temporary, harmless pain can usefully be employed in this case without harmful consequences to the family of the guilty person, provided it is applied without serious harm to bodily health. This punishment, if sufficient, is the best.

2551. *Prison*, whether mild or harsh, has no harmful consequences for the families of unmarried delinquents whether they live with their families or not. Nor is it harmful in the case of idle, non-productive delinquents who are a burden rather than a help to their families. As Romagnosi says, they are of no 'social worth.'[450]

suffered by the execution of its father, but the great philosopher thinks that it should be compensated and comforted by civil society and thus confirmed in its own good ways. Modern legislation is still a long way from such just, elevated feelings.

[449] *Delle leggi*, bk. 9.

[450] 'By *social worth*, I mean the faculty a man has of working for others while working for himself and, while exercising a single kind of work, of enjoying civil independence' (*Genesi del D. P.*, §962).

2552. *Detention* and *prison* can, however, cause very serious damage to innocent families when the guilty member is useful to the others by supporting them with his work, and providing the other members with work. This is especially the case if he alone is capable of directing them, or has the ability to maintain the shops, workshops and earnings on which they live.

To say that the damage suffered by the innocent is *indirect* (the normal hair-splitting of lawyers) is baseless. It remains just as harmful, and unjustly harmful, if it can be avoided, as it often can be — and more often than one imagines. But this can only be done through wise legislation, by believing that it *is* possible, and by taking account of the pain and anguish pressing down upon innocent creatures. Let me say briefly what comes to mind immediately on this subject, about which lengthy thought and solid, collective study by the civil legislator is a sacred duty. If prison is believed necessary for a man who works, let him work sufficiently to compensate with his earnings the damage and punishment of the family whom he has to abandon. If this does not suffice, is it absurd for a human, civil, Christian society to think of some other way in which to compensate the unhappy, non-culpable family?

2553. We have seen that civil society is obliged to be careful in eliminating harm which may come to a family as a result of punishment inflicted on the guilty. Criminal legislators, however, also have the duty to see that punishment helps the guilty to emend rather than grow worse.[451]

This noble duty also descends from the general duty of the end of society, and from the special end of punishment, the aim of which is to diminish crime. Society operates against its own end therefore if, in applying punishment, it worsens the person it punishes and nourishes rather than decreases the criminal drive in him. It operates in accordance with its end if it betters this person. Civil society neglects its duty if it does not regulate punishment in accordance with its end. But how will it succeed in doing this?

2554. I think it will succeed if the concept underlying punish-

---

[451] 'No punishment imposed by the law tends to evil. Its normal effect is always to produce one of two results: either it makes better the person punished, or renders him less wayward' (Plato, *Delle leggi*, bk. 9).

ment by incarceration is predominantly the following: 'Prison must be a place of work and education for delinquents.'

2555. It is not, therefore, *punishment* of the prisoner that has to be sought in prison. Punishment is necessarily connected with 1. reclusion and privation of physical freedom; 2. assiduous work, ordered and imposed by others; 3. the privation of restoratives such as wine and tobacco that could cause disorder;[452] 4. moral education accompanied by forceful means wisely applied. In this system, punishment is secondary; prison becomes a means for the betterment of the guilty. This does not diminish it as punishment, but simply ensures its human dignity and gives it worth in the eyes of the criminal himself. It may indeed be milder, but it is more effective; the manner of inflicting it has decreased the need for rigour. The virtue inspired in the guilty, the moral habits imposed upon them, are far more powerful in repressing any possible criminal drive in them than material, angry pain. The good conduct of released prisoners will serve as good example in lowering the criminal drive that their bad example had previously incited.

2556. *Negative* and *positive* means have to be employed if prison is to be a place of education and moral betterment. One of the most necessary negative means is the separation of the delinquent from contagion by other prisoners. Without separation, there is no hope for his emendment; he will certainly get worse. A communal prison is a school of wickedness.[453]

The advantage, and indeed the necessity of the cell system

---

[452] Wine and tobacco were forbidden in French prisons by the law of 19th May, 1819. The many advantages of this enactment were indicated by Tocqueville in his *Report* on the *Progetto di legge relativo al regime penitenziario*.

[453] Prisons in France were seriously affected in this way between 1828–1841:

	Accused Recidivists	Condemned Recidivists	Prisoners	Recidivists
1828:	1,000	108	1,000	60
1841:	1,000	227	1,000	154
1843:	18,322	7,365		

In addition, crime had been organised in France. Criminals come to understand one another's position, and communicate. Their society can have its origin only in prison. All this can be found in Tocqueville's *Report*, quoted above, and in the accompanying documents, supplied by the Interior Ministry.

[2555–2556]

must be immediately obvious to everyone, even if it is not used with the same constant rigour as in Philadelphia, but tempered in accordance with the proposal made by Tocqueville in his admirable *Report*. However, I think there should be some kind of wise classification of prisoners. There should also be some gradation of solitary confinement from absolute to lesser solitude. As prisoners improve, they should be moved at various times to different stages of social life, but without being allowed any contact whatsoever with other prisoners. No one with evil tendencies can be improved by evil company; only by good.

Nevertheless, round-the-clock separation of inmates is, as we said, only a negative means. It impedes greater evil, and even prepares the way for good. But it cannot be expected to better these sad people. We have to trust more in *positive* means, which, thanks to our modern materialism and unbelief, are the least studied by the philanthropists of our century.

Amongst these positive means the most influential is that of religion. Priests, religious men and women, pious Christians, male and female, are the true friends of humanity. Their help can provide prisoners with instruction, comfort, good motivation and finally true conversion to God and virtue. If the spirit of the Catholic Church is allowed to penetrate prisons, inmates will be seen to change into penitents. This is the only way to form true penitentiaries.

2557. *Penal colonies.* — This kind of punishment has immense advantages without the drawbacks of prison. It can perhaps be used more successfully than any other punishment for reclaiming the worst cases for society by sending them to a new world where they are forced to forget the instigation to vice found in the old world. However, not all governments have the opportunity of unloading the lowest elements of their populations in distant, uncultivated lands.

2558. *Loss of political rights.* — These political rights of the criminal are either some *duty* entrusted to him by civil society, or simply his *state as a citizen*. If his crime shows that he is *unsuitable* for office he should be stripped of his job without compensation. But is this loss of a post, which is more a consequence of the manifestation of the criminal's unsuitability than of the crime itself, a sufficient punishment? The answer depends, as always, on the great rule of the end of social punishment, that is, restraint of the criminal drive. Certainly, the loss of one's post seems a necessary consequence of unsuitability, not a criminal punishment. Nevertheless, it *is* painful, and need not be increased by further punishment if it can be shown to have produced its effect as counter-thrust to the kind of crime in question amongst officials.

2559. I consider the total loss of *citizenship* neither useful nor necessary. However, granted that civil society is constituted in such a way that radical power is divided according to the citizens' income or capital (cf. 1687–1693), this power must naturally decrease in proportion to the many fines levied on the capital of the delinquent, and to other punishments affecting his material possessions.[454]

E.
Organisation

2560. We can now summarise what we have said so far. Acts of autocratic power are the material and executive activities carried out by this power, and the commands, judgments and laws which emanate from it directly.

A fifth kind of acts, the *organisation* of society, has to be added to these four. This will be achieved by a simple, changeable command if the society is small and in its infancy. More often, it will depend upon organic laws. As we said, it soon becomes obligatory, as civilisation develops, to organise by means of law (cf. 2427–2428).

2561. It is clear that conceiving an autocratic power in charge of a civil society without need of a ministry is practically impossible. Bonald notes, acutely enough, that every society includes of its nature some kind of trinity: the autocrat (the person who wills), the minister (the person who executes) and the subject (the person or people who obeys).

2562. The autocrat communicates some of his own power to the organic offices. Note, however, that autocratic power is in part essential to the autocrat as supreme power, and in part not

[454] Cf. Blackstone, t. 1, p. 238–240.

essential. *Legislative* power, for example is essential; *executive* power is not. The communication of power therefore can be either *delegation* of all or part of autocratic power, or *communication* of simple executive power.

2563. Supreme-delegated power pertains to what we have called *government-mandatory* power (*USR*, 313). An example of this are *deputies* who in constitutional States represent the people having a part in the autocracy.

2564. In the second case, the power communicated is properly called *ministry*. This ministerial, executive power is found in the three social subjects which I have called the *executive*, the *tribunal* and *military force* (*USR*, 367).

2565. The *executive* is divided into two branches:

I. The first is the office of *political vigilance* (*political magistrate*). This office is responsible

1. For seeing that members of a society fulfil their social duties, and do nothing opposed to them.

2. For recognising the cases in which government intervention is necessary to regulate the modality of rights.

3. For establishing and putting into execution the modalities which, without prejudice to the *value* of anyone's rights, are necessary or useful for the maintenance of public order and the good of all, and prevent disorder.

II. The second is the office of *administration* of *public goods* (*economic magistrate*).

F.

Nomination to social offices

2566. We move now to the sixth act of autocratic power, provision of suitable persons for the various responsibilities established along with the organisation (cf. 2151–2153). Can the autocratic power nominate persons to offices at will?

Here we have to distinguish between *seigniorial* and *social Right*. A *master* can nominate whomsoever he wishes as procurator of his own affairs. Doing this, he does not offend anyone's right, although he may offend against prudence and culpably harm himself and his family by preferring favourites of his own who are unsuitable for dealing usefully with his interests. But if the *master* is also a *civil autocrat*, he must execute his social duties faithfully.

2567. The civil administrator must be guided in his rule by social, not seigniorial Right. Consequently, he does not have a seigniorial choice in nominating persons to social offices or responsibilities. Rather, he has a strict jural obligation to choose the persons whom he judges impartially to be the best, all things being considered, for carrying out the offices.

2568. Again, he has the jural obligation to use all the means of which he has knowledge, and over which he has power, to discover with the greatest possible safety the most suitable persons. This is the case even if such persons seek modestly and virtuously to avoid honorific and profitable public responsibilities.

2569. Granted all this, the autocrat, or his proxy, remains the *competent judge* of the greatest possible suitability that can be found. And this is the basis of distributive social justice.

2570. The *greatest possible suitability* is therefore the only rule according to which the autocrat, or the person he has delegated, must choose the officials. It is true that a great number of elements enter into the calculation of this suitability, each one of which must be attributed its exact weight. In the end, however, the choice must always fall on the greatest comprehensive suitability that can be found; it must not be made according to the personal taste of the autocrat. It would appear that one of these elements must be nationality. If, however, the autocrat were to find definitely more suitable persons amongst foreigners, after nationality has been given due weight in the calculation, he would have to prefer a foreigner. A worthy foreigner could, of course, soon become a national, and thus be acquired for the country. Enlightened rulers sometimes enriched their States by inviting great men to their countries from all parts. This was to the glory of the rulers and the immense social advantage of their countries.

2571. Have those chosen for social responsibilities and offices the jural duty to accept this work? The responsibilities can be considered either as public burdens, or as honorific, well-paid, advantageous posts in so far as they put people in the public eye and offer economic advantages to their holders. Everyone can renounce well-paid jobs and honours. No one can renounce public burdens, but he can require them to be distributed proportionately. The competent judge of this proportionality is the autocrat alone (cf. 2153). The citizen can ask to be dispensed from the office or responsibility offered to him, but will have to accept it if the autocrat does not willingly grant him the dispensation.

2572. The most onerous of these burdens in civilised nations is military service, which must be distributed more scrupulously than other burdens.

1. It must be distributed equally amongst all the citizens. Accordingly, it conforms to social justice, it would seem, if families not subject to call-up, or exempt for any reason, pay some compensatory tax, justly calculated. This will be slightly higher than the tax paid to the State by families who suffer by conscription, and will be calculated either on the principle that it is distributed to these families or to the individuals they provide (cf. 2154), or put into the State treasury for the general alleviation of public taxes.

2. Conscription must be kept to the lowest possible level, that is, sufficient to provide for wars which have a true social reason.

2573. We have to distinguish here between wars which a master wages in defence of his own seigniorial Right (dynastic wars), and those fought by civil society in self-defence (national wars). A master, even if he is not head of civil society, must be defended by those of his bond-servants whose servitude includes this burden (cf. 2159). If he wishes to hire mercenaries, as families often did before the constitution of civil associations, he has to form a free contract with them. He cannot force them to fight for him. A modern example of this is Lord Cochrane, when he came to the help of the Greeks and used his own money to arm a frigate.

2574. On the other hand, it is very fitting that civil society should defend its autocrat even if it has no servile tie towards him.

G.
Social vigilance

2575. The seventh act of autocratic power, which is as much a duty as a right, is vigilance or social inspection. This supreme, universal vigilance applies to the execution of commands, judgments, laws, and extends in a special way to officials nominated by an autocratic power. As Baroli shrewdly says:

> The actions of individuals which have no influence at all over the social end are not a legitimate object of such power.
> This right is limited to those objects over which the autocrat's activity can be jurally extended, and to the means which the ruler is authorised to use to obtain knowledge of the true position of the City, and of the individual actions of the subjects. These means must be approved by right reason, that is, they must not be contrary to jural, moral law. — The ruler must on no account use what he knows to be base and corrupt to attain this end. Immoral means of this kind degrade and debase the ruler in the eyes of the people, who themselves become accustomed to immorality, seduction and perfidy. In the last analysis, such means are lethal relative to the prosperity of the State.[455]

§2. *Governmental acts that an autocratic power can carry out through others*

2576. Autocratic power contains all governmental powers, all the acts that we have so far enumerated. Some of them, however, are so *essential* to this power, that they cannot be alienated; some can be communicated to ministers.

The essential powers of an autocrat are the following: *supreme command, supreme judgment, supreme legislation* and *supreme inspection.* These supreme acts can be delegated, but if alienated, bring about cessation of autocratic power. Other commands can be entrusted to other people. The autocratic power can

---

[455] Baroli, *Diritto naturale pubblico interno*, §130.

work through organs by instituting a ministry. *Social ministry* extends therefore to the following: 1. the acts of material execution; 2. lesser commands and ordinances; 3. lesser judgments; 4. lower levels of inspection.

Other matters that could be required relative to the exercise of such offices are dealt with in treatises on the subject. My own lengthy work may therefore be considered finished.

PART THREE

APPENDIX TO THE PHILOSOPHY OF RIGHT — THE BETTER CONSTRUCTION OF CIVIL SOCIETY

2577. At this point, the philosophy of Right comes to an end for us. But I cannot bring myself to drop the thread of these various branches of knowledge which, although methodologically separate, must not be regarded as different sciences. They form a single science, a single light of the mind diffused as it were throughout a vast space, a single wisdom. I see the glorious beauty of its image, its single light, its wisdom unfolded, imperfectly indeed, to my spirit. No books or words of mine — those lumbering, fragmented signs — can ever fittingly describe or faithfully convey it. Let me simply remind my readers before concluding this book on civil, social Right, of how far the work is from exhausting the *science of civil society*.

CHAPTER 1

The philosophy of Politics begins where the philosophy of Right ends

2578. The vast and noble science of civil society is divided into two parts because the City can be ordered in the best way only according to two sublime virtues, *justice* and *prudence*. Justice is the object of Right, prudence the subject of Politics. *Prudence*, however, can only follow *justice*. If it wished to precede justice, it would cease to be virtue and become cunning and crookedness. The *Philosophy of Politics* begins, therefore, where the *Philosophy of Right* ends. It is the second part of civil, social science. The first part is Right.

2579. To see how the teaching of Right allows space to the teaching on social prudence, or Politics, we have to reflect that the norms of justice do not determine everything determinable

[2577-2579]

in civil society. Many things are left undetermined by these norms in the composition and action of the social body, but then receive their determination from the norms of prudence. Thus, nothing is left to chance in the City; everything is drawn out and ordered with beautiful precision.

2580. Indeed, civil society can be just in many ways, not in one alone. We have to search, therefore, amongst all the cases free from injustice in civil society, for that particular one which best protects justice from disturbance and more easily facilitates the progress of human happiness. This case, this determination of society, which we call its *regular state*, is indicated only by civil prudence.

CHAPTER 2

How the norms suggested by politics can be considered as the norms of right, and the norms of right as the norms of politics

2581. Civil prudence forms part of Right under yet another aspect. It is clear that the norms of prudence, if they help to direct governmental action in such a way that civil society attains its end more fully, become jural obligations for government.

2582. On the other hand, there is not a single principle of justice which cannot be considered an excellent norm in politics. There are three reasons for this: 1. civil society comes about in the first place for the maintenance of justice; 2. civil society flourishes when justice is universally maintained; 3. associated human beings must not and cannot by nature consider their association a good if it can be preserved only through injustice. Politics itself must first want to obtain the remote end of society. This is the principal end and consists in moral good; it must be preferred to the proximate end which is simply a means.[456]

2583. This explains why we placed the teaching on the remote and proximate ends of civil society, and on the relationship

---

[456] *SP*, 204–213.

between these two ends (the second of which must serve the first), amongst the principal parts of the Philosophy of Politics. In this way, Politics itself shares in the nobility of Right, and is sanctified by it.

2584. Nevertheless, there is nothing to prevent Right from being treated separately from Politics. It is even necessary to consider them as separate branches of knowledge, or better as distinct parts of a single social science. Although it is certain that every principle of right is an excellent rule for direction in politics, the nature of this principle is jural and its political value is only an accessory relationship. On the other hand, political principles, that is, the norms according to which governed society flourishes, are political of their nature. In other words, they tend to social utility, and acquire jural quality only relative to governors for whom they become jurally obligatory.

2585. In the last analysis, the principal political norms indicated here at the end of the book will serve to complete and crown the Philosophy of socio-civil Right because these norms pertain under certain aspects to this science. At the same time, it will be a kind of introduction to that part of the Philosophy of Politics which we have not yet published.

CHAPTER 3

An outline of the regular construction of civil society —
The first condition: justice

2586. The first and most elementary duty of those who rule is to preserve society. Societies exist, and it is sufficient to preserve and better them. Our first endeavour in the Philosophy of Politics was, therefore, to investigate the summary reason for the stability or downfall of human societies. We then considered the principle governing their preservation. According to us, this consists in a force (whose nature can be determined later) which in every society, and in every period of society, prevails over all the other forces. Governmental wisdom has to 1. distinguish this force from all others which contemporaneously impinge upon society, 2. take possession of it and 3. make it the aim of all its provisions. It does this to prevent the force perishing through neglect or slipping from its hand. Our investigation furnished us with the following comforting conclusion: in our age, the prevalent force in European civil societies is located in respect for justice in all the extension and sublimity of this word.[457]

2587. Civil society, however, has its nature determined by its end in such a way that it is no longer civil when it abandons its end. We have to say, therefore, that government denatures society to the extent that through its work it has weakened its intention of preserving society's existence. And the more it turns society away from its end, the more it denatures it. We then endeavoured to determine the nature and end of civil society. This brought us to the same conclusion as that of the preceding investigation. We recognised with total evidence that justice, morality, religion (the supreme human goods, which alone are capable of making human beings happy) constitute the final end to which governments must direct and make serve the proximate end of civil society, that is, the acquisition of social goods and pleasures. Thus, the *teaching on the end* and the *teaching on the prevalent force*, taken together, provided us with a single, simple conclusion with which we established the principle and supreme criterion of the Philosophy of Politics.[458]

2588. According to the summary table placed at the end of the Preface to the Philosophy of Politics, which shows the outline and distribution of the work, the treatise on the end of civil society should be followed by that on the *natural construction* of civil society. It is at this point that Right and political science, although in perpetual alliance, are most strongly distinguished from one another, and take forms proper to the two teachings. This will become more clear if we imagine a nation that has decided to give itself the best possible form of government and, with the consent of all who are interested in the public good, chooses a commission of wise, just men whose duty it is to compose the new constitution. In our hypothesis all the fathers take part *per compromissum*, with their natural and domestic rights safeguarded. Whatever constitution is proposed by the assembly of wise men, provided it is conscientiously dictated,

[457] *SC*, 127–147.
[458] *SP*.

would be just. Injustice cannot be present if all the persons interested give their consent. Nevertheless, it still remains to see if it is prudent. As we said, society can be founded on equable but imprudent conventions (*USR*, 346–366). The aim of the Philosophy of Politics, therefore, is to assist the work of these wise men. It has to answer the question: 'Granted a just, civil constitution ('just' because legitimate and already constituted), how can this constitution be prudent?' The prudent constitution will be that which organises a society in the way most natural to that society. This is what we call its *regular* constitution; all other constitutions are irregular. We shall now outline this constitution as a kind of preface to the part of the Philosophy of Politics which will serve as a continuation of what we have already published.

CHAPTER 4

Continuation — Second condition: the principle of balance between mutually attractive things

2589. To discover this state or *regular mode* of civil society, we have to recall the three summary forces at work in society. As we said, they are: 1. the human spirit; 2. things included in the notion of good and evil; 3. the social organism.[459] We must return constantly to these three final forces, the sole operatives in society, when we want to investigate what can improve or worsen society's condition. As long as they are not related to one another in certain ways, these forces possess the power to produce both good and evil. Determining these relationships is the object of the Philosophy of Politics.

2590. The *organism*, the form of government or, more generally speaking, social compaction, must not be the first thing to attract our attention. We cannot determine the best form of compaction in civil society without having solved the problem about the distribution of the second force, that is, the problem of what *things are desirable* or not to the members. In other

---

[459] *SC*, 93–107.

words, we have to: 'Find in society that collocation of objects included in the notion of good and evil which has more influence on social good.'[460]

2591. The relationship between the first, completely internal, force (the *spirit*) and the other two external forces (good and evil, and the organism), is discovered by considering the human spirit in its two distinct qualities as active and passive. *Activity* forms the force of the spirit; *passivity* is what provides a place for the second and third forces. In other words, passivity occasions the force of things included in the notion of good and evil, and the force of the organism. These things do not, in fact, influence civil society before first influencing the human spirit, which in their regard is *passive*.

2592. It is not sufficient, however, to consider only the best disposition of the spirit of the individuals who compose society if we want to discover the regular construction of civil society. This disposition does indeed have the greatest influence on civil society. Nevertheless, the principal element in the regular construction of society is to be sought in the second force, that is, in the things included in the notion of good and evil. We have to solve this problem by asking: 'What is the best collocation or distribution in civil society of all those objects which can be included, for men and women, in the notion of good and evil.'

2593. The first condition for this collocation is presupposed; the collocation must conform to justice. The problem is, therefore, to see which distribution, amongst all those which can exist in harmony with justice, is preferable for attaining social happiness. Once this is known, all the means at hand for this purpose, proper to the government of society, can be employed.

2594. What principle will help us solve such a general problem? For what reason must one given distribution of these matters be preferred to another, and consequently judged the most regular? The only reason, it would seem, is the following. The things included in the notion of good and evil are divided into different species, each of which, when possessed by someone, inclines that person to desire and want the possession of the next thing, which he does not yet possess. This inclination and

[460] *Ibid.*

impulse, this temptation verified in a multitude of persons, is always the force at work to disturb society. The disturbance lasts until the mass of persons tempted in this fashion obtains what it wants. When this occurs, tranquillity is restored. The state of civil society, when the persons composing it are involved in this endeavour or tendency, is an irregular state subject at every instance to disturbance and change. The contrary is the regular state. Hence the political criterion: THE KINDS OF GOOD WHICH NATURALLY ATTRACT ONE ANOTHER MUST BE CONJOINED IN CIVIL SOCIETY, OR GIVEN THEIR RIGHT BALANCE. If one kind of good is accumulated in great quantities in the hands of certain persons, and another kind in the hands of other persons, on every insignificant occasion which acts as a channel, tension suddenly breaks out between the two kinds of good to rectify the imbalance.

2595. Note that the tumult and disturbance occurring in society when one accumulated good tends to find its balance with some other accumulated kind close to it, is not to be attributed simply to a *perverse activity* of the human spirit, but rather, as we said, to its *passivity*, to its weakness. If an individual is tempted to evil, there must be some force independent of him which draws him, even though he is capable of resisting. This force, precisely because it is independent of him, is felt by the individual, according to nature, as good or bad. So, even though we may not know the goodness or evil of the persons who make up a society, we can reasonably conjecture that this society will be subject to greater disturbance and movement in so far as the individuals composing the society have more temptations to produce upheaval. This is the great defect of *irregular society*. Its irregularity consists in the greater temptations to disturbance felt by the members who have greater means of producing disruption. This state is verified whenever one of these kinds of mutually attractive, mutually desired goods is divided from another.

CHAPTER 5

Continuation — Enumeration of the goods which tend to balance one another

2596. What we have said becomes clearer if we enumerate the principal kinds of these goods, and consider how each kind inclines human beings to take possession of its neighbouring kind. These kinds of good can be reduced to the following: 1. population; 2. wealth; 3. civil authority; 4. material (military) force; 5. knowledge; 6. virtue.

Knowledge and virtue are invisible forces of the spirit. What can be said about them is strictly connected with what regards the activity of the spirit.

Relative to the first four forces (population, wealth, civil authority and material force), it is not difficult to understand how one easily draws the other to itself and how each one of these goods provides human beings with the means, and hence the temptation, to take possession of the other.

CHAPTER 6

Continuation — Balance between population and wealth

2597. If we consider the relationship between *population* and *wealth* in domestic society, we find that their balance provides the law by which the *family* is constituted in a regular, tranquil mode. This is the first balance necessary for the perfect constitution of humanity.

2598. In fact, a glance at the condition of family societies in their reciprocal relationships before the institution of civil society shows that the number of children was the source of their wealth. In other words, numerous children constituted the family force which in turn attracted wealth. Servitude was a substitute for the scarcity of children. As a result, families whose wealth was not in proportion to family force (children and bond-servants), were subject to impoverishment and incapable of resisting the prevalent family force of other families. When proportional balance between *family force* and *wealth* is lacking, the social constitution of a family can be just, but irregular. In other words, it is not constituted according to the natural laws which provide it with security and tranquillity.

2599. If we now apply this consideration to civil society, we see that the imbalance between the number of children and wealth causes disturbance when this is verified in a great number of families. Amongst workers, disruption is frequent because population is great and wealth small. War takes place between people and nobles because population has accumulated amongst the former, and wealth amongst the latter; they tend to find their balance.

2600. We could offer many considerations deduced from this law to explain certain relationships, events and struggles between nations.

CHAPTER 7

Continuation — Balance between wealth and civil power

2601. It is not repugnant to the laws of justice that the administration of civil society should be placed in the hands of those who have no wealth. Wealth and the right to govern are not essentially united and indivisible. Moreover, they are acquired through different titles (*USR*, 311–314, 354–366).

However, if this does occur, civil society, although just in its constitution (provided jural titles are not lacking), cannot be said to be regular. As just, society will not be subject to the changes sometimes produced by the force which love of justice has over the human spirit. But as irregular, society will not be altogether safe from the disruption and turmoil arising from the *weakness* of human beings who may find themselves greatly deceived, and tempted to cause upheaval.

2602. Thus, in the case we have supposed, those who have accumulated wealth and are nevertheless excluded *de facto* from civil government, will be greatly tempted to use their wealth to despoil poor people of the authority with which they have been invested. This will undoubtedly occur even when the rich themselves have imprudently consented to be ruled by poor people, or are themselves the authors of such government. As time passes, they will be unable to resist temptation.

On the other hand, persons invested with civil authority, but without corresponding wealth, will be inclined and tempted to use their authority to enrich themselves, rather than for the common good. In other words, they will try to acquire what they lack, which they see as necessary if they are to defend their right to govern against the ambition of the rich.

2603. Wealth, therefore, is a means for defending one's right to govern, and the right to govern is a means to defend wealth. It follows that neither the right to govern nor wealth are secure from avidity and ambition as long as they are unbalanced, that is, as long as civil power is not distributed in *fact* with the same proportion as wealth. Moreover, it conforms to the nature of the case and to equity that civil power should be divided according to the proportion of wealth (*USR*, 213–254).

CHAPTER 8

Continuation — Balance between civil power and material force

2604. The same can be said about the material (military) force and civil power. It is obvious that civil power will never be secure if military power is not distributed in the same way as civil power. However, we mention this in passing. It is very evident. The praetorian guard in the Roman empire, janissaries in the Ottoman empire, and commanders-in-chief of great armies, especially in republics where they are particularly dangerous, have all been able to exercise political command because military power was found *de facto* in hands different from those of civil power. In such a situation, military power tends forcefully to unite with civil power and re-establish balance.

[2603–2604]

CHAPTER 9

Continuation — Balance between military-civil power and knowledge

2605. Those accustomed to reflect will also find it easy to see how *knowledge* necessarily influences government. This influence does in fact bring about balance between *knowledge* and *military-civil power*. Persons with greater knowledge have a large share in civil authority.

2606. This balance is without doubt only approximate. Perfect balance is impossible. We are simply saying that all social organs tend towards this balance. Their inclination is to prevent the kind of imbalance which, when very marked, breaks out and causes great damage.

2607. It is impossible for a government to survive or remain in the same state if all the most enlightened men of the nation are set aside, despised and unheard. Educated people left in such conditions will spend their time censuring and satirising the government as though truth were obviously on their side. Reforms, social theories and new constitutions will burst forth from their imagination and draw people's attention in so far as they are opposed to the reality that people have to come to hate. New Encyclopaedists will appear, and philosophers of revolution will rise and spread like locusts. The middle class is now so dangerous to governments because of its superabundant education. It can be satisfied only by aspiring to a corresponding quantity of social influence.

CHAPTER 10

Continuation — Balance between knowledge and virtue

2608. *Knowledge* which is not balanced by *virtue* falsifies itself to become mankind's greatest enemy. This imbalance pertains properly speaking to universal, theocratic society, not to civil society. Just as the law of the regular construction of the family consists in the balance between population and wealth, so the law of the natural, regular state of the society of the human race and of the Church consists in the balance between knowledge and virtue.

2609. But just as the irregular state of families upsets civil society, so the irregularity thrust into theocratic society through the imbalance between knowledge and virtue brings about immense disasters in civil association.

2610. On the other hand, those governing the City who possess wealth and knowledge but are devoid of virtue, will simply abuse their force and authority, corrupt the citizenry and tyrannise society.

Chapter 11

Recapitulation of social balances

2611. We can sum up by stating the following which, we think, can be considered a cosmic law, that is, a law of both the physical and the moral world: 'Every movement or action, regular or irregular, arises from the effort made by two forces endeavouring to attain the balance they lack.'

2612. By applying this law of the universe to the particular characteristics of mankind as we investigate the causes of continual social disturbances amongst the human race, we first recognised an innate human tendency to justice, and discovered the necessity for a fundamental balance:

The first-order balance
necessary for the perfect constitution of civil society:
FACT MUST BE BALANCED WITH RIGHT

2613. We first imagined a state of civil society in which this balance was fully achieved, and then asked if other causes of disturbance could be present after justice had been established. We saw that it was not sufficient for society to be in a state of justice, that is, for all its goods to be possessed under a just title, if society was to remain tranquil. Even without the presence of injustice, society could still be subject to disturbance as a result of certain kinds of mutually attractive goods. These goods have to be balanced if they are not to cause turmoil. If divided, they cause disturbance through the vehement urge with which they attract one another. Hence:

The second-order balance
necessary for the perfect constitution of civil society:
THE KINDS OF GOOD THAT ARE MUTUALLY ATTRACTIVE MUST BE
BALANCED WITH ONE ANOTHER

2614. We went on to ask what kinds of good possessed such a great tendency to unite, and found that they were reduced to six, that is, population or family force, wealth, civil power or the right to govern, material force, knowledge and virtue. Five balances are, therefore, equally necessary, for the best constitution of humanity.

2615. The first balance is between family force and wealth. This renders the state of families *regular* and secure, and is expressed as follows:

The first part of second-order balance:
BALANCE SHOULD EXIST BETWEEN THE MULTIPLICATION OF THE
HUMAN SPECIES IN INDIVIDUAL FAMILIES, AND THE WEALTH OF
THESE FAMILIES

This balance, although proper to domestic society, is necessary to civil society, which is an aggregate of domestic societies.

2616. The second balance is a balance between wealth and civil power; the third requires equilibrium between civil power and material force. These are the two balances which, by removing two special causes of turmoil, properly speaking place *external* civil society in a *regular* state. They are formulated as follows:

The second part of second-order balance:
BALANCE SHOULD EXIST BETWEEN WEALTH AND CIVIL POWER

The third part of second-order balance:
BALANCE SHOULD EXIST BETWEEN CIVIL POWER AND
MATERIAL FORCE

2617. Material force has two objects: internal tranquillity and defence against external enemies. Relative to the first object, material force is simply a part of civil power. In can also be

[2614–2617]

considered as such relative to the second object, except that this second object is not necessary to full civil power. If there were no external aggression, government would still be fully constituted with internal administration as its aim. If we consider material force as a defence against external enemies, it can be called the *national force*, and in the nation corresponds to *family force* in the family. These two balances can therefore be considered as one if military power is taken as a part of civil power.

2618. Two balances remain: that between military-civil power and knowledge, and that between knowledge and virtue. The latter brings regularity to the universal society of mankind, of which civil societies are only parts. By noting here these two last balances, readers will have some idea of the principal threads of our politico-jural system.

The fourth part of second-order balance:
BALANCE SHOULD EXIST BETWEEN MATERIAL-CIVIL POWER AND KNOWLEDGE

The fifth part of second-order balance:
BALANCE SHOULD EXIST BETWEEN KNOWLEDGE AND VIRTUE

All five balances are part of the general balance between different kinds of mutually attractive goods which, as we have seen, is necessary for social tranquillity.

CHAPTER 12

Continuation — Third condition for the regular construction of civil society: social inequalities dependent on nature

2619. As we saw, a general second-order balance, brought about by the five applications we have enumerated, is necessary to determine and resolve the problem: 'Wherein lies the tranquil state of society?' We began our solution to this problem by referring to first-order balance, that is, the balance between fact and right, but were unable to answer it completely. In establishing that society required justice in all its parts, we assigned to the problem only one of the conditions needed for a state of tranquillity. This was insufficient to pin-point a single state. It is, in fact, possible to imagine a society organised in different ways, all of which verify the condition of justice. We still had to see which organisation amongst equally just, although different, organisations of society would be preferable relative to the tranquillity and stability that we were seeking.

We found this new condition for public tranquillity in proportional balance between the different kinds of goods that we enumerated. We concluded that the tranquil state of society would be that in which 1. all good was distributed according to justice; 2. the different kinds of goods already indicated would be divided proportionately amongst themselves. Everywhere the number of children would be proportioned to wealth; wealth would be proportioned to civil power and to material force, which is civil power's sanction; civil and material power would be proportioned to knowledge; finally, knowledge would be proportioned to virtue.

2620. Now, although our imagined state of civil society, in which both the condition of justice and the second condition about the five balances are present, is less subject to turmoil, can we say that nothing more is needed to resolve our problem fully and completely? In other words, is the state in which the two conditions are verified the only possible one, or can we imagine still further states of society in which the two conditions of justice and balance are actuated?

If, granted the two conditions, we cannot imagine more than one state of civil society, the problem has certainly been determined and resolved. If, moreover, society remains subject to turmoil in this unique state, we have to conclude that such disturbance is necessary and intrinsic to society. In fact, because the form of society is determined by these two conditions, it will be impossible to remove either without uncovering a greater source of disturbance and disquiet.

On the other hand, if many possible states of civil society can be imagined in which the two conditions are equally verified, a new effort can be made to find a third condition which will eliminate other possible states containing further germs of disquiet. At this point, we can either determine a single state by fixing precisely the ideal of civil society where total security of rights, tranquillity and happiness is brought about in the best possible way, or we can indicate other states from which we then have to make a choice.

2621. I am quite sure that the condition about balances does not fully determine the problem; it does not indicate our imagined, unique state of civil society. In fact, it is easy to see that different states of civil society can be imagined in which this condition is equally verified. First, we think of such a state and then immediately change (in its distribution, not in its absolute quantity) one of the six kinds of goods which we have mentioned. For example, let us imagine that wealth passes from the rich to those who previously were poor. Given this new distribution of wealth under a just title, it follows that, if the condition about balances is to be verified, the primitive order has to be changed and all other kinds of goods put in balance with wealth. In this way, we obtain a new state of society different from the first in which, however, the two conditions of justice and balance will still be verified.

This reasoning about wealth can be applied in the same way to any other kind of good. To imagine a state of society in which the condition about balances is verified, it is sufficient to begin from any one of the six kinds of good. Each of them will serve as a primitive, arbitrarily chosen starting point. It is clear that whatever mode of distribution is arbitrarily chosen, I can, by beginning from it, conceive a society which is not only just, but such that all other kinds of goods in it are distributed in the same proportion as that established by me as my norm. Innumerable states of civil society are thus possible in which the two conditions about justice and balances are conceived as equally verified.

2622. The law about balances presupposes, therefore, a primary, arbitrary distribution of goods. We have to see which of all possible kinds of distribution of goods is preferable to the rest. If we find this preferred distribution, we shall have found the third condition enabling us to determine the problem left undetermined by the first two conditions.

2623. Finding this third condition is much more difficult than uncovering the first two. Granted the preservation of balance between the various kinds of goods, satisfactory knowledge of degrees of equality and inequality amongst human beings is extremely difficult to calculate. Such a task is far more suitable for divine Providence than for human knowledge.

2624. Moreover, we should note that the famous question about the best form of government is only a part of this problem. The form of government results from the distribution of civil power which itself is one of the six kinds of goods to be distributed amongst members of a society in the same proportion as the other five kinds. Knowing how these six kinds of goods have to be distributed amongst the members of civil society if they are to be balanced, we have to solve yet another problem: 'What is the best absolute distribution of this unique type of goods made up of the six kinds already indicated?'

2625. The best distribution is that which is least man-made and arbitrary, and conforms better to the indications of nature. But we still have to point to these natural indications.

2626. Military and civil power cannot indicate them because these powers are entirely the result of human work. Nor can we find them in differing sizes of families. Although important during the period when families lived in the state of nature, this loses its importance in civil society, where over-large families easily divide. We must look for these natural indications, therefore, in the other three goods: virtue, knowledge and wealth. We have to see how nature distributes each of these goods amongst the families that make up nations, how she accidentally accumulates these goods in greater quantities, and how she then tends to balance them.

2627. Nature gives neither virtue nor knowledge, but provides dispositions towards both. Nevertheless, within a single race, she divides these gifts with some kind of equality (cf. 1358–1368). At the same time, we see very noticeable differences between the intellectual and moral character of different races. One, with fewer vices and more virtuous dispositions, is better than another; some are more watchful and penetrating, others less so. We can conclude, therefore, that when a nation is composed of several, still unfused races, social inequalities will be greater. Nature herself has already posited greater inequality by her distribution of gifts of mind and heart.

2628. Climate is one of the elements which influence the mind and spirit. But there are many others of greater importance. Geography is one example. Mountain people are very different from plains people; those who live by lakes or the sea are very different from those in the hinterland. Qualities of mind and forms of spirit will therefore differ greatly in those nations which contain more geographical variety, and sometimes have populations enclosed within natural boundaries that to a great extent prevent communication and intermingling with other peoples. This is another cause of natural inequality.

2629. Wealth is another matter. It is natural that wealth should accumulate more in industrial and trading nations than in agricultural countries. But even in these, inequality of fertile land sometimes leads to small patrimonies of more or less the same size, and sometimes (in great plains, for instance) to large-scale farming and great estates. In industrial and trading nations, as well as in nations where land and products require large-scale farming, nature herself will ensure great *inequalities* of wealth.

2630. According to the principle laid down ('follow nature') inequality of fortune is preferable in these conditions, provided that provision is made for the serious evils inevitably associated with inequality. The first of these is the extreme misery found at the lower end of the social scale. Several remedies can alleviate this, principally: 1. the promotion of religious and ecclesiastical celibacy for both sexes among the lower class of society; 2. care of poor families by society, which has still not been considered sufficiently.

2631. These natural indications must lead to the solution of the question we have proposed: 'What degree of social inequality in various nations is most suitable and opportune in the distribution of the six kinds of goods that we have mentioned?'

CHAPTER 13

Continuation — Fourth condition for the regular construction of civil society

2632. We have found an ideal state of society in which three conditions are verified: 1. everything is distributed justly; 2. in each of the different kinds of goods, inequality is relatively distributed in a uniform way to ensure their balance; 3. the degree of inequality depends upon the indications given by the very nature of things in different nations. We return now to our question: 'When the three conditions are verified, is the resulting state of civil society unique? Or can we still point to different possible states of society in which the three conditions are equally verified? In other words, has the problem we proposed been fully solved by the three conditions assigned to it, or does it need some further determination?'

Each of the three conditions has brought us nearer to the solution of the social problem by diminishing the number of possible states, but they are still not sufficient to establish the unique state that we are seeking as the ideal of civil society.

2633. The condition about justice has eliminated from civil society all the turmoil that could arise from love of justice; the condition about relatively equal distribution of the different kinds of goods has eliminated the turmoil that could be produced by the weakness of the human spirit, tempted as it is to abuse its force when some overt, easy opportunity for this arises; the condition about social inequalities according to the degree indicated by nature prevents the discontent and struggle with nature herself which arises when people wish at all costs to submit her to arbitrary modifications and laws. Nevertheless, something still remains to be regularised, defined and determined in society if it is not to be disturbed, and its compaction is to be totally regular. Let me describe this missing element.

2634. As we said, proportional balance is required between the number of children and wealth and other kinds of goods. But what is the ratio of this proportion? What I mean is that the wealth, for example, of a house and the number of its members must preserve the same ratio that exists between the wealth and numbers in every other house. If, however, the *proportion* is left intact, this *ratio* may vary.

Proportional balance leaves undetermined the *ratio* that must exist between wealth and the number of children or members of a house. This makes possible very many states of society in all of which the three conditions are verified.

Our endeavour to find some way of determining the ratio of which we have spoken means answering the following question: 'What is the best *ratio* to be assigned to the individual kinds of goods which are to be balanced in each family?' In other words,

[2633-2634]

we are trying to find a fourth condition still lacking to a final determination of the problem.

2635. It is easy to see that the ratio between the portions of goods assigned to any family whatsoever will be self-determined if we take for granted both the absolute quantity in any given society of each of the kinds of goods, and the same quantity distributed proportionately amongst the families. Our problem is senseless if we interpret it in this way. In fact, we are endeavouring to determine the ratio to be preserved amongst the portions of goods assigned to each family so that civil society may live in tranquillity and peace. But we do this without taking as unchangeable the absolute quantity of these goods. We leave the absolute quantity to be determined by that *ratio* between the portions of goods which is necessary, in each family, for maintaining public order.

2636. Although we cannot respond adequately to such a difficulty, we can establish certain limits which determine in part the ratio that we are seeking.

2637. The ratio that must exist between wealth and the numbers in a family can be assigned, up to a point, by the following principle: the number of children should not increase beyond that degree of wealth which is necessary for their nourishment, education and the payment of the social contribution.

2638. Having determined wealth in this way through the population of a family, it is not difficult to see the ratio that must exist between the family and authority, or civil power. This power is of its nature unchangeable, especially if it is considered at its point of greatest development.

2639. The quantity of national force is determined by the need which society has of it.

2640. The lower limit of knowledge must be fixed by the need to administer that part of civil power held by each family.

2641. The lower limit of virtue, if we are allowed this expression, must be such that it allows both individual and family sufficient virtue to use the knowledge that they have for the sake of good.

CHAPTER 14

Continuation — The fifth condition for the best construction of civil society.

2642. The foregoing, however, are all lower limits. What are the higher limits? The lower limits indicate the *smallest* quantity of goods to be found in civil society if there is to be a *suitable ratio* between the portions of goods assigned to individual families. Could this suitable ratio be rendered better? In other words, what is the most desirable *absolute quantity* of these goods? Is it true, as our dominant political theory has held until now, that the goods we have mentioned can never increase too greatly in a nation?

2643. This would be a disastrous, although very attractive error. There is in fact only one absolute good, that is, moral good, virtue, which can never be too much. This final, essential good is the only good that admits no upper limit because it is man's very perfection, which all other goods must serve.

2644. The unlimited nature of this good requires that the ideal of perfect human society cannot be attained absolutely speaking unless it is pushed to the infinite. It is impossible, therefore, for our minds to succeed in determining the entire ideal of society unless the beauty of this ideal, losing itself in the infinite, causes all the finite parts of society, which we have outlined with such effort, to vanish from our grasp; this beauty brings us to such a sublime, happy condition that all external goods and evils seem to disappear. In such a state, it would be useless to proportion and distribute them amongst human beings who are no longer deceived or attracted by them.

2645. Although we have to leave aside, therefore, this state of infinite goodness unattainable by human beings, we can still draw an extremely important corollary from the teaching we have developed: that is, other kinds of goods can usefully increase, in proportion to the increase of moral virtue amongst human beings, provided they are commanded by this first, sovereign good. The other kinds must not, however, exceed the

moral power that human beings have for dominating and directing them.[461]

2646. Summarising, we can say that the forces in society are
three: 1. the human spirit; 2. things included in the notion of
good and bad; 3. the social organism.

The organism, or form of government, is perfectly constituted
if it results from the optimum distribution of things. This distribution is obtained by: 1. their balances; 2. opportune social
inequalities; 3. a suitable ratio between various kinds of things
in the same family; 4. maximum increase in moral virtue.

The human spirit, when moved by love of justice, disturbs an
unjustly constituted society; it disturbs a justly but irregularly
constituted society when such a society, impelled by a principle
of weakness, gives way to the temptation produced in the spirit
by an unnatural distribution of things; finally, the human spirit
disturbs society even when society is justly and regularly
constituted, but finds itself without a moral, virtuous counter-
balance to the other goods. Virtue alone is the final guarantee
that society will remain totally without turmoil. Only virtue
solves perfectly the problem of finding a state of secure, perfect
tranquillity; only virtue prevents politics from being a vain,
deceptive art; only virtue provides politics with a fulcrum, and
the ideal of society with infinite beauty.

CHAPTER 15

Progress towards the natural construction of civil society

2647. Our argument has brought us back to our starting point,
that is, to the knot that binds WHAT IS JUST so beautifully with
WHAT IS USEFUL. We can now understand better the nature of
such an important link. In fact, the argument shows:

2648. 1. The law of justice, which human beings can never
obliterate from their spirit, produces in them a feeling of re-
action towards every injustice. Society cannot resist this force
for long without serious upheavals.

[461] *SP*, 708–814.

2. While justice contributes to the aim of politics by helping society maintain a secure, tranquil state, politics in turn assists and helps the desire of justice that goods should spontaneously distribute themselves amongst people in such a way that people experience the least possible temptations to break the order of justice and disturb society. Politics achieves this, as far as possible, by giving these goods an impulse to dispose themselves little by little according to the law of the five assigned balances. Human weakness is thus less compromised and tempted. The aim of sound politics is to remove from human beings occasions and temptation of evil, and can therefore be defined as 'the art of ensuring in the world the least possible need of virtue.' In fact, the fewer the temptations and occasions of evil, the less virtue needed to avoid evil.[462]

3. All that politics can do, if we prescind from virtue, is to reduce temptations opposed to what is upright and just. If the human spirit is perverse and corrupt, the impetus of its wayward desire will plunge it into evil notwithstanding the best possible politics. The human spirit, maddened by perversity, and acting thoughtlessly, will ruin what is well-ordered. Human good-sense has no defence against it. Virtue alone, as we said before, is the only unshakeable rock on which to raise a solid, majestic, social edifice.

2649. Is there any hope that this rock will be posited, and that happy, secure, civil associations will be raised up on it? Only madness and delirium would cause our spirit to reject such a desirable thought. For my part, I think I see a stable law, founded on the nature of human things, by which *justice* and *regularity* in civil constitutions tend continually to actuate

---

[462] When Montesquieu said that the principle behind republics must be virtue, and that the principle behind monarchies is honour, not virtue, he stated, without realising it, that monarchy is a more perfect form of government than republic precisely because monarchy keeps society in a state of tranquillity with less need for virtue. It is obvious that where a form of government is less perfect, the need of individual virtue to supply for the imperfections of government is greater. If people were perfectly virtuous, government would be practically useless, or at least dispensed from its primary aim, that is, those measures which render crime more difficult and rare.

themselves with such harmony that one continually helps the other.

2650. It is true that there appears to be no connection between a balanced, regular distribution of goods and titles to rights, which when respected render a society just. Nevertheless, I think the affinity between them is greater than it appears. I believe that each entails the other, and I regard as exceptions those cases in which civil society is constituted according to the rules of justice, but not according to those of politics (a *just*, but *irregular* state). I have no hesitation in calling the *natural constitution* of society that in which the rules of both justice and politics are maintained. The very nature of things leads society imperceptibly to such a constitution.

CHAPTER 16

The leading principle of social progress is justice, maintained coherently

2651. There is no doubt that social *irregularities* often arise from the titles of right acquired over things. These titles are accidental facts and do not seem to distribute goods with due regularity. Moreover, since the state of society results from the existence of these titles to right, it can be said to result from equivalent *irregularities*. Careful consideration shows, however, that the same irregularities, accumulated according to a provident law of nature, are mutually destructive and gradually lead society to regular formation. Each individual case, considered separately from the others, is fortuitous and could be irregular. When many cases are taken together, there is an obvious, wonderful tendency to bring about a total entity which approaches regularity.

2652. I say 'a wonderful tendency to bring about a total entity which approaches regularity' because the complete, perfect regularity we have described is perhaps never realised. The statesman, who has to begin from existing irregularities in the society he is commissioned to govern, certainly cannot carry out his abstractly conceived plans without taking account of these irregularities; he must build upon what he has, not on what he would like to have. Practical political wisdom does not consist so much in establishing a regular society *ex novo* (there may be no chance of this), but of providing an existing, irregular society with an impetus that enables it to go on regularising itself. This must be done without injury to justice which stimulates society's natural tendency to regularity.

2653. However, to understand better the relationship of which we have spoken between the just and the regular construction of society, let us go back to the imaginary case of a group of people still without government whose entire ownership is well-founded in justice, but amongst whom no one has yet acquired a title to government. Granted this case, political orders can be given to the multitude without any prior intention of following the rules of politics aimed at utility and reduced to the five balances we have mentioned. The intention will be to follow the rules of justice alone. If this were the case, I maintain that we would arrive at a result similar to that obtained by following political rules. In other words, we would be borne towards the five balances. Let us examine this briefly by reference to the balance between ownership and civil power.

2654. The right to govern is a good, as wealth, etc., is a good (*USR*, 159, 311). It must not be given to people at random, but according to the rules of *distributive justice* and equity.

2655. Government must bestow some good on the individual, the group and the people as a whole. Its first responsibility, therefore, is to keep evil at bay by defending the rights of all.

2656. Our first consideration will be to ensure that

1. government does not exceed the limits of its power, and does not use any other means in obtaining its desired *good* than those which regulate the modality of people's rights. It has no power over rights themselves;

2. government not only does not abrogate for itself more authority than it actually possesses, but, as far as possible, is inclined by its constitution to make good use of its authority in such a way that harmful governmental constitution does not provoke those who govern to injustice by tempting their passions.

2657. Every governmental ordinance contains two distinct acts: 1. a judgment by which government decides that the ordinance is within its competence and does not harm the rights of any member of society (first heading); 2. the execution of the ordinance itself. With the first act, government *acts as judge*, and comes to a decision about justice between itself and the members of its society; with the second, it acts as *administrator*, whose duty it is to reject useless ordinances and put useful ordinances into practice.

2658. Until now these two parts of civil government have always been confused. Although the distinction between them, which is extremely important and very evident, is as clear as that between justice and utility, Montesquieu traced his own celebrated division of three powers. I think, however, that the division between these two parts of government is even more important and necessary. The division is suggested by the very nature of things because deliberations about judging what is just and judging what is useful are highly diverse and have different consequences. Different means are required to ensure correct judgment in the two cases. It is absurd to dispense the executive part of government from rendering an account of its activity to the judicial part. The former cannot remain independent of the latter. The two acts of government have to be separated. They have to be actuated in different ways, and finally constitute two supreme powers around which all others revolve. They will be independent but harmonious powers, and as such help one another reciprocally within the limits of their aim (*USR*, 309–310, 357–364).[463]

---

[463] These two powers correspond to *jural* and *constitutive* equality (cf. 2182–2187). We saw that all human beings are equal in the first, but not in the second way. All are equal when judgment has to be passed on the possession or not of a right; they are unequal when judgment about the possession of a right has already been passed. In this case, the inequality enables the person who has a right to use it, while the person without a right has to abstain from using it and respect the use that the other makes of it. The question about who possesses a right requires a judgment *relative to justice* because it is about what is *mine* and what is *yours*. Granted this judgment, the person considered to have the right is now free to use it as he likes, as he finds more agreeable and useful. This is an *act of administration*. If we now apply this argument now to the two acts of social government that we have distinguished, we find that the former is a *judgment*, the second an *administrative act* which presupposes the judgment. Relative to the first power, government is considered as a person endowed with jural equality, that is, equal to any other collective

2659. We have to establish two offices or ministries in the population which, in our supposition, has to organise its own government. One office will take the form of a *tribunal* destined to judge political questions between the administration of the society and the members; the other will take an *administrative* form directed, relative to justice, by the social tribunal.

2660. Having recognised and fixed the two principal and essentially distinct parts of civil government, we now have to examine the form or constitution best fitted to them. This will be done, as always, according to the rules of justice and equity that we have proposed.

First, it is immediately obvious that we cannot follow the same principles in establishing a just tribunal and a prudent administration. The procedure will be totally different because judges and administrators require very different and sometimes opposite gifts. Judges have to remain outside the interests they judge; administrators must have some interest in the business they deal with. An owner always makes the best administrator of what is his own.

2661. This opposition and almost incompatibility between the two offices shows that when a way has been found of separating the two offices as far as possible, an immense step will have been taken towards the best, most just constitution of civil society. They must be made independent of one another, and allocated to two distinct jural persons; civil society will remain very distant from its ideal as long as these two offices are joined in the same person, whether individual or collective. The less interest a person has in business, the better his judgement and the worse his administration. The more interest he has in business, the more his jural acts will give grounds for fear, and his administration, grounds for confidence.

2662. Until now civil government has been seen only from the point of view of administration; there has been no consideration of any political tribunal present in government prior to admin-

or individual person, great or small, inside or outside of society (*RI*, 1647–1660). Relative to the second power, government is considered as a collective person endowed with constitutive inequality. The decision is made that the government's projected ordinance is concerned with an administrative act, with the use that government makes of one of its certain rights.

istration. Although the judgment proper to this tribunal precedes all administrative acts of government, no theorist has yet thought of conceiving a tribunal in which serious consideration would be given to the one element towering above all others, that is, the element dealing with *public justice*. The natural consequence of the lack of a political tribunal, or its confusion with other governmental powers, has made and makes civil society an immense weight upon its members who have no satisfactory way and manner of appeal against it. Human nature, despite consistently resenting this, rebelling against it and tearing itself apart, has always been unable to recognise clearly what it lacked and was searching for. It tried palliatives, and even poisonous remedies, whose disastrous effects led it to bear peacefully troubles which it considered necessary and irremediable. Civil society sagged, as it were, into a kind of timid, inert resignation.

It is, of course, obvious that the true needs of mankind first show themselves in the crude protests of rebellious, unrestrained people, long before the wise make themselves heard; it is obvious that the mercilessness of the most viciously corrupt, always on the alert for the chance of spreading ruin and devastation, is first to take hold of the feeling aroused by social needs which it then brazenly abuses by using this obscure, powerful feeling as a support and cover for its own hidden designs. Nevertheless, the need for a court of *political justice*, despite its bad interpretation and expression by unhappy people, is naturally felt in human hearts. And the voice of nature, as always, is faithful, merciful and friendly.

2663. But surely this political tribunal would be judging government? This objection can only spring from the imperfect idea of civil government that has been prevalent until now. Government, it has been wrongly supposed, is solely administration, not a tribunal of public justice. As far as I can see, it is both. The idea of complete government is present only when the two parts of which we are speaking have been united by a co-ordinating principle.

2664. But surely, the objection continues, it is impossible to establish such a tribunal to judge cases between administration and the members of society. Is it impossible? Would the tribunal find it difficult to decide justly in all cases? This objection, if valid, would prove too much because it would also be applicable in the case of civil tribunals where again the well-being of citizens is entrusted to the integrity of judges. This was almost entirely the case when laws were still unwritten and not yet clearly ordered in a single body. Despite occasional injustices, civil tribunals retain their worth and necessity. As we said, the difficulties simply prove that the final, solid guarantee of all human institutions is solely uprightness and virtue. If we cannot suppose some virtue in society as a firm basis on which to place its institutions, society itself would be impossible.

2665. This comment allows us to understand better the difference between a court of justice and an administration. A judge's first quality must necessarily be *integrity*; an administrator's, considered solely as administrator, *foresight*, An excellent judge, always accustomed to follow a direct line, and decide straightforwardly and unambiguously what conforms to the laws of justice, may well be a hopeless administrator; an excellent administrator, with considerable talent in calculating the balance of utility and finding prudent ways of action, will scarcely ever be an honest, loyal judge. The spiritual endowments and intellectual talents of these two personages are normally very different. Justice possesses something universal, independent of all human things, and can therefore be known to people of every condition provided they have the same talent and sentiments. The administrator's talent lies in something quite different. His instinct enables him to see the long-term consequences of things, and calculate the effect of many interacting events. His talent, therefore, is entirely dependent on the practice of human things, on relative experience. It is not common to all and sundry, but proper to those who are accustomed to command, govern and administer, which is normal in higher ranks of society. The judge pronounces his decisions according to fixed, unchangeable, absolute rules; the administrator makes his ordinances on the basis of changeable rules, relative to circumstances. The norms of justice, precisely because they deal with a universal object, are common to all, and almost inborn; the norms of utility are infinitely variable, according to the ambit of affairs to which they refer and, because acquired only through experience, differ according to human conditions.

As a result, concurrence for the political tribunal must be left open to every single member of the society, and even to foreigners, whatever their condition. The only criterion for the most suitable persons for this responsibility is, relative to the spirit, their virtue, integrity and solid incorruptibility; relative to their mind, jural knowledge. Every endeavour directed at instituting a *political tribunal*, will therefore aim at: 1. deciding the best way of discovering which people best possess the two requirements of integrity and moral science, and ensuring that these candidates are chosen for the court; 2. deciding the best way of rendering the tribunal inviolable. This will be done by giving support to its judges in their human weakness, protecting them as far as possible from temptations to injustice and ensuring their commitment to their work with various but principally religious means which impose on them the duty of never consciously violating justice without their crime appearing very serious indeed to their own conscience and that of the public.

2666. Administration on the other hand will not be open equally to all members of society. It will take into account the different economic circumstances of the citizens; participation in administration will depend on the extension of their ownership. Those who belong to more wealthy families have by their habitual attitude more to offer public administration.

We have thus been led, by reasoning from principles of justice alone, to establish the political criterion which we first found on the basis of political principles. In other words, we have arrived at establishing proportional balances, especially that between ownership and civil power.

2667. I realise that prejudices still present in spirits since the revolution will at this point raise an enormous clamour, and cry out for my crucifixion. Why should the rich be preferred to the poor in public administration? What frightens the objectors is the oppression of the poor by the rich, of the weak by the strong. — This, however, is an irrational fear. It is not difficult to show, and here theory and practice go hand in hand, that injustice will more probably be committed by a poor rather than a wealthy administration. The former is much more to be feared than the latter. Moreover, the difficulty put forward vanishes completely when the faculty for judging what is just and unjust has been removed from governmental administration. We have entrusted this judgment to people taken from all classes without distinction. Their sole distinction consists in their greater degree of proven uprightness and integrity, and their greater degree of jural ability or knowledge.

When governmental administration has been deprived of supreme political judgment, that is, the power of judging in its own cause, all that remains is a body of citizens who together regulate the modality of their own rights, and in which each citizen influences the modality in proportion to the rights he possesses, the same rights that regulation is intended to assure and assist. This administration is truly a society in which each member enters with some capital. It is therefore reasonable and conforms to justice that each member should influence proceedings with a vote commensurate with his contribution (*USR*, 213–366). There is nothing unjust in the government of such a society. It is reasonable that owners should be administrators of what is their own. It is just that those who possess the greater part of a common social capital should prevail when different co-owners administer it and cannot reach agreement. Depriving them of this right would certainly be an injustice. Do we really want to begin to constitute a society based on injustice under the pretext of fearing injustice?[464]

2668. It is clear, therefore, that social administration can be

---

[464] This is so clear and conforms so well with common sense that it seems impossible for a person of good faith to think in any other way. The opinion of those who claim that social administration should be regulated by votes of equal weight for each of the co-owners is absurd. In this case, a member who possesses thirty times as much of the common social capital as another would not have a greater voice in the administration than the other. If this were so, the member who possesses more would have lost some of his capital on entering the society, and the member who possesses less would have gained. The member who possesses more would have ceded to the other's will a proportion of government over his own possessions which would not be compensated by the portion of government acquired over the other's possessions. Equally, the one who possesses little would have ceded part of a small administration and acquired part of a large administration. In other words, one of the members would have gained, the other lost. As a result, equality between the two members would not be maintained; the new disposition would include a blameworthy inequality, against the principles of distributive justice. Civil society differs from the society of which we are speaking (in which various co-owners administer a common social capital) only in its extension and in the nature of the social capital administered.

divided in this way only, if we wish to follow the principles of distributive justice in setting it up. It is also clear that such a division, by assuring the rights of all, renders injustice less probable, and hence less to be feared. Injustice is always a matter for fear to the extent that administration is entrusted to mercenary persons, or even to persons other than the owner. If, in fact, an owner were to make some mistake in administration, he would be the only one to suffer. This in turn would not cause social upheaval because a person easily forgives himself. If it were possible to exclude all non-owning administrators from human affairs, every administration would make progress, or would at least exist peacefully, because no owner would complain about his administrator. Applying the same principle to the great administration of civil society, we would have constituted it in the best possible way, and as far as possible have outlawed from it all injustice, by ensuring that owners administer it themselves. This is achieved precisely by dividing administration amongst the members of the society in proportion to the quantity of rights which they bring to it.

2669. Let us suppose the contrary, and imagine that governmental administration is invested in those who possess the least. We would now have a form of administration in which the owner is divided from the administrator; we have opened the door to all the injustices we are trying to avoid.

This would not be the case if the owner were the administrator. This is so true that injustice would be lessened even on the supposition that the political tribunal we proposed did not actually exist. The door would certainly be left opened to injustice, but this would be caused only by lack of a tribunal, not by a less perfect form of administration. It would always remain true that this form of administration would reduce the danger of injustice to a level below that in any other form, although it could not eliminate it absolutely.

2670. This residue of injustice adhering to the best form of administration is what we want to avoid by instituting a political tribunal, or Senate. Such injustice is very far from damaging the administrative form of which we are speaking. Indeed, it constitutes a counter-proof that this form is the best of all. Why is it, we may ask, that there is always some danger of injustice even when this form of administration has been set up? Because, whatever form of civil administration comes about, it is never possible to ensure that the *owner* alone is at the same time the *administrator*. It is clear that an owner cannot commit an injustice against himself.

It is not absurd for an owner to administer his own capital when it belongs entirely to him. We thus find the two states of owner and administrator incorporated in the same person. If, however, the capital has many masters, each of which possesses an unequal portion, it is impossible to establish a single administration with such a form that the owner is incorporated in it in exactly the same way as the administrator. All the forms which can be given to this kind of administration are reduced to the following: 1. administration by persons not belonging to the group of masters; 2. administration by persons chosen from the masters, but without their influencing matters in proportion to the share that each master possesses; 3. administration by masters themselves in proportion to their share in the social capital. None of these forms allows the owner to be fully incorporated with the administrator. The second, however, is closer to this than the first, and the third than the second.

Relative to the first, the matter is clear: the owner is totally excluded from administration. A comparison can be made only between the second and third. As we can all see, every time that a master co-administers power which exceeds the proportion of his ownership, he becomes to that extent an administrator of others' goods, not of his own. Thus the administration is misplaced and put in the hands of non-masters. Let us imagine, for example, a society with only two masters, one of whom posits thirty units as his contribution to the social capital, the other, two; the two masters administer with equal authority. The total authority is as great as the social capital which has to be administered, and can here be expressed as thirty-two (because the social capital is thirty-two). Each of the owners enjoys sixteen parts and administers, as it were, sixteen parts. But the ownership of one person extends only to two units; he is thus administering fourteen parts belonging to his companion. The ownership of the other comprises thirty parts, of which he administers only sixteen. As a result of this irregularity, the master ceases to be administrator of fourteen parts of his capital.

2671. It is true, of course, that not even the third manner of administration attains perfect incorporation between owner and administrator. It does, however, draw near to it because a common administration, while requiring each person to cede in part the administration of what is his own, allows each to acquire in compensation some part of the administrative power of the others.

2672. In every common administration, however, there is an opening for some injustice because each person, by influencing the entire capital, produces an effect on something not his own. Where does this injustice fall? It must fall on one of the three aims of civil society: the common good, the public good, and the private or particular good (cf. 1643–1663). It is natural that the *common good* be desired by all the owners. There can be no violation of the common good, therefore, except by an administrator who is outside the society. Moreover, the outsider who wishes to sin against the common good, will want to sin even more seriously against public and private good. This is the extremely serious defect of the first of the three forms of administration that we have indicated.

The social administration can only sin against the *public good* when it is instituted in the second of the forms we have indicated, that is, where deliberative votes are not distributed in accord with ownership. If they were distributed in accord with ownership, it would be impossible to make any ordinance voluntarily endangering the public good, that is, endangering a mass of rights greater than half the common social capital. The greater number of votes would always be favourable to the greater number of rights. But in the case where the value of the votes is not in proportion to the rights possessed by the voters, it could well be that the greater number of votes was opposed to the greater number of rights. In the second form of administration, therefore, the greater part of rights, far from being assured by society, would be exposed to the decision of the person who obtained a disproportionate degree of influence in the social balance. Particular good would be even less assured in this form of administration where public good is insufficiently assured.

It remains, therefore, that only *particular good* is insufficiently protected under the third form of administration, in which administration is distributed according to ownership. Private good, the lesser mass of rights, can always be oppressed by the greater mass. This is the only opportunity, however, that remains for the strong to assail the weak, and the powerful to harm the impotent. There is no human counsel or foresight that can save the weak from the envious desires of the strong; no external foresight or precaution whatsoever will be able to save them unless justice herself, the heavenly ruler of the moral world, gives them shelter and protection under her mantel.

2673. It is necessary, therefore, to establish a venerable, sacred, political Tribunal alongside governmental administration. Here eternal, immutable justice, the most sublime of all powers, calls to herself all mankind whom she judges equally without consideration of persons or social bodies. Here the poor may find refuge against the rich, the weak against the strong, the minority against the majority; here, to the honour of the Christian world, it becomes clear that the law which commands all, before which everything on earth bows low and trembles, has finally an invincible sanction in consciences and an incorruptible interpreter in society.

It is the responsibility of the philosophy of politics to develop more extensively *the natural construction of civil society* which we have barely outlined. This will enhance the dignity and utility of Right because it will be seen ever more clearly that what has been decided about the best construction of civil society, by reasoning with the principles of justice, will be fully in harmony with that suggested by strictly political principles whose immediate aim is utility.

CONCLUSION

SOCIAL RIGHT

2674. I shall add nothing more to the conclusion of this work on the special Right governing civil association. Instead, I shall bring together the threads of the various volumes in which I have divided and examined briefly, as far as I could, the whole of the philosophy of social Right. These threads of thought will be united under a single heading and, as it were, bound together: the heading is the majesty of the Creator.

In fact, every right receives its authority and its unshakeable consistency from God himself. This authority is made known to us by reason and divine revelation. Reason shows us the divine authority of the moral law and of Right both directly and indirectly. Directly, in the self-evident principle of the moral law, that is, BEING AS MANIFESTATIVE OF ESSENCES, to which we can assent (moral good) or from which we can dissent (moral evil); indirectly, when we first know through reason that the essence itself of Being is alive in the fullest sense of the word, and wills itself eternally, and then, second, know that assenting to *manifestative Being* means assenting to the supreme will, just as assenting to the supreme will means assenting to manifestative Being. The moral law which we know directly is, therefore, divine; its indirect consequences share in divine authority itself (with the result that every right is divine); on right is founded not only the prosperous state of human societies, but also their existence and all the powers that rule them. How praiseworthy, therefore, the wisdom of ancient Rome which asserted with

[2674]

such good sense: 'A city is bounded more securely by religion than by its own walls.'[465]

2675. The social atheism of our own times is very different; it reveals itself as unfounded, totally ignorant nonsense. It also shows its petty narrowness of mind when it maintains, as some authors do, that rulers have their authority from *divine Right*, and that the divinity of right is restricted to protecting the civil power or, even more narrowly, the thrones of civil rulers. They mean that this power alone comes from God, and clutter up with ambiguities and interminable questions the entire science of human rights, from the clarity of which ensues peace, from the obscurity and confusion of which comes war upon the world. The abuse of the phrase 'divine right', subjugated to the service of rulers, both deprives many other powers of their legitimate value, and throws together confusedly in a single concept that which comes from God through the divine light of reason, and that which comes from God positively, that is, the authorities of the Church of the Redeemer. Divine Right, in the proper and common sense of the word, pertains only to these authorities.

2676. The abuse of this *divine right*, exclusively used by some writers to maintain human sovereignty, is very strange. Authors use it to cut, but not untie, the knot of the most difficult and important socio-jural questions. To know that the power of rulers, like every other lawful power, comes from God, seems to mean, according to these writers, that we also know the *jural title* of this power.

It would seem odd to send these Europeans, and 19th century masters at that, to China for clarification of their ideas, to some very ancient disciples of Confucius, whose knowledge was extant centuries before Christ. But there they would learn that knowledge of power which comes from God does not dispense them from investigating its origin amongst human beings.

In fact, ancient Chinese philosophers taught in agreement with the whole of antiquity that civil rule comes from God, whom they called *heaven*; they also called the emperor the *son of heaven*. At the same time, they harmonised this teaching in

[465] Cicero, *De Nat. Deor*, 3: 40.

the best possible way with that on jural, natural titles. The following dialogue between Wen Chang and Confucius' disciple, Mencius, is sufficient to illustrate the point:

> *Wen Chang.* Is it true that the emperor Yao gave the empire to Shun?
>
> *Mencius.* Not at all. The son of Heaven cannot confer the empire on anyone.
>
> *Wen Chang.* Well, Shun was in charge of the empire, so who gave it to him?
>
> *Mencius.* Heaven.
>
> *Wen Chang.* If Heaven gave it to him, did Heaven explain Shun's mandate in clear, resounding words?
>
> *Mencius.* No. Heaven does not speak. It makes its will known through the actions and great events in a man's life. Nothing more.
>
> *Wen Chang.* What do you mean?
>
> *Mencius.* The son of Heaven can only propose a man to Heaven; he cannot ordain that Heaven give him the empire. The vassals of the empire can propose a man to the son of Heaven; they cannot ordain that the son of Heaven confer the dignity of vassal-ruler upon him. — So Yao proposed Shun to Heaven, and Heaven accepted him. He showed him covered with glory to the people, and the people accepted him. That's why I said that Heaven does not speak and that it makes its will known through the actions and great events in a man's life.
>
> *Wen Chang.* Let me ask you another question. What do you mean by the words: he proposed him to Heaven, and Heaven accepted him? Did he show him covered with glory to the people, so that the people accepted him?
>
> *Mencius.* I mean this: he ordered him to rule over the administration of public affairs. When all the families of the empire saw how well he administered, they were tranquil and content.[466] That is how the people accepted him. — Shun helped Yao in the administration of the empire for twenty-eight years. This was not the effect of human power, but of Heaven. Three years after the death of Yao, when the period of mourning was over, Shun left the son of Yao and withdrew to the southern part of the southern

---

[466] Note here the characteristic which we used to discern lawful *occupancy*, that is, lack of jural resentment and tacit consent.

river in order to leave the empire to him. The great vassals who came in spring and autumn to swear loyalty and homage did not, however, go to the son of Yao, but to Shun. People with complaints and lawsuits did not go to the son of Yao, but to Shun. The poets who praised great events in their works, and sang of them, did not sing of the son of Yao, but celebrated and sang the undertakings of Shun. That is why I said that the exaltation of Shun was the effect of the power of Heaven. Afterwards Shun came to the middle empire, and sat on the throne of the son of Heaven. If he had gone on living in the palace of Yao, and had oppressed and harmed his son, he would have usurped the empire. He would not have received it from Heaven.[467]

This passage of a very ancient book clearly expresses the divine right of rulers. At the same time, it reconciles with this right the jural and natural rights in which God, the author of nature and reason, speaks and manifests his will.

2677. The titles of social rights lie in human nature. Indeed, this nature is, as it were, a complex of such titles. Human nature is essentially jural, essentially social.

2678. I do remember, of course, that I once wrote that the quality, 'social', should not be put in the definition of human nature.[468] But I was speaking there of the *individual*. Here, I am speaking about society and *human society*. Human society leads us back to the *species*. Now it cannot be denied that the reason for every *human society* has to be found finally in the fact that many human beings are a single species subsisting in many individuals (*RF*, 1554). Let us grant also that some society of different species could be conceived through the identity of the intellectual good which they enjoy (*RGC*, 635–670). Nevertheless, *human society* possesses this as its own in a particular way; the quite special characteristic of *human society* is to place in communion *human nature* itself, the identical species.

2679. This explains why pagan sages, confined to nature, were unable to extend their vision beyond humanity, or scarcely beyond it. The foundation of their arguments about social life was the innate, human quality of sociableness, a quality based

[467] *Mencius*, bk. 2, c. 3.
[468] *Anthropology*.

on the fact that each human being sees his own species in others; he see another self.[469] This unity of species which brings together individuals is truly the principle not of every society, but of every *human society*. In the most cultured nations of the ancient world, however, the *City* prevailed, and every human society was reduced to the City. The City became the source of justice precisely because all justice was reduced to the *human justice* included in *human society*. This explains why Plato, Aristotle and other sages made *civil life* the height of virtue, and considered political science as the continuation and apex of moral science. For us, enlightened by Christ, these are extremely limited, narrow concepts. Our mind goes out beyond the finite and human to associate with pure intelligences and enjoy the bliss of true society with God.

2680. Only by removing every limit to the association of intelligent natures is it possible to attain that concept of society which, stripped of every injustice, is totally full of justice. We have seen that every social element is an element of justice, that every limitation of society is accompanied by something unjust and that, as society extends, justice too is fulfilled.[470]

2681. Three societies are necessary for complete organisation of the human race (*USR*, 20). Of these, family society, which is the most natural, is also the most restricted, although this was not intended according to the first design of the Creator who provided a single father for the whole human race (*RF*, 994). That father became mortal, however, along with his children,

---

[469] This is how Cicero expresses the teaching in Latin: *Nam cum sic hominis natura generata sit, ut habeat quiddam innatum quasi CIVILE ET POPULARE, quod Graeci* πολιτικον *vocant: quidquid aget quaeque virtus, id a communitate et ea, quam exposui, caritate atque SOCIETATE HUMANA non abhorrebit: vicissimque justitia, ut ipsa se fundet usu in ceteras virtutes, sic illas expetet* [Human nature is generated in such a way that something almost CIVIL AND POPULAR is innate to it. The Greeks call this πολιτικον. Whatever any human capacity does, it has no dread of community and of that love and HUMAN SOCIETY which I have explained. The same is true about justice. Just as it comes forth in use through the other virtues, so it searches for them](*De finib.*, 5: 23). Here the Greek word πολιτικον, which corresponds to *civil* and *popular*, is obviously taken to mean 'human society' which, in turn, is taken erroneously for every society, for that society which includes every other society.

[470] *SP*, 37–49.

[2680–2681]

and the great, single domestic society, which should have embraced the whole of mankind, was split into many divided families whose limitations and restrictions went on increasing.

2682. This separation and restriction of family societies gave rise to all that was unjust in the nature and tendencies of families — *family selfishness*, as we have called it. How could this intrinsic evil, this profound defect in the family, be removed? The family could not be extended beyond certain limits because nature would not allow this. All that remained was some kind of mediation between families. Hence the institution of civil society, a broader society, which would undertake such mediation and be responsible for healing the radical defect of the family.

Family pride, however, is untamed and ferocious. Every time civil society attempts to dress the wound, this pride, aggravated by deep pain, rises up in fury. Its only desire is to destroy its healer. The consequence is the obstinate, angry strife between domestic and civil society that we have described (cf. 1963–2016).

This war to the death would have ended with the destruction of both societies unless a third society, even more extensive than civil society, had appeared in the world in good time. This society, universal and extremely powerful, assumed in its turn the responsibility of mediation between civil and family societies which had come to blows, just as civil society had assumed responsibility for mediation amongst different family societies. This new, most widely extended society was Christianity.

The Church reconciled family and civil principles, rendered possible their co-existence and by saving them both brought them to such accord that they were of help to one another. Civil society completed its mission of mediatrix between families, and domestic society communicated its force and consistency to civil society.

This, however, was not sufficient. The universal society of Christ, ('theocracy', as we have called it), still had to fulfil the role of mediation between civil societies. These societies, although more extensive than family societies, were still confined within certain limits which added to their multiplicity and exclusiveness. This limitation became a source of injustice and war between them. Combat and strife would have torn them to pieces unless a more magnificent society had intervened to pacify them. This society was of its nature universal and totally just. It excluded no one, admitted all to its embrace, rendered justice to all alike, and gathered all to itself in its immense benevolence and beneficence.

Thus family society, no longer enclosed within domestic walls, was gradually perfected by civil society which in turn was perfected by the Church of JESUS Christ, a society not confined to a single place by mountains, rivers, seas or even human treaties and conventions. It spread all over the globe to humanity itself but, better still, is as universal as the truth, justice and charity of God himself. Thus, the perfect organisation of mankind is brought to completion.

2683. But has this great work of Providence truly been completed? Not yet, but it is being brought to fulfilment every day. Some idea of the progress made in this great work can be gained by noting how family selfishness has been put down and conquered forever. Yes, it still slithers around like a beheaded snake or like a hydra trying to grow heads again. But I regard it as overcome because it can never reassert itself to any great degree; civil society prevails and is always ready to humiliate it again. The first step, therefore, has been completed.

Now, however, civil society is itself puffed up by its victory. Selfishness has passed from *families* to *nations*. Our own time is a period of *national selfishness* which flourishes and increases, and invades everything. It thinks itself all-powerful, and becomes irritable and bitterly suspicious about anything that may temper it or rein it in. Nevertheless, it must be and will be refrained by the law of universal justice proper to theocratic society, and by the progress of universal charity incessantly preached by the Church of Christ. This second operation is still to be completed. Theocratic society does not want to destroy civil society, but root out the vice of selfishness that defiles it with injustice. In the same way, civil society did not want to destroy family society, but heal in it the same disease of even narrower selfishness.

Universal justice and *universal love* are the powerful remedies brought from heaven by the teacher of mankind who bears,

[2683]

written on his thigh, the words: 'King of kings, and Lord of lords'. His medicine alone is capable of healing the nations.

There can be no doubt, therefore, of the importance of the philosophy of Right which we have outlined as best we could. Nor is its end uncertain. I repeat, civil society still has to grow towards perfection by befriending universal society (perfect, theocratic society) from which alone it can draw complete justice and attain purification from every spirit of injustice. To indicate the path to such a glorious rejuvenation of the nations, I have tried to determine the end within which civil society and its government must limit themselves, that is, 'the regulation of the modality of rights.' It is only a little seed, but one that I entrust to the logic of time and to the charity of Christians. Charity will water it, and time will allow it to unfold. I have no doubt of this. And perhaps future generations will enjoy its fruits.

Appendix

1. (1635).

Kant, Schmalz, Rotteck and others see the concept of servitude in the obligation imposed on citizens of remaining forever in the civil society in which they find themselves without hope of leaving it. It seems certain that the opinion of those authors who deny the right of emigration to citizens comes from their attributing some kind of true seigniory to social government and of true servitude to citizens. Recently, an Italian author explained Rotteck's thought as follows:

> A person once belonging to a State either through birth or admission was considered a slave (*Leibeigener*) of the State and, in practice, of the ruler himself. In other words, he was obliged towards it with his whole person even till death, without any right of separation or emigration. It seemed that the perpetual end of the City required this because the social pact either demanded such a duty or declared the person the property of the lord of the territory or servant of the glebe. The law of circumscription, present also in the constitutional German States, rests on the same foundation. It declares the children of the fatherland servants of the glebe even before they have fulfilled the obligatory manifestation of their desire to belong to the State of their birth. Again, all laws requiring the permission of the supreme power before emigration (because these laws do not recognise the simple right to emigrate) derive from the same maxim, which is false and to be rejected without qualification.
> (*Lehrbuch des Vernunftrechts*, vol. 2, p. 133)

Several things can be noted in these words, I think:

1. To declare as false the maxim 'the subject is bound personally to his ruler,' and to reject it unconditionally, is to go too far. Because rational Right certainly recognises the Right of seigniory and the duty of servitude (rights and duties which are

not absurd), it is necessary to limit oneself to an investigation of the fact. In other words, does a given special civil society have the jural title of seigniory and its relative servitude? Once the fact is determined, the corresponding Right is also determined. The false maxim, and the only one to be rejected unconditionally, is the general dictum: 'Seigniory and servitude are present in all civil societies to the extent that they are civil societies.' This principle is the foundation of *unjust absolutism*. Viceversa, the maxim: '*De facto* civil societies are never mingled with an element of lawful seigniory' is also false and to be rejected unconditionally. This principle, which claims that all civil societies must be pure, is the principle of *ultra-liberalism*, and is as excessively unjust as the preceding principle. Jural reason, therefore, proceeds between the two extremes. It distinguishes the notion of civil society from the notion of seigniory, but shows that the two elements can be mixed in fact. Consequently, the practical jurisconsult has to examine the civil and seigniorial titles which subsist in a given, real, civil society and use them to determine if lawful seigniorial elements are present, what kind they are, and the extent to which they limit the freedom of others.

2. The Napoleonic law of conscription is eminently civil in its substance, but some notion of seigniorial right could have been added to it in those places where its introduction caused, for masters, the cessation of rights of defence and support from their subjects who were obliged, as in all feudal States, to supply a certain contingent of soldiers to him. But granted conscription as a civil law, as it is in its spirit and institution, it can indeed oblige citizens to undertake military service if they are still members of the State in the years when the law is in force. Having finished their military service, they are free, just as they are free from the law if they have emigrated before being subject to it.

3. Permission to emigrate does not seem to me to be opposed to civil liberty whenever such permission is referred to the right a society has to examine if the would-be emigrant owes the society anything. In this case, emigration could be impeded (*RI*, 501–507). However, the departure of a citizen free from debt or obligations towards the civil society cannot be impeded by the society. This permission, therefore, must be reduced to a

declaration by the society that it has no outstanding credit or claims upon the citizen.

2. (1729)

Those who depend upon a *tacit convention* do not err as grossly as those who presuppose an expressed social contract which, according to Bossuet, is not preserved in any archive. I say they do not err so grossly because I cannot see how they can be absolved from all error. The word *convention*, or *contract*, in its proper meaning, presupposes an actual, positive adherence of will. It is indeed true that the presence of obligation amongst human beings requires a *presupposed* tacit consent between them; it is repugnant to imagine moral, rational, human nature acting contrary to itself. But to attribute the name of contract to this *consent of* human *nature* rather than to the actual, free *consent* of the individual *will* does not seem to me to accord with linguistic propriety. Monsignor Marchetti's use of *stipulate*, for example, in the following passage is simply metaphorical:

> We ought not to say that stipulation (of the social contract) is unknown in public registers. This argument would be valid for those who think of it as a real, factual event, but not for one who finds it in the register of the human mind which lays down stipulations for all that we do, and for everyone. Why is it *the oddest thing in the world* to suppose that reason has stipulated something for a father *relative to his baby son*? Does nature not speak on behalf of the child against the parent in China and in the Congo who drowns a superfluous child or leaves him exposed in the street? Can even the slave *iure bello* be treated unnaturally because you have the right to take away his life? Kill him if you like, but as long as life remains it is the life of a human being who falls under the stipulation established by his reason, a human being whom you must use as a human being. You tread on the stool when you get into your carriage because the stool is made of wood; its nature makes no stipulation with the person who uses it. A *human being*, however, even as a slave whose life you can take, stipulates because of the respect his nature demands.

The tribunal of the whole of humanity will always condemn as barbarians those conquerors, such as Sapor the
Persian or other Eastern monsters, who trod on their
prisoners, treating them like animals or even killing them
without reasonable, proportionate intent.

(*Della Chiesa quanto allo stato politico*,
Confer. 9, section 2, n. 68)

3. (1895).

The sixteenth century saw the first appearance of authors who
were to proliferate a century later. They are aptly called 'sophists', a word in wide use today. The external cause influencing
the emergence of this kind of wrong-headed writer is the
disharmony between the state of civil society (principally its
organisation) and the correspondingly excessive intellectual
development of its members. Ill-at-ease in society, they have to
show their displeasure, but express it indirectly and captiously
in their writings and teaching because they are not free to do so
openly. Corrupt, they are vexed by the social ills in which they
share and which they exaggerate, as though to appease their
bitterness. Unable to give free vent to their poison, they become
enraged. On the other hand the feeling of deep disgust they have
for themselves, for their contemporaries and for public matters
is even more confused. They can neither say what they want,
nor express their opinions clearly. Their consequent embarrassment increases the exaggeration and acerbity of their claims and
of the new systems they dream up every day. Their satirical,
mocking style, when carefully examined, is simply a continuous
argument *ad hominem*, a discussion about generally accepted
principles from which they deduce absurdities to overthrow
principles. Their reasoning is always far removed from what in
fact they feel and want; their subtleties are simply an attempt to
torment and confuse their contemporaries, to shatter prevalent
opinion and the society in which they live. They give no thought
to applying themselves seriously to solid doctrine which might
substitute something useful and enduring for what they want to
destroy.

Hobbes, one of the first sophists, is a perfect example of this type of person. The very title of his book, *Leviathan*, indicates a satire of unrestrained civil power. The mockery in a book which acknowledges as civil power only an unlimited monarchy, not even restricted by natural justice, is patent to all. For him, tyranny and monarchy do not differ in any way (*De Cive*, cc. 7 and 10). The absolute monarchy he establishes originates from a contract, but he says:

1. This contract must be made by everyone with everyone, 'because no one is obliged by a pact of which he is not the author' (*De Cive*, c. 6).

2. The pact is invalid without external signs, which however have no value *per se* but only through fear of the harm caused by their violation (*Leviath.*, pt. 1, c. 14; *De Cive.*, c. 2).

3. A contract in which a person gives to another without receiving anything is absurd. Hence, the social contract is possible only in so far as those making it fear death if they do not make it (*ibid.*).

4. A strong person whom another cannot resist is free to break the pact (*De homine*, 14, 15).

5. There is no law except *natural* law, which consists in doing what is helpful and avoiding what is harmful. Keeping a pact pertains to natural law simply because it is useful to keep it, not otherwise (*ibid.*).

6. In many places Hobbes very clearly satirises rulers whose vices and exaggerated power he undertakes to justify, for example, in *Leviath.*, pt. 1, c. 11, and in the Dedication of *De Cive*.

Finally he himself advises his readers to use his system by bawling it aloud like the geese who saved the Capitoline with their squawking. This is the clearest expression of his thought: 'I can do nothing better than sing the praises of civil power (ITS POSSESSOR desires it to be as great as possible). And I am discussing mere right, not HUMAN RIGHT (note this). I squawk like the GEESE ON THE CAPITOLINE at the sound of the climbers' (*Leviath.*, Dedic.).

It is very strange that this sophist has been understood as a serious teacher. Many have made him their master, others have refuted him. I repeat, there is no system in what he says, simply the appearances of a system, under which he tries to demonstrate the enormous absurdities and wickedness of principles which, in his opinion, reign over or rather undermine society as it was in his country at the time. Rousseau, despite saying the opposite, grasped his spirit and made himself his interpreter. Rousseau, although he saw that Hobbes' principles would have the opposite result to those intended, was deceived by the principles themselves. These were copied (or at least the author thought they were copied) from the fact of existing society, not from the author's mind and persuasion. Rousseau was unable to distance himself from the dialectic artifice of his master and exemplar; at the cost of choking himself he gulped down great chunks as though they were sugar-coated pills. In fact, Rousseau, as I have said elsewhere, cannot be classed among philosophers but among literary critics or satirical poets — call him whatever you please. In this respect his eloquent exaggerations contain something moral, a kind of deposit of virtue (cf. *SP*, 81–90).

4. (1985).

This personal, *seigniorial Right* was naturally modified as soon as the nomad peoples, conquered by the Romans, learned about ownership of land, an element of civil society, and about agriculture. Luigi Cibrario thus describes the political state of the Germans and the modification brought about by ownership of the conquered territories.

> In Germany, whence the conquerors came, the common holding of land rendered governmental organisation *personal*, not *real*.

The groups were *seigniories* rather than societies.

> In general, the Germans were not agricultural peoples, although some Germanic nations, such as the Franks and the Burgundians did eventually dedicate themselves to agriculture. Nevertheless, in all cases they preserved for a long time *tribal* rather than *State* organisation.
>   The organisation was as follows. Germany was divided into *peoples* corresponding to the ancient italic *cities*.

These *cities* were, however, true civil societies; the *peoples* were *seigniories*, or great tribes.

> Each people consisted of various tribes, or great families called *fare*. The heads of the families were called *farones*, from which we have 'barons'. This was the natural division.
>
> Governmental division was manifest in a king, the supreme head in time of war. During peace, his authority was extremely limited.
>
> Various *fare* formed a *gau* corresponding first to the Latin *pagus* and in later centuries to the *comitatus*. It was governed by a *graf*, or count, with a counsel of sworn assistants, or *skapins*, who can be likened to assessors. Other officials, known as *centenarii*, or *sculdassii (scultheis)*, and *decani*, were heads and judges over a hundred families or over ten families. The jurisdiction of these officials was AT FIRST PERSONAL, AND THEREFORE MOBILE AND PERIPATETIC. It became real and geographic as a result of the conquest of sections of the Roman empire where the immigrant Germanic nations acquired ownership of a third (in the case of the Heruli, Goths and Lombards) or two thirds (in the case of the Burgundians) of the lands they had conquered. In these cases, either there was no common land-holding, or it soon disappeared. Every family of *harimans*, that is, of free soldiers, had its own portion of land.
>
> *Dell'Economia politica del medio evo*,
> Bk. 1, c. 1 (Turin edition, 1839)

5. (fn. 165).

Montesquieu observed that under the barbarians the law was *personal* rather than *territorial* (*Espr. des Lois*, 28, 2). This was denied by some erudite people because riparian, Salic, Frankish and other laws speak of territories to which the law applies (Chabrit, *De la Monarch. franc.*, bk. 8, c. 21). However, these savants fail to notice that a *territorial* law is not such because it applies to a given territory. It means that all the inhabitants of a given territory are subject to it as a result of the territory they inhabit. Barbarian laws, after the conquest, did not oblige all persons, but only certain classes dwelling in the given territory. In other words, each person could choose the law under which to live. This choice was made public according to the constitution of Lothaire I (*Leges Longobard.* bk. 2, c. 57).

Did this *personalism* of barbarian laws exist before the conquest or only afterwards? Montesquieu makes it depend on the condition of the barbarians before the conquest:

> The spirit of personal laws was present in these peoples before they began to move from their native lands to the territories they conquered.
>
> (*Espr. des Lois*, 28; 2)

He also makes it depend on the separate life led by the tribes:

> These nations were divided by marshes, lakes and forests. One can see in Caesar how they liked separate lives (*De Bello Germ.*, bk. 6). All these peoples were free and independent when they were on their own. When they intermingled, independence remained. The fatherland was common, and the republic particular. The territory was the same, the nations different.
>
> (*Ibid.*)

Savigny (*Introd. gener. allo studio del Diritto*), in opposition to Montesquieu, claims that the barbarian laws became personal only through necessity, as a result of the clash between the conquerors and the defeated Romans. Montesquieu is right, however. He is speaking of the *spirit* not the *fact* of the laws. The spirit of personal law had to precede the conquest. It is easy enough to see this if we consider that barbarian life, in great part nomadic, was not bound to territory, and that it embraced *family* and *tribal* society, but not *civil society*, or at least not to any notable stage of development. The family, however, is ruled by paternal right, and therefore by seigniorial and personal right. This is what we said about seigniorial legislation and government. As we saw, the master as such does not lay down laws other than those which affect his seigniory, nor does he extend the care of his government except in relationship to the grandeur of his own family. This is a fact pertaining to *seigniorial instinct*. Hence, a people whose culture and development does not extend further than the limitations of seigniorial laws and government is forced to do what it can for itself when other civil needs show themselves. The master consents by granting the people certain laws, judges and officials of their own, provided they show no sign of weakening his dominion. This occurred when the leaders of barbarian families conquered Roman territories.

Later, the barbarians came to appreciate the worth of agriculture and a settled life as well as the importance of civil government. At this point, the dominant families embraced the civil element, broke away from their family restrictions and began to see in their subjects both a certain dignity and other families and rights. In fact, the importance and esteem of territorial wealth grew to such an extent that the opposite defect manifested itself. The law, which had first followed the free person, now required the person to be fixed to the soil. The law became *territorial*.

When the law as a whole became territorial, it also became tyrannical. Clearly, if land is appreciated more than personal dignity, person is sacrificed to land. The governing, seigniorial families became dependent on land alone for their wealth and riches. This kind of excess is corrected later, but normally only through the tremendous upheavals of revolution.

In the last century Rousseau found a sign of servitude and despotism in the fact that kingdoms took their names from territories rather than from government by persons. Actually, only the owner of land has the right to live from its produce; others either receive alms from him, or leave the territory, or die of hunger.

This explains the incessant struggle between *personal* and *territorial laws* in social history. Each tends to regulate society to the exclusion of the other. As soon as one succeeds and then goes to excess, a social movement towards the other is initiated, and vice-versa. For example, *territorial laws* had become excessive and almost dominant as a result of feudalism. As we saw recently, society reacted against this excess with the deliberation taken in France in 1830: the head of the nation was no longer to be called king of France, but king of the French.

Should civil laws, therefore, be territorial or personal? Neither one nor the other; they should be mutually tempered. It is precisely this tempering, this just mean, that society often seeks in the midst of its agitation. The wisdom of the Catholic Church has preceded civil legislators in this matter also; its legislation has always been a mixture of personal and local laws.

6. (2080).

Shortly before the period of the French revolution, civil society had given clear indications in almost every European nation of readiness to move forward. But the unjust violence into which it erupted in France horrified good people and alarmed every powerful family, who saw themselves attacked by a gang of assassins. Another cause which did great harm to civil progress was the fact that the revolution was led throughout by false philosophers, thanks to whom Frederick said, 'The greatest punishment possible for a province is to entrust its government to philosophers' (*Dialogues des Morts par le roi de Prusse*), adding that he 'feared philosophical principles might bring back the barbarities from which Europe had only recently emerged' (*Lettres à D'Alembert*). The civil movement under discussion was led disastrously by the sophists of the time. We refer the reader to C. L. Haller's excellent description in his *Ristorazione*, t. 1, c. 7 & 8. In Russia, progress was revealed through the influence of contemporary ideas and needs not on the people but on the monarch who took the initiative. Haller says:

> A little later, at the opposite end of Europe, Catherine II presented the rare spectacle of a kind of *National Convention* in order to form a new code of law (1776 AD). Because she was unsuccessful, this code has not been discussed as much as the French code, but it remains a phenomenon worthy of recall, if the dominant sprit of the period is to be known.
>
> Castera, in his *Histoire de Cathérine II*, t. 2, p. 33–35 speaks about this philosophical drama. According to him, the assembly was dissolved precipitously because some deputies had made it known that the Empress could have been dethroned. Thirty years later, Paul I created a new legislative commission (1797), which was confirmed and enlarged by Alexander on the 5th June 1801.

Finally, the French movement was irreligious and wicked, the foremost reason why France struggles even today to have a clear conception of real social freedoms and, while bitterly opposing some of them, equally often mistakes *licence* for *freedom*.

7. (2159).

In antiquity we see kings receiving *gifts* but not gathering *taxes*. These gifts show that in these societies the king considered himself *lord* rather than *supreme governor of civil society*. In modern civil societies sovereigns are considered more as supreme governors. The difference is immense. I will simply note one distinctive characteristic between the right to receive gifts as lord and the right to impose taxes as governor of a society. Granted that the title of lord is founded on justice, the right to receive gifts is unalterable. The quantity of gifts is fixed, and cannot be increased by the lord or reduced by the subject, whatever the needs of civil society. *Civil taxation* however is subject neither to prescription nor usucaption; annual needs determine its increase or decrease. It is therefore a patent and immense injustice that the Catholics of Ireland pay tithes to the Anglican Church. The Anglican Church cannot use possession or usucaption or prescription as a legal title for collecting tithes; Catholics do not need Anglican ministers, and do not acknowledge them as pastors. The Catholics' duty to pay them ceases because tithes are only a voluntary contribution, a voluntary taxation of theocratic society, which ceases when the need for it ceases. We know, for example, that the Anglican Church draws more than twenty million francs annually from Ireland, although it has only 700,000 followers, of whom 400,000 are concentrated in the province of Armagh. Catholics, on the other hand, total more than seven million. The Anglican Church in Ireland is divided into four ecclesiastical provinces (Armagh, Dublin, Cashel and Tuam), thirty-two dioceses, 1,387 benefices and 2,430 parishes. The Anglican clergy is composed of four archbishops, eighteen bishops, 326 deacons, canons, etc., 1,333 ministers, 752 vicars. During the debates in the Houses of

Parliament in 1835 concerning appropriation, it was acknowledged that the average income of each bishop reached 175,000
francs annually. In some parishes there are 1,500 Catholics but
not a single Anglican; in others, 3450 Catholics and 15 Anglicans; in others, 5393 Catholics and 12 Anglicans, and so on. The
contributions of the faithful, by title of the service of God and
care of souls, are voluntary gifts to their church and motivated
by faith. — There is therefore an enormous double injustice in
the conduct of the English civil government towards Catholic
Ireland: 1. an injustice which changes a purely theocratic tax (a
free offering) into an obligatory, civil impost; 2. an injustice
which extracts this free, faith-motivated offering of the people
to their Church in order to give it to another Church which they
condemn.

8. (2240).

During the civil wars of the Roman empire one party sought
to destroy the power of the other. Even the magistrates were put
to the sword, which is what happened when Severus captured
Byzantium from Niger and Albinus. Gibbon writes:

> For forty years, if we except the short, doubtful respite
> during the reign of Vespasian, Rome groaned under a
> continual tyranny which exterminated the ancient families
> of the republic and was almost fatal for every virtue and
> talent that appeared at that unfortunate period.
>
> (*Storia della Decad.*, c. 3)

The crime of *lèse-majesté* was the pretext for numerous public
and solemn assassinations. The fratricide, Caracalla, considered
extirpating all the families related to his slaughtered brother.
Commodus had been attacked by a man who cried out as he
struck the blow, 'This comes from the senate'; this was sufficient
for the emperor to carry out an horrendous butchery against the
senate. Gibbon says, 'Suspicion replaced proof; accusation was
condemnation. The torture of an illustrious senator meant the
destruction of all those who would weep or revenge his action.'
Describing the reign of Gallienus, whose cruelty in extinguish-
ing illustrious families was extreme, he says, 'The only family,

among all the ancient families of Rome, to survive the tyranny of the Caesars was the Calpurnia' (c. 10). The last branch of this family was killed at the order of the tyrant Valens. The author of *Delle morti de' persecutori* says that Maximian, who could exercise his cruelty only on new families, 'extinguished the lights of the senate through trumped-up crimes'.

The barbarians completed the work. The Goths, Vandals and Huns reduced to slavery everything they found illustrious in the Roman empire. Nobles less capable of mechanical work were humiliated and despised by the barbarians who were at a loss to appreciate or even know what culture was. The well-known author of *Discorso storico*, the preface to *Adelchi*, narrates two facts concerning the barbarians' slaughter of the leaders of the cities they conquered. He then says:

> These two facts alone do not allow us to suppose that the killing of the principal owners was part of the Lombard system of conquest. But if we had more facts to establish this, we cannot deny that it would help us to explain why, among all the stories of barbarian domination, the indigenous population is less evident where the Lombards hold sway. It would be even more easy to argue to the condition to which those left alive were reduced.

9. (2437).

All writers of any worth admit that conventions between an autocrat and civil society, and members of civil society, are possible and valid. Johann Brunnemann makes this comment on the ruler:

> But he can be bound by positive law if he has obliged himself, even without an oath, to observe the law. The obligation is stronger still if it has been made under oath. In these cases he is obliged not by the law, but BY THE PROMISE he has made. Let no one say that a ruler is not obliged BY CONTRACT OR CONVENTION.

A little later he adds:

> I would say with men of old (*cum veteribus*) no one is

more obliged by convention and promise than God; he is truth and trustworthiness itself, and the God of truth. After God, no one is more strictly obliged amongst mortals than a ruler. The greater the trustworthiness of a person, the more he is bound by obligation. For this reason the learned tell us: 'The trustworthiness of nobles is obligatory even when they are not on oath.' The nobleman therefore is more obliged than the rustic.

(Comm. in Pandect., bk. 1, t. 3, bk. 3)

This comment is not to be understood in the sense that obligation, objectively considered, does not oblige all equally. The law of fidelity is the same for all, although the factual bond changes as the circumstances of the subject change, that is:

1. Through *awareness* of one's duty. — A person more clearly and profoundly aware of his own obligation is more gravely obliged. This higher awareness is presupposed in the ruler.

2. As a result of a clearer, more repeated and more assured *expression* of the promise. — Both the ruler and the great man give evidence and even boast of the value of their word. A person's condition does indeed render his promise more authoritative. It is not just an individual who makes a promise, but the entire group whose dignity invests the one making the promise.

3. As a result of the *greater trust* of the people in the promises of such persons who in violating their promises betray the great trust placed in them.

4. Finally, because the people themselves must not use violence to obtain what has been promised — breaking the promise shows a lack of response to the people's delicacy and generosity towards the ruler, who provokes them to crime.

10. (2509).

There are very serious philosophers who maintain not only that penalties are unsuitable for preventing the rare cases of crime into which weak human nature plunges (the more depraved a people is, the more this happens), but that multiplying

and stressing the rigour of their punishment sometimes produces an effect opposite to that intended. Seneca, for instance,
states (*De clementia*, bk. 1, c. 23–24):

> Moreover, you will often see frequent punishment of
> crime followed by frequent outbreaks of the same crime.
> — Where people are rarely punished, there is a kind of
> consensus about innocence, which is favoured as a kind of
> public good. Let a City think it is innocent, and it will be.
> There is more anger about people who turn away from
> upright conduct when they are seen to be few. I think it is
> dangerous to show a City how many evils exist in it. —
> The human spirit is obstinate by nature. It tends towards
> what is contrary and rash, and follows more easily than it
> is led.

These are profound, beautiful thoughts. Punishment, therefore, and the manner of administering penal justice, must be so
tempered that:

1. it does not educate people to commit crime; 2. it does not
darken the imagination with too many examples of wickedness
(*images* are principles of *instincts* and of *actions*); 3. it does not
accustom people to over-frequent examples of serious corporal
punishment (punishment loses its terror and is more easily
undergone when many suffer together); 4. it does not give rise
in the social body to an exaggerated persuasion of wickedness
(this provides the body with a low image of itself and weakens
its moral forces — when society has a good opinion of itself, it
senses the price of its own moral dignity which it feels honoured
to preserve); finally, 5. it does not provoke human sensitivity
which is more forceful where it finds greater resistance and
intolerance.

What should we say, therefore, about the publication in the
press of complete criminal trials? — There is no doubt that it
opens to the whole nation a very ominous school of crime. —
But surely, publicity assures better justice in the trial? — It may
be that *publicity* will be favourable to the guilty party, or it may
be thought that it will provide an incentive to unprejudiced
action on the part of judges if the arguments for or against are
made public, even contrary to the guilty party's wishes. These
are matters which we can let pass. There is nothing, however,

which justifies to my eyes the detailed circumstances in which newspapers reporting trials put the most horrible turpitude and wickedness committed in a nation before the eyes of adults and even of children who have scarcely learnt to read. Yes, let the guilty person who thinks he has been treated unjustly by the courts publish his entire trial in the newspapers. This will be his appeal to public opinion, the truly supreme tribunal of civilised nations, which can restore his honour and bring shame upon unjust or ignorant judges. But publishing the trial without any request from the guilty party, or even against his will, is both fatal to public decency and unjust towards the guilty person whose punishment is increased by consequent notoriety. It is an invitation to lay aside shame forever because it prevents any possible restoration of honour whatever efforts are made at emendation.

11. (2514).

Everyone knows how severely the Almighty forbade the shedding of blood at the beginning of the world (Gen 9: 5–6). Hugo Grotius comments on these verses with his usual common sense: 'In those first days, either because of the scarcity of human beings or because there was less need of an example for THE FEW MURDERERS, God suppressed with an edict something that was naturally lawful. He did indeed want people to avoid contact and dealings with murderers, but he did not want their life to be taken' (*De iure B. et P.*, bk. 1, c. 2, §5). This command of God to spare the life of the murderer, but avoid contact with him, suggests two considerations: 1. The nature of the first penal laws did not tend properly speaking to suppress criminal activity, but to prevent its birth or, granted its birth in some individual, to forestall any increase in others through bad example or through dealings with the delinquent. The supposition here is that the social body is still unharmed and that criminal activity has not spread. 2. The constancy of divine legislation. The separation of the delinquent from society was the punishment perpetually adopted both by the ancient and the new Church, but more by the latter which is altogether intent on saving the delinquent, and preserving society from scandal and the contagion of imitation. It is our hope that civil society and criminal legislation will one day reach its ideal. When that day comes, the greatest, most effective, most human punishment will be EX-COMMUNICATION. Legal positivists will laugh at this, but that is only because their vision sees no further than the present moment. Grotius notes that this extremely ancient punishment of excommunication and exile was established by Plato in place of the death penalty, although our Greek philosopher did not exclude the death penalty for certain crimes such as patricide, and for certain persons such as bond-servants (*De Leg.*, 9). Grotius offers an example from Euripedes (*Orest*, v. 511 ss.), where he praises the first legislators because they inflicted exile, not death, on murderers:

> How well our FATHERS IN THEIR FORESIGHT
> compelled the murderer to flee
> the ways and sight of men
> and expiate with exile, not with death,
> the crime that tainted him.

Lactantius, speaking of exile imposed on offenders from the beginning, says: 'It still seemed wrong to execute even evil men' (*De Institut. div.*, bk. 2, c. 20: 23). Pliny records the first death penalty, carried out, it would seem, by the Council of the Areopagus (*Hist. nat.*, 7: 56).

12. (2518).

Barbarously *cruel* punishments normally offend human dignity. This is much more true when punishments are *capricious* and strange. Taken to the extreme, this renders punishment a *game*, a public amusement, rather than a severe public lesson in morality. Pagan society at its basest reached this third stage of waywardness in inflicting punishment (cf. Count De Maistre, *Sur le délais de la Justice divine* of Plutarch). In a note added towards the end by the editor, we read:

> Because commentators have said nothing about this passage, which explains a little-known usage amongst the Romans, I think I should go into a little more detail. It is

well-known that Romans used the punishment inflicted on criminals as a source of amusement, and that the sight of delinquents being torn apart by savage beasts was one of the ordinary pleasures at games in the circus. But Plutarch is alluding in this case to a refinement of barbarism of which we have traces in antiquity, and which I can only mention here. In the tragedies, for example, criminals condemned to death were made to take the parts of Hercules on Mount Oeta; of Creusa who fell victim to Medea; of Prometheus on Mount Caucasus. The ancients took delight in seeing these events depicted literally. In Martial (*Spectaculorum Liber*, ep. 7), we see a certain Laureolus take the part of Prometheus, except that he was torn to pieces by a she-bear rather than a vulture; another person took the role of Orpheus torn to bits by the Bacchantes, represented by she-bears (ep. 11). Tertullian remarks on this subject (*Apologia*, c. 15): 'Your very gods are represented by criminals.' He mentions Atys, god of Pessinus, mutilated in the theatre; Hercules, burnt alive, and so on. Clavier believes, along with de Maistre, that Plutarch is speaking of a similar representation, and that these are the clothes Juvenal indicates with the words: *tunica molesta* (*Sat.* 8, v. 235).

Index of Biblical References

Numbers in roman indicate paragraphs or, where stated, the appendix (app.); numbers in italic indicate footnotes. Bible references are from RSV (Common Bible) unless marked †. In these cases, where the author's use of Scripture is dependent solely upon the Vulgate, the Douai version is used.

Index of Persons

General Index

Numbers in roman indicate paragraphs or, where stated, the appendix (app.); numbers in italic indicate footnotes

criminal, 2134, 2425
obligatory and free, 2422, 2425
rights and, 2424

Judicial Power
people and, 1689
rights and, 2423
see also **Power**

Justice
civil society and, 2579–2580,
  2586–2587, 2593
commutative, 1789, 2185
distributive, 1789, 2148, 2153–2154,
  2164, 2185, 2300, 2544, 2569, 2655,
  2688
humanity and, 2101, 2648
norms of, 2665
passions and, 1814
perfect mediator, 2098–2106
politics and, 2582
prevalent force, 2096, 2121
prudence and, 2578
rigorous, *274*
social progress and, 2651–2673
statesmen and, 2163
theoretical and practical principle of,
  2101
truth and, 2100
universality, 2665, 2683
virtue and, 1734

Knowledge
good of civil society, 2596
military power and, 2605–2607
monopoly of, 2383
nature and, 2627
single science of, 2577
virtue and, 2608–2610

Languages
division of, 1809
reason and, *117*
society and language, *117*

Law
act required by, 2488
circumscription, *app.* no. 1
civil Code and, *354*
civil-jural and civil-political,
  2477–2479

civil society and equality before,
  2064, 2069
classification of civil, 2448–2559
coercive, 2363
compilation of, 2443–2447
consent in marriage and, *396*
cosmic, 2611
criminal, 2505
facultative, 2473–2476, 2493
form of, 2447
God and, *373*
immediately obligatory, 2475–2476
individual and, 2487
interpretation of, *377*
lawmaker and, 2350; *357, 371*
master and, *359*
meaning of word, *354*
obligation of civil, 2450–2476
obtaining end of, 2446
permissive, 2370–2472, 2493
personal, *app.* no. 5
politico-civil, 2496, 2503–2505
precepts versus, 2427–2428
reason and, *354*
territorial, *app.* no. 5
universality and abstraction of, 2427
willed decisions and, *357*
wisdom and, 2443, 2445
  see also **Codes of Law, Moral Law,
  Natural Law, Penal Law,
  Rational Law, Roman Law**

Lawmaker
laws and, 2350; *357, 371*

Legislative Authority
exercise of, 1711
fathers and, 1705, 1714
  see also **Authority, Civil Authority,
  Ecclesial Authority**

Levy, *see* **Tax**

Liberalism
ultra, *app.* no. 1

Litigation
facultative laws and, 2473
payment for, *389*

Loans (forced)
taxation, 2265